Lecture Notes in Information Systems and Organisation

Volume 44

Lecture Notes in Information Systems and Organization—LNISO—is a series of scientific books that explore the current scenario of information systems, in particular IS and organization. The focus on the relationship between IT, IS and organization is the common thread of this collection, which aspires to provide scholars across the world with a point of reference and comparison in the study and research of information systems and organization. LNISO is the publication forum for the community of scholars investigating behavioral and design aspects of IS and organization. The series offers an integrated publication platform for high-quality conferences, symposia and workshops in this field. Materials are published upon a strictly controlled double blind peer review evaluation made by selected reviewers.

LNISO is abstracted/indexed in Scopus

More information about this series at http://www.springer.com/series/11237

Vikas Kumar · Jafar Rezaei · Victoria Akberdina ·
Evgeny Kuzmin
Editors

Digital Transformation in Industry

Trends, Management, Strategies

Springer

Editors
Vikas Kumar
Bristol Business School
University of the West of England
Bristol, UK

Jafar Rezaei
Faculty of Technology, Policy
and Management
Delft University of Technology
Delft, The Netherlands

Victoria Akberdina
Department of Regional Industrial Policy
and Economic Security
Institute of Economics of the Urals Branch
of the Russian Academy of Sciences
Ekaterinburg, Russia

Evgeny Kuzmin
Department of Regional Industrial Policy
and Economic Security
Institute of Economics of the Urals Branch
of the Russian Academy of Sciences
Ekaterinburg, Russia

ISSN 2195-4968 ISSN 2195-4976 (electronic)
Lecture Notes in Information Systems and Organisation
ISBN 978-3-030-73260-8 ISBN 978-3-030-73261-5 (eBook)
https://doi.org/10.1007/978-3-030-73261-5

This Springer imprint is published by the registered company Springer Nature Switzerland AG
The registered company address is: Gewerbestrasse 11, 6330 Cham, Switzerland

Introduction

The emergence of advanced technologies has marked a new era of global development. The large-scale use of digital and information communication solutions is fundamentally changing social life and restructuring economic relationships. Digitalization is exerting a profound effect on all the industrial sectors and is changing traditional business models. It opens a whole world of opportunities and challenges. While many enterprises are eagerly following the new developments to strengthen their competitive advantage, some are facing obstacles to digitalization and forced to alter their business processes. Typically, the sustainable introduction of digital innovations is driven by best practices. The theoretical and empirical analyses of digitalization case studies will therefore allow forming effective support mechanisms and drive digitalization. Learning from successful real-world cases as well as anticipating the future effects of digitalization prepare enterprises better manage the challenges and benefit from new opportunities.

This book provides a selection of the best papers presented at the International Scientific Conference *Digital Transformation in Industry: Trends, Management, Strategies*, which was held in Ekaterinburg, Russia, on November 27, 2020. Our vision was to provide a platform to researchers and practitioners to collaboratively explore new approaches to study digitalization and to substantiate successful strategies of digital transformation in industrial enterprises. The conference hence focused on evaluating trends in the use of digital technologies, discussed the prospects dissemination of Industry 4.0, and sketched the image of the economy of the future.

The various papers selected in this book provides readers with an overview of how Industry 4.0 technologies are transforming the competitive landscape in various industries across the globe and creating new opportunities. It also provides an understanding of the key challenges and potential mitigation strategies. The topics covered in this book include the perception of Industry 4.0 basic technologies and the extent to which they affect digitalization processes; the prerequisites for forming the system of digital platforms as a universal environment for creating new products; modeling the procedure and structural links between digitalization components and its factorial influence on the entire industrial sector, as well as industrial enterprises and regions; examining the cases of using neural networks and artificial intelligence;

the demand for human capital and the peculiarities of intellectual capital formation amid digitalization; evaluated the effects and risks of digital solutions in supply chains; the closeness of relationships between companies in production chains; the role of digital innovation in the sustainable development of the industrial sector; investigating the issues of competence training of Industry 4.0 specialists using project-based approach; exploring the practice of using digital technologies in the oil industry, education, finance, chemical industry, etc.; and formulating the principles of new industrial policy in the era of digitalization. These topics will be of great interest to academics, researchers, policymakers, and practitioners.

Contents

About the Editors

Dr. Vikas Kumar is Director of Research and Professor of Operations and Supply Chain Management at Bristol Business School, University of the West of England, UK. He is also visiting Professor at Ton Duc Thang University, Ho Chi Minh City, Vietnam. He holds a Ph.D. degree in Management Studies from the University of Exeter and a Bachelors of Technology degree in Metallurgy and Materials Engineering. He serves on the editorial board of several international journals and is a regular speaker at international conferences. He has guest-edited a number of special issues in high-impact journals. He is also a reviewer of more than 15 international journals. He has published more than 200 peer-reviewed papers and contributed four books. His current research focus is on sustainable supply chain management and supply chain 4.0. Among his other research interests are short food supply chains, circular economy, and operational excellence.

Dr. Jafar Rezaei is Associate Professor and Head of the Section Transport and Logistics at the Department of Engineering Systems and Services, Faculty of Technology, Policy and Management (TPM), Delft University of Technology (TU Delft). He did his Ph.D. at TPM, TU Delft, has a background in operations research, and has published in several peer-reviewed journals. He is founding Editor of *Journal of Supply Chain Management Science*. In 2015, he developed the Best Worst Method (BWM), which has become a popular multi-criteria decision analysis method. His main research interests are supply chain management, logistics, sustainability, and decision analysis.

Dr. Victoria Akberdina is Deputy Director of the Institute of Economics of the Ural Branch of the Russian Academy of Sciences. She heads the Department of Regional Industrial Policy and Economic Security. She performs fundamental and applied research on the problems of industrial policy formation, forecasting methodology and modeling the evolution of the economic and technological development of industrial complexes, and conducts research on the structural proportions of economic development. In 2019, she was awarded the title of Corresponding Member of the Russian Academy of Sciences.

Evgeny Kuzmin is Researcher (Academic) of the Department of Regional Economic Policy and Economic Security of the Institute of Economics of the Ural Branch of the Russian Academy of Sciences and Senior Lecturer of the Department of Enterprises Economics of the Ural State University of Economics. He is a reviewer of high impact international journals including *Journal of Cleaner Production* (Elsevier), *Entrepreneurship and Sustainability Issues*, etc. His research interests are risk, uncertainty, economic crises, sustainability, public–private partnerships, investments, business planning, industrialization, industrial policy, industry markets, modeling, economic growth and development, entrepreneurship, and business activity.

Industry 4.0: Individual Perceptions About Its Nine Technologies

Francisco Diniz, Nelson Duarte, António Amaral, and Carla Pereira

Abstract Industry 4.0 is a trendy concept that everyone is talking about. However, there are several concepts and technologies attached to Industry 4.0. The concept is considered as the most recent industrial revolution and takes us to the domains of automation, digitalization, information, etc. The concept is gaining in popularity, but sometimes firms and employees are not able to follow new trends. The paper summarizes a research on the concepts of Industry 4.0 and 9 technologies commonly associated with the Industry 4.0 umbrella. Most of the literature recognizes it as something that can bring several benefits to firms. However, it is also pointed out that the adoption of these technologies relies on several factors. The current study focuses on the human factors. A group of 260 respondents participated in a questionnaire and were asked about their perceptions of Industry 4.0 and its technologies. The main purpose was to find different responses to Industry 4.0 technologies, according to age, education level, gender or field of studies. In general, all the individuals present a

F. Diniz (✉)
CETRAD, UTAD, Pólo II da ECHS, Quinta de Prados, 5000-801 Vila Real, Portugal
e-mail: fdiniz@utad.pt

N. Duarte
CIICESI, ESTG, Politécnico Do Porto, Rua do Curral, Margaride, 4610-156 Felgueiras, Portugal

IRIEM, Hong-Kong, China

N. Duarte
e-mail: nduarte@estg.ipp.pt

A. Amaral
Departamento de Engenharia Mecânica, Politécnico Do Porto, Instituto Superior de Engenharia Do Porto, Rua Dr. António Bernardino de Almeida, 431, 4249-015 Porto, Portugal

CIICESI, Politécnico Do Porto, Rua do Curral, Margaride, 4610-156 Felgueiras, Portugal

C. Pereira
CIICESI, ESTG, Politécnico Do Porto, Felgueiras, Portugal
e-mail: cpereira@estg.ipp.pt

INESCTEC, Rua Dr. Roberto Frias, 712, 4200-465 Porto, Portugal

A. Amaral
e-mail: sal@isep.ipp.pt

V. Kumar et al. (eds.), *Digital Transformation in Industry*, Lecture Notes in Information Systems and Organisation 44, https://doi.org/10.1007/978-3-030-73261-5_1

similar approach. The Main differences were found on Big Data, Augmented Reality and Simulation technologies.

Keywords Industry 4.0 · Technologies · Profile

1 Introduction

This new revolution—Industry 4.0 (I4.0) is leading us to the digital era: business models, production systems, smart and autonomous machines, augmented reality to support operators, smart products and services integration, big data analytics, value chain information—most of these activities are now being performed digitally.

According to Alcacér and Cruz-Machado [2], in 2011, the German government brought into the world a new heading called Industrie 4.0. This concept was assumed as the fourth industrial revolution because it is possible to identify four main industry changes throughout history [17].

"Since I4.0 boom, the research community has experienced different approaches to I4.0 concept; however, the general society may be confused based on the lack of understanding on this area." [2]. On the one hand, it is clear that new (digital) technologies are in a way to increase the productivity of modern organizations; on the other hand, a question arises: are human resources fully committed to these new technologies? How open are we as human beings to accept, welcome and adapt to this new environment? The population, depending on the propensity to innovate, digital skills and the use of digital technology, varies considerably according to several factors, such as age, level of education, income, role in the company among others.

Considering that the concept of I4.0 is composed of different technologies and that not all of them are easy to understand by the overall population, this paper addresses this topic by intending to measure: how familiar are different groups of people with I4.0 and its technologies?

2 Industry 4.0 and Its Technologies

Some variations could be found in the literature regarding I4.0 Technologies [5]. According to some authors [2, 19], it is generally accepted for successful implementation of I4.0, nine fundamental technologies are required to be part of the entire system. I4.0 also brings increments in the development of automation, digitalization and digitization processes [13, 14], intelligent communication systems/technologies [6, 19], and Cyber physical systems [1, 5].

The framework for Industry 4.0 might be presented as follows [2]:

- Internet of Things (IoT):

A global system serving users worldwide with interconnected computer networks using Standard Internet Protocol. As individually distinguishable by the real world, the "things" can be anything like an object or a person.

- Augmented Reality:

Augmented Reality increases the perception of reality by making use of artificial information about the environment, where the real world is fulfilled by its objects. It can help in closing some gaps, e.g., between product development and manufacturing operations, due to the ability to reproduce and reuse digital information and enhance knowledge creation while supporting assembly operations.

- Big Data Analytics:

Huge amount of (un)structured data from different types of sources that can come from interconnected and heterogeneous objects describes Big Data. Data collection or storage has no meaningful value, but the core characteristic of Big Data is to perform data analysis.

- Cloud:

Cloud computing is an alternative technology for companies who intend to invest in IT outsourcing resources. The adoption of Cloud service has several advantages related to cost reduction, e.g., the direct and indirect costs on the removal of IT infrastructure from the organization.

- Cybersecurity:

Cybersecurity is a high-level attribute of information security, and through the word "cyber" it spreads to apply also on industrial environments and IoT. Cybersecurity is a combination of technology and management protocols laying on protecting, detecting and responding to attacks.

- Simulation:

Computer simulation, is becoming a technology to better understand the dynamics of business systems. Simulation allows experiments for the validation of products, processes or systems design and configuration. Simulation modeling helps with cost reduction, decrease development cycles and increase product quality.

- Systems Integration (Vertical and Horizontal):

Engineering, production, marketing, suppliers, and supply chain operations, everything connected must create a collaborative scenario of systems integration, according to the information flow and considering the levels of automation. In I4.0 systems integration has two approaches: horizontal and vertical integrations.

- Additive Manufacturing:

Additive Manufacturing is an enabling technology helping on the development of new products, business models and supply chains. A set of technologies that enables "3D printing" of physical objects form the collective term Additive Manufacturing. Products such as one-of-a-kind can be manufactured without conventional surpluses, so it is a big advantage.

- Robotics:

Robots with Artificial Intelligence increase the adaptability and flexibility, of production systems that could facilitate the manufacturing of different products and consequently decreasing its production costs reduction. Fully autonomous robots make their own decisions to perform tasks in constantly changeable environments with or without operator's interaction.

Recognizing the relevance of I4.0, as well as the benefits it can bring to firms [4, 8, 9, 15, 16], there are some dimensions to consider in the digitization process towards the I4.0 implementation [6]: (1) organization of work—new technologies need to rethink how the organization will operate; (2) human factors—new technologies require new competences and skills from the workers; (3) external environment—adoption of new technologies is dependent of the maturity of the environment, where they are implemented. In this paper, the central focus is on the human factors dimension which were already identified as a relevant factor by other authors [18, 21].

As stated by Kamble et al. [11] "*the workforce lacks the adequate skills required to cope up with the upcoming automation and there is a lack of clarity in the standards for the implementation of industry 4.0 which has created ambiguity in many organizations*". For effective and successful adoption of I4.0 "*A collaborative, explorative, and entrepreneurial mindset is a success factor that has to be established among a company's most important resource: the* employees" [16]. The same authors argue that managers should train and develop employees' competences on specific I4.0 technologies (data analytics, IT, software, and human–machine interaction). Standing in line, new job profiles with novel requirements for training and education are expected to emerge, mostly referring to decreasing importance of manual labor that will be replaced with workers with IT-skills [7, 12, 16]. Age, training and education factors, are also regarded as factors to take into consideration [7].

Different authors also identified other differences, such as on the definition of I4.0 across academic disciplines, namely Operations Management, Industrial Engineering, Data Science, Operations Research and Control [10]. Differences in the adoption are also identified according to firms' size, business sector, or role (user or provider) at I4.0 [16, 20]. Another relevant issue is related to SME due to their typical style of management and short-term strategy that differs from their larger counterparts [15]. The same authors also conclude that "*despite the growing number of new tools and technologies, most of them are under-exploited, if not ignored by SMEs.*" Their study shows "*that the least expensive and least revolutionary technologies (simulation, cloud computing) are the most exploited in SMEs whereas those allowing profound business transformations (CPS, Machine-To-Machine, bigdata, collaborative robot) are still neglected by SMEs*" [15].

Considering the factors pointed out in the literature, some questions can be raised, namely: Is there any difference towards I4.0 Technologies according to gender? And according to the generation factor? Will the level of education or field of studies play a role in the openness to I4.0 Technologies on individuals? These are some questions that we will try to answer in this paper.

3 Methodology

The present paper results from a broader project aiming to identify specific characteristics among different generations. This project includes a multicultural team (Portugal, Poland, and Latvia). The questionnaire was updated from a previous project. In the most recent version, in the Portuguese questionnaire, were added some questions to identify some issues related to I4.0.

The Portuguese survey was applied to 260 individuals, mainly by using the social networks. The main purpose for the inclusion of these items is related to the aim of this paper that is the identification of possible patterns among the respondents' characteristics (gender, generation, level of education and field of studies) with the nine technologies of I4.0.

In order to study the relationships, statistical analysis was performed, using the SPSS Statistics software v.25, mainly using a crosstab's analysis.

The purpose of the study was to explore the existence of specific patterns associated with specific characteristics. Therefore, the following research hypotheses were put forward:

H1–4: Is there any variable association between Gender (1); Generation (2); (Level of Education (3); Field of Studies (4) and the Knowledge people claim to have about I4.0?
H5–8: Is there a variable association between Gender (5); Generation (6); (Level of Education (7); Field of Studies (8) and IOT
H9–12: Is there a variable association between Gender (9); Generation (10); (Level of Education (11); Field of Studies (12) and Augmented Reality
H13–16: Is there a variable association between Gender (13); Generation (14); (Level of Education (15); Field of Studies (16) and Big Data Analytics
H17–20: Is there a variable association between Gender (17); Generation (18); (Level of Education (19); Field of Studies (20) and Cloud
H21–24: Is there a variable association between Gender (21); Generation (22); (Level of Education (23); Field of Studies (24) and Cybersecurity
H25–28: Is there a variable association between Gender (25); Generation (26); (Level of Education (27); Field of Studies (28) and Simulation
H29–32: Is there a variable association between Gender (29); Generation (30); (Level of Education (31); Field of Studies (32) and Systems Integration
H33–36: Is there a variable association between Gender (33); Generation (34); (Level of Education (35); Field of Studies (36) and Additive Manufacturing
H37–40: Is there a variable association between Gender (37); Generation (38); (Level of Education (39); Field of Studies (40) and Robotics.

For the realisation of the main objective of the study, a diagnostic survey was applied using a likert scale (from 0 to 5) and asked the respondents to mark a value within that range, in order to identify how comfortable they were with each of the nine technologies of I4.0.

In order to explore variable association, cross tabulations tests will be performed based on the following hypotheses:

H0: The variables are independent (variable association does not exist) *versus.*

H1: The variables are dependent (association exists).

As stated in the literature, in order to analyse these hypotheses, one must run a χ^2 test. The decision will be taken according to the p-value obtained with the χ^2 test.

The survey was conducted from March to July 2020 through social networks in order to get the snowball effect.

4 Results

In this section the first figure being presented results from simple, but quite important analysis, in order to frame the subsequent analysis. Firstly, it is important to understand the perceptions that inquired individuals present about the basics of I4.0.

On a second stage it will be presented a brief characterization of the respondents, and after that we will present some results in order to identify the existence of patterns among different groups of individuals and their perceptions about I4.0.

Considering the answers to those nine technologies the average figure (even being an average from a Likert scale) presents a result of 2.93 and a standard deviation of 1.24. Analyzing the frequencies from the Likert scale answers was verified that 30% of the respondents scored 4 out of 5 in a variable that combined into one of the nine technologies [(V1+ … +V9)/9]. Other curious but somehow expected results are the extremes: 4.6% of the respondents have no idea about I4.0 (scored 0), while 7.3% are fully committed, since they scored 5 out 5 in the nine technologies. At a first glance, the results seem to be positive; however, 62% of respondents scored 3 or above. These first results suggest that further analysis might identify specific patterns, but this hypothesis will be explored later on.

When it comes to the technologies, at an individual level, the analysis shows that might be some differences towards the familiarization to each technology among respondents. The first results are presented in Table 1.

Based on Table 1, where mean and mode for each technology is presented, it is possible to verify that the most familiar concept (among the nine technologies) is **Cloud** (the only technology with a mode of 5), followed by the concept of **IoT**, while the less familiar is **Additive Manufacturing** and **Robotics**.

These first results are in some way related and divergent to some findings from the literature review. For instance, Moeuf et al. [15] identified Cloud Computing and Simulation as the most frequent technologies in SMEs. Being Portugal a country where the overwhelming majority of firms are SMEs, Cloud technology seems to be aligned, but Simulation is one of the technologies with the lowest results.

From the previous results it was not possible to disclose any pattern. But if we start to consider variables such as gender, age (or generation) or level of studies will we be able to find patterns? Those patterns might be interesting to identify the type of individuals and skills that are aligned with the employer's or project's requirements in

Table 1 Mean and mode for each technology of I4.0

Technology	Mean	Mode
IoT	3.40	4
Augmented reality	2.89	3
Big data analytics	2.70	4
Cloud	3.71	5
Cybersecurity	3.18	4
Simulation	2.67	3
Systems integration	2.85	4
Additive manufacturing	2.42	3
Robotics	2.60	3

terms of I4.0 technologies. In order to explore these possibilities, it will be important to describe/characterize our group of respondents.

From the data available in Table 2, an overview of the respondents' profile could be

Table 2 Respondents' brief characterization

	%
Gender	
Male	48.1
Female	51.9
Generation	
Baby Boomer	0.4
Gen. X	20
Gen Y. (Millennial)	26.5
Gen Z	53.1
Education	
Basic school	3.8
High school	39.6
University degree	36.9
Master or doctorate	19.2
Missing	0.4
Field of education	
Economics/management	20.4
Social sciences/law	1.9
Tourism	0.4
STEM	33.1
Health	2.3
Others	8.8
Missing	33.1

seen. The main idea was to present a brief description from the respondents in order to explore the patterns (and hypothesis) suggested in the previous chapters. Next, we will try to identify the existence of relations among some variables, according to the hypothesis and tests presented in the methodology section.

The first variable dependence test was related to I4.0 variable as a whole. At first was considered the variable that aggregates the nine technologies in order to find a possible variable association with gender, generation, education or field of studies. The results are as follows:

- cross-tabulation I4.0 versus Gender:

  The results observed and expected do not present a significative difference. By requiring the χ^2 test we got a p-value of 0.492. Since this result is higher than 0.05 it means that H0 may not be rejected. So, the results suggest that on what regards I4.0 there are no differences between genders.

- cross-tabulation I4.0 versus Generation:

  The first test considering the 4 generations and the 6 levels of I4.0 (0 to 6) presented a result without statistical validity, since 37.5% of the cells presented a count of less than 5. In order to try a valid result, the levels of I4.0 were reduced from 6 to 3: [0 and 1 1; 2 and 3 2; 4 and 5 3]. After this reduction the test keeps without statistical validity. Looking to the results obtained, were not identified unexpected patterns.

- cross-tabulation I4.0 versus Education:

  In what regards Education the results are similar to those obtained in the Generation tests. There is no statistical validity, but there are not unexpected patterns identified so, does not make sense to readjust any variable.

- cross-tabulation I4.0 versus Field of Studies:
  The first analysis of this relation presented a result without statistical validity. In this case were reduced both variables (I4.0 as in the previous ones, and the field of education to 3 categories: Economics and Management, STEM and others that now also aggregates Tourism, Health and Social Sciences/Law). The second test led to a statistical valid result, but with a p-value (on the χ^2 test) of 0.426—higher than 0.05 which means that H0 may not be rejected. Anyway, there is a slight tendency for a pattern: On the categories of Economics and Management and Others the number of cases in the lower levels of I4.0 is higher than the expected ones, and we got a lower (than the expected) count in the higher levels of I4.0. The opposite scenario was identified in the STEM category. Once again, this results origin from a detailed figures observation, rather than a statistical valid test.

The results from these analyses lead us to assume that with H0 (variable independence) no rejection, one can assume that the familiarization with the concept of Industry 4.0 is not a particular characteristic of a specific group of people. It seems to be a concept that is equally known by different groups of people in this sample study.

The next step consists of a similar analysis but this time considering each one of the nine technologies individually. In order to reduce the results without statistical

Table 3 Results from the Cross-tabs among I4.0 technologies and respondents' characteristics

Technology	Gender	Generation	Education	Field of studies
IoT	H0 not rejected	H0 not rejected	H0 not rejected	H0 Not rejected
Augmented reality	H0 Not rejected	**H0 Rejected (10%)**	Without statistical validity	H0 Not rejected
Big data analytics	**H0 Rejected (5%)**	H0 Not rejected	Without statistical validity	H0 Not rejected
Cloud	H0 Not rejected	H0 Not rejected	H0 Not rejected	H0 Not rejected
Cybersecurity	H0 Not rejected	H0 Not rejected	H0 Not rejected	H0 Not rejected
Simulation	H0 Not rejected	**H0 Rejected (10%)**	H0 Not rejected	H0 Not rejected
Systems Integration	H0 Not rejected	**H0 Rejected (5%)**	H0 Not rejected	H0 Not rejected
Additive Manufacturing	H0 Not rejected	H0 Not rejected	H0 Not rejected	H0 Not rejected
Robotics	H0 Not rejected	H0 Not rejected	H0 Not rejected	H0 Not Rejected

Comments: IoT: No variable association, Augmented Reality: It was identified a pattern: Generation Z are the ones that assume to be more familiar with this concept (p-value = 0.097), Big Data Analytics: Men are more familiar with this concept p-value = 0.038). Even without statistical validity there is an identified tendency to be more familiar to those with higher levels of education, Cloud: No variable association, Cybersecurity: No variable association, Simulation: The younger generations (Y and Z) are more familiar with this technology, Systems Integration: Y Generation (millennials) is the one that is more familiar with this concept (p-value = 0.030), Additive Manufacturing: No variable association, Robotics: No variable association

validity, the levels of familiarization with these concepts were reduced from 6 to 3. In the category of generation considering that only one respondent classified as baby-boomer, this generation was excluded from the analysis. To simplify the results are presented in Table 3.

The results obtained and presented in Table 3 are aligned with the results on the Industry 4.0 variable as a whole. When the technologies are considered by themselves, in most cases the variable independence (no association) is the result. On those results with variable association, the most relevant is the Generation (or age). While younger people (Generation Z—born after 1994) are more familiar with the concept of Augmented Reality, the so-called Millennials (born between 1980 and 1994) are more familiar with Systems integration. Both Y and Z are comfortable with the Simulation concepts. On what regards Gender, men are more familiar with the Big Data concept.

5 Conclusion

As first conclusion in general it can be said that taking into consideration the results from this sample, there are no significant differences among the level of education or field of studies, towards to I4.0 and its technologies. On what regards gender and generation some differences were identified. On gender, it was verified that men are more comfortable with the concept of big data analytics than women. It was also identified that younger generations (Y and/or Z) are more confident in the following technologies: Augmented Reality, Simulation and Systems Integration.

A research developed in two large universities in Eastern Europe concluded that students from business, finance, economics, statistics, marketing, and similar disciplines did not reject the inclusion of technical content (cloud computing, big data, social networks, cybersecurity) [3]. This outcome in some way justifies the results obtained in the field of studies analysis. Students, even those that are not in STEM, are aware and interested in the I4.0 technologies.

Notwithstanding, the results point out a subliminal importance of technology embedding throughout generations which could produce expressive differences between perceptions and skills development among its members and generate difficulties to standardize the use of such technologies.

It is also important to point out that the digital transformation of society, industry and services, as well as in the education field is in a development/transition phase which means that some of these previous results could vary through time. In our view, it will be important to measure these variables longitudinally towards picturing the tendencies and the degree of alignment between the perceptions and skills of people and the work requirements in the digitalized world.

Acknowledgements This work is supported by national funds, through the FCT – Portuguese Foundation for Science and Technology under the project UIDB/04011/2020 and under the project UIDB/04728/2020.

References

1. Acatech (ed.). (2011). *Cyber-physical systems driving force for innovation in mobility, health, energy and production*. Acatech Position Paper. Springer Verlag.
2. Alcácer, V., & Cruz-Machado, V. (2019). Scanning the industry 4.0: A literature review on technologies for manufacturing systems. *Engineering Science and Technology, 22*(3), 899–919. https://doi.org/10.1016/j.jestch.2019.01.006.
3. Bologa, R., Lupu, A., Boja, C., & Georgescu, T. (2017). Sustaining employability: A process for introducing cloud computing, big data, social networks, mobile programming and cybersecurity into academic curricula. *Sustainability, 9*(12), 2235. https://doi.org/10.3390/su9122235.
4. Brettel, M., Friederichsen, N., Keller, M., & Rosenberg, M. (2014). How virtualization, decentralization and network building change the manufacturing landscape. *International Journal of Mechanical, Industrial and Aerospace Sciences, 7.0*(1). https://doi.org/10.5281/zenodo.1336426.

5. Costa, M., Santos, L., Schaefer, J., Baierle, I., & Nara, E. (2019). Industry 4.0 technologies basic network identification. *Scientometrics, 121*(2). https://doi.org/10.1007/s11192-019-03216-7.
6. Dalenogare, L., Benitez, G., Ayala, N., & Frank, A. (2018). The expected contribution of industry 4.0 technologies for industrial performance. *International Journal of Production Economics, 204*(3), 383–394. https://doi.org/10.1016/j.ijpe.2018.08.019.
7. Dombrowski, U., & Wagner, T. (2014). Mental strain as field of action in the 4th industrial revolution. *Procedia CIRP, 17*, 100–105. https://doi.org/10.1016/j.procir.2014.01.077.
8. Ejsmont, K., Gladysz, B., & Kluczek, A. (2020). Impact of industry 40 on sustainability-bibliometric literature review. *Sustainability, 12*(14), 5650. https://doi.org/10.3390/su12145650.
9. Ghobakhloo, M. (2018). The future of manufacturing industry: A strategic roadmap toward Industry 4.0. *Journal of Manufacturing Technology Management, 29*(6), 910–936. https://doi.org/10.1108/JMTM-02-2018-0057.
10. Ivanov, D., Tang, C., Dolgui, A., Battini, D., & Das, A. (2020). Researchers' perspectives on Industry 4.0: Multi-disciplinary analysis and opportunities for operations management. *International Journal of Production Research,* 1–24.
11. Kamble, S., Gunasekaran, A., & Sharma, R. (2018). Analysis of the driving and dependence power of barriers to adopt industry 4.0 in Indian industry. *Computers in Industry, 101*, 107–119. https://doi.org/10.1016/j.compind.2018.06.004.
12. Kubicek, B., & Korunka, C. (2017). The present and future of work: Some concluding remarks and reflections on upcoming trends. In *Job demands in a changing world of work: Impact on workers' health and performance and implications for research and practice.* https://doi.org/10.1007/978-3-319-54678-0_9.
13. Lasi, H., Fettke, P., Kemper, H., Feld, T., & Hoffmann, M. (2014). Industry 4.0. *Business & Information Systems Engineering, 6*, 239–242. https://doi.org/10.1007/s11576-014-0424-4.
14. Lu, Y. (2017). Industry 4.0: A survey on technologies, applications and open research issues. *Journal of Industrial Information Integration, 6*, 1–10.
15. Moeuf, A., Pellerin, R., Lamouri, S., Tamayo-Giraldo, S., & Barbaray, R. (2018). The industrial management of SMEs in the era of Industry 4.0. *International Journal of Production Research, 56*(3), 1–19. https://doi.org/10.1080/00207543.2017.1372647.
16. Müller, J., Kiel, D., & Voigt, K. (2018). What drives the implementation of Industry 4.0? The role of opportunities and challenges in the context of sustainability. *Sustainability, 10*(1), 247. https://doi.org/10.3390/su10010247.
17. Qin, J., Liu, Y., & Grosvenor, R. (2016). A categorical framework of manufacturing for industry 4.0 and beyond. *Procedia CIRP, 52*, 173–178. https://doi.org/10.1016/j.procir.2016.08.005.
18. Ras, E., Wild, F., Stahl, C., & Baudet, A. (2017). Bridging the skills gap of workers in industry 4.0 by human performance augmentation tools: Challenges and roadmap. In *PETRA '17: Proceedings of the 10th International conference on pervasive technologies related to assistive environments* (pp. 428–432). https://doi.org/10.1145/3056540.3076192.
19. Salkin, C., Oner, M., Ustundag, A., & Cevikcan, E. (2018). A conceptual framework for industry 4.0. In *Industry 4.0: Managing the digital transformation* (pp. 3–22). Springer International Publishing.
20. Sony, M., Naik, S. (2019). Key ingredients for evaluating Industry 4.0 readiness for organizations: a literature review. *Benchmarking, 27*(7). https://doi.org/10.1108/BIJ-09-2018-0284.
21. Wei, Z., Song, X., & Wang, D. (2017). Manufacturing flexibility, business model design, and firm performance. *International Journal of Production Economics, 193*. https://doi.org/10.1016/j.ijpe.2017.07.004.

Industrial Policy: A New Reality in the Context of Digital Transformation of the Economy

Olga A. Romanova and Evgeny Kuzmin

Abstract The latest technological and globalization trends have entailed a sharp increase in various regulatory functions, which enhances the content and significance of state industrial policy. Amid these conditions, it is becoming increasingly important to identify the key features of a new reality that determine the necessity for industrial policy to be adjusted under digital transformation. We hypothesize that the transformation of the priorities, goals and economic content of industrial policy is due to a new reality affected by changing core factors of technological development, the influence of recent globalization trends, and the growing importance of human capital. The fourth industrial revolution, globalization and human capital are believed to be the major drivers of today's economic development, despite the differences in their institutional nature. Their combined impact provides a new direction for the development of industrial policy and encourages the formation of a system of public instruments for supporting priority industrial areas. The driving force of today's economy is not only technology or the production sector, but also sophisticated organizational-economic models and advanced mechanisms for coordinating manufacturers based on a cross-platform network business model. Addressing the experience of developed and developing countries, we demonstrate the changing importance of production factors transforming industrial policy. The study substantiates the need for a proactive industrial policy that takes into account economic and social interests.

Keywords Digital transformation · Globalization · Industrial policy · Innovation technology · Industry 4.0 · Network-based business models

O. A. Romanova · E. Kuzmin (✉)
Institute of Economics of the Ural Branch of the Russian Academy of Sciences, Moskovskaya St. 29, 620014 Ekaterinburg, Russian Federation
e-mail: kuzmin@usue.ru

E. Kuzmin
Ural State University of Economics, 8 Marta/Narodnoy Voli St. 62/45, 620144 Ekaterinburg, Russian Federation

V. Kumar et al. (eds.), *Digital Transformation in Industry*, Lecture Notes in Information Systems and Organisation 44, https://doi.org/10.1007/978-3-030-73261-5_2

1 Introduction

The modern stage of the global economy's development is gaining in popularity as the age of disruption. Such changes seem to be fully consistent with the term "black swan" introduced by Taleb [35] to describe events that are characterized by anomalies, a tremendous ascendancy and a retrospective nature. The emergence of a black swan in 2020 in the form of the COVID-19 pandemic has affected the entire planet by provoking large-scale economic, technological, socio-cultural and political changes. They will undoubtedly accelerate the outlined structural shifts in these areas and result in a sharp increase in regulatory and administrative functions of the state.

In this context, industrial policy is of special importance. An overview of the evolution of industrial policy models in different countries, the ambiguous consequences of its implementation and the specificity of the formation of the industrial policy institution underlie the hypothesis of the current study [2, 13, 15, 22, 23, 36, 41]. A certain influence was exerted by the peculiarities of policies during the second, third and fourth industrial revolutions, as well as by the corresponding changes in the significance of the reproduction process factors [12, 38]. The hypothesis is that priorities, goals and economic content of industrial policy are transforming themselves in response to a new reality influenced by changing key factors of technological development, the influence of recent globalization trends, and the growing importance of human capital.

Of numerous factors affecting the industrial policy transformation, one can single out the key drivers that determine the emergence of elements of a new reality in economic development. They influence the change in the fundamental technologies of industrial development, form new particularities of manufacturing and new institutions of industrial development, and determine the largest shifts and the depth of structural changes in global and national industrial production.

Drivers may differ depending on certain spatial boundaries or at different historical stages. For instance, in the 1990s, the economic growth factor was the production of computers and electronics; but in 2000, the main drivers were software and databases [40]. The period from 2010 to 2020 is characterized by the strengthening of such institutionally different factors as the fourth industrial revolution, globalization and human capital [40]. With all the specificity of the impact each of these factors has on economic growth, the common feature typical of all of them is the ever-increasing significance of digital transformation. This establishes a new direction for the development of industrial policy and stimulates the formation of a system of public instruments for supporting digital transformation of industrial production.

2 Key Drivers of the Transformation of Industrial Policy

Despite their conflicting institutional nature, the three mentioned drivers of economic development are supposed to fully reveal new realities that have a transformative effect on industrial policy.

2.1 *The Fourth Industrial Revolution*

The first decades of the twenty-first century are characterized by global technological changes that are increasingly interpreted as the fourth technological revolution—Industry 4.0 [28]. It is based on cyber-physical systems, the Internet of Things, 3D printing, and networks. According to Soloviov [33], the digital economy is being formed against the backdrop of the revolution considered as the completion of just another cycle of technological bifurcations.

At the present stage of the development of the world industrial system, there are four groups of crucial technological systems: digital technologies, advanced materials, biotechnology, and technologies in the field of environmental protection and new energy. It is digital technologies that can cause the transformation of traditional industrial production [32].

The introduction of such technologies supported through the use of industrial policy tools allows forming new generation industries (advanced manufacturing) designed to stimulate economic growth [42]. The formation of new generation industries is intertwined with the evolution of industrial development institutions. While during the second industrial revolution (1920–1960) institutions of industrial development enjoyed a substantial support and aimed to promote vertical integration and concentration of production, in the time of the third revolution (1960–2010) they switched to the support for the global outsourcing of business processes. In the period of the fourth industrial revolution (since 2010), industrial policy has been concentrating on supporting new institutions, which encourage the formation of network structures of business, science and education, and informal networks of customized products manufacturers.

The wide spread of ICT, digital platforms, integration of digital technologies into business processes predetermined the transformation of economic systems into dynamic network-based systems with a flexible structure of internal relationships. These systems are able to quickly respond to change in the external environment and increased uncertainty, which allows them to adapt to the constant emergence of new technologies and changing demands in the market. Digitalization of economic processes makes it possible to ensure a horizontal mobility of knowledge and technology between territories and sectors of the economy, which leads to the emergence of a network multiplier effect. This generally recognized fact of the new reality strengthened the positions of horizontal industrial policy and resulted in the development of new tools to support the digitalization of the economy.

In many countries, the digitalization of the economy and, above all, industry, is viewed as a pivotal point on the national economic agenda [18]. The growing significance of the digitalization of the economy is confirmed by empirical studies by the McKinsey Global Institute [18]: digitalization as a tool for enhancing the productivity and competitiveness of the economy is equivalent in terms of its impact to the creation of technological innovation. Today's reality lies behind the integration of vertical and horizontal industrial policy, since the equivalent priorities in industrial policy are, on the one hand, the support for the latest production technologies, and, on the other hand, an improvement in the business environment for their continuous renewal and successful functioning.

The importance of creating a network environment conducive to uninterrupted innovation activity is highlighted using the case of the EU industrial policy implementation, where the strengthening of the barrier-free horizontal connectivity of national economies facilitates the development of new network ecosystems [3, 25, 27, 30, 39]. This leads to changes in the industrial policy's object of support. The new object is collaboration mechanisms. The network-based nature of new industrial policy shifts its focus from supporting large-scale production and supply chains to servicing customized consumers partially involved in the production process [38]. In doing so, innovative production networks are formed that support the initiatives uniting industrial companies and research institutes in order to design and develop breakthrough technology. This is one of the factors of the new reality that establish a network trajectory of industrial policy's transformation [31, 38].

When framing a new agenda related, inter alia, to the coronavirus pandemic, the following aspects should be also taken into account. Quarantine measures are already changing the pace of structural change in the economy. The growth rates of the telecommunications sector, as well as the production and sales of digital content have increased worldwide. Digital services in the public sector, medicine, education and trade are gaining in demand. Distant learning technologies have witnessed an explosive growth. Meeting the growing demand in the timely manner identifies a range of primary objectives of the new industrial policy. The list of the objectives is also expanded by the fact that the ability of workers to adapt to digital technologies, artificial intelligence, remote solutions and big data becomes critical for the competitiveness of the country's economy at large and individual companies, in particular.

Another aspect of the new reality affecting the transformation of industrial policy is that the key driver of economic development today is not just technology or the manufacturing sector, but novel organizational-economic models and modern manufacturer coordination mechanisms based on cross-platform business models. Such business allows for interaction, providing all participants with an open infrastructure and setting rules uniform for all of them. The primary purpose of a platform is to establish relationships between users and promote the exchange of goods, which creates value for all participants. Measures and tools of industrial policy supplemented with the instruments for supporting industrial digital platforms can significantly enhance policy efficacy in terms of both performance and cost effectiveness.

In our view, high-tech industries are in need for special support. The experience of developed countries indicates that the key driver of the economy is high-tech companies enjoying government support [6, 8, 9, 14, 20, 26]. At that, most of such companies are usually private. However, these firms demonstrate the highest growth rates, ensure the ever-growing share of non-resource exports and create high-paying jobs, which improves the quality of life. In recent years, Russia has also witnessed the sector of private high-tech companies forming, which are more efficient than companies with state participation: the average revenue per employee in private high-tech companies is four times higher [37]. It is noteworthy that private high-tech companies in Russia are more active in funding R&D and launch new products to the market, 70% of which are already present in the global market. Using the industrial policy toolkit to support private high-tech companies should take its rightful place when forming a new industrial policy agenda.

2.2 *Globalization*

The early 1980s are widely believed to be the beginning of the modern stage of economic globalization. This stage was initiated due to the intensification of scientific-technological development, in which the widespread use of computers played a leading role. As noted by Schwab [29] at the 2018 World Economic Forum, globalization is a phenomenon driven by technology and the movement of ideas, people and goods. Despite all contradictions, globalization remains a dominant trend in the development of the world economy, which forces most nations to adapt their economic and, therefore, industrial policies to new realities.

One of these realities is the problem of the revival of protectionism. Today's protectionism results from both the policy of globalization and the development of the digital economy. In contrast to the traditional interpretation of protectionism, the concept of Protectionism 2.0 is analyzed from different angles [19]. Narrowly defined, this term denotes the application of protective measures in the production and trade of digital technologies. However, amid the growing global competition, most countries are pursuing a more aggressive policy that implements a set of measures protecting not the national economy alone. The measures of this policy are used to support companies operating within both the domestic market and global value chains. Such a proactive and goal-oriented public policy is referred to as Protectionism 2.0. Its main distinguishing features are as follows: a focus shifted from protecting the domestic market to protecting the interests of national business; support for business through political and economic pressure on competitors; going beyond the economic domain in order to protect historical and cultural values (cultural protectionism [4]), etc.

Hence, the new reality of the age of globalization characterized by deepening international competition and the struggle for economic dominance predetermines the need to change the forms, methods and mechanisms of industrial policy. In the face of increasingly aggressive forms of protectionism emerging, industrial policy should go beyond supporting only national business, but provide for methods and mechanisms of economic pressure on foreign competitors in their territories.

2.3 Human Capital

The success of the digital transformation of industry is largely affected by the quality of human capital. Its formation depends on such resources as knowledge, information and scientific-technological progress used in the reproduction process, as well as traditional resources such as labor and capital. All these resources taken together, but to varying degree, affect not only the economy, manufacturing and environment, but also society, which largely shapes a person and their perception of the world and lays the foundations for human capital.

At different stages of economic systems' development, the role of factors affecting industrial digital transformation varies significantly, which is reflected in the change in the priorities of industrial policy. For example, the reorganization of the technological structure of industry and its digitalization resulted in workforce being intensively replaced with means of labor; this, in turn, reduced the importance of workforce as a factor of production. In addition, the development of economic digitalization processes has led to a radical change in the seemingly unshakable statements about the created product distributed between labor and capital in the stable proportion. The experts from the International Monetary Fund argue that technological progress, along with varying exposure to routine occupations, explains about half the overall decline in advanced economies [5]. The ILO statistics on the share of GDP-weighted labor income in 185 countries indicates that between 2004 and 2017 this share decreased in 117 countries [10]. The downward trend in the share of labor income in GDP is also typical of Russia, where the percentage of total labor income in GDP over the past decade has fallen from 52.6 to 46.4% [12]. Such shifts in the structure of primary income show that a growing number of the benefits associated with the use of digital technologies are being concentrated in the hands of capital owners, while the share of benefits received by workers in the form of wage is decreasing. Such a state of affairs cannot contribute to the formation of human capital in the long term. If this trend persists, this will deepen the contradictions between labor and capital and elevate the level of income polarization and inequality.

Stiglitz's theory on the great divide [34] demonstrates that the US economy has long been developing in the interests of 1% of the wealthiest people, without due regard to the needs of the remaining 99% of the population. A similar situation, but with a different ratio of social inequality, is characteristic of developing countries, including Russia. Amid the emerging digital economy, unacceptable income inequality and information inequality, when users are differentiated in terms of access to information, are becoming increasingly dangerous. These and other radical challenges of the modern world require industrial policy to timely modify its content and goals, since the new reality poses interdisciplinary problems, which excludes the possibility to resolve them independently, within the conventional context.

As for human capital, it is noteworthy that the ability of workers to adapt to digital technologies, artificial intelligence, remote solutions, and big data amid the shift in competencies becomes critical for the digital transformation of industry. At the same time, employees working in finance, education, law, corporate governance, etc. are highly qualified specialists adapted to remote work. However, staff with lower qualifications needs to be prepared to working under new conditions. This is going to be a task for not only companies, but also the state in terms of regulating educational practice, which requires a special emphasis within the framework of industrial policy.

Changes in the goals of industrial policy are largely corrected by the emergence of the newest trend towards shrinking the "old" labor market: for the first time ever, modern technologies do not lead to the creation of new jobs. The labor market is shrinking due to the appearance of creative professions and fundamentally new engineering specialties, on the one hand, and as a result of the robotization of production, on the other. According to some experts, introduction of digital technologies will result in the disappearance of professions for the maintenance of traditional production machinery, as well as a number of specialties [17]. Understandably, in such conditions, timely support for continuous education is becoming one of the top priorities of industrial policy. Nevertheless, the downward trend in the number of employees engaged in production of goods highlights, on the one hand, the severity of the employment problem, and on the other, decreases the resources for forming human capital. Currently, in the world's leading economies, 2 out of 100 people are employed in agriculture, providing for not only themselves but also everyone else, 10 people work in industry, and 13 people—in management [11]. The question is what are the other 75 people supposed to do?

Such a situation creates a dangerous source of social instability for the state. In order to avoid this uncertainty, some attempts are made to smooth it out (for example, a social experiment on the introduction of universal basic income). With all the ambiguity of the findings, the main conclusion has confirmed the position shared by the overwhelming majority of researchers: even with financial support for each member of society, in general, it is not ready for the fact that most of its members will be unemployed [11].

3 Proactive Industrial Policy

With the obvious inevitability and all the indisputable advantages of digital transformation of the industry, some consequences of this process are difficult to predict. To make sure that the claims that most modern technologies are a deferred sentence [35] are false, interdisciplinary studies on the outcomes of the latest digital technologies introduction should be performed. This should become an imperative when transforming traditional industrial policy and shaping modern one. Such an approach is fully consistent with the ideology of socio-economic development. Realization of such goals is important from the perspective of both human capital formation and, as the global experience shows, the prevention of possible social conflicts [1, 16, 21, 24, 43].

There is a well-known global trend towards synchronization of the previous three industrial revolutions with social explosions, which led to radical socio-economic transformations. If the cycles of cardinal technological transformations are consistent with the cycles of alarming social instability, then in order to escape from possible social calamities, the state concentrates on creating proactive industrial policy, rather than pursuing a reactive one.

Thus, the growing number of new realities of today's world makes it increasingly relevant to develop a proactive industrial policy on an interdisciplinary basis. Under these new conditions, the role of state support enhances significantly. The number-one priority is to advance such technological solutions, which, when implemented, keep the balance between economic and social interests. The development of proactive industrial policy is starting to be seen as a process where government, business and society are increasingly involved in strategic interaction.

4 Conclusion

We believe that the development of a new generation industry on a digital basis entirely fits into the emerging paradigm of social dynamics in the post-crisis world, i.e. the paradigm of responsible development [7]. Responsible development provides unlimited opportunities for forming human capital, developing knowledge economy, solidarity economy, etc. The sources of their functioning are intellectual resources. Obviously, this is not yet a new reality. We can only talk about the necessity to sort out priorities and tools of responsible development policy that stems from digital transformation. Researchers agree on the fact that the anticipated technological transformation will be in line with the growing social responsibility of the state, society and business. This is fully consistent with our hypothesis that the transformation of the priorities, goals and economic content of industrial policy is due to a new reality affected by volatile key factors of technological development, new globalization trends and increasing importance of human capital.

Acknowledgements The paper was funded by the Russian Foundation for Basic Research (RFFI), project No. 20-010-00719 "Modeling the processes of cross-industrial networkization in the industrial complex based on hybrid technologies".

References

1. Arntz, M., Gregory, T., & Zierahn, U. (2020). Digitization and the future of work: Macroeconomic consequences. In: K. Zimmermann (ed.). *Handbook of labor, human resources and population economics*. Springer. https://doi.org/10.1007/978-3-319-57365-6_11-1.

2. Beath, J. (2002). UK industrial policy: Old tunes on new instruments? *Oxford Review of Economic Policy, 18*(2), 221–239. https://doi.org/10.1093/oxrep/18.2.221.
3. Borrás, S. (2007). Governance Networks in the EU: The Case of GMO Policy. In: M. Marcussen, J. Torfing (eds.). *Democratic Network Governance in Europe*. Palgrave Macmillan. https://doi.org/10.1057/9780230596283_12.
4. Burri, M. (2012). Cultural Protectionism 2.0: Updating cultural policy tools for the digital age (pp. 182–202). In S. Pager, A. Candeub (eds.). *Transnational culture in the Internet age*. Edward Elgar Publishing. https://ssrn.com/abstract=2020991.
5. Dao, M., Das, M., Koczan, Z., & Lian, W. (2017). Why is labor receiving a smaller share of global income? https://www.imf.org/en/Publications/WP/Issues/2017/07/24/Why-Is-Labor-Receiving-a-Smaller-Share-of-Global-Income-Theory-and-Empirical-Evidence-45102.
6. Demidova, E. V., & Oleynikova, M. A. (2017). High-tech companies as a potential driver for the further development of the Russian economy. *Scientific Notes of Young Scientists, 2*, 28–34.
7. Dynkin, A. A., & Telegina, E. A. (2020). Pandemic shock and the world after crisis. *World Economy and International Relations, 64*(8), 5–15. https://doi.org/10.20542/0131-2227-2020-64-8-5-16.
8. Gu, Q., & Dong, R. (2017). High-tech industries: New space and opportunities for NGEs' growth and development in the new stage. In Y. Liu (ed.). *New interpretations on the development of China's non-governmental enterprises. Research series on the Chinese dream and China's development path*. Springer. https://doi.org/10.1007/978-981-10-3872-3_11.
9. Horobet, A., Popovici, O., & Belascu, L. (2020). Drivers of competitiveness in European high-tech industries. In A. Śliwiński, P. Polychronidou, A. Karasavvoglou (eds.). *Economic development and financial markets. Contributions to economics*. Springer. https://doi.org/10.1007/978-3-030-32426-1_4.
10. ILO. (2019). International Labour Organization. The global labor income share and distribution. https://www.ilo.org/global/statistics-and-databases/publications/WCMS_712232/lang--en/index.htm.
11. Ivanov, V. V., & Malinetsky, G. G. (2017). Digital economy: From theory to practice. *Innovations, 12*(230), 3–12.
12. Klavdienko, V. (2020). Digitalization of economy and the distribution of primary income between labor and capital. *Innovations, 5*(259), 20–26. https://doi.org/10.26310/2071-3010.2020.259.5.004.
13. Kuznetsov, B. V., & Simachev, Yu. V. (2014). Evolution of state industrial policy in Russia. *Journal of the New Economic Association, 2*(22), 152–179.
14. Kwon, S. S., & Yin, J. (2015). A comparison of earnings persistence in high-tech and non-high-tech firms. *Review of Quantitative Finance and Accounting, 44*, 645–668. https://doi.org/10.1007/s11156-013-0421-5.
15. Lenchuk, E. B., ed. (2016). *New industrial policy of Russia in the context of ensuring technological independence*. Aleteya.
16. Livingstone, D. W. (2012). Debunking the 'knowledge economy'. In D. W. Livingstone, D. Guile (eds.). *The knowledge economy and lifelong learning. The knowledge economy and education* (vol. 4). Sense Publishers. https://doi.org/10.1007/978-94-6091-916-2_5.
17. Luksha, P. (Ed.). (2015). *Atlas of new professions*. Moscow: Olymp Business.
18. MGI. (2015). McKinsey Global Institute. *Digital America: A tale of the haves and have-mores*. McKinsey & Company.
19. Milovidov, V., & Asker-Zade, N. (2020). Protectionism 2.0: New reality in the age of globalisation. *World Economy and International Relations, 64*(8), 37–45. https://doi.org/10.20542/0131-2227-2020-64-8-37-45.
20. Oh, D., & Masser, I. (1995). High-tech Centres and Regional Innovation: Some Case Studies in the UK, Germany, Japan and Korea. In: C. S. Bertuglia, M. M. Fischer, G. Preto (eds.). *Technological change, economic development and space. Advances in spatial science*. Springer. https://doi.org/10.1007/978-3-642-79760-6_14.
21. Pianta, M. (2018). Technology and employment: Twelve stylised facts for the digital age. *The Indian Journal of Labour Economics, 61*, 189–225. https://doi.org/10.1007/s41027-018-0124-5.

22. Romanova, O. A. (2018). Industrial policy priorities of russia in the context of challenges of the fourth industrial revolution. Part 1. *Economy of Region, 14*(2), 420–432. https://doi.org/10.17059/2018-2-7.
23. Romanova, O. A., & Ponomareva, A. O. (2020). Multi-vector industrial policy in Russia in an emerging new industrial landscape. *Russian Journal of Economic Theory, 17*(2), 276–291. https://doi.org/10.31063/2073-6517/2020.17-2.3.
24. Roy, I., & Consoli, D. (2018). Employment polarization in Germany: Role of technology, trade and human capital. *The Indian Journal of Labour Economics, 61*, 251–279. https://doi.org/10.1007/s41027-018-0133-4.
25. Rumford, C. (2000). Trans-European networks and cross-border projects. In: *European cohesion?* Palgrave Macmillan. https://doi.org/10.1057/9780333981733_3.
26. Rybalka, A. I. (2020). Relationship of property structure and performance of high-tech technology companies. *Studies on Russian Economic Development, 31*, 264–270. https://doi.org/10.1134/S1075700720030144.
27. Sautter, B. (2016). Futuring European industry: Assessing the ManuFuture road towards EU re-industrialization. *European Journal of Futures Research, 4*, 25. https://doi.org/10.1007/s40309-016-0100-6.
28. Schwab, K. (2017). *The fourth industrial revolution. World Economic Forum.* New York: Crown Publishing Group.
29. Schwab, K. (2018). *Globalization 4.0 - what does it mean?* World Economic Forum, 5 November 2018. https://www.weforum.org/agenda/2018/11/globalization-4-what-does-it-mean-how-it-will-benefit-everyone/.
30. Siokas, E. (2018). Network analysis of EU-funded R&D collaboration in the European security research programme: Actors and industries. In N. Karampekios, I. Oikonomou, E. Carayannis (eds.). *The emergence of EU defense research policy. Innovation, technology, and knowledge management* (pp. 221–245). Springer. https://doi.org/10.1007/978-3-319-68807-7_12.
31. Smorodinskaya, N. (2014). Network innovation ecosystems and their role in dynamisation of economic growth. *Innovations, 7*, 27–33.
32. Smorodinskaya, N. V., & Katukov, D. D. (2017). Key features and implications of Industrial Revolution 4.0. *Innovations, 10*(228), 81–90.
33. Soloviov, V. P. (2020). On some background of the fourth industrial revolution. *Innovatsii – Innovations, 5*, 14–19. https://doi.org/10.26310/2071-3010.2020.259.5.003.
34. Stiglitz, J. E. (2015). *The great divide: Unequal societies and what we can do about them.* New York: W.W. Norton & Company.
35. Taleb, N. N. (2010). *The Black Swan. Second Edition: The Impact of the Highly Improbable Fragility.* New York: Random House Publishing Group.
36. Tambovtsev, V. L. (2017). Industrial policy: Towards new interpretation. *Journal of the Ural State University of Economics, 5*(73), 54–67. https://doi.org/10.29141/2073-1019-2017-17-5-5.
37. Titov, B., & Popova, N. (2020). *Special report to the President of the Russian Federation: Regulatory and law enforcement issues constraining the development of high-tech companies in the Russian Federation.* https://doklad.ombudsmanbiz.ru/2020/6.pdf.
38. Tolkachev, S. A. (2018). Network industrial policy in the age of the new industrial revolution. *Journal of the New Economic Association, 3*(39), 155–162. https://doi.org/10.31737/2221-2264-2018-39-3-9.
39. Tukker, A. (2003). First EU network on sustainable product-service development launched. *The International Journal of Life Cycle Assessment, 8*, 112. https://doi.org/10.1007/BF02978437.
40. Varnavskii, V. (2020). Drivers of global economy. *World Economy and International Relations, 64*(7), 5–16. https://doi.org/10.20542/0131-2227-2020-64-7-5-16.
41. Warwick, K. (2013). Beyond industrial policy: Emerging issues and new trends. *OECD science, technology and industry policy papers. No. 2.* OECD Publishing.
42. WEF. (2012). *The Future of Manufacturing: Opportunities to Drive Economic Growth.* Geneva: World Economic Forum.

43. Wierzbicki, A. P. (2015). Threats and challenges of the new era. In *Technen: Elements of recent history of information technologies with epistemological conclusions. Intelligent systems reference library* (vol. 71). Springer. https://doi.org/10.1007/978-3-319-09033-7_14.

A Framework for Continuous Assessment of IT Value in Industry 4.0

João Lemos, Filipe Baptista, and João Barata

Abstract Assessment of the value of information technology (IT) is one of the most challenging priorities for modern organizations. The topic has been studied for decades but the continuous nature of digital transformation in industry (DTI) has added a new dimension to the problem. This paper presents a framework to capture IT value over time, supporting industries in (1) monitoring the outcomes of their digital transformation and (2) evaluating the need for new investments. The framework is inspired in the literature of IT value and extended to the dynamic, integrated and boundary spanning logic of Industry 4.0. The difficulty to prove the holistic value of IT investments is an obstacle to the necessary developments in industry. Moreover, similarly to DTI, IT value assessment is multidimensional and should be the result of an ongoing evaluation supported by evidence. Our proposal offers a starting point to create new tools to assist C-level managers steer their investments and make visible the inevitability of digitalization to compete.

Keywords IT value · Continuous assessment · Industry 4.0

1 Introduction

Sustainable digital transformation requires to achieve social, economic, and environmental outcomes [8, 19]. Industry worldwide is interested in this trend that promises to transform organizations using information technologies (IT) and redesigned business processes [10]. Industry 4.0 is a possible term to describe the phenomena that

J. Lemos (✉) · F. Baptista · J. Barata
University of Coimbra, CISUC, Department of Informatics Engineering, Pólo II, Pinhal de Marrocos, 3030-290 Coimbra, Portugal
e-mail: jflemos@student.dei.uc.pt

F. Baptista
e-mail: lfgb@student.dei.uc.pt

J. Barata
e-mail: barata@dei.uc.pt

V. Kumar et al. (eds.), *Digital Transformation in Industry*, Lecture Notes in Information Systems and Organisation 44, https://doi.org/10.1007/978-3-030-73261-5_3

"is a long term programme, and it is envisaged that it will only become fully implemented from about 2025 onwards" [46]. Therefore, new frameworks are necessary to support industry managers in their vision and assessment of digital transformation.

The outcomes of Industry 4.0 can be measured [8]; however, the concept of value is complex and several researcher claimed for integrated approaches. For example, in the extant literature of IT value [5]. Assessing the value of IT is even more important in the digital transformation era that involves major investments and long term vision [46]. Surprisingly, integrated approaches to assess the value of IT in Industry 4.0 are still rare, particularly when it is necessary to go beyond the scope of individual projects and create routines of assessment that support continuous investments in IT. Important governance frameworks like COBIT 2019 suggests regular meetings to evaluate how digitalization can be adopted [18], requiring advanced data analytics capabilities and useful indicators to support decisions.

To address the above-mentioned challenges, this paper puts forward the following research objective: *to propose an integrative framework to assess IT value in Industry 4.0*. These results are the first step to create a digital platform that delivers a comprehensive assessment of digital transformation over time. The remainder of this paper is structured as follows. Next, background literature on Industry 4.0 and its adoption are offered. Section 3 begins with a revision of IT value and provides the foundations for the new framework included in Sect. 3.2. The paper closes stating the main conclusions, the study limitations, and the opportunities for future work.

2 Background

2.1 Industry 4.0

Digital transformation in industry (DTI) is now a top priority for different zones of the globe [10, 22, 52]. It can be defined as the development of smart factories that provide smart services and smart products to satisfy the needs of each client [50]. Characterized by the extensive use of advanced resources of information and communication technologies, Industry 4.0 is also a social transformation process with major impacts in work practices [27].

Industry 4.0 was originated by a technology strategy project of the German Government aiming to promote innovation and improve competitiveness [39]. The term was firstly used in the Hannover fair in 2011 and, in April 2013, a final report about the development of Industry 4.0 was published. The concept become popular in many countries and is a growing research stream [23].

Important guidelines and recommendations for this initiative have been proposed [1], describing how companies can create intelligent and autonomous networks by connecting machines, systems, and IT resources. According to Acatech [1], "[i]*ndustrie 4.0 will also result in new ways of creating value and novel business models. In particular, it will provide start-ups and small businesses with the opportunity to develop and provide downstream services.*"

Upgrading to Industry 4.0 requires vertical, horizontal, and end-to-end digital integration of manufacturing systems [3]. Moreover, industries must foster digital engineering throughout the product lifecycle and, lastly, the decentralization of production and computing resources. Through complex innovation processes based on disruptive technologies (e.g., cloud, mobile, artificial intelligence, robotics), numerous companies will be forced to rethink their strategy, processes, and position through their business value chain, and how they think about the development of new products and introduce them in the market, adjusting the marketing and distribution actions. According to Klaus Schwab, there are four main effects on business across industries [44], namely, *(1) customer expectations are shifting, (2) products are being enhanced by data, which improves productivity, (3) partnerships are being created as companies learn the importance of new forms as collaboration, and (4) operating models are being transformed into new digital models.* Products and services are being empowered with digital capabilities. Intelligent sensors are now able to monitor information in real time, providing statistical information of performance [32]. Nevertheless, Industry 4.0 requires proper planning to evolve organizational maturity [43], as presented in the next section.

2.2 The Adoption of Industry 4.0

Industry 4.0 is expanding in the global manufacturing industry but there are also barriers, particularly for small and medium-sized companies [29], as presented in Fig. 1.

Important challenges arise when designing a 4.0 industry architecture, requiring a system of systems and models that continuously adapt [33]. The first is "*due to the necessity of defining the required business entities: how these entities participate during the value creation process can be challenging to map and requires the perception of the real implication within the value chain network. The second challenge pertains systems integration and interoperability*" [15]. A deep restructuring of IT and work organization is possible, but the lack of standardization, workers skills, insufficient financial resources, and the possible security issues must be evaluated in detail [2, 15]. To understand IT value applied to Industry 4.0, some reflection questions seek for answers by the companies that want to adopt it [13]:

- "How much technology do I need, and why?
- Am I spending too much on technology?
- What benefits will the institution realize?"

It became clear that the decisions to invest in Industry 4.0 require a continuous analysis of costs and benefits. However, the analysis of value is extremely difficult and it has been suggested that companies "*must identify a clear business objective,*

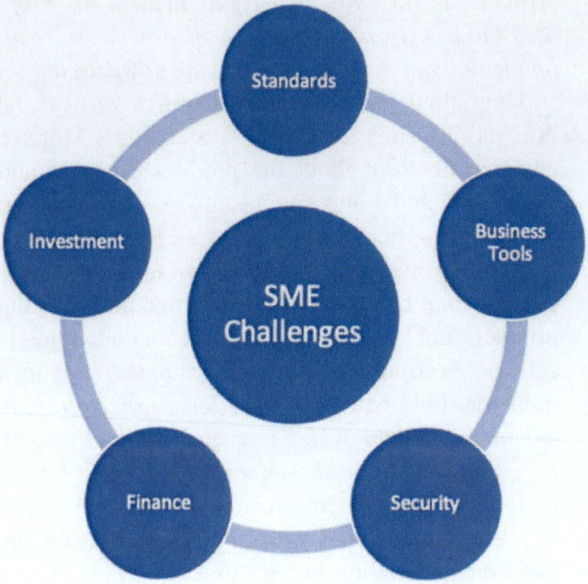

Fig. 1 Challenges faced by small and medium enterprises when adopting Industry 4.0

start small, focus on one area to begin with, get that area right, and prove the value of digital transformation before expanding to other parts of the enterprise" [7]. How to assess IT value in Industry 4.0 is the focus of the next section.

3 IT Value Assessment in Industry 4.0

3.1 The Traditional Approach

There is a temporal gap between IT costs and its benefits realization that must be taken into account [49]. For example, IT that was newly implemented is expected to have different evaluation when comparing to another system already fully implemented and learnt by all the members of a team. Depending on the lifecycle stage of the IT investment, benefits vary.

Figure 2 describes a sequence of steps for value assessment of IT in Industry 4.0 that we identify in the literature.

Four main phases are pinpointed. First, contextualization, depends on the setting in which IT is being implemented. For example, solutions that automate manufacturing lines using advanced sensors and artificial vision may be relevant for quality management, while systems involving augmented reality for product service may require an evaluation based on customer satisfaction. Subsequently, data collection needs to include both tangible (e.g., IT spending, improvement measures) and intangible elements (e.g., improved worker satisfaction and motivation). Business intelligence techniques are then essential to capture value of digitalization. When the context

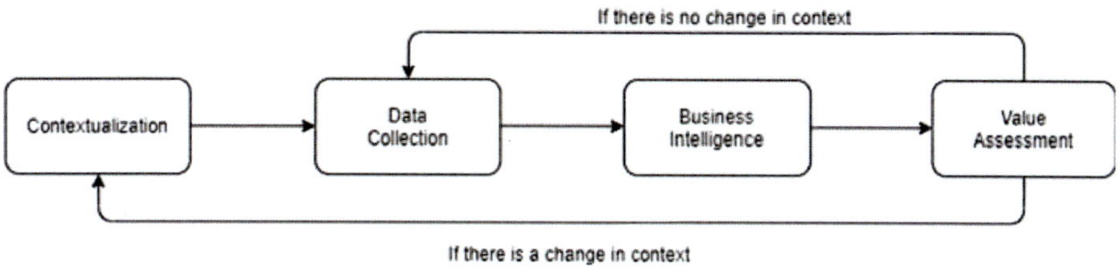

Fig. 2 Diagram representing the IT value assessment flow

changes or the company requires an evaluation (e.g., new IT system introduced), the cycle must restart. A review on each of the four phases is presented below.

Context

Value assessment is related to a particular context of digital transformation. Therefore, managers must determine the priorities of the company stakeholders since their definition of value may vary [26]. Improving sales, customer satisfaction, or accident prevention are examples of concerns. The clarification of business strategy is vital to the success of IT implementation and evaluation, as showed by Kyratsis, Ahmad, and Holmes [20]. These authors conducted a study addressing technology adoption on 11 health Trusts concluding that choosing IT before breaking down priorities tend to lead to unsuccessful implementations.

The type of IT system is another important variable. Li, Yang, Sun, and Sohal [21] performed a hypothesis testing based on data collected from 182 companies to explore the type of value generated by a supply chain management system. Other authors focused their efforts in developing four layers that assist in evaluating the value generated by multi-firm IT [48]. The examples are vast revealing the different possible benefits of IT that may be deliberate (achievement of organizational goals) or emergent from their use and adaptation by users.

Table 1 illustrates some examples of IT value in different contexts.

Data collection to assess IT value usually involve costs and benefits, as described in the next two subsections.

Table 1 Examples of research of IT value in different contexts

Contextualization	Description	Authors
IT Type	Multi-firm Integration IT	[48]
	Quantifying the financial impact of cloud IT investment	[40]
	How established companies leverage IT for value co-creation	[47]
Priority	Priority Ranking for IT	[42]
	Role of competitive priorities on IT implementation	[14]
Organization	IT value management model for Universities	[35]

Costs

Li et al. [21] define direct costs as those costs that can be reasonably measured and allocated to specific output, product, or work activity, while indirect costs cannot.

Direct costs are easier to identify in a precise way and can be classified into 4 categories [9]:

- Hardware: The costs related to the purchase of computers and equipment.
- Software: The cost related to the acquisition and maintenance of software.
- In-House Labor: The cost of labor used in the operations related to IT.
- External Providers: The cost of services hired to external entities.

These four categories of direct costs need to be wide enough to be common to every company. Then, it is necessary to divide them in sub-categories to be chosen and filled by the CIO according to their unique case. This approach is also intended to be used for indirect costs and benefits. Nevertheless, indirect costs cannot be underestimated [24]. Hochstrasser [16] defends that they can be up to four times greater than the direct ones. Contrasting to direct costs, indirect measures are very difficult to assess and categorize and have been a topic of research for the past decades. Activity based costing is a possible solution to adopt [38].

Benefits

It is difficult to find a complete benefit categorization model for IT. However, the categorization made by Weill [51] may assist in the IT value analysis:

- *Strategic* IT contributes to the position of a company as part of the market whether to increase competitive advantage or to increase market share.
- *Informational* IT developed to optimize information related operations.
- *Transactional* IT focusing on cutting on labor costs by automating transactional processes. Mirani and Lederer [28] selects this classification for the development of a benefit measuring classification, while Mooney, Gurbaxani, and Kraemer [30] also introduces the concept of automation and transformational effects of IT.

Table 2 Examples of indirect costs to measure IT value in different contexts [24] and possible methods to use

Typology	Method
Time	Time tracking practices such as timesheets
Learning costs	
Effort and dedication	
Costs of resistance	Satisfaction surveys and performance monitoring
Deskilling	
Reduction in knowledge base	
Missed-costs	Reference guide for IT associated expenditure
Moral hazard	Inquiries directed to the decision makers

Irani [17] argues that focusing benefit evaluation on a financial viewpoint is insufficient. The author suggests two additional levels: tactical that refers to the systems used to achieve the business objectives, such as improvements in productivity, and operational, which refers to the benefits in the core of the operations to keep the business running.

However, the pervasiveness of IT is creating difficulties to value assessment. The emphasis in automatizing business processes is shifting to digital transformation of supply chains and products, as presented in the new logic of innovation [53]. This change in IT led to an expansion of its costs (e.g., renting, pay-per-use) and impacts, making the prior categorizations restrictive. The recent proposal presented by Töhönen et al. [49] suggests classifying outcomes according to organizational performance, process (e.g., efficiency and effectiveness), and individual users. This vision can be expanded to the societal outcomes [25].

Business Intelligence

Chen et al. [4] defines Business Intelligence (BI) as "*technologies to analyze critical business data to help an enterprise better understand its business and market and make timely business decisions.*" Assessing IT in increasingly digitalized companies requires exploring a large amount of input data. New tools can be developed to explore contextualization, and the more recent contributions in IT value assessment can assist managers. Nevertheless, value is not a static measurement. To be valid to assist managers, BI must be able to capture value over time, according to the needs of the stakeholders. Static evaluation is lacking since the context in which IT is inserted has a great impact on its business value, can change unexpectedly, and depends in the users adaptation of IT and the business processes [34]. Our literature review allowed us to propose an updated framework, as described in the next section.

3.2 *The New Logic of IT Value Assessment in Industry 4.0*

The new logic requires a continuous assessment of IT value, not restricted to punctual changes in context (e.g. process redesign, new IT investment). Moreover, there are evidences suggesting that "*IT alone is not able to sustain a competitive advantage*" [36], requiring a boundary spanning perspective and the creation of capabilities in the organization to take advantage of digital transformation [31]. Both, IT *resources* and the investments in the organizational *capabilities* driven by IT are crucial to generate value. Figure 3 presents the proposed framework.

Figure 3 summarizes the extension proposed by the authors to the traditional approach of IT value assessment. The framework suggests a cyclic evaluation and improvement [6, 45] of IT systems tailored to a specific context of the industry. Contextualization is followed by the economic assessment of IT resources (e.g. IoT acquisition, enterprise systems, manufacturing execution systems) and capabilities [12, 31].

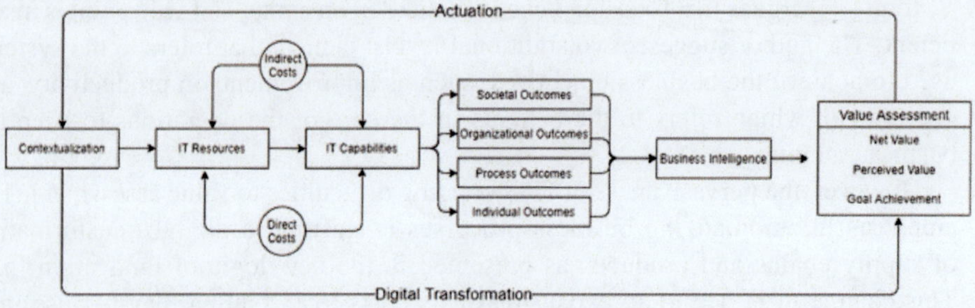

Fig. 3 Framework for continuous IT value assessment in industry 4.0

The lens to evaluate IT value in Industry 4.0 are not restricted to projects or departments. In fact, there are new drivers to invest in digital transformation that expands the boundaries of the organization to more complex supply chains, societal challenges, and human protection [11, 37, 41]. Business intelligence will need to include the value perceived by the systems users in combination with the achievement of desired organizational goals and the net value of digital transformation [49].

4 Conclusions, Limitations, and Next Steps

This paper presented a framework for the continuous assessment of IT value in Industry 4.0. The results are based on a literature review of IT value and three main trends found in Industry 4.0, namely (1) the long-term effect of digital transformation in industry, (2) the boundaryless nature of change that impacts the entire society, and (3) the combination of assessment perspectives. The latter incorporates the users perceived value, the goal achievements according to the desired strategy, and the net value.

Our exploratory research has limitations that must be stated. First, despite the care taken in the selection of the literature sources, this is the version of the framework. Second, the focus of our study is Industry 4.0. The concept of IT value may be different in other sectors of the economy, for example, services or Government administration. Third, this research is essentially explorative, aiming to provide the foundations for a new system to support C-level executives in their decisions. Therefore, the next steps of our research include (1) the development of an IT platform to record and continuously evaluate digital transformation data, and (2) testing the proposed framework in industries adopting Industry 4.0. Two companies already confirmed their interest in supporting the implementation of the framework and validate if the new logic proposed in this paper is more effective to capture IT value when comparing to the static analysis of particular projects and time frames.

IT value is difficult to assess in yearly reports or ad-hoc measurements. Moreover, when used independently, current evaluation approaches (perception, goal achievement, net value) are limited. For example, users may perceive IT value according to the use at that moment, goals may have been achieved but its value depends on the capacity of establishing those goals (and may not have a direct relation to IT investments), and net value is extremely dependent on time because some costs/benefits only become visible in the future. It is possible and desirable to explore synergies combining multiple levels of analysis (internal/external to the organization), forms of value, and progress over time. The proposed approach seems promising to assist managers' decisions in uncertain and dynamic environments and create new BI tools that capture the all-inclusive value of DTI.

Acknowledgment This work is co-funded by national funds through the FCT - Foundation for Science and Technology, I.P., within the scope of the project CISUC - UID/CEC/00326/2020 and by European Social Fund, through the Regional Operational Program Centro 2020.

References

1. Acatech. (2013). *Recommendations for implementing the strategic initiative INDUSTRIE 4.0*. Frankfurt, Germany. https://www.acatech.de/fileadmin/user_upload/Baumstruktur_nach_Website/Acatech/root/de/Material_fuer_Sonderseiten/Industrie_4.0/Final_report__Industrie_4.0_accessible.pdf.
2. Bauer, H., Baur, C., Mohr, D., Tschiesner, A., Weskamp, T., & Mathis, R. (2016). *Industry 4.0 after the initial hype - Where manufacturers are finding value and how they can best capture it. McKinsey Digital*. Whitepaper. https://www.mckinsey.com/~/media/mckinsey/businessfunctions/mckinseydigital/ourinsights/gettingthemostoutofindustry40/mckinsey_industry_40_2016.ashx.
3. Brettel, M., & Friederichsen, N. (2014). How virtualization, decentralization and network building change the manufacturing landscape: An industry 4.0 perspective. *International Journal of Mechanical, Aerospace, Industrial, Mechatronic and Manufacturing Engineering, 8*(1), 37–44.
4. Chen, H., Chiang, R., & Storey, V. (2012). Business intelligence and analytics: From big data to big impact. *MIS Quarterly, 36*(4), 1165. https://doi.org/10.2307/41703503.
5. Davern, M. J., & Wilkin, C. L. (2010). Towards an integrated view of IT value measurement. *International Journal of Accounting Information Systems, 11*(1), 42–60. https://doi.org/10.1016/j.accinf.2009.12.005.
6. Deming, W. E. (1988). *Qualité: La Revolution du Management (J. M. Gogue, Trans.)*. Paris: Economica. (Original work published 1982).
7. Demirkan, H., Spohrer, J. C., & Welser, J. J. (2016). Digital innovation and strategic transformation. *IT Professional, 18*(6), 14–18. https://doi.org/10.1109/MITP.2016.115.
8. Felsberger, A., Qaiser, F. H., Choudhary, A., & Reiner, G. (2020). The impact of industry 4.0 on the reconciliation of dynamic capabilities: Evidence from the European manufacturing industries. *Production Planning and Control, 0*(0), 1–24. https://doi.org/10.1080/09537287.2020.1810765.
9. Flanagan, R., & Marsh, L. (2000). Measuring the costs and benefits of information technology in construction. *Engineering, Construction and Architectural Management, 7*(4), 423–435. https://doi.org/10.1108/eb021164.
10. Popkova, E.G., & Sergi, B. S. (2018). Will Industry 4.0 and Other Innovations Impact Russia's Development? In *Exploring the future of Russia's economy and markets* (pp. 51–68). Emerald Publishing Limited. https://doi.org/10.1108/978-1-78769-397-520181004.

11. Ghobakhloo, M. (2018). The future of manufacturing industry: A strategic roadmap toward Industry 4.0. *Journal of Manufacturing Technology Management, 29*(6), 910–936. https://doi.org/10.1108/JMTM-02-2018-0057.
12. Goh, J. M., & Arenas, A. E. (2020). IT value creation in public sector: How IT-enabled capabilities mitigate tradeoffs in public organisations. *European Journal of Information Systems, 29*(1), 25–43. https://doi.org/10.1080/0960085X.2019.1708821.
13. Goldstein, P., Katz, R., & Olson, M. (2003). Understanding the value of IT. *Educause Quarterly, 26*(3), 14–18.
14. De Haro, M. R., Basáez, M. O., & Aranda, D. A. (2019). IT implementation and customer results: the mediating role of the competitive priorities achieved by the firm. *International Journal of Business Environment, 10*(4), 329. https://doi.org/10.1504/IJBE.2019.101644.
15. Hernández, E., Senna, P., Silva, D., Rebelo, R., Barros, A. C., & Toscano, C. (2020). Implementing RAMI4.0 in Production - A Multi-case Study. In *Progress in digital and physical manufacturing. ProDPM 2019. Lecture notes in mechanical engineering* (pp. 49–56). https://doi.org/10.1007/978-3-030-29041-2_6.
16. Hochstrasser, B. (1994). Justifying IT investments. In *Information management* (pp. 151–169). Springer US. https://doi.org/10.1007/978-1-4899-3208-2_8.
17. Irani, Z. (2002). Information systems evaluation: Navigating through the problem domain. *Information & Management, 40*(1), 11–24. https://doi.org/10.1016/S0378-7206(01)00128-8.
18. ISACA. (2019). COBIT® 2019 Framework Governance and Management Objectives.
19. Kamble, S. S., Gunasekaran, A., & Gawankar, S. A. (2018). Sustainable Industry 4.0 framework: A systematic literature review identifying the current trends and future perspectives. *Process Safety and Environmental Protection, 117*, 408–425. https://doi.org/10.1016/j.psep.2018.05.009.
20. Kyratsis, Y., Ahmad, R., & Holmes, A. (2012). Technology adoption and implementation in organisations: Comparative case studies of 12 English NHS Trusts. *British Medical Journal Open, 2*(2), e000872. https://doi.org/10.1136/bmjopen-2012-000872.
21. Li, G., Yang, H., Sun, L., & Sohal, A. S. (2009). The impact of IT implementation on supply chain integration and performance. *International Journal of Production Economics, 120*(1), 125–138. https://doi.org/10.1016/j.ijpe.2008.07.017.
22. Li, L. (2018). China's manufacturing locus in 2025: With a comparison of "Made-in-China 2025" and "Industry 4.0." *Technological Forecasting and Social Change, 135*(October), 66–74.
23. Liao, Y., Deschamps, F., de Loures, E. F. R., & Ramos, L. F. P. (2017). Past, present and future of industry 4.0 - a systematic literature review and research agenda proposal. *International Journal of Production Research, 55*(12), 3609–3629.
24. Love, P. E. D., Ghoneim, A., & Irani, Z. (2004). Information technology evaluation: Classifying indirect costs using the structured case method. *Journal of Enterprise Information Management, 17*(4), 312–325. https://doi.org/10.1108/17410390410548724.
25. Majchrzak, A., Markus, M. L., & Wareham, J. (2016). Designing for digital transformation: Lessons for information systems research from the study of ICT and societal challenges. *MIS Quarterly, 40*(2), 267–277.
26. Marthandan, G., & Meng Tang, C. (2010). Information technology evaluation: issues and challenges. *Journal of Systems and Information Technology, 12*(1), 37–55. https://doi.org/10.1108/13287261011032643.
27. Melnyk, L., Kubatko, O., Dehtyarova, I., Matsenko, O., & Rozhko, O. (2019). The effect of industrial revolutions on the transformation of social and economic systems. *Problems and Perspectives in Management, 17*(4), 381–391. https://doi.org/10.21511/ppm.17(4).2019.31.
28. Mirani, R., & Lederer, A. L. (1998). An instrument for assessing the organizational benefits of IS projects. *Decision Sciences, 29*(4), 803–838. https://doi.org/10.1111/j.1540-5915.1998.tb00878.x.
29. Moeuf, A., Pellerin, R., Lamouri, S., Tamayo-Giraldo, S., & Barbaray, R. (2018). The industrial management of SMEs in the era of Industry 4.0. *International Journal of Production Research, 56*(3), 1118–1136.

30. Mooney, J. G., Gurbaxani, V., & Kraemer, K. L. (1996). A process oriented framework for assessing the business value of information technology. *ACM SIGMIS Database: The DATABASE for Advances in Information Systems, 27*(2), 68–81. https://doi.org/10.1145/243350.243363.
31. Nwankpa, J. K., & Roumani, Y. (2016). IT capability and digital transformation: A firm performance perspective. In *ICIS—International conference on information systems.*
32. Oztemel, E., & Gursev, S. (2020). Literature review of industry 4.0 and related technologies. *Journal of Intelligent Manufacturing, 31*(1), 127–182. https://doi.org/10.1007/s10845-018-1433-8.
33. Panetto, H., Iung, B., Ivanov, D., Weichhart, G., & Wang, X. (2019). Challenges for the cyber-physical manufacturing enterprises of the future. *Annual Reviews in Control, 47*, 200–213. https://doi.org/10.1016/j.arcontrol.2019.02.002.
34. Paul, R. J. (2007). Challenges to information systems: Time to change. *European Journal of Information Systems, 16*(3), 193–195.
35. Pereira, C., Ferreira, C., & Amaral, L. (2018). An IT value management capability model for Portuguese universities: A Delphi study. *Procedia Computer Science, 138*, 612–620. https://doi.org/10.1016/j.procs.2018.10.082.
36. Perez-Arostegui, M. N., Benitez-Amado, J., & Tamayo-Torres, J. (2012). Information technology-enabled quality performance: an exploratory study. *Industrial Management & Data Systems, 112*(3), 502–518.
37. Peruzzini, M., Grandi, F., & Pellicciari, M. (2020). Exploring the potential of operator 4.0 interface and monitoring. *Computers and Industrial Engineering, 139*(December), 105600. https://doi.org/10.1016/j.cie.2018.12.047.
38. Raz, T., & Elnathan, D. (1999). Activity based costing for projects. *International Journal of Project Management, 17*(1), 61–67. https://doi.org/10.1016/S0263-7863(97)00073-2.
39. Reischauer, G. (2018). Industry 4.0 as policy-driven discourse to institutionalize innovation systems in manufacturing. *Technological Forecasting and Social Change, 132*(March), 26–33. https://doi.org/10.1016/j.techfore.2018.02.012.
40. Rosati, P., Fox, G., Kenny, D., & Lynn, T. (2017). Quantifying the financial value of cloud investments: A systematic literature review. In *2017 IEEE international conference on cloud computing technology and science (CloudCom)* (pp. 194–201). IEEE. https://doi.org/10.1109/CloudCom.2017.28.
41. Savastano, M., Amendola, C., Bellini, F., & D'Ascenzo, F. (2019). Contextual impacts on industrial processes brought by the digital transformation of manufacturing: A systematic review. *Sustainability, 11*(3), 891. https://doi.org/10.3390/su11030891.
42. Schreieck, M., & Wiesche, M. (2017). How established companies leverage it platforms for value co-creation—insights from banking. In *Proceedings of the 25th European conference on information systems, ECIS 2017, 2017*, (pp. 1726–1741).
43. Schumacher, A., Erol, S., & Sihn, W. (2016). A maturity model for assessing industry 4.0 readiness and maturity of manufacturing enterprises. *Procedia CIRP, 52*, 161–166.
44. Schwab, K. (2017). *The fourth industrial revolution.*
45. Shewhart, W. (1939). *Statistical method from the viewpoint of quality control.* Graduate School, Department of Agriculture.
46. Smit, J., Kreutzer, S., Moeller, C., & Carlberg, M. (2016). *Industry 4.0—Study for the ITRE Committee.*
47. Sobczak, A., & Berry, D. M. (2007). Distributed priority ranking of strategic preliminary requirements for management information systems in economic organizations. *Information and Software Technology, 49*(9–10), 960–984. https://doi.org/10.1016/j.infsof.2006.10.006.
48. Thomas, B., & Johnson, J. (2012). Cocreating IT value: New capabilities and metrics for multifirm environments. *MIS Quarterly, 36*(1), 225–232.
49. Töhönen, H., Kauppinen, M., Männistö, T., & Itälä, T. (2020). A conceptual framework for valuing IT within a business system. *International Journal of Accounting Information Systems, 36*, 100442. https://doi.org/10.1016/j.accinf.2019.100442.

50. Wang, S., Wan, J., Li, D., & Zhang, C. (2016). Implementing smart factory of industrie 4.0: An outlook. *International Journal of Distributed Sensor Networks, 12*(1), 3159805.
51. Weill, P. (1992). The relationship between investment in information technology and firm performance: A study of the valve manufacturing sector. *Information Systems Research, 3*(4), 307–333. https://doi.org/10.1287/isre.3.4.307.
52. Xu, L. D., Xu, E. L., & Li, L. (2018). Industry 4.0: State of the art and future trends. *International Journal of Production Research, 7543*(2018), 1–22.
53. Yoo, Y., Henfridsson, O., & Lyytinen, K. (2010). The new organizing logic of digital innovation: An agenda for information systems research. *Information Systems Research, 21*(4), 724–735.

Prerequisites and Principles of Digital Platformization of the Economy

Victoria Akberdina and Anna Z. Barybina

Abstract The article explores transformation processes of the economy and industry in the context of the digital technology introduction. It substantiates the methodological basis of the research, including the process, technological and sector-specific approaches. The study formulates the fundamental hypothesis about the possibility to integrate the three approaches and form an ecosystem based on the platform organization of the economy and industry. The authors propose a definition of the concept of digital platform, distinguish the types of digital industrial platforms and justify the effects of the platform organization of the economy.

Keywords Industry · Digitalization · Economic transformation

1 Introduction

Informatization and automation processes have been deeply embedded in industrial processes. The next stage in the transformation of the real sector economy is digitalization. The primary goal of this process is to cut costs by optimizing the processes of production, management, sales and promotion of products in the market.

Amid globalization of the world economy, economies of scales are achieved, whereas the growing service sector is forcing companies to diversify their supply sources and operate in various geographical markets. Toughening competition is making industrial enterprises to introduce new development strategies in the context of digitalization of the economy, including reorganization of production chains using firms involved in the network. This results in the emergence of partnership strategies and new relationships of power that affect the production and technological capabilities of countries and societies.

V. Akberdina (✉) · A. Z. Barybina
Institute of Economics of the Ural Branch of the Russian Academy of Sciences, 29 Moskovskaya St, Ekaterinburg 620014, Russian Federation
e-mail: akberdina.vv@uiec.ru

V. Akberdina
Ural Federal University, 19 Mira St, Ekaterinburg 620002, Russian Federation

V. Kumar et al. (eds.), *Digital Transformation in Industry*, Lecture Notes in Information Systems and Organisation 44, https://doi.org/10.1007/978-3-030-73261-5_4

With the convergence of industrial technologies, it is impossible to look at each industry in isolation; therefore, there is an urgent need for cross-industrial innovations from different technological segments referred to as end-to-end digital technologies simultaneously covering several industries. In Russia, within the framework of the National Technology Initiative (NTI), end-to-end digital technologies were defined as key scientific and technical areas that have the most significant effect on market development.

Basic technologies underpinning the previous stages of industrial transformation are being replaced with new digital solutions. Based on the principles of the fourth industrial revolution, we propose the following interpretation of the concept of cross-industrial open production and service ecosystems: these are intersectoral networks of real material and immaterial objects, vertically and horizontally connected through the industrial Internet of Things into digital platforms that manage the entire life cycle of the product.

Studying the best practices of digital transformation leaders, examining and monitoring the world's largest companies and markets for high-tech products and services, as well as comprehending the standpoints of leading entrepreneurs, analysts, visionaries and experts lead to the realization of the special role of industry digital platforms in the new economy. The present study aims to consider the substance of the term "digital platform", types of platforms and their classifications, as well as to scrutinize the principles of digital platformization of the economy. The central objective of the research is to determine the essence of digital platform in the economy. The study discusses the features of digital platforms distinguishing them from one another, identifies categories of platforms and compiles a classification of platforms by the types of value proposed. It is concluded that there is a necessity to develop a methodology for creating digital platforms for production.

2 Literature Review

A digital platform is a system of algorithmic mutually beneficial relationships of a significant number of independent participants in an economic sector (or field of activity) implemented in a single information environment, which reduces transaction costs by using a package of digital data processing technologies and changes in the division system.

Introduction of the principles of Industry 4.0 to organization of industry, the use of end-to-end digital technologies immediately in the production process, and the use of artificial intelligence in making optimal decisions ensures a change in the technological paradigm [1, 2]. *Researchers distinguish between three methodological approaches to assessing this process.*

1. *Process approach* is based on the process of value creation in industrial production [3–7]. The approach enables creating (in a digital environment) value from research, development and design prior to production, sale and operation.

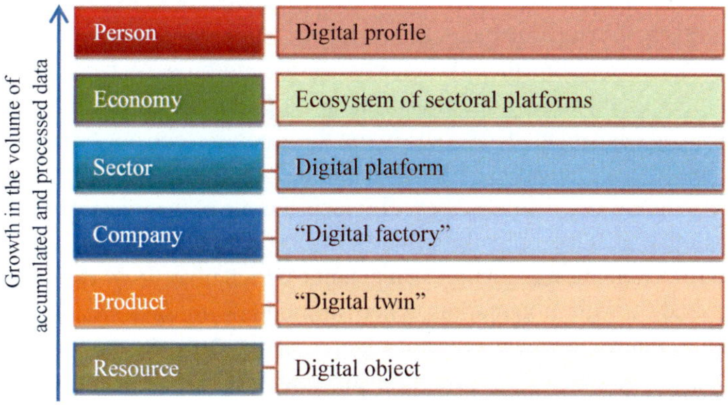

Fig. 1 Levels of industrial production digitalization

2. *Technological approach* suggests studying clusters of digital technologies that ensure qualitative transformation of the industrial complex [8–12]. The level of the digital technologies application is a condition for the growth of competitiveness and prospects of companies, sectors and entire national economies.
3. *Sector-specific approach* is based on the identification of the existing and emerging industrial markets involved in digital transformation [13–16]. The dynamics of digital transformation in particular industrial sectors is due to the differences in the conditions of implementation, specifics of big data and the ability of digital technologies to alter processes and business models.

The digital transformation of industrial markets should ultimately create a digital ecosystem of interrelated industries. The levels of industrial production digitalization are shown in Fig. 1.

End-to-end digital technologies embrace several segments simultaneously, which predetermines the vertical and horizontal openness of a production system. Horizontal channels for the industrial ecosystem's formation are linked with the diffusion of digital technologies within the same sector from innovation-companies to imitation-companies, which increases productivity of the entire segment. Regardless of the fact that horizontal transfer is traditionally interpreted as an intra-sectoral phenomenon, digital technologies broaden its scope.

Vertical channels for a production ecosystem's development are based on value chains formed in various sectors. End-to-end digital technologies demonstrate the vast potential for penetration that catalyzes the transformation of the entire "cross-sectoral vertical". In this case, productivity gains are achieved by introducing digital technologies to the entire chain from primary producers to end users.

Our review indicates that the economic-mathematical modeling of cross-industrial network-based production and service ecosystems is possible only on a composite methodological platform incorporating three approaches: reproductive, institutional and synergistic. On the one hand, the variety of technologies and innovations emphasizes the need for using the whole range of technologies that build "a network of technologies" in the process of industrial development. The network should be based not only on the high-tech sector, but also on the medium-tech ones (the so-called structural technological inclusion). Moreover, all markets of the future will be arranged as network communities—this is a new crucial principle of the innovation-technological development that starts prevailing in nearly all spheres. In the high-tech sector, there is a need for a transition from industrial giants, which involve working with suppliers, to networked coordination models, where individuals produce small batches of goods while coordinating their activity through the network. Many companies, especially those in new industries, are adopting the principles of network organization that lacks the prior role of vertical management. On the other hand, the research sector itself as the generator of technologies should undergo organizational changes and introduce the networked coordination model premised on the principles of S2B (science-to-business).

Thus, *we hypothesize that it is possible to integrate the three above-mentioned approaches and create an industrial ecosystem based on the platform organization of the economy.*

3 Materials and Methods

The central method of the present study is the analysis of scientific publications.

To analyze the formation of industrial digital platforms in world practice, it is first necessary to delimit the definition of the term "digital platforms" and then, among them, identify a category of those related to industry.

Numerous researchers propose their own definitions of the phenomenon of digital platforms [17–24]. According to the generally accepted interpretation, a digital platform refers to a system of algorithmic relationships between market participants operating in a single information environment, which entails a decrease in transaction costs. A digital platform is a system focused on creating value through direct interaction between the buyer and the supplier, and on performing transactions between them and several groups of third-party users.

A digital platform also refers to a set of interrelated information technologies that allows creating new types of businesses (activities) based on the interaction between material and digital worlds, provides access to digital technologies and produces synergistic effect from their application. Digital platforms unite subjects of the digital economy.

Within the framework of the system-based approach adopted in the paper, it is also necessary to establish the boundaries of ecosystems based on digital platforms [25]. This is due to the fact that all business segments are, in one way or another, connected to each other, which makes the analysis of all the segments a very resource-intensive process.

We have identified the vertical and horizontal boundaries of the digital platform represented by the level of technical architecture and fields of application, respectively. In a certain context, digital platforms should be regarded at the level of the ecosystem core, which concentrates the most significant relationships. This will limit the external relationships and the additional functions of platforms that can affect the categorization of digital platforms.

Organization principles should also be taken into account. Digital platformization of the economy is premised on the principles of digitalization universality, sustainability of the information space, regularity/availability of digital services, expediency and efficiency. The principle of digitalization universality implies that digitalization processes embrace all existing sectors of the economy. The principle of sustainability of the information space suggests the presence of the developed infrastructure to implement the processes of digitalization both at the level of regions and enterprises. The principle of regularity/availability of digital services assumes the continuity of information and communication services and their affordability. Network effects arising while digital technologies are operating have their power due to the scale, in particular, the scale of the number of consumers of these services. The principle of expediency indicates the need for evaluating the introduction of particular innovations and their relevance. Many digital processes might be quite resource-intensive and load the current infrastructure with unnecessary processes. The principle of efficiency shows the need to monitor the demand for certain processes, comply with the established rules in terms of technology application and support the trends towards increasing efficiency from the introduction of digitalization processes into the activities of an economic entity.

4 Results and Discussion

Currently, there are numerous classifications of platforms; however, most of them lack the category of organizations adopting the "digital environment" business model. This aspect is difficult to pinpoint among the large number of startups that use the term "platform" in their company name as a marketing ploy, and fall under the formal description of platforms.

In the sphere of technological platforms, there are two types of them fundamentally different from each other: these are hardware that forms the infrastructure for information networks to function, and software that animates information networks and lets them function in an uninterrupted mode. The fact that almost every new startup is called a "platform" creates confusion. This results from the vogue and tactics for raising funds and attracting attention to a popular topic. In most cases, a platform refers to technology, but not business model. The examples of platforms as technology are presented in Table 1.

The examples presented in Table 1 are associated with a product or technology that can serve as the basis for building other modular components. Platform business models also use similar modular modifications, which creates a confusion of

Table 1 Types of platforms as technology

Name of technology	Essence and examples
Computing platform	A computer system to set up applications (e.g. Simbian)
Product platform	Common design, formula or generic product as the basis for a product line (e.g. car chassis used in the production of different vehicle models)
Sectoral platform	Products, technologies or services as the basis for creating additional products, technologies or services (e.g. Intel)
Platform as a service	A category of cloud computing services that provide a computing platform and a set of solutions in the format of online service (e.g. Amazon Web Services)
SaaS model (software as a service)	An integrated set of software products (Salesforce (sales and customer relationship management), Cloud budget (accounting for small businesses), Kontur-Extern (online reporting), Elba (SaaS accounting)

definitions. The most common mistake is that the term "platform" is misused when describing products of SaaS companies. Such firms utilize the word "platform" as a marketing ploy only, since they operate according to a linear model.

The business model visualizes the processes of value creation for customers and describes how to capitalize on these processes. It also characterizes the structure of a firm's expenditures and relationships with other companies and partners. Speaking of the platform business model, it implies not just any sort of technologies, but a holistic description of the processes of creating, proposing and preserving the company's values.

The asset of such an organization is software that works on the Internet, carries a unique value available to any user, both the seller and the buyer. To exchange value, platform organizations generate accessible, large and exponentially growing networks of users, within which communities and markets are organized. Platforms do not possess the means of production—they create the means of communication instead.

Within the platform, a business model is defined as a company that uses a system algorithm accelerating the exchange of values between two or more groups of users, consumers and producers, in order to increase profits of all participants.

At the moment, digital platforms are developed in numerous spheres and new ideas emerge every day. Not each of them turns into a viable project, but breakthrough ideas are being searched relentlessly. In this regard, the functional classifications of platforms available in the scientific literature are rather heterogeneous.

According to the approaches to defining and categorizing digital platforms proposed by Rostelecom's Center for Information Infrastructure Competences, there are three types of digital platforms: instrumental (Java, Andriod), infrastructural (Gosuslugi, Predix), and applied (Yandex, Avito, Booking).

Deloitte University has developed its own functional classification of digital platforms: aggregated (Alibaba), social (Facebook, Instagram), mobilization (Bitrix24), and educational (YouTube, Coursera) [26, 27].

The classification of digital platforms presented by the Center for Global Enterprise includes the following categories: operational platforms (Uber, Gett, Yandex), innovation platforms (Android, IOS, Microsoft Windows), integrated (Apple: App Store, iCloud), and investment (Kickstarter) platforms [28]. This classification is based on the study of 176 world platforms: the list comprises large trading companies, as well as small private companies, such as Uber or Airbnb. Geographical distribution of platform companies is quite uneven: 82 platforms are registered in Asia, 64—in North America. Although Europe is the main consumer of services, only 27 of the platforms surveyed are registered there.

Having reviewed the major classifications of digital platforms, we arrived at the conclusion that the category *Platform as a Business Model* contains only applied digital platforms in the classification by Rostelecom's Center for Information Infrastructure Competences (Russia).

To single out the companies using platform business models and further develop approaches to creating organizations, there is a need for a focused specialization, which reflects the specifics of the value provided by a particular platform. This will also allow identifying digital platforms within large ecosystems combined into large complexes. The core of a platform is a unique value it provides to user. To some extent, this is its mission.

To propose our own classification, we have analyzed a multitude of existing digital platforms and sorted them out by the types of value they propose. The authors' classification is given in Table 2.

To identify the distinctive features of the platform business model, it is required to look at organizations operating in a certain area and their specifics in creating value for customers. It is important to ascertain if they are really platform business models or platform products or services.

Platform organizations can be categorized into two groups: platforms for reducing transaction costs (exchange platforms) and those creating infrastructure for user creativity to encourage direct communication between customers and producers and create value [11]. The key difference can be traced through the purpose of the transactions: whether the outcome of the transaction is intended for one consumer or for many.

As for industry, there are several avenues for applying digital platforms: digitization of production processes; creation of an enterprise's digital twin; a marketplace platform; and a gadget/application platform (providing conditional value which requires the output for its implementation).

Table 2 Classification of digital platforms by the type of value proposed

Platform	Type of value	Examples
Public	Providing public services in a single window	Gosuslugi.ru, data.gov.ru, IAS Labour Market, IAS Corporate System of Information-Analytical Support for Public Authorities, Electronic Budget, ILS Russian Legislation
Social	Opportunity to find partners to communicate and build social relationships	OkCupid, LinkedIn, Facebook, Twitter, WeChat, Skype, MySpace, Instagram and WhatsApp, Snapchat, Tencent QQ
Trade (services)	Opportunity to find an executor of certain services	Airbnb, Craigslist, Fiverr, Sberbank Telecom, Foodplex
Trade (products)	Opportunity to find particular products	Threadless, Amazon Marketplace, Alibaba, eBay, Yandex.Market, Avito, Ula, Cian
Educational	Gaining knowledge in various fields of education	Minerva, TopCoder, Salesforce, Microsoft Xbox, Duolingo, MOOC, Skillshare, Udemy, Coursera, adX, Khan Academy, Intuit, OptnDo
Healthcare	Receiving medical aid at any moment and place	Medicast, HealthKit, Fitbit, Jawbone and MyFitnessPal, DocDoc
Information (consulting)	Deriving information and operational details on any issue of interest	Clarity, Thompson Reuters, Cleversite, Frell, Jivosite, LiveTex, OnlineSeller, RedHelper, StreamWood, Wikipedia
Crowd funding	Opportunity to attract investors to implement a project, charity fundraising, non-profit activity, environmental safety project	Kickstarter, Indiegogo, Crowdfunder.com, Rockethub, Crowdrise, Somolend, Appbackr, AngelList, Invested.in, Quirky, Boomstarter, Kroogi, Planeta.ru, Appsfunder, Yandex.Money
E-mail services	Formal data transmission in the form of electronic messages	Yandex.Mail, Gmail, Mail.ru, Dropmail, Crazymailing, Mohmal, Minuteinbox, Hotmail (Outlook), Yahoo! Mail, Runbox
Cloud services	Storing, accumulating and processing the existing databases	SberCloud, pCloud, MEGA, MediaFire, Box, Cloud.Mail, Yandex.Disk, iCloud, Dropbox, OneDrive, Google Drive
Payment/financial	Making financial transactions, loans, insurance	PayPal, Square, MasterCard, ShopThis!, Mint, Yandex.Money

(continued)

Table 2 (continued)

Platform	Type of value	Examples
Lending	Hunting for lending schemes using the treasury of digital data they collect	Zopa, Lending Club, AngelList, Fingooroo, Vdolg
Labor exchanges	Search for jobs or employees	LinkedIn, HeadHunter, Upwork, zarplata.ru, YouDo, Freelancer
Logistics and transportation	Food delivery, cargo transportation. Economic functions contributing to transportation of passengers and cargo	FedEx, Munchery, Go-Jek,
Cartographic	Pinpointing geographical location, searching for new objects on the map	Google Maps, Apple Maps, Yandex.Maps
Production (industrial)	Digitizing production processes, creating a digital twin	SAP, 1C, Otchet.ru, OFD, Kontur.Postavki, Kontur.Prizma, Kontur.Pulse, Kontur.Reestro, Kontur.Diadoc, Kontur.Bukhgalteriya, Kontur.Alkosverka, Kontur.Zakupki
Energy industry	A platform that collects, distributes and transmit free electricity	No alternatives
Agriculture	The market of agricultural products: planning the future demand for agricultural products and distributing available resources to complete the order	Fasal
Infrastructure technology	Third-party developers are capable of creating applications	Cisco AXP, Apple iOS, Google Android, Microsoft, Intel
Internet of Things	Opportunity to interconnect devices installed within the home ecosystem	GE Industrial Internet, Nest
Entertainment/mass media/news	Receiving up-to-the-minute information on the news agenda, accessing entertainment content	Netflix, PlayStation, Xbox, Nintendo (Wii), YouTube, Rutube, ivi.ru, Divan.tv, Megogo.net, TVZavr, AYYO, Tvigle, Zoomby, Now.Ru, Amediateka, iTunes, BBC TV, Vimeo OnDemand, Disney+, Amazon Prime Video, HBO Max, Hulu and Peacock

(continued)

Table 2 (continued)

Platform	Type of value	Examples
Search engines	Searching for information, objects, applications, platforms; internet navigators	Google, Yandex, Rambler, Mail.ru, Baidu, Bing, DuckDuckGo, Boardreader, Dogpile, Creative Commons Search, Giphy, Quora, Vimeo, WolframAlpha, StartPage, Ask.com, SlideShare

5 Conclusion

In prospect, digitalization will ensure a significant increase in labor productivity in industry. It is worth noting that there is a strong correlation between the level of digitalization and the level of material production development—the state and rates of fixed assets renewal, the rate of investment in fixed assets, labor productivity in industry, etc. Digital solutions should be introduced in the context of commensurate development of the material sector; otherwise the overall economic effect of digitalization will not be as profound. We suppose that the industries already forming the high-tech segment and reaching high labor productivity should be provided with all the necessary conditions for large-scale digitalization. Alternatively, digitalization of production lends a powerful impetus for the development of medium- and low-tech sectors thus guaranteeing the efficiency of industrial enterprises.

In light of this, the formation of digital platforms is expected to become a necessary condition for a large-scale digital transformation of industry. Digital platforms show the potential to process big data. A platform is able to combine information and distribute the flow of orders not only in line with the available production capacity, but also the quality characteristics in the most efficient way. In this context, a platform is figuratively referred to as "an invisible hand of the market". Or a digital platform will become a universal planner on a global scale.

The present study has revealed the need to develop a methodology for creating digital platforms for production. It has proved that there is a necessity to analyze the international experience and architecture for building digital platforms in various areas of the industrial sector.

Acknowledgements The paper was funded by the Russian Foundation for Basic Research, project No. 18-010-01156 "Modeling the technological transformation of the Russian industrial complex in the context of the digitalization of the economy".

References

1. Akberdina, V. V. (2018). Digitalization of industrial markets: regional characteristics. *The Manager, 9*(6), 78–87. https://doi.org/10.29141/2218-5003-2018-9-6-8.

2. Lasi, H., Fettke, P., Kemper, H., Feld, T., & Hoffmann, M. (2014). Industry 4.0. *Business & Information Systems Engineering, 6*, 239–242. https://doi.org/10.1007/s11576-014-0424-4.
3. Banga, K. (2019). Digital technologies and «value» capture in global value chains: Empirical evidence from Indian manufacturing firms. *WIDER Working Paper No. 2019/43*. https://doi.org/10.35188/UNU-WIDER/2019/677-7.
4. Núñez-Merino, M., Maqueira-Marín, J. M., Moyano-Fuentes, J., & Martínez-Jurado, P. J. (2020). Information and digital technologies of industry 4.0 and Lean supply chain management: A systematic literature review. *International Journal of Production Research, 58*(16), 5034–5061. https://doi.org/10.1080/00207543.2020.1743896.
5. Ranjan, K. R., & Read, S. (2016). Value Co-creation: Concept and Measurement. *Journal of the Academy of Marketing Science, 44*(3), 290–315. https://doi.org/10.1007/s11747-014-0397-2.
6. Rodrik, D. (2018). New Technologies, Global Value Chains, and Developing Economies. *Working Paper 25164*. October. https://doi.org/10.3386/w25164.
7. Schmidt, M.-C., Veile, J. W., Müller, J. M., & Voigt, K.-I. (2020). Ecosystems 4.0: redesigning global value chains. *The International Journal of Logistics Management* (in print). https://doi.org/10.1108/IJLM-03-2020-0145.
8. Genz, S., Janser, M., & Lehmer, F. (2019). The impact of investments in new digital technologies on wages – worker-level evidence from Germany. *Jahrbücher für Nationalökonomie und Statistik, 39*(3), 483–521. https://doi.org/10.1515/jbnst-2017-0161.
9. Kiel, D., Müller, J. M., Arnold, C., & Voigt, K. I. (2017). Sustainable Industrial Value Creation: Benefits and Challenges of Industry 4.0. *International Journal of Innovation Management, 21*(08), 1740015. https://doi.org/10.1142/S1363919617400151.
10. Li, Y., Dai, J., & Cui, L. (2020). The impact of digital technologies on economic and environmental performance in the context of industry 4.0: A moderated mediation model. *International Journal of Production Economics, 229*, 107777. https://doi.org/10.1016/j.ijpe.2020.107777.
11. Sorbe, S. (2019). Digital dividend: Policies to harness the productivity potential of digital technologies. In *Economic Policy Paper No. 26*. OECD Publishing. https://doi.org/10.1787/273176bc-en.
12. Wiesböck, F., & Hess, T. (2020). Digital innovations. *Electron Markets, 30*, 7586. https://doi.org/10.1007/s12525-019-00364-9.
13. Akatkin, Y. M., Karpov, O. E., Konyavsky, V. A., & Yasinovskaya, E. D. (2017). Digital economy: Conceptual architecture of the digital industry ecosystem. *Business Informatics, 4*(42), 17–28. https://doi.org/10.17323/1998-0663.2017.4.17.28.
14. Alexandrova, E., & Poddubnaya, M. (2020). Digital Technologies Development in Industry Sectors and Areas of Activity. In T. Antipova (ed.). *Integrated Science in Digital Age 2020. ICIS 2020. Lecture Notes in Networks and Systems,* (vol. 136). Springer. https://doi.org/10.1007/978-3-030-49264-9_10.
15. Bughin, J., Manyika, J., & Catlin, T. (2019). *Twenty-five years of digitization: Ten insights into how to play it right*. McKinsey Global Institute (MGI). https://www.mckinsey.com/business-functions/mckinsey-digital/our-insights/twenty-five-years-of-digitization-ten-insights-into-how-to-play-it-right.
16. Paunov, C., & Planes-Satorra, S. (2019). *How are digital technologies changing innovation?: Evidence from agriculture, the automotive industry and retail*. OECD Science, Technology and Industry Policy Papers, No. 74. OECD Publishing. https://doi.org/10.1787/67bbcafe-en.
17. Bygstad, B. (2017). Generative innovation: A comparison of lightweight and heavyweight IT. *Journal of Information Technology, 32*(2), 180–193. https://doi.org/10.1057/jit.2016.15.
18. Eaton, B., Elaluf-Calderwood, S., Sorensen, C., & Yoo, Y. (2015). Distributed tuning of boundary resources: The case of Apple's iOS service system. *MIS Quarterly: Management Information Systems, 39*(1), 217–243.
19. Gawer, A. (2014). Bridging differing perspectives on technological platforms: Toward an integrative framework. *Research Policy, 43*(7), 1239–1249. https://doi.org/10.1016/j.respol.2014.03.006.
20. Ghazawneh, A., & Henfridsson, O. (2015). A paradigmatic analysis of digital application marketplaces. *Journal of Information Technology, 30*(3), 198–208. https://doi.org/10.1057/jit.2015.16.

21. JPMorgan Chase & Co. (2016). *Paychecks, paydays, and the online platform economy. Big data on income volatility*. № 1.
22. Martens, B. (2016). An economic policy perspective on online platforms. *Digital Economy Working Paper* (Vol. 5). Institute for Prospective Technological Studies.
23. de Reuver, M., Sørensen, C., & Basole, R. C. (2018). The digital platform: A research agenda. *Journal of Information Technology, 33*(2), 124–135. https://doi.org/10.1057/s41265-016-0033-3.
24. Vermesan, O., Friess, P., Guillemin, P., Serrano, M., et al. (2016). IoT digital value chain connecting research, innovation and deployment. *Digitising the Industry Internet of Things Connecting the Physical, Digital and Virtual Worlds, 49*, 15–129.
25. Basole, R. C., Russell, M. G., Huhtamäki, J., Rubens, N., Still, K., & Park, H. (2015). Understanding business ecosystem dynamics: A data-driven approach. *ACM Transactions on Management Information Systems (TMIS), 6*(2). https://doi.org/10.1145/2724730.
26. Hagiu, A., & Wright, J. (2015). Multi-sided platforms. *International Journal of Industrial Organization, 43*, 162–174. https://doi.org/10.1016/j.ijindorg.2015.03.003.
27. McCabe, M. J., & Snyder, C. M. (2018). Open access as a crude solution to a hold-up problem in the two-sided market for academic journals. *The Journal of Industrial Economics, 66*(2), 301–349. https://doi.org/10.1111/joie.12167.
28. Evans, P. C., & Gawer, A. (2016). The rise of the platform enterprise. A global survey. *The Center for Global Enterprise No. 1*. https://www.thecge.net/app/uploads/2016/01/PDF-WEB-Platform-Survey_01_12.pdf.

Modeling the Digital Transformation of the Region's Industry

Grigoriy Korovin

Abstract The paper studies the issues of modeling the digital transformation of the regional industrial sector. The polystructural nature of the research object requires the use of a methodological toolkit capable of adequately simulating comprehensive socio-economic systems. To simulate the digital transformation of a regional industrial sector, an agent-based approach is applied. When developing a model, the study proposes to take into account the elements of the irrational behavior of firms when making a strategic decision on digitalization, considering the formed opinion of managers and the general level of digitalization in the region. In the author's opinion, these factors are of a psychological nature and can be assessed using a multidisciplinary approach. As a result of developing the model, the author proposed 4 classes of agents, their parameters, strategies used, possible states, estimated assets, and liabilities. In the model, an enterprise's choice of a digitalization strategy and an operational decision on starting digital transformation are separated. The transition to a digitalization strategy is based on the actions of other industrial enterprises and the probability of a positive decision of the CEO identified as a result of the survey. The decision to start a digitalization program is determined by a strategic decision, the current financial capabilities of a particular enterprise, and the level of subsidies for the digitalization of the industry by regional authorities. The results of the study enrich the methodological toolkit for modeling the digitalization of the industrial sector, expand the ideas about the rational choice of an enterprise's digitalization strategy, and make it possible to use the opinions of CEOs in an agent-based model.

Keywords Agent-based modeling · Industry · Digitalization

1 Introduction

The study of the issues of transformation of the industrial sector, due to its complexity, involves the use of modern tools that can adequately model comprehensive systems

G. Korovin (✉)
Institute of Economics of the Ural Branch of the Russian Academy of Sciences, Moskovskaya St. 29, 620014 Ekaterinburg, Russian Federation
e-mail: korovin.gb@uiec.ru

V. Kumar et al. (eds.), *Digital Transformation in Industry*, Lecture Notes in Information Systems and Organisation 44, https://doi.org/10.1007/978-3-030-73261-5_5

of interconnections, take into account the conflicting interests of the stakeholders of industrial development, strategies, and algorithms of their behavior. One of such approaches is agent-based modeling, which has very wide capabilities and effective computer tools for their implementation. The construction of such models involves the choice of classes of agents, the identification of their properties and algorithms of behavior that are close to real ones. Such models, using simple algorithms of agent behavior, can demonstrate the specific dynamics of the system as a whole.

The task of finalizing the methodology for constructing agent-based models of the digital transformation of an industrial sector is urgent. A significant requirement is the use of interdisciplinary approaches, since the functioning of regional socio-economic systems and transformation processes in them depend not only on economic and social factors but also on institutional, political, and psychological ones. For Russia, this problem is of particular importance, since, along with strategic management, elements of direct management remain, leading to an imbalance in the processes of economic development and the disproportionality of transformation processes.

In this paper, on the basis of the previously developed architecture of the agent-based model, the main elements of the model have been detailed, the characteristics of interactions and the state of industrial enterprises in the course of digital transformation have been formalized.

2 Literature Review

2.1 Digital Transformation of the Industry

The author considers the digital transformation of the industry as a process of increasing competitiveness through the use of advanced information technologies. The new digital paradigm is a combination of advanced technologies that provide efficient and accurate economic and technical decisions in real time. One can say that now the industrial sector is undergoing a digital transformation. Matarazzo et al. [6] showed that digital tools were driving the modification of enterprise business models by creating new distribution channels and new ways to create and deliver value. Industrial enterprises, accepting this challenge, are forced to adjust their strategies according to the concept of Industry 4.0. Zhou and Le Cardinal [7] compared various programs of the fourth industrial revolution in different countries and identified some technologies that are important for this process. Kang et al. [4] investigated the general concept of intelligent manufacturing, established key technologies associated with it, and trends linked with intelligent manufacturing. Designing and implementing a digital transformation strategy has become a key challenge for many pre-digital organizations in traditional industries. Chanias et al. [3] assessed the transition to a digital strategy, related it with planning the implementation of information systems and the importance of taking into account the emerging new challenges.

2.2 *Application of Agent-Based Modeling*

The agent-based approach chosen here is, in modern conditions, one of the most universal, since it allows establishing a wide range of agent parameters, behavior algorithms, and connections of a different nature. In addition, agent-based modeling software environments allow the use of a wide range of economic and mathematical methods. The local behavior of agents working according to their own laws determines the behavior of the system as a whole, making it possible to observe new systemic effects and identify emergent properties. As one of the basic ideas, one can cite the theory of cellular automata, which reveals that a set of agents obeying the simplest rules can form rather complex structures in the visual field. The agent-based approach is widely utilized in the areas of defense, marketing, social sciences, logistics, modeling of sustainable industrial development, etc.

In the industrial sector, Makarov et al. [5] implemented a number of projects on agent-based modeling of industrial development within the framework of regional and municipal models. Among the models that formalize transformation processes is the work by Bertani et al. [1], who, on the basis of the agent-based macro model, tried to identify the micro and macro effects of digital transformation. The results show an increase in the profitability of digital technology manufacturers, a desire for market concentration. At the macro level, there is an increase in unemployment rates as digital production assets are not balanced by the new jobs created in the digital sector. Unemployment is growing in the long term within the model due to the increased productivity of digital assets. The agent model of transformation of the labor market under the influence of technological development by Caiani et al. [2] confirmed that investment by firms in R&D led to an increase in productivity in the real sector and, in the absence of compensatory measures, to distortion of labor markets and an increase in inequality. They outlined the need to introduce a digital asset developer as a new type of capital producer within the macroeconomic model.

3 Materials and Methods

The main advantage of agent-based modeling over other classes of models is the ability to create a model that is as close to reality as possible. The study of the digital transformation of the industry on the basis of an agent-based approach requires solving problems of choosing classes of agents and constructing adequate algorithms for their behavior. This approach will take into account the multi-level and polystructural nature of the industrial digitalization process in the context of unpredictable institutional and technological leaps.

As a theoretical paradigm, the author used the provisions of the neoclassical economic theory on the rational preferences of producers and consumers (the subjects of relations maximize their own gain) and independence and possession of complete and relevant information. Taking these provisions as the main ones, the author proposes to integrate into the model the elements of irrational behavior, the acquired rules of behavior, norms, and requirements. For the subjects of the model, this is realized in assessing the probabilities of choosing a digitalization strategy, striving to save the company from additional damage, taking into account the experience of digitalization of other agents. In the author's opinion, these factors are of a psychological nature and can be assessed on the basis of an analysis of the results of interviews with CEOs of industrial enterprises. The spatial aspect, determined by the territorial location of production facilities, the resources necessary for it, will not be taken into account by the development of the transport infrastructure.

As an information base of the study, the author used the state statistics data of the Russian Federation and data from questionnaires filled by CEOs of industrial enterprises, making it possible to identify the psychological aspects of adopting a digital transformation strategy by industrial enterprises.

4 Results

4.1 Characteristics of Classes of Agents in the Model

During the creation of the model, the architecture was formed and the main subjects of industrial development were identified: large industrial enterprises, small and medium-sized industrial enterprises, manufacturers of digitalization means, regional authorities. Regional authorities are a single agent; they are able to redistribute federal and regional subsidies for digitalization (Fig. 1).

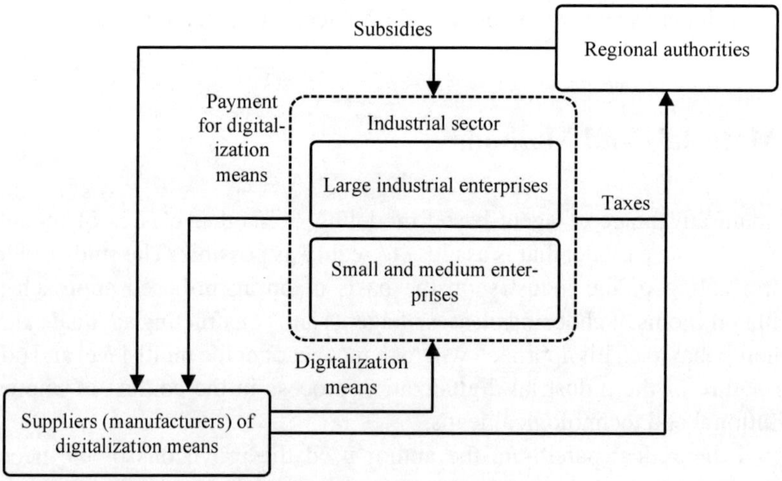

Fig. 1 Graphical view of the agents and resource flows of the model

Table 1 Parameters of an agent-based model of transformation of the industrial sector

Agent class	Parameters	Strategies	States	Assets	Liabilities
Large industrial enterprises/small and medium industrial enterprises	Digitalization indicators Volume of sales Profit Costs of particular digital technologies	Inert Active	Pre-transformation state Transformation period Transformed state	Fixed assets Own (cash) funds Productive reserves Subsidies for digitalization	Debt service Taxes
Digitalization means manufacturers	Volume of sales Profit R&D costs	Active			
Regional authorities	Parameters of the development of industry in the region: production volumes, employment, labor productivity, investments, etc	Active stimulation of digital development Hampering digital development		Tax revenues Federal budget subsidies	Subsidies for digitalization

Each of the selected agents—industrial enterprises has its own spatial and industry specificity, that of competitive strategies, business models, and resource opportunities. Here the author will use only the basic financial and individual technological indicators (Table 1).

4.2 *Formalization of Agents' Behavior*

The factors considered for choosing a digitalization strategy, and accumulating experience in digitalizing other agents, which have a psychological basis, should be included in the structure of the model as those influencing the algorithm of action of industrial enterprises. One can assume the type of agents' behavior strategy based on the analysis of statistics and the study of the opinion of CEOs of industrial companies. A study by a Russian company "Strategy Partners" showed that 91% of Russian enterprises continued to operate according to an outdated business model and did not include digitalization in their business strategy. Thirty percent consider digitalization as a priority for 3–5 years, while 78% of respondents intend to use digital solutions for certain production processes. According to 22% of survey participants, one of the main barriers is the lack of financial resources.

A survey by the regional Union of Industrialists and Entrepreneurs of the Sverdlovsk Region shows that only 11% of industrial enterprises are focused on the digitalization of their business. Only 15% of companies indicated that they were introducing information technology into the main production; 2.2% are digitalizing R&D; 7.4%—HR; 14%—sales. About 33% of companies limit themselves to accounting automation. The state is expected to develop specialized education and support corporate R&D, initiatives to introduce technological solutions: 35% of the surveyed managers think so, 22% expect incentives for technological entrepreneurship (grants, acceleration programs). At the same time, as the CEOs assume, digitalization can give business new competitive advantages: a multiple increase in productivity and a decrease in operating costs by a third.

The survey data allow including the evaluated psychological factors in the model algorithm. Industrial enterprises at each cycle of the model can choose the transition to a digitalization strategy $Strategic\_Decision_i$, taking into account the actions of other agents of industrial enterprises and the general level of digitalization $DigLevel$ and based on the probability of adoption of the strategy by the CEO $\Pr obability_i$:

$$Strategic\_Decision_i = f(DigLevel, \Pr obability_i), \quad (1)$$

The very decision to start a digitalization program is determined by the adopted strategy, the current financial capabilities of a particular enterprise $\text{Res}Adequacy_i$ and based on the level of subsidies for digitalization of the enterprise by the regional authorities $DigSubsidy$:

$$DigitalStart_i = f(Strategic\_Decision_i, \text{Res}Adequacy_i, DigSubsidy_i) \quad (2)$$

The IT manufacturing agent plays the role of an executor of digitalization projects, strengthens its financial condition, increases R&D costs and releases a new version of the digitalization tool.

The regional authority is guided by the socio-economic indicators of the region $I_1, I_2, ..., I_n$, own strategy of digitalization of the industry $GovDigStrategy$ and decides on the size of the subsidy to stimulate digitalization of the industry in the region $DigSubsidy$:

$$DigSubsidy = f(GovDigStrategy, I_1, I_2, ..., I_n) \quad (3)$$

5 Discussion and Conclusion

In the author's opinion, the elements of agents' behavior taken into account in the model, associated with the beliefs of enterprise managers about the feasibility of digitalization, will allow a more adequate modeling of the transformation processes implemented in the industry. The proposed version of the formalization of algorithms for agents' actions will allow using not only past statistical data, but also the managers' ideas about the future of industrial enterprises.

The next stage of the study will be devoted to the refinement and verification of the model based on retrospective data, scenario calculations, and the study of the possibilities of state policy in the management of digitalization processes in the industrial sector of the economy. As a result, a flexible, adaptable model can become the basis for predicting transformation processes in a regional industrial sector.

Acknowledgements The article is supported by the Russian Foundation for Basic Research, project no. 20-010-00719 "Modeling of crossindustrial networking processes in the industrial complex based on hybrid technologies".

References

1. Bertani, F., Ponta, L., Raberto, M., Teglio, A., & Cincotti, S. (2020). The complexity of the intangible digital economy: An agent-based model. *Journal of Business Research*, (In Press). https://doi.org/10.1016/j.jbusres.2020.03.041.
2. Caiani, A., Russo, A., & Gallegati, M. (2019). Does inequality hamper innovation and growth? An AB-SFC analysis. *Journal of Evolutionary Economics, 29*, 177–228. https://doi.org/10.1007/s00191-018-0554-8.
3. Chanias, S., Myers, M. D., & Hess, T. (2019). Digital transformation strategy making in pre-digital organizations: The case of a financial services provider. *The Journal of Strategic Information Systems, 28*(1), 17–33. https://doi.org/10.1016/j.jsis.2018.11.003.
4. Kang, H. S., Lee, J. Y., Choi, S., et al. (2016). Smart manufacturing: Past research, present findings, and future directions. *International Journal of Precision Engineering and Manufacturing-Green Technology, 3*, 111–128. https://doi.org/10.1007/s40684-016-0015-5.
5. Makarov, V. L., Bakhtizin, A. R., & Sushko, E. D. (2013). Computer simulation of interaction between municipalities, regions, government authorities. *Control Sciences, 6*, 31–40.
6. Matarazzo, M., Penco, L., Profumo, G., & Quaglia, R. (2021). Digital transformation and customer value creation in made in Italy SMEs: A dynamic capabilities perspective. *Journal of Business Research, 123*, 642–656. https://doi.org/10.1016/j.jbusres.2020.10.033.
7. Zhou, R., & Le Cardinal, J. (2019). Exploring the impacts of industry 4.0 from a macroscopic perspective. *Proceedings of the Design Society: International Conference on Engineering Design, 1*(1), 2111–2120. https://doi.org/10.1017/dsi.2019.217.

Visual Methodology for the Multi-factor Assessment of Industrial Digital Transformation Components

Andrey I. Vlasov and Vadim A. Shakhnov

Abstract The paper offers a visual method for multi-factor assessment of digital transformation components of the industry. The authors consider the aspects of its application in assessing the implementation of digital information systems in the electronic industry and give recommendations for analyzing the existing business processes at an enterprise. The study proposes an approach to the implementation of the electronic digital space system in the enterprise's information structure, which allows increasing the efficiency of enterprise management processes and simplifying the system for monitoring the state of its activities. The article briefly discussed the main factors of efficiency of introduction and modernization of the enterprise's digital information space and shows the main difficulties of implementation and the planning principles for the transition to digital transformation in the enterprise. The authors recommend on the development of visual diagrams for multi-factor assessment of digital transformation components taking into account the needs of a particular enterprise.

Keywords Industrial digital transformation · Visual models · Multi-factor analysis · Life cycle · Information systems · Digital space · Smart systems

1 Introduction

The first industrial revolution brought significant changes to the industry using steam as an energy source. The second industrial revolution used electricity and a conveyor belt for mass production. The integration of information technology and computers into manufacturing was the foundation of the third industrial revolution. The fourth industrial revolution is just around the corner, taking production to a new level where machines redefine their ways of interacting and performing individual functions. However, the fourth industrial revolution concerns not only the industry [1, 5, 21]. General transformation using digital integration and intelligent engineering is

A. I. Vlasov (✉) · V. A. Shakhnov
Bauman Moscow State Technical University, Baumanskaya 2-ya St. 5/1, 105005 Moscow, Russian Federation
e-mail: vlasovai@bmstu.ru

V. Kumar et al. (eds.), *Digital Transformation in Industry*, Lecture Notes in Information Systems and Organisation 44, https://doi.org/10.1007/978-3-030-73261-5_6

considered [12, 17, 19, 21, 22]. This transformation involves a level of production where machines are autonomously reconfigured, depending on the performance of individual functions. The Industry 4.0 concept was initially defined as a means of increasing the competitiveness of the manufacturing industry through the enhanced integration of "cyber-physical systems" into factory processes [23]. For any Industry 4.0 system, continuous connectivity, human assistance, and decentralized decision-making are essential. The main components of Industry 4.0 include cyber-physical systems, virtual and augmented reality, cloud computing, Big Data analysis, etc. [3, 23].

The work objective is to formalize a visual methodology for the multi-factor assessment of industrial digital transformation components, based on systematization and generalization of trends in the transition to a new digital industry and the formation of proposals for introducing smart factories.

Achieving this objective involves analyzing the provisions of the Industry 4.0 concept, analyzing the technology of digital tool production and their use in Industry 4.0, comparative analysis of the types of factories of the future and their classification, analyzing the features of implementing smart factories in modern Russia, analyzing the stages of the digital transformation of the economy, analyzing the problems of transition to a new digital industry and their solutions, developing methods for integrating classical production in Industry 4.0 with the creation of "smart factories of the future" [1, 2, 4, 6–8, 11, 15, 24].

The practical significance of the proposed method of multi-factor assessment of industrial digital transformation components is aimed at formalizing methods for assessing the degree of digital transformation. The key to training high-quality specialists necessary in the conditions of the fourth industrial revolution is hidden in the advanced educational "Factories of the future" as new approaches to training and reproduction of personnel in the concept of "inevitability of accumulation and transfer of knowledge" [5, 10, 14, 16, 18, 20, 25].

Electronic instrumentation is one of the most important branches of modern industry, characterized by high dynamics of changes, fierce competition, saturation with modern technologies, and a constant reduction in the market for new products. In such an environment, the role of technological and managerial, economic, socio-psychological knowledge and solutions increases significantly [21]. A modern radio engineering enterprise needs to consider processes holistically as components of the product lifecycle management, united by bidirectional links—digital information flows and logistics chains to realize competitive advantages. This approach can be implemented within the framework of the modern concept of industrial digital transformation [21] by digitizing the specified components of the life cycle, creating mathematical, physical, and simulation models of objects with the corresponding sets of parameters, inputs/outputs, control actions, criteria, constraints, and optimization variables. Based on these models, it is possible to conduct simulation modeling, predict characteristics, select promising options, optimize the parameters of both the product itself and its production processes and other components of the life cycle, without the need for expensive testing of prototypes, field experiments and making expensive changes to the already formed production, sales, and service infrastructure.

2 Literature Review

The Industry 4.0 concept, which originated in Germany, has attracted much attention in the scientific community [3, 5, 12, 17, 22–24]. Industrial production is currently driven by global competition and the need to quickly adapt production to constantly changing market requirements. These requirements necessitate a radical transformation of modern production.

Industry 4.0 is a prospective approach based on the integration of social and production processes and the integration of all participants in the company's value chain (suppliers, customers, etc.) [16, 22].

The technical aspects of these requirements are fulfilled by applying cyber-physical systems and the industrial Internet of Things to industrial production systems [2, 10, 14–16, 18, 20, 25].

Digital transformation is a fundamental rethinking of the organization's model (from the business model and business processes to sources of financing and the formation of an intelligent personnel reserve), for which digital technologies are only a catalyst, and non-digital aspects become key, determining the success of implemented innovations, the transition to new business models, and the speed of reaction to external changes [2, 10, 14–16, 18, 20, 25].

The stages of digital transformation are analyzed below. The first stage is aimed at defining values, including forming a clear justification for the need for transformation, determining the key team from the top and middle level, setting the organizational scope of transformation, and allocating investment (financial and human) in the company for the implementation of the corresponding program [1, 12, 21].

The second stage aimed at launching and accelerating the transformation program (Launch and Acceleration) is designed to avoid the rollback of transformations, maintain the momentum of transformational efforts and ensure the first significant results that finally convince the bulk of the organization's employees of the need and inevitability of digital transformation [1, 12, 21].

The third stage should be focused on scaling up. As a rule, companies reach it after about 18 months of implementing the transformation program, and by this time, they have accumulated experience, which should be used to bring all the initiatives of the transformation program to a new level, as well as ensure that all new practices are consolidated in the operational, routine, activities of the organization [1, 12, 21].

A decade ago, it was widely believed that it was enough to create a digital model of the product, design/production object to solve the above problems. This approach made it possible to effectively solve the problems of computer-aided engineering, engineering analysis, and partially the pre-production, mainly machine-building production [21]. With this approach, communication with production is implemented as a unidirectional process, which allows assessing how well this product is suitable for the existing production structure. Flexible readjustment, adaptation, and production variability are significantly limited here.

The production specificity of electronic equipment in terms of modules on printed circuit boards and blocks involves a large number of assembly operations with the creation of permanent connections by soldering, welding, gluing, diversified small- and medium-batch production, quick readjusting to new products, a broad range of automated assembly equipment, combined into production lines and flexible manufacturing areas, a certain proportion of manual operations of assembly, inspection, and repair [21]. In addition to the digital product model, it is necessary to possess a digital model of production with all its technical and economic aspects of equipment, facilities, personnel, components, processes and routes, material and logistics flows within the site/warehouse, performance, accuracy, reliability, minimize readjusting times, downtime of equipment, optimization of technological routes, the quantity of staff, etc. [8, 21].

This changing "digital twin" of real production is the basis of the modern Industry 4.0 concept, which involves the introduction of various cyber-physical systems in production structures. Simultaneously, one of the leading factors of effective development is the economic and social aspects of management in close connection with the subject and operational technical proficiency [3, 9, 12, 16, 22–24]. Each of the life cycle production components is reflected in a single information management production infrastructure, which provides information transparency, reproducibility, manageability, and reliability of the entire production system [12, 13].

3 Methods

The visual method of multi-factor assessment of industrial digital transformation components assumes reflection of state properties in the 3D space of the level of digital transformation following the starting point of the digitization process:

- F-axis is factual information (characteristics, object properties that are collected, systematized, and processed to form digital maps (mapping));
- D-axis is full-text sources of information (containing text descriptions, forming digital archives of documents);
- R-axis is regulations for the life cycle of digital documents (form the rules for creating, processing, accounting, and storing digital documents).

For each axis, its tools are allocated: archives and electronic storage, mail systems, word processors, etc. Movement along each of the axes separately does not affect the essence of the digital transformation of the enterprise and cannot contribute to complex digitalization. A study of the experience of many enterprises has confirmed that the creation of a digital transformation system in a complex should be based on a spatial model that combines all three components.

4 Results

A method for building a digital transformation model for an enterprise based on movement along three F-R-D axes is considered [2]. They provide for accounting for factual information, the ability to work with full-text documents, support for document processing regulations, and define a 3D space of properties where a complex digital transformation criterion moves along a certain trajectory, going through various stages in its development (Fig. 1).

The position of the point in the system (F, D, R) indicates the current state of digital transformation. The position of this point can track the level of development and effectiveness of digitalization implementation.

The presented model allows understanding the finishing point, what is missing, and how to use the results already achieved. It is enough only to know the current state of the work organization at each necessary enterprise. At the same time, the steepness of the curve proportionally affects the speed of the modernization process, and the values of the three coordinates directly indicate the level of digitalization, which can be used to determine the number of issues.

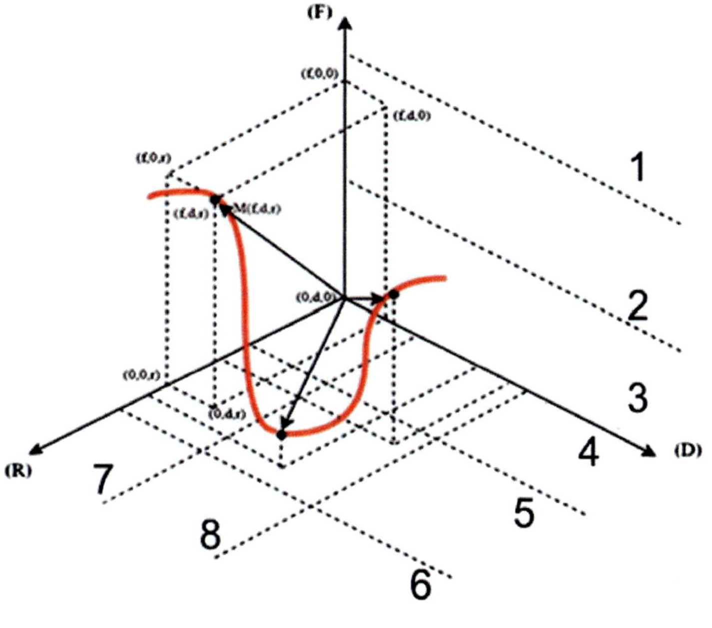

Fig. 1 A spatial model of the digital environment in the 3D space of properties (F (Factual account (storage organization level)); D (Document flow); R (Regulations); 1—Linked to processes; 2—Primary file accumulation; 3—Full-text documents; 4—Data generation and transmission; 5—Simplified regulations; 6—Unified management system; 7—Simple archive; 8—Corporate archive)

5 Discussion

The issues of estimating the indicators values along the F-R-D axes must be analyzed using the proposed visual methodology for multi-factor assessment of industrial digital transformation components. If the activities of a company whose task is to produce products are considered, then all three coordinates must have balanced values. The "F" and "D" axes define the specifics of the organization's activities, regulated by the position of the third coordinate (R) of the model space. In the simplest case, it can be used to evaluate the levels of factual account, archive, and regulations discretely, for example, using the expert panels methods, "Delphi," etc. However, such assessments are largely subjective. In the proposed method, a complex ratio is introduced for each of the axes, estimated by the effective area of the quality circle (Fig. 2).

For example, digital transformation indicators can be grouped:

F Axis:

- navigation tools provide ease of use for applications and include basic tools, such as personal and group queues for document processing tasks, tools for navigating

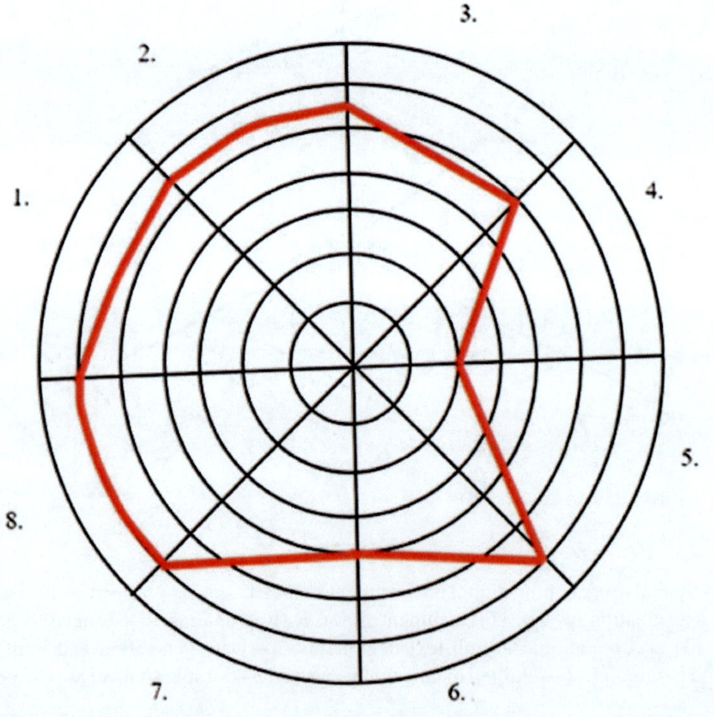

Fig. 2 Quality circle for a group of digital transformation indicators (1. Navigation tool. 2. Card index/accounting. 3. Archive/processing. 4. Routing/control. 5. Process automation. 6. Group work. 7. Knowledge search/management. 8. Openness)

the hierarchy of data in the system, the right to manage data views, and initializing document processing functions;
- the card file or accounting allows recording the accompanying information of documents, attributes, and links. It determines the correctness of filling in fields, ensuring uniqueness, automatic numbering, and determining document processing operations;
- automation tools.

D Axis:

- document archiving involves the orderly storage of files; processing is determined by scanning and recognizing the document content. Locks and versions are managed here;
- search and knowledge management allows using full-text, attribute, and filter searches. It provides smart search and complex search queries, classification of documents;
- additional functionality is the most important parameter, the presence of only standard application configuration tools is often not enough, and hence there is a need for software interfaces of platforms.

R Axis:

- document routing and status monitoring are responsible for transmitting documents to users and monitoring the user's work and actions. Online and offline documents editing;
- group work functions allow employees to interact on organizational issues through conferences and other discussion methods.

In reality, no system implements all the functions in full. For example, the figure shows the executable functions of a virtual model of a radio engineering enterprise.

Qualified personnel, the knowledge of tools offered by the platform, and experience with the platform process automation have a large impact on the successful implementation of the enterprise's digital transformation. Before implementing the system, the company or the external market must ensure a sufficient number of qualified specialists in this field.

6 Conclusion

An approach has been developed to assess the digital transformation of an industrial enterprise based on a set of complex indicators. This solution allows tracking the evolution of the transformation with the decomposition of the general problem into several specific subtasks solved by separate subsystems. The resulting RFD model in the 3D space of properties can be used to prepare, analyze, and improve the production of electronic equipment at the stage of creating a new production and launching new products into existing production.

The availability of an effective tool for quantitative assessment and identification of possible problem areas for the implementation of Industry 4.0, both in Russia in particular and worldwide, allows predicting and building theories for the rapid and smooth development of the industrial digital transformation.

The application of the proposed model creates conditions for ensuring effective management and transparency of the company's activities at all levels. A promising direction in further research is to refine the composition of functional coefficients used in the quality circle to improve the effective evaluation of the system as a whole.

Acknowledgements Some project results were obtained with the Ministry of Science and Higher Education's financial support for project No. 0705-2020-0041 "Fundamental research of the digital transformation methods of the component base of micro and nanosystems."

References

1. Akberdina, V. V., Kalinina, A. V., & Vlasov, A. I. (2018). Transformation stages of the Russian industrial complex in the context of economy digitalization. *Problems and Perspectives in Management, 16*(4), 201–211.
2. Baena, F., Guarin, A., Mora, J., Sauza, J., & Retat, S. (2017). Learning factory: The path to industry 4.0. *Procedia Manufacturing, 9*, 73–80. https://doi.org/10.1016/j.promfg.2017.04.022.
3. Bogoviz, A. V., Osipov, V. S., Chistyakova, M. K., & Borisov, M. Y. (2018). Comparative analysis of formation of industry 4.0 in developed and developing countries. In E. G. Popkova, Yu. V. Ragulina, & A. V. Bogoviz (Eds.). *Industry 4.0: Industrial revolution of the 21st century* (pp. 155–164). https://doi.org/10.1007/978-3-319-94310-7_15.
4. Brinca, P., Duarte, J. B., & Oliveira, J. G. (2019). Investment-specific technological change, taxation and inequality in the US. *Journal of Eurasian Economic Dialogue, 4*(2), 29–48.
5. Cheng, G.-J., Liu, L.-T., Qiang, X.-J., & Liu, Y. (2016). Industry 4.0 development and application of intelligent manufacturing. In *International conference on information system and artificial intelligence (ISAI)*.
6. Chernova, V. Y., Golodova, Z. G., Degtereva, E. A., Zobov, A. M., & Starostin, V. S. (2018). Russian industry in global value-added chains. *European Research Studies Journal, 21*(3), 165–178. https://doi.org/10.35808/ersj/1051.
7. Chernova, V. Y., Zobov, A. M., & Starostin, V. S. (2019). Dynamics of digital inequality in Russia. *Media Watch, 10*(2), 225–234. https://doi.org/10.15655/mw/2019/v10i2/49622.
8. Demin, A.A., & Vlasov, A.I. (2017). Visual methods of formalization of knowledge in the conditions of the synchronous technologies of system engineering. In *CEE-SECR '17: Proceedings of the 13th central and eastern European software engineering conference in Russia*, No. 3166098. https://doi.org/10.1145/3166094.3166098.
9. Guseva, V. E., Kuzmin, E. A., & Vlasov, A. I. (2019). Study of operational efficiency of large-scale publicly owned companies in Russia. *Advances in Systems Science and Applications, 19*(3), 23–37. https://doi.org/10.25728/assa.2019.19.3.747.
10. Jerman, A., Bertoncelj, A., & Bach, M. P. (2018). A bibliometric and topic analysis on future competences at smart factories. *Machines, 6*(3), 41. https://doi.org/10.3390/machines6030041.
11. Lambert, T. E. (2018). Monopoly capital and innovation: An exploratory assessment of R&D effectiveness. *Journal of Eurasian Economic Dialogue, 3*(6), 20–35.

12. Lee, J., Davari, H., Singh, J., & Pandhare, V. (2018). Industrial artificial intelligence for industry 4.0-based manufacturing systems. *Manufacturing Letters, 18*, 20–23. https://doi.org/10.1016/j.mfglet.2018.09.002.
13. Litau, E. (2018). The information problem on the way to becoming a "Gazelle." In *Proceedings of the European conference on innovation and entrepreneurship, ECIE* (Vol. 2018-September, pp. 394–401).
14. Nouiri, M., Trentesaux, D., Bekrar, A., Giret, A., & Salido, M. A. (2019). Cooperation between smart manufacturing scheduling systems and energy providers: A multi-agent perspective. *Studies in Computational Intelligence, 803*, 197–210.
15. Paelke, V. (2014). Augmented reality in the smart factory: supporting workers in an industry 4.0 environment. In *Proceedings of the 2014 IEEE emerging technology and factory automation (ETFA)*. https://doi.org/10.1109/ETFA.2014.7005252.
16. Palmgren, G. (1997). Transgenic plants: Environmentally safe factories of the future. *Trends in Genetics, 13*(9), 348. https://doi.org/10.1016/S0168-9525(97)01232-8.
17. Prinz, C., Morlock, F., Freith, S., Kreggenfeld, N., Kreimeier, D., & Kuhlenkötter, B. (2016). Learning factory modules for smart factories in industrie 4.0. *Procedia CIRP, 54*, 113–118. https://doi.org/10.1016/j.procir.2016.05.105.
18. Raslavičius, L., Felneris, M., & Striūgas, N. (2018). New insights into algae factories of the future. *Renewable and Sustainable Energy Reviews, 81*, 643–654. https://doi.org/10.1016/j.rser.2017.08.024.
19. Romanova, O. A., Korovin, G. B., & Kuzmin, E. A. (2017). Analysis of the development prospects for the high-tech sector of the economy in the context of new industrialization. *Espacios, 38*(59), 25.
20. Schallock, B., Rybski, C., Jochem, R., & Kohl, H. (2018). Learning factory for industry 4.0 to provide future skills beyond technical training. *Procedia Manufacturing, 23*, 27–32. https://doi.org/10.1016/j.promfg.2018.03.156.
21. Shakhnov, V. A., & Kurnosenko, A. E. (2019). Digital production modeling of electronic equipment in the framework of the "industry 4.0" concept. In V. V. Akberdina (Ed.), *2nd International scientific and practical conference, digital transformation of the industry: Trends, management, strategies* (pp. 585–594).
22. Simons, S., Abé, P., & Neser, S. (2017). Learning in the AutFab – The fully automated industrie 4.0 learning factory of the university of applied sciences Darmstadt. *Procedia Manufacturing, 9*, 81–88. https://doi.org/10.1016/j.promfg.2017.04.023.
23. Stroiteleva, T. G., Kalinicheva, E. Y., Vukovich, G. G., & Osipov, V. S. (2018). Peculiarities and Problems of Formation of Industry 4.0 in Modern Russia. In E. G. Popkova, Yu. V. Ragulina, & A. V. Bogoviz (Eds.), *Industry 4.0: Industrial revolution of the 21st century* (pp. 145–153). Springer. https://doi.org/10.1007/978-3-319-94310-7_14.
24. Wang, S., Wan, J., Li, D., & Zhang, C. (2016). Implementing smart factory of industrie 4.0: An outlook. *International Journal of Distributed Sensor Networks,* Article ID 3159805. https://doi.org/10.1155/2016/3159805.
25. Zhuravleva, L. V., Kirilin, V. D., Repnikov, P. O., & Usyukin, M. A. (2020). Integration analysis of "factories of the future" and "industry 4.0" technologies. *Information Technologies in Design and Production, 3*(179), 45–51.

Modeling the Factors Behind Digitalization of the Real Sector of the Economy

Svetlana S. Kudryavtseva, Marina V. Shinkevich, and Sofia Sh. Ostanina

Abstract The relevance of the article is associated with the increasing influence of digitalization on the development of the real sector of the economy. The paper aims to determine the key factors in the development of digital technologies at industrial enterprises and to identify, on their basis, the dependencies between these indicators, which will allow the list of key drivers of digitalization of the industrial sector in the short and medium term to be codified. The following research methods were used: the description method for analyzing the dynamics of changes in the digitalization indicators of enterprises in the real sector of the economy; correlation analysis; and regression analysis. Among the key drivers of digitalization of the real sector of the economy based on modeling, the authors have identified the following: the share of organizations using customer relationship management systems in the total number of organizations surveyed; the share of organizations that placed orders for goods (work, services) on the Internet in the total number of organizations surveyed; the share of organizations that had special software for managing the procurement of goods (works, services) in the total number of organizations surveyed.

Keywords Digitalization · Real sector of the economy · Information and communication technologies · Modeling

1 Introduction

The use of digital technologies in the management of business processes of modern enterprises in the real sector of the economy has an important national economic purpose. First, it increases the degree of management flexibility and adaptability to changes in the external environment. Second, informatization contributes to involving all participants in the product supply chain in production and management processes,

S. S. Kudryavtseva (✉) · M. V. Shinkevich · S. Sh. Ostanina
Kazan National Research Technological University, K. Marx St. 68, 420015 Kazan, Russian Federation

V. Kumar et al. (eds.), *Digital Transformation in Industry*, Lecture Notes in Information Systems and Organisation 44, https://doi.org/10.1007/978-3-030-73261-5_7

increasing the level of their integration. Third, in the age of the fourth industrial revolution, the digitalization trend is the key to the level of competitiveness of economic systems and individual business entities.

In this regard, analysis of the key trends in the development of the digital economy at the level of enterprises in the real sector is timely and relevant. The purpose of the article is to determine the key factors in the development of digital technologies at industrial enterprises and to identify, on their basis, the dependencies between these indicators, which will allow the list of key drivers of digitalization of the industrial sector in the short and medium term to be codified.

2 Literature Review

Scientific literature widely discusses the key areas of digitalization in various industries of the real sector of the economy, including the information transformation of technological processes [11], innovative strategies for industrial modernization in the context of digitalization of the economy [1], the role of production management in industry 4.0 [2, 3], modeling of efficiency factors of production and technological processes [10], the specifics of the fourth industrial revolution [4], etc. Numerous studies examine narrow areas of introducing digital technologies into the real sector of the economy: Big Data technology [5], additive manufacturing [6], integrated data structures in enterprise resource planning (ERP) [9], digital competencies [7], etc.

However, scarce attention is paid to identifying the key drivers behind the development of the industrial sector of the economy at the microlevel of management amid the digitalization of economic systems and business entities. This provision served as a choice in formulating the goals, object, and subject of the article.

3 Material and Methods

The following research methods were used in the article.

1. The descriptive method for analyzing the dynamics of changes in the indicators of digitalization of enterprises in the real sector of the economy.
2. The correlation analysis method. To solve diverse business problems, it is necessary to assess the relationship (ratio) between two or more features. To solve this problem, correlation indicators are most often used (from the Latin *correlation*—ratio). With such a relationship, the average value (mathematical expectation) of the random variable of the effective attribute y changes depending on the change in another random variable x_i or a set of random variables x_v $x_2, \ldots, x_n$. Correlation is a special case of stochastic communication, when the change in the average value of the effective trait is correlated with the change in the average values of the factorial traits. In the general case, the stochastic

relationship can also manifest itself in changes in other characteristics of the studied traits.

The correlation coefficient is calculated using formula

$$r_{xy} = \left[n\Sigma xy - \Sigma x \Sigma y\right] / sqr\left(\left[n\Sigma x^2 - (\Sigma x)^2\right] \times \left[n\Sigma y^2 - (\Sigma y)^2\right]\right. \quad (1)$$

where x is the value of the factor attribute; y is the value of the effective feature; n is the number of data pairs.

3. The regression analysis is a set of statistical methods for studying the influence of one or more independent variables x_1, x_2, ….x_p on the dependent variable Y. The independent variables are otherwise called regressors or predictors, and the dependent variables are criterion variables.

In practice, the regression line is most often looked for as a linear function

$$Y = b_0 + b_1x_1 + b_2x_2 + \ldots + b_nx_n \quad (2)$$

(Linear regression) that best approximates the desired curve. This is done using the least-squares method, when the sum of the squares of deviations of the actually observed values from their estimates is minimized (meaning estimates using a straight line, claiming to represent the desired regression relationship).

The time series for the analysis included indicators for the Russian economy in 2010–2019 [8] (https://rosstat.gov.ru).

The software products used for the simulation were Statistica and JASP.

4 Results

The proportion of people employed in the information and communications technology (ICT) sector in the period of 2010–2019 remained stable and averaged 1.7% of the total employed in the economy. The share of organizations that used means for protecting information transmitted over global networks in the total number of organizations surveyed in 2019 amounted to 89.5%, an increase in comparison with 2010 by 26.6%. The share of organizations using the Intranet and Extranet in the total number of surveyed organizations was 31.8% and 19.5%, respectively, having increased in comparison with 2010 by 2.4 and 3.7 times. An insignificant increase (within 7–8%) is noted in the use of software products in commerce in the procurement and sales activities of enterprises in the real sector of the economy. Thus, the share of organizations that had special software tools for managing the procurement of goods (works, services) in the total number of surveyed organizations in 2019 amounted to 39% (in 2010—36.1%), for sales management—26% (in 2010—24.3%). A significant increase is noted in the use of digital technology in managing relationships with consumers, corporate systems, and integrated supply chains—on average, their use in 2019 compared to 2010 increased 2.3-fold. The share of organizations using ERP systems in the total number of surveyed organizations reached 14.8% in 2019; used customer relationship management (CRM) systems—13.9%; electronic document management systems—70%; electronic data exchange between their own and external information systems by exchange formats—67%; supply chain management (SCM) systems—6.6%. The share of organizations that placed orders for goods (work, services) on the Internet in the total number of surveyed organizations increased from 35 to 43.3% by 2019 (an increase of 23.7%). The share of organizations that received orders for manufactured goods (work, services) via the Internet in the total number of surveyed organizations increased from 16.9 to 23.7% (an increase of 40.2%).

Table 1 presents descriptive statistics for the indicators analyzed and modeled are presented.

In Table 1, the variables are designated as follows:

The share of those employed in the ICT sector in the total employed population—X1;
The share of organizations that used means for protecting information transmitted over global networks in the total number of organizations surveyed—X2;
The share of organizations using the Intranet in the total number of organizations surveyed—X3;
The share of organizations using the Extranet in the total number of organizations surveyed—X4;
Percentage of organizations using third-party open-source operating systems (e.g., Linux) of the total organizations surveyed—X5;

Table 1 Descriptive statistics (%)

Variable	Mean	Minimum	Maximum	Std. Dev
X1	1.7	1.6	1.7	0.0
X2	84.8	70.7	89.5	6.1
X3	20.8	13.1	31.8	6.8
X4	12.6	5.3	19.5	5.6
X5	14.7	8.8	18.9	4.0
X6	37.3	36.1	39.0	1.2
X7	23.2	20.3	26.0	1.9
X8	9.6	5.1	14.8	3.3
X9	8.3	4.1	13.9	3.5
X10	63.8	58.9	70.0	3.7
X11	48.2	24.3	67.0	17.8
X12	4.3	2.5	6.6	1.4
X13	41.0	35.0	43.4	2.4
X14	19.2	16.9	23.7	2.3

The share of organizations that had special software for managing the procurement of goods (works, services) in the total number of organizations surveyed—X6;
The share of organizations that had special software tools for managing sales of goods (works, services) in the total number of organizations surveyed—X7;
The share of organizations using ERP systems in the total number of organizations surveyed—X8;
The share of organizations using CRM systems in the total number of organizations surveyed—X9;
The share of organizations using electronic document management systems in the total number of organizations surveyed—X10;
The share of organizations that used electronic data exchange between their own and external information systems by exchange formats in the total number of organizations surveyed—X11;
The share of organizations using SCM systems in the total number of organizations surveyed—X12;
The share of organizations that placed orders for goods (work, services) on the Internet in the total number of organizations surveyed—X13;
The share of organizations that received orders for manufactured goods (works, services) via the Internet in the total number of organizations surveyed—X14.

For the digital economy, it is proposed to use the indicator of gross value added per enterprise in the real sector of the economy as the dependent variable Y. The dynamics of gross value added per enterprise demonstrate a constant upward trend and are described by a linear positive trend with a model determination coefficient of 96%, which is a high indicator and allows characterizing these dynamics as favorable and stable (Fig. 1).

Based on the correlation analysis performed, it was found that all independent variables X have a positive effect on the growth of gross value added in the real sector of the economy. The correlation coefficients are statistically significant ($P \leq 0.05$) and exceed 0.6. The exceptions were the variables: the share of the employed in the ICT sector in the total employed population (X1) and the share of organizations that had special software tools for managing sales of goods (works, services) in the total

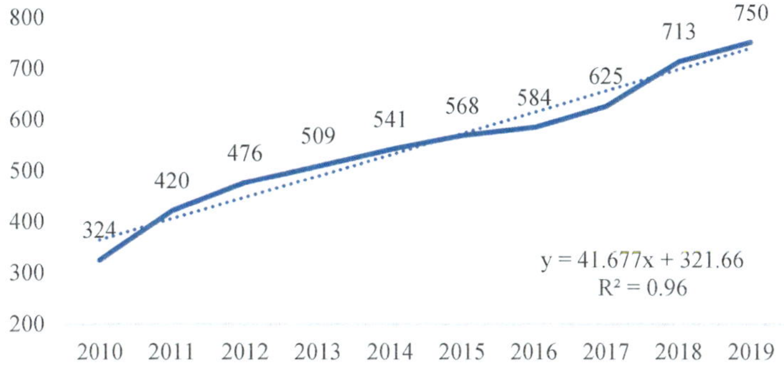

Fig. 1 Gross value added per enterprise (million rubles)

Table 2 Correlation matrix

Variable	Y	p
Y	1.0000	–
X1	−0.3903	0.265
X2	0.8537	0.002[a]
X3	0.9321	0.000[a]
X4	0.9144	0.000[a]
X5	0.9156	0.000[a]
X6	0.6526	0.041[a]
X7	0.2390	0.506
X8	0.9707	0.000[a]
X9	0.9558	0.000[a]
X10	0.7824	0.007[a]
X11	0.8229	0.003[a]
X12	0.7946	0.006[a]
X13	0.7754	0.008[a]
X14	0.9094	0.000[a]

[a]Statistically significant correlation ($P \leq 0.05$)

number of surveyed organizations (X7) and these will be excluded from subsequent analysis (Table 2).

On the basis of regression analysis using the step forward method, we obtained a regression model that determines the drivers of the formation of gross value added in the real sector of the economy in the context of digitalization:

$$Y = 37 \cdot X9 + 18 \cdot X13 + 13 \cdot X6 \quad (3)$$

This model is statistically significant: the coefficient of determination (R2) of the model was 90%, Fisher's test ($F \leq 0.05$) and the average value of the model residuals tends to zero.

5 Discussion

Thus, based on the simulation, the following conclusions may be drawn. Among the indicators of digitalization, the greatest influence on the growth of gross value added in the real sector of the economy is exerted by the share of organizations using CRM systems in the total number of surveyed organizations. An increase in this indicator by 1% point will lead to an increase in gross value added by 37 thousand rubles. The indicator of the share of organizations that placed orders for goods (work, services) on the Internet in the total number of surveyed organizations is next in terms of the strength of influence. Its increase by 1 percentage point will lead to an increase in gross value added per enterprise in the real sector of the economy by 18 thousand rubles. The key drivers of digital technologies that affect the growth of gross value added in the real sector of the economy include the share of organizations that had special software for managing the procurement of goods (works, services) in the total number of surveyed organizations—an increase in this indicator by 1% point will lead to an increase in the dependent variable by 13 thousand rubles. The total effect of the identified factors behind the digitalization of the real sector of the economy when all variables of the model change by 1% point is 68 thousand rubles.

The authors believe that the obtained modeling results can be used to develop forecasts of the digitalization of economic systems and individual economic entities. These models can also be used for developing scenarios for the digitalization of individual sectors of the economy based on the use of the elasticity coefficients of the model.

6 Conclusion

Thus, based on the analysis performed, the following trends were identified in the development of digital technologies in the real sector of the Russian economy.

There is a focus on the use of all types of digital technology, the biggest increase among which is noted for the implementation of CRM systems, the Extranet, and ERP systems. At the same time, the share of those employed in the ICT sector does not exceed 2% and remains stable. Among the key drivers of digitalization of the real sector of the economy based on modeling, the authors have identified the following: the share of organizations using CRM systems in the total number of surveyed organizations; the share of organizations that placed orders for goods (work, services) on the Internet in the total number of surveyed organizations; the share of organizations that had special software for managing the procurement of goods (works, services) in the total number of surveyed organizations.

The main directions of the digitalization of the real sector of the economy are expected to be the following:

(1). expanding the use of integrated supply chains based on information technology and virtual contracting;
(2). expanding cross-border cooperation and greater cooperation between enterprises;
(3). increasing the importance of cross-channel communications and mobile technologies;
(4). development, along with information technologies used in the field of procurement and sales, production technologies (digital design, digital twins, etc.);
(5). increasing importance and actualization of digital transformation, complex management systems, and lifelong learning.

Acknowledgements The reported study was funded by RFBR, project number 20-010-00655.

References

1. Barsegyan, N. V., Salimyanova, I. G., & Kushaeva, E. R. (2020). Typology of innovation strategies for petrochemical enterprises. *Journal of Physics: Conference Series, 1515*, 042090. https://doi.org/10.1088/1742-6596/1515/4/042090.
2. Gölzer, P., & Fritzsche, A. (2017). Data-driven operations management: organisational implications of the digital transformation in industrial practice. *Production Planning and Control, 28*(16), 1332–1343. https://doi.org/10.1080/09537287.2017.1375148.
3. Gráda, C. (2016). Did science cause the industrial revolution? *Journal of Economic Literature, 54*(1), 224–239. https://doi.org/10.1257/jel.54.1.224.
4. Klochko, E., & Brizhak, O. (2019). Prospects of using virtual technologies in modern corporate business systems. *Advances in Intelligent Systems and Computing, 726*, 308–319. https://doi.org/10.1007/978-3-319-90835-9_36.
5. Lamba, K., & Singh, S. P. (2017). Big Data in operations and supply chain management: current trends and future perspectives. *Production Planning and Control, 28*(11–12), 877–890. https://doi.org/10.1080/09537287.2017.1336787.
6. Liravi, F., Toyserkani, E., & Darleux, R. (2017). Additive manufacturing of 3D structures with non-Newtonian highly viscous fluids: Finite element modeling and experimental validation. *Additive Manufacturing, 13*, 113–123. https://doi.org/10.1016/j.addma.2016.10.008.
7. Narandja, M. E., Howes, S., & Fattahi, B. (2015). The role of soft skills in a challenging environment. *Journal of Petroleum Technology, 67*(9), 102–108. https://doi.org/10.2118/0915-0102-JPT.
8. Rosstat. https://rosstat.gov.ru.
9. Samaranayake, P., & Laosirihongthong, T. (2015). Production planning and scheduling using integrated data structures in ERP: Implementation and numerical simulation. *International Journal of Management Science and Engineering Management, 10*(3), 176–190. https://doi.org/10.1080/17509653.2014.939726.
10. Shinkevich, A. I., Kudryavtseva, S. S., & Ershova, I. G. (2020). Modelling of energy efficiency factors of petrochemical industry. *International Journal of Energy Economics and Policy, 10*(3), 465–470. https://doi.org/10.32479/ijeep.9396.
11. Tolstykh, T., Savon, D., Shkarupeta, E., Safronov, A., & Savelyeva, O. (2020). Digital transformation of managerial, technological and logistical processes based on formation of ecosystem of digital twins for individual systems. In *Proceedings of the 33rd International business information management association conference, IBIMA 2019: Education excellence and innovation management through vision* (pp. 7751–7758).

Research on the Impact of Digital Services on the Economic Performance of Industrial Enterprises

Alexey I. Shinkevich, Sergey V. Kiselev, and Farida F. Galimulina

Abstract The research is based on analysis of the scientific literature, world-class reports, analysis and processing of statistical data on the research topic. The subject of the research is the process of digitalization of industrial enterprises. The purpose of the study is to develop a model for managing digital services in order to improve the efficiency of industrial enterprises. The hypothesis is that digital services management determines the vector of competitiveness of industrial enterprises' products. The main research methods were comparison, a systemic approach, the decomposition method, economic and mathematical modeling, and forecasting. The use of the methods allowed us to achieve new scientific results: a decomposition diagram of the process of digitalization of industrial enterprises, economic and mathematical models that reflect the contribution of digital services to the development of industry, a predictive model of the development of industrial enterprises taking into account acquisition of digital services that complement the existing approaches to assessing the effect of digitalization. Managers of industrial enterprises can take into account the presented findings when implementing the corporate development strategy along the digital transformation vector.

Keywords Digital services · Digitalization · Industry · Mining · Manufacturing

1 Introduction

Digitalization trends contribute to tougher competition, which is caused by the risk of "non-digitized" industrial enterprises losing their appeal to consumers and profits against the background of competitors adapting to new technological trends. As a result, there is a need to find resource opportunities for supporting the digitalization processes of an industrial enterprise.

The essential approach to the study of digitalization of industry is reduced to consideration of this process in two aspects:

A. I. Shinkevich · S. V. Kiselev · F. F. Galimulina (✉)
Kazan National Research Technological University, K. Marx St. 68, 420015 Kazan, Russian Federation

V. Kumar et al. (eds.), *Digital Transformation in Industry*, Lecture Notes in Information Systems and Organisation 44, https://doi.org/10.1007/978-3-030-73261-5_8

- material—acquisition of computers, peripheral and communication equipment;
- intangible (service)—services received using computer technology, communication networks ("cloud services", software, data processing, communication services, implementation of geographical information systems, etc.).

The prevailing share of the information and communication technology sector of the Russian economy is accounted for by services. According to data published by the Higher School of Economics, in 2018, data processing accounted for 6% in the structure of goods and services in the sector, software development—18%, and telecommunications services—59% [3]. This highlights the special significance of the development of digital services in industry.

At the same time, there are barriers to trade in digital services and regulatory mechanisms. According to the Digital Services Trade Restriction Index, Russia is among the top-10 countries with the highest level of the index, which characterizes a relatively closed mode of the trade in digital services.

Thus, the subject of research is the process of digitalization of industrial enterprises. The purpose of the research is to develop a model for managing digital services in order to improve the efficiency of industrial enterprises. The goal is achieved by solving the following objectives: to build a logical and informational model of the process of digitalization of an industrial enterprise, taking into account provision of digital services; to develop economic and mathematical models that reflect the specifics of digitalization of economic sectors; to build a predictive model for managing the efficiency of industrial enterprises' development, taking into account acquisition of digital services.

The above allows us to formulate the hypothesis of the study: digital services management determines the vector of the competitiveness of industrial enterprises' products.

2 Literature Review

Owing to the relevance of the research issues, scientific works on digitalization of the service sector, in particular public, financial, logistics, tourism, educational and others, are widely presented in the literature. To a lesser extent, scientists explore the specifics of providing digital services to industry. The resource-saving effect of digitalization of industry is revealed in the work by Barsegyan et al. [1]. Some aspects of the problem under study are disclosed in a work by a team of authors headed by J. Wan that reflects the possibilities of smart production and its preventive maintenance through Big Data [11]; the work by Petrik et al. [4] examines the Internet of Things platform; there is a popularization of the study of the essence and definition of digital services, which is reflected in the works by Williams et al. [12], and Singhal and Kar [8]. The authors conclude that digital services are online activities. In the report on the development of the digital economy in Russia prepared by the World Bank

Group, digital services are analyzed through the prism of public administration and digital government [10].

From the perspective of the issues under consideration, research works that pay attention directly to the methodology for assessing the digital transformation of industry are of special interest. Thus, Remane et al. [5] assess the digital maturity of organizations and, in two aspects, the impact of digitalization on organizations and their readiness for transformation. Schumacher et al. [7] proposed an expanded methodology for assessing the digital maturity of enterprises, combining nine dimensions, in particular, basic and organizational ones. The applicability of methods based on a review of digital maturity models is assessed by Chanias and Hess [2].

An analytical review of scientific papers on digitalization of industry allows us to put the research focus on automation of production processes without specifying digital services. Methodological developments concentrated on business processes and organizational issues are presented. However, there is no obvious link between digital services and the performance of industrial enterprises. In this regard, there is obviously a need to develop a model for managing digital services in order to improve the efficiency of industrial enterprises in the Russian economy.

3 Material and Methods

The research is based on analysis of Russian and foreign literature and theoretical research on diagnostics of the scientific and practical aspects of digital services management in industry, as well as on analysis of empirical data published on the official websites of Rosstat [6] and the Higher School of Economics [3], in reports published by the World Bank [10] and the Eurasian Economic Commission [9].

The research methods were comparison methods, a systems approach, a decomposition method (using the AllFusion Process Modeler (BPwin) tool), economic and mathematical modeling (implemented using Statistica), and forecasting (using Microsoft Excel). Modeling includes step-by-step tasks:

1) building regression models of form (1):

$$y = a + b * x_1 + c * x_2, \quad (1)$$

where y is product profitability (dependent variable); a, b, c are coefficients of regression; x_i is indicators of digitalization of industry (independent variables);

2) scenario forecasting of the level of profitability using constructed economic and mathematical models; in our case, it is based on construction of two types of trend line:

   - polynomial approximation, the trend line is described by an equation of form (2):

$$y = a * x^2 + b * x + c, \quad (2)$$

where y is the predicted variable; a, b, c are the coefficients of the trend line equation (constants); x is the period number;

- logarithmic approximation, the curve is described by an equation of form (3):

$$y = a * \ln(x) + b, \quad (3)$$

where y is the predicted variable; a, b are the coefficients of the trend line equation (constants); x is the period number.

The initial data set consists in a set of observations for 2014–2018 (the choice of a number of dynamics is due to the relatively small experience of digitalization of industries in the Russian economy).

For modeling purposes, we selected data that characterize the digitalization of industrial sectors (mining and processing industries):

y_1—profitability of mining and quarrying products, %;
y_2—profitability of manufacturing products, %;
x_{1i}—expenditures on purchasing software in organizations of the i-th sector (bln rubles);
x_{2i}—use of cloud technology in organizations of the i-th sector (percentage of the total number of surveyed organizations of the relevant activity);
x_{3i}—use of CRM-system in organizations of the i-th sector (percentage of the total number of surveyed organizations of the relevant activity);
x_{4i}—use of ERP-system in organizations of the i-th sector (percentage of the total number of surveyed organizations of the relevant activity);
x_{5i}—use of SCM-system in organizations of the i-th sector (percentage of the total number of surveyed organizations of the relevant activity);
x_{6i}—receipt of public services completely in electronic format by organizations of the i-th sector (percentage of the total number of surveyed organizations of the relevant activity);
x_{7i}—use of an electronic document management system in organizations of the i-th sector (percentage of the total number of surveyed organizations of the relevant activity).

The quality of models is evaluated using the coefficient of determination R^2, Fisher's F-test, and student's t-test.

4 Results

Based on the study of theoretical approaches to the management of digital services, it is proposed to consider provision of digital services to industrial enterprises at all stages of the production cycle: purchase of raw materials, production and sale of finished products. Digital services include information and telecommunications services and processes such as robotics, blockchain, cognitive computing, intelligent data extraction from physical documents, and sensor-based material tracking.

At the input—the needs of the enterprise for digital technologies and services, and data and information about the business processes of the enterprise (Fig. 1), the Diagram is constructed using the AllFusion Process Modeler (BPwin) and reflects a systemic approach to provision of digital services to an industrial enterprise. The regulatory and legal documents governing the company's activities, the list of digital services available on the market, and the technical requirements for digitalization of the company's processes are highlighted as control actions. These mechanisms include telecommunications services, software and hardware, support for a reliable Internet connection and, equally important, availability of qualified IT specialists.

The process of digitalization of an industrial enterprise covers a number of stages, sequential implementation of which requires digital maintenance. The decomposition of this process with indication of the services at all stages of implementation and operation of digital technologies is performed in the IDEF0 notation (Fig. 2). It is noteworthy that the diagram implies but, owing to clutter prevention, does not reflect human resources.

The projects "digital factory", "digital warehouse" and "digital transport", "electronic Commerce" [9] are modern tools for digitally transforming industry. Digital services may also be considered as a separate stage of product sales (consumer service). In this regard, we consider it necessary to emphasize the dual nature of digital services:

(1). automated activities carried out online as part of the digital transformation of an industrial enterprise at all stages of the production cycle;
(2). services that accompany the material flow at the stage of sales of finished products to the consumer.

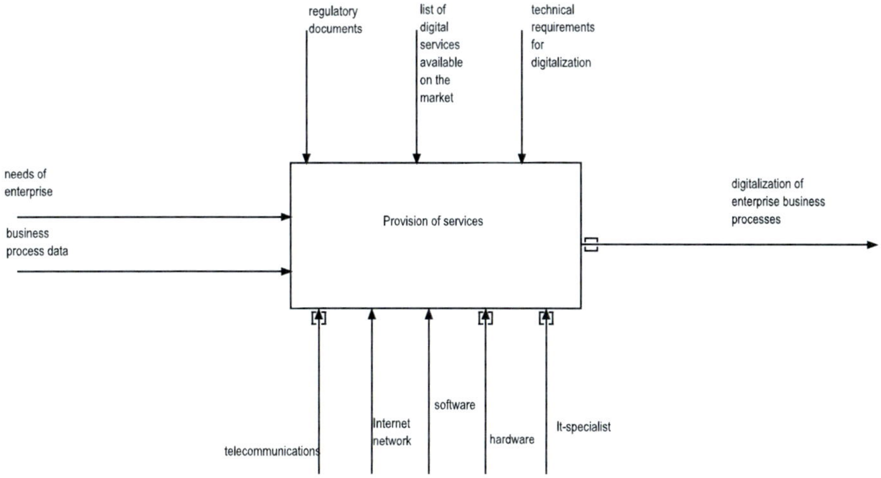

Fig. 1 Context diagram of digital services rendered to an industrial enterprise

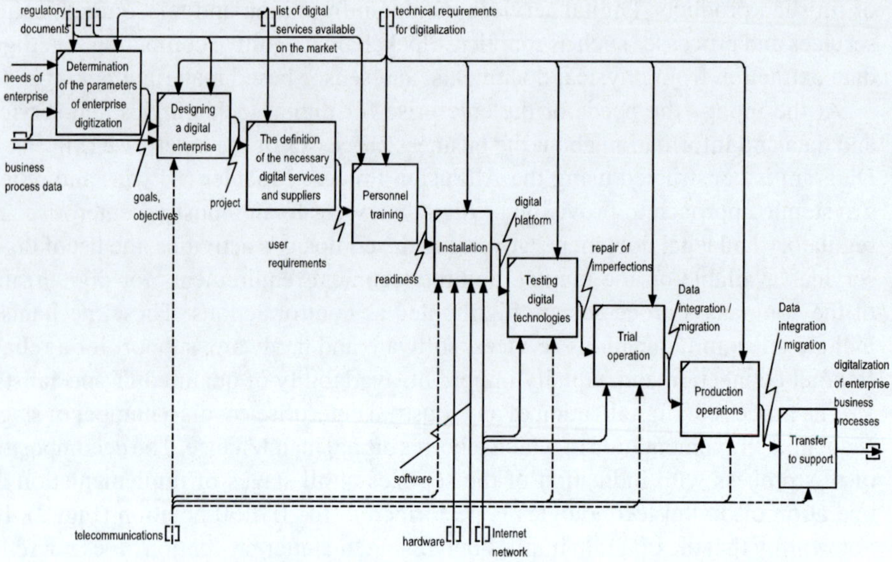

Fig. 2 Diagram of the decomposition of the digitalization process of an industrial enterprise

From the point of view of production processes, "cloud" technologies and services, as well as supercomputer solutions with high socio-economic potential, are recognized as an advanced type of digital service. The industry-specific nature of the digitalization process is obvious (Fig. 3). Manufacturing industries are more deeply integrated into the digital space and are ahead of mining enterprises in all the indicators presented: cost of digital services (software), development of cloud technologies,

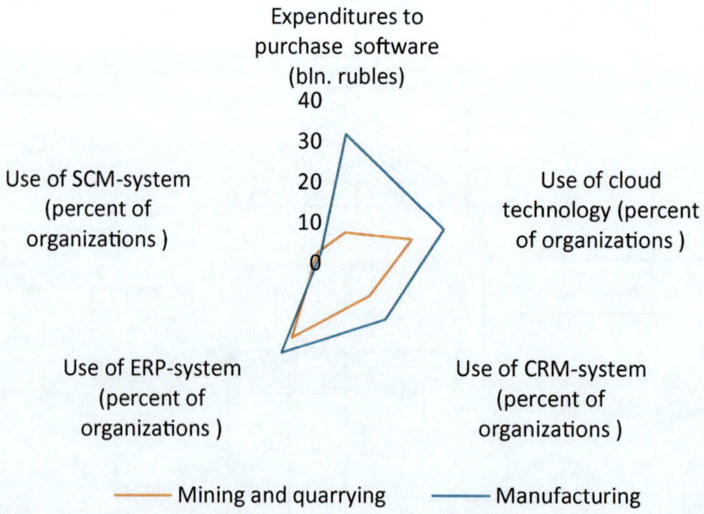

Fig. 3 Indicators of industrial digitalization in the Russian economy, 2018

Table 1 Correlation coefficients between product profitability and digitalization indicators

	Mining and quarrying (y_1)		Manufacturing (y_2)
x_{11}	0.716755	x_{12}	0.984583
x_{21}	0.836030	x_{22}	0.503477
x_{31}	0.212141	x_{32}	0.690453
x_{41}	0.166361	x_{42}	0.003367
x_{51}	0.489176	x_{52}	0.597686
x_{61}	0.646617	x_{62}	0.439367
x_{71}	−0.481732	x_{72}	0.545344

introduction of SCM-, ERP- and CRM-systems. At the same time, software costs are quadruple the corresponding indicator of mining enterprises.

In order to identify cause-and-effect relations and dependence of economic performance of industrial enterprises on consumption of digital services in the context of types of activity, economic and mathematical modeling based on correlation analysis and construction of multiple regression equations was carried out. The correlation coefficients obtained from data analysis in the context of two economic sectors are presented in Table 1.

There are contradictory dependencies in the industries studied. Mining and processing enterprises demonstrate a weak impact of ERP, SCM-systems and electronic document management on the profitability of products.

Excluding multicorpora signs, we find that:

(1). in both cases, the profitability of products is somewhat determined by the cost of software: $r(y_1; x_{11}) = 0.72$ and $r(y_2; x_{12}) = 0.98$;
(2). in the field of mining, the profitability of products depends on receiving public services in electronic format: $r(y_1; x_{61}) = 0.65$;
(3). in the field of manufacturing, the profitability of products is determined by using CRM systems $r(y_2; x_{32}) = 0.69$.

The results of the correlation analysis served as a preparatory stage for constructing dependence models. For the extractive industry, the results of the regression analysis are presented in Table 2. A sufficiently high coefficient of determina-

Table 2 Results of regression analysis of the impact of digital services on the profitability of the extractive sector of the economy

	Regression summary for dependent variable: y_1 R = 0.98573455 RI = 0.97167260 Adjusted RI = 0.94334520 F(2.2) = 34.302 p < 0.02833 Std. Error of estimate: 1.0366					
	b*	Std. err	b	Std. err	t(2)	p-value
Intercept			−38.9385	8.814530	−4.41753	0.047614
x_{11}	0.772692	0.119417	3.0638	0.473507	6.47053	0.023062
x_{61}	0.679017	0.119417	1.1203	0.197026	5.68608	0.029565

tion indicates a high quality description of the actual trends in development of the industry. The F-test allows us to judge that the null hypothesis is refuted, the correlation between the resulting variable and factor features is close, and the regression equation is adequate. The regression coefficients are significant because the p-value for all coefficients is below 0.05. The equation should be used as a predictive model.

The economic and mathematical model of the dependence of the profitability of production in the extractive sector on digital services consumed by enterprises in the sector will take form (4):

$$y_1 = -38.94 + 3.06 * x_{11} + 1.12 * x_{61}, \tag{4}$$

where y_1 is profitability of production in the extractive sector of the Russian economy; x_{11} is software costs for enterprises in the extractive sector (bln rubles); x_{61} is receipt of public services completely in electronic format by the mining and quarrying sector.

A similar procedure is applied to manufacturing industries (Table 3). In this case, you should also recognize the high quality of the model (for all criteria) and its applicability for forecasting purposes.

The dependence equation for manufacturing industries will take form (5):

$$y_2 = 5.48 + 0.13x_{12} + 0.13x_{32}, \tag{5}$$

where y_2 is profitability of manufacturing products (%); x_{12} is expenditures on purchasing software in manufacturing organizations (bln rubles); x_{32} is use of CRM-systems by enterprises in the manufacturing sector.

In order to forecast the financial performance of enterprises, predictive models are built. According to Eq. (4), the best predictor of production profitability in the extractive sector is the cost of purchasing software, a further increase in which (for automating business processes) will contribute to a rise in the resulting financial indicator (Fig. 4).

There are three development scenarios in Fig. 4:

(1). optimistic: the forecast value of the financial indicator is calculated based on the logarithmic approximating curve ($R^2 = 0.78$);

Table 3 Results of regression analysis of the impact of digital services on the profitability of manufacturing products

	Regression summary for dependent variable: y_2 R = 0.99856470 RI = 0.99713145 Adjusted RI = 0.99426290 F(2.2) = 347.61 p < 0.00287 Std. error of estimate: 0.07414					
	b*	Std. err	b	Std. err	t(2)	p-value
Intercept			5.476038	0.402871	13.59252	0.005369
x_{12}	0.882142	0.044465	0.134406	0.006775	19.83921	0.002531
x_{32}	0.195505	0.044465	0.128055	0.029124	4.39688	0.048030

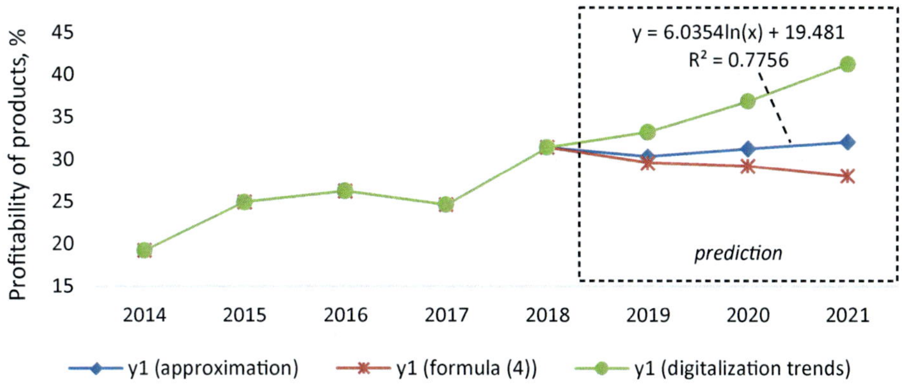

Fig. 4 Forecasting production profitability in the extractive sector of the economy, taking into account the volume of digital services purchased

(2). pessimistic: the forecast values of independent variables reflecting acquisition of digital services are calculated (the tendency of the cost of software to increase and the tendency of the purchase of public services in electronic format to decrease based on polynomial approximation), on the basis of which the predicted value of y_1 is calculated using formula (4);

(3). optimistic: assumptions are made that the purchase of public services in electronic format is not reduced in the context of digitalization but, taking into account the projected increase in software costs and the predicted level of product profitability obtained, taking into account of industry digitalization trends.

Thus, scenario forecasting of product profitability allows one to take into account three scenarios, including an increase in the volume of digital services purchases.

The procedure for calculating predictive values is also performed in relation to the processing industries. Since the coefficient of determination of the approximation for five analyzed years was low, data for a number of previous years were taken into account, which, as a result, provided a high-quality approximation (Fig. 5).

Two scenarios of (optimistic) development of manufacturing industries were obtained:

(1). the predicted level of product profitability is determined based on a polynomial approximating curve ($R^2 = 0.72$);

(2). the forecast values of independent variables reflecting acquisition of digital services (the trend towards increasing software costs and CRM-systems based on polynomial approximation) are calculated, on which basis the predicted value of y_2 is calculated using formula (5).

According to the two alternative scenarios, the financial performance of manufacturing industries will grow, which also confirms the hypothesis about the positive impact of digital services purchased by industrial enterprises on their economic performance.

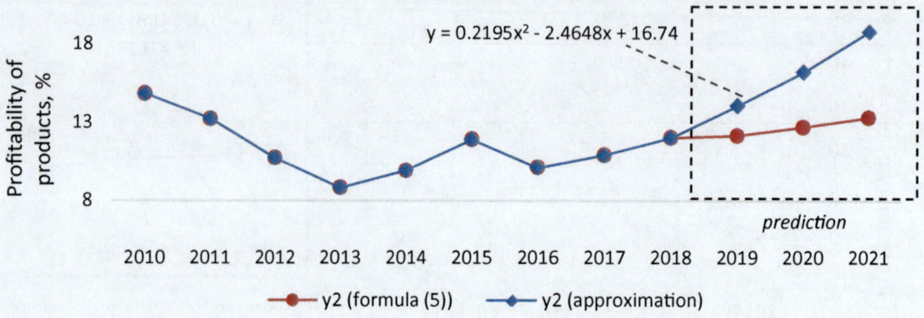

Fig. 5 Forecasting the profitability of manufacturing products, taking into account the volume of digital services purchased

5 Discussion

The process of digitalization is becoming a central focus of research papers covering modernization of various subsystems of industrial enterprises. These are production (operations and technologies), customers, organizational culture, and human resource management [7]. However, it is important to assess the digital maturity of industrial enterprises from the standpoint of not only business processes, but also of the final result of activity expressed in the level of competitiveness and profitability of products, which is the theoretical and methodological core of the current study.

By digital services, we mean a set of intangible flows that enter the internal environment of an industrial enterprise online or in the form of software, communication services, cloud technologies, and data processing. We measure the intensity of the use of these services through the corresponding costs and activity of enterprises in the field of integration of information systems that serve communications in both the internal and external environment of an industrial enterprise.

This research is of practical value for industrial enterprises and the manufacturing sectors of the economy as the main industries that ensure the competitiveness of the Russian economy. Undoubtedly, innovation and modernization are capital-intensive processes that require investment assessment and are not of interest to all industrial enterprises. However, absolute digitalization can be negative [5]. Even so, the results of the study confirm the hypothesis that digital services have a direct impact on business performance.

6 Conclusion

The presented research results allow us to conclude that the goal of developing a model for managing digital services in order to improve the efficiency of industrial enterprises has been achieved. Solving the problems allowed proving the hypothesis of the study. As a result, we received:

(1). a logical and informational model that reflects refinement of the digitalization process, taking into account digital services;
(2). economic and mathematical models of industrial digitalization management are constructed through the prism of improving enterprise efficiency;
(3). scenario forecasts of the impact of digital services on the financial results of enterprises in the mining and processing sectors of the Russian economy are presented, allowing us to clarify the areas of concentration of financial and organizational resources in the process of industry digitalization.

Thus, our contribution to improving the methodology for evaluating the effectiveness of digital services in industry is obvious, owing to clarification of the directions of development of enterprises at the current stage of growth. Managers of industrial enterprises can take into account the presented findings when implementing the corporate development strategy along the digital transformation vector.

Further research is planned to focus on the mechanism of internal business processes digitalization at industrial enterprises.

Acknowledgements The research was carried out within the framework of the grant of the President of the Russian Federation for state support of leading scientific schools of the Russian Federation, project number NSH-2600.2020.6.

References

1. Barsegyan, N. V., Salimyanova, I. G., & Kushaeva, E. R. (2020). Typology of innovation strategies for petrochemical enterprises. *Journal of Physics: Conference Series, 1515*, 042090. https://doi.org/10.1088/1742-6596/1515/4/042090.
2. Chanias, S., & Hess, T. (2016). *How digital are we? Maturity models for the assessment of a company's status in the digital transformation*, from https://www.wim.bwl.unimuenchen.de/download/epub/mreport_2016_2.pdf.
3. HSE. (2020). Retrieved from https://ww.hse.ru.
4. Petrik, D., Straub, D., & Herzwurm, G. (2020). Potentials of platforms for the realization of digital services for component manufacturers. *The 53rd CIRP Conference on Manufacturing Systems, 93*, 652–657. https://doi.org/10.1016/j.procir.2020.04.096.
5. Remane, G., Hanelt, A., & Wiesboeck, F. (2017). Digital maturity in traditional industries—an exploratory analysis. In *Twenty-Fifth European conference on information systems (ECIS)*. https://www.en.wim.bwl.uni-muenchen.de/pubdb_en/art_proc_i/2017-04.html.
6. Rosstat. (2020). https://rosstat.gov.ru.
7. Schumacher, A., Erol, S., & Sihn, W. (2016). A maturity model for assessing industry 4.0 readiness and maturity of manufacturing enterprises. *Procedia CIRP, 52*, 161–166. https://doi.org/10.1016/j.procir.2016.07.040.
8. Singhal, H., & Kar, A. (2015). Information security concerns in digital services: Literature review and a multi-stakeholder approach. In *International conference on advances in computing, communications and informatics* (pp. 901–906). https://doi.org/10.1109/ICACCI.2015.7275725.
9. The Eurasian Economic Commission. (2017). *Analysis of the world experience of industrial development and approaches to digital transformation of the industry of the member states of the Eurasian Economic Union*. https://www.eurasiancommission.org.

10. The World Bank. (2018). *Competing in the digital age: Policy implications for the Russian Federation*. https://www.worldbank.org/en/country/russia/publication/competing-in-digital-age.
11. Wan, J., Tang, S., Li, D., Wang, S., Liu, C., Abbas, H., & Vasilakos, A. V. (2017). A manufacturing big data solution for active preventive maintenance. *IEEE Transactions on Industrial Informatics, 13*, 2039–2047. https://doi.org/10.1109/TII.2017.2670505.
12. Williams, K., Chatterjee, S., & Rossi, M. (2008). Design of emerging digital services: A taxonomy. *European Journal of Information Systems, 17*(5), 505–517. https://doi.org/10.1057/ejis.2008.38.

Coverage of Production Chains in Cooperation Industrial Enterprises

Evgeny Kuzmin and Olga A. Romanova

Abstract The complexity of production processes substantiates the need for a joint industrial activity for developing innovative products. According to the common practice, the major source of breakthrough innovative solutions is small and medium-sized enterprises (SME). The intra-corporate transfer of such solutions can significantly reduce the time needed to establish new production facilities and become a key factor in the competitive struggle in the market. The formation of SMEs cooperation networks falls within the framework of industrial cooperation research. Using the case study of Russia, we address the issue of an effective production network of cooperation between SMEs and large companies. The research sample comprised 14 enterprises distributed according to the industries dominating in the Russian economy. The data obtained show that large enterprises partially owned by the state and acting as cooperation centers are assigned a specific "anchor" role. Anchor companies tend to lower the level of production localization. However, this does not have a significant effect on increasing their financial performance and does not depend on the share of state participation. Russia's experience clearly highlights the weakness of cooperation, albeit with trends towards positive change. In 2015–2019, there was an increase in the share of orders placed by large manufacturers with SMEs. The share of SMEs within the production chains is substantially differentiated and varies between 5.5 and 79.5% for the enterprises under consideration.

Keywords Cooperation · Production chains · SMEs · Production networks

E. Kuzmin (✉)
Ural State University of Economics, 8 Marta/Narodnoy Voli St. 62/45, 620144 Ekaterinburg, Russian Federation
e-mail: kuzmin@usue.ru

E. Kuzmin · O. A. Romanova
Institute of Economics of the Ural Branch of the Russian Academy of Sciences, Moskovskaya St. 29, 620014 Ekaterinburg, Russian Federation

V. Kumar et al. (eds.), *Digital Transformation in Industry*, Lecture Notes in Information Systems and Organisation 44, https://doi.org/10.1007/978-3-030-73261-5_9

1 Introduction

Transformations in the economy that occur under the influence of globalization processes encourage enterprises to look for effective forms of organization of production activities. Such forms of integration as subcontracting, franchising, leasing, venture financing, technology parks, joint ventures, tolling, etc. are becoming more and more popular [1]. Cooperation develops along the entire value chain. The system of functional production of cooperative relations has become widely used.

The phenomenon of intercompany network relations attracts researchers who are trying to explain the reasons for its occurrence [2]. The intensive growth of industrial cooperation raises questions about the blurring of lines of the economic agent, the formation of hybrid structures, which are increasingly referred to as networks. In the most general terms, intercompany networks are perceived as a way to regulate the interdependence between companies. It should be taken into account that initially, the definitions of intercompany networks differ both in the terminology used and in the emphasis [3–5].

The development of network production cooperation with the participation of SMEs is presented in the works of many scientists [6–8]. Petrishcheva [9] attempts to set the concept of industrial cooperation and points out the potential for its development. It is generally agreed [10–14] that subcontracting is one of the most promising organizational forms of integration of small, medium, and large enterprises. This form of cooperation is designed to use a wide network of suppliers [9, 15, 16].

In developed countries, cooperation is a tool for improving the efficiency of industrial production and ensuring overall economic growth [17–19]. Since SMEs are initiators of many innovations and provide the basis for sustainable economic development [20], they must be adequately protected in order to survive in the industrial market. This can be achieved through government policies encouraging industrial sectors to increase the pace of production cooperation with SMEs. One of the mechanisms is the regulation of public procurement.

In Russia, this is facilitated by the procurement system of state-owned companies, which obliges large enterprises to purchase from SMEs, which in turn can be carried out by transferring part of the production cycle to a subcontractor (subcontract). The volume of purchases from SMEs, including purchases in which the contractor must engage the SME as a subcontractor, must be at least 20% of the total annual value of contracts concluded by customers based on the results of purchases. At the same time, at least 18% of the total annual value of contracts should be allocated to procurement involving only SMEs [21].

However, these measures have not yet significantly changed the role of SMEs in the economy as a whole. According to the Analytical Center for the Government of the Russian Federation, in comparison with foreign countries, the share of public procurement by SMEs is low—about 1–5% against 20%. The reasons for these discrepancies are both institutional and structural [22]. It is obvious that for sustainable economic development, it is necessary to search for optimal mechanisms for expanding cooperation between industrial enterprises of various levels.

Therefore, the purpose of the study is to assess the effects of cooperation between SMEs and large industrial enterprises in Russia. To do so, the authors analyzed the purchasing activities of large enterprises with state participation in key Russian sectors—oil, gas, minerals and related activities (petroleum products transportation); industrial production, and electric-power supply industry. Preliminary data indicate that the degree of cooperation between enterprises is relatively low. The identified impact factors will allow understanding better the mechanism of forming production chains through cooperation and assessing its potential in the Russian economy.

2 Materials and Methods

To assess the degree of development of cooperation between industrial enterprises and SMEs in Russia, "anchor" large enterprises were selected and divided into key industries: oil, gas, minerals and related activities (petroleum products transportation); industrial production, and electric power (Table 1). The list includes such companies as Bashneft, Vankorneft, Gazprom, Rosneft, Russian Helicopters, NGO Almaz, United Aircraft Corporation (UAC), United Engine Corporation (UEC), Eastern Energy Company (EEC), Mosenergo, Rosseti Moscow Region (MOESK), Rosseti, RusHydro, and Transneft.

The choice of "anchor" companies is contingent on their contribution to the Russian economy. All these companies are among the top-100 largest companies in Russia; their revenue for the last report in 2019 varies from 39 billion to 4.8 trillion rubles. Moreover, all industrial enterprises have a share of state participation. This feature is also an area of research restrictions. In addition to the selection of industrial enterprises with state participation, the analysis of the degree of cooperation with SMEs is carried out only among legal entities (companies); individual entrepreneurs and individuals are ignored (although they perform work, provide services and produce products for "anchor" companies).

The study used the following indicators of enterprises: revenue, cost of production, works (services); the amount and share of revenue of large industrial enterprises attributable to SMEs; the amount and share of the cost of production, works (services) of large industrial enterprises attributable to SMEs. The data panel was supplemented with information on the volume of purchases from SMEs, the share of state participation in the capital of industrial enterprises, and the number of employees. The sources of information were the news agencies SPARK-Interfax and Interfax Corporate Information Disclosure Center [23].

3 Results and Discussion

The level of internal production localization (autonomy) for all the considered enterprises decreased (Table 2), and enterprises increased the share of orders placed with

Table 1 Selected large industrial enterprises of Russia for the analysis of industrial cooperation with SMEs

Enterprise	Share of state participation in the capital, %	Average number of employees, people	Revenue in 2019, million rubles	Cost of sales in 2019, million rubles
1. Production of oil, gas, and minerals				
Bashneft	60.5	9183	703,151	514,467
Vankorneft	0.01	1600	383,329	308,751
Gazprom	50.0	26,691	4,758,712	2,657,654
Rosneft	40.4	4553	6,827,526	4,782,222
2. Production				
Russian Helicopters	85.71	427	39,854	23,885
NGO Almaz	1.16	11,387	101,586	92,535
United Aircraft Corporation (UAC)	8.99	661	54,734	53,083
United Engine Corporation (UEC)	87.45	14,297	94,039	63,188
3. Electric-power supply industry				
Eastern Energy Company (EEC)	0.08	3962	97,746	90,981
Mosenergo	26.4	7922	189,782	172,256
Rosseti Moscow Region (MOESK)	88.4	14,377	160,376	139,861
Rosseti	88.4	642	39,435	4,658
RusHydro	62.2	5396	155,180	93,884
4. Other activities				
Transneft	78.55	1257	960,812	787,368

Source SPARK-Interfax [26], Center for Corporate Information Disclosure Interfax [23]

SMEs in the cost price. However, the degree of localization varied heterogeneously over the period under review.

Based on the collected data, the share of revenue and the share of the cost of "anchor" large industrial enterprises accounted for by SMEs was calculated—separately for medium-sized, small, and micro enterprises according to the classification adopted in Russia [24]. The criteria for a medium-sized enterprise are that the average number of employees is not more than 250, and the annual income is not more than 2 billion rubles. The share of organizations in the capital of medium-sized enterprises that are not related to SMEs should not exceed 49%, the share of the state, regions, or non-profit organizations shall not exceed 25%. The small business criteria are that

Table 2 Production localization degree of large industrial enterprises with state participation in 2015–2019, %

Enterprise	2015	2016	2017	2018	2019
Bashneft	8.42	9.38	6.89	2.92	79.53
Vankorneft	4.09	61.35	0.92	0.35	74.85
Russian Helicopters	10.97	3.13	8.52	33.22	134.75*
Gazprom	0.34	0.57	0.31	0.03	5.50
EEC	0.55	0.65	0.63	0.78	36.01
Mosenergo	1.68	1.56	1.72	0.30	75.15
MOESK	13.63	7.639	8.99	23.76	78.22
NGO Almaz	1.94	1.13	1.13	0.11	73.15
UAC	8.76	3.60	5.07	0.60	67.96
UEC	1.85	1.80	3.99	0.59	51.99
Rosneft	5.43	1.55	0.26	0.02	6.40
Rosseti	16.41	9.86	10.26	1.62	735.63*
RusHydro	17.61	15.44	8.37	4.27	157.79*
Transneft	0.04	0.71	0.32	0.25	7.01

Note *For holding companies, the cost of production, works (services) has a heterogeneous distribution within the group
Source Center for Corporate Information Disclosure Interfax [23]

the average number of employees is not more than 100, and the income does not exceed 800 million rubles. The micro-enterprise criteria are the average number of employees—no more than 15, and annual income—no more than 120 million rubles. Restrictions on the structure of the authorized capital are similar.

The largest share of orders for medium-sized enterprises in the revenue of large industrial enterprises in revenue in 2019 was observed in Rosseti (48.48%), UAC (39.6%), RusHydro (39.69%). The largest share of orders for medium-sized enterprises in the cost of large industrial enterprises was observed in Russian Helicopters (36.75%), RusHydro (31.38%), and MOESK. Gazprom, Transneft, and Rosneft placed the smallest share of orders with medium-sized businesses (Fig. 1).

A similar situation is observed for small businesses. The largest share of orders for small businesses in the revenue of large industrial enterprises in 2019 was recorded in Russian Helicopters (39.12%), RusHydro (44.79%), Rosseti (33.28%). Mosenergo (36.95%), RusHydro (32.33%), and Bashneft (26.16%) accounted for the largest share of orders for small enterprises in the cost of large industrial enterprises. Gazprom, Rosneft, and Transneft demonstrated the worst work with small enterprises (Fig. 2).

Gazprom (0.30%), Rosneft (0.19%), and Transneft (0.32%) showed a low share of the revenue from large industrial enterprises attributable to micro-enterprises. Such a low share of micro-enterprise participation is also observed in the cost of these companies (Fig. 3). RusHydro (10.99%), NGO Almaz (7.04%), and EEC (6.16%)

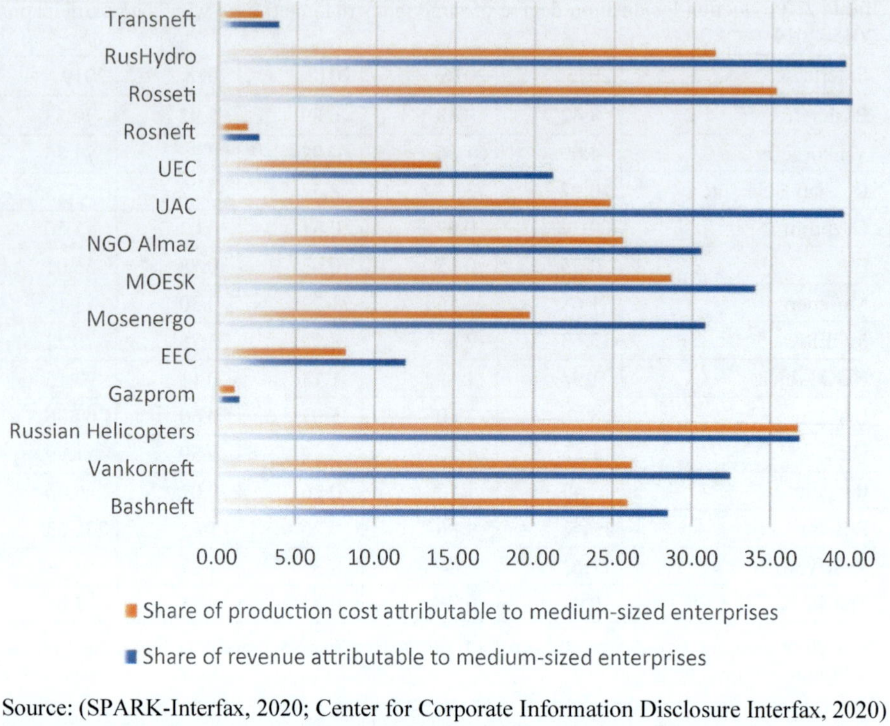

Fig. 1 Shares of revenue and cost of large industrial enterprises attributable to medium-sized enterprises in 2019, %. *Source* SPARK-Interfax [26], Center for Corporate Information Disclosure Interfax [23]

show the best positions in working with micro-enterprises in terms of the revenue share. In terms of cost, the degree of participation of these companies is close—RusHydro (7.32%), Mosenergo (6.66%), and NGO Almaz (5.11%).

In general, the leaders in placing orders for the SME sector in 2019 were such enterprises as RusHydro (95.46% of revenue), Rosseti (86.90% of revenue), Russian Helicopters (80.76% of revenue), Mosenergo (68.21% of revenue), MOESK (68.22% of revenue), NGO Almaz (66.64% of revenue), and UAC (65.91% of revenue). The smallest share of orders attributable to SMEs in revenue is observed in the "anchor" companies in the oil and gas sector.

The average order amount placed with one small enterprise in 2019 was 249,114.9 thousand rubles, with one medium-sized enterprise—943,719.6 thousand rubles, and with one micro-enterprise—30,243.6 thousand rubles. Thus, the structure of the distribution of orders for SMEs is dominated by medium-sized enterprises. Recall that medium-sized enterprises are characterized by the presence of an average number of employees up to 250 people and an annual income (revenue) of no more than 2 billion rubles.

Based on the study, it can be concluded that production cooperation in Russia between "anchor" large industrial enterprises with state participation through the

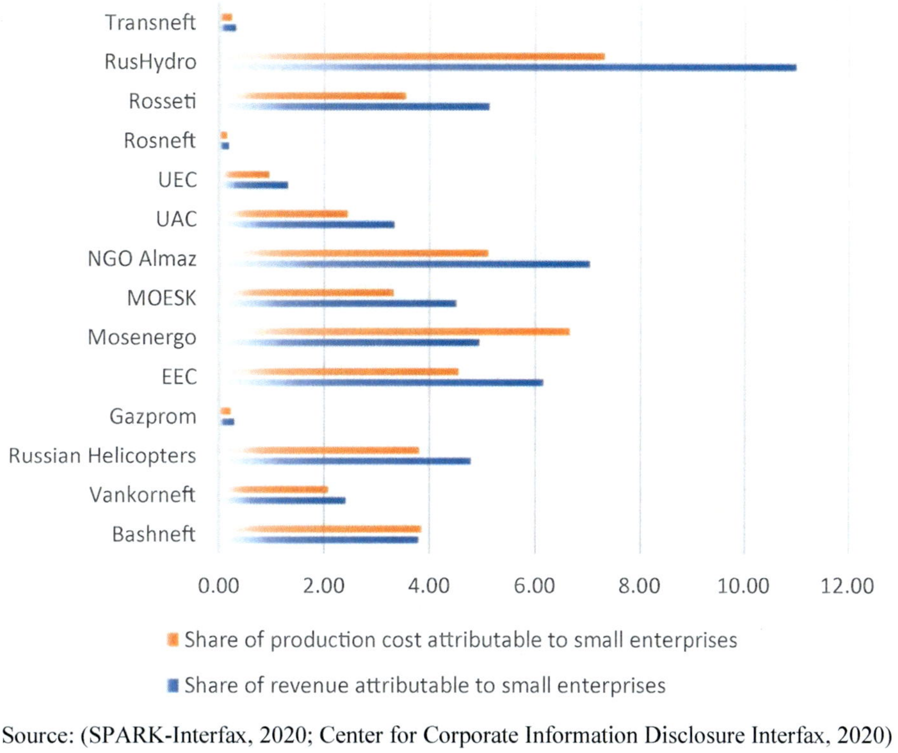

Fig. 2 Share of revenue and cost of large industrial enterprises attributable to small enterprises in 2019, %. *Source* SPARK-Interfax [26], Center for Corporate Information Disclosure Interfax [23]

use of subcontracting with the SME sector is not carried out effectively. Many of the expected internalities that are characteristic of cooperative relations in developed countries, both for contractors and subcontractors, are not reflected in the specifics of the Russian economy or their manifestation is limited.

4 Conclusion

The development of specialization and cooperation of small, medium and large enterprises in the modern conditions of the global market is becoming an economic necessity and is a consequence of the new competitiveness paradigm [25]. This statement finds convincing arguments in world practice. Production cooperation is formed along the entire value chain and leads to the emergence of a new phenomenon of intercompany relations—production networks. However, the strength and scale of cooperation are not uniform. The Russian experience clearly demonstrates the weakness of cooperative partnership, although with positive trends of change. The results

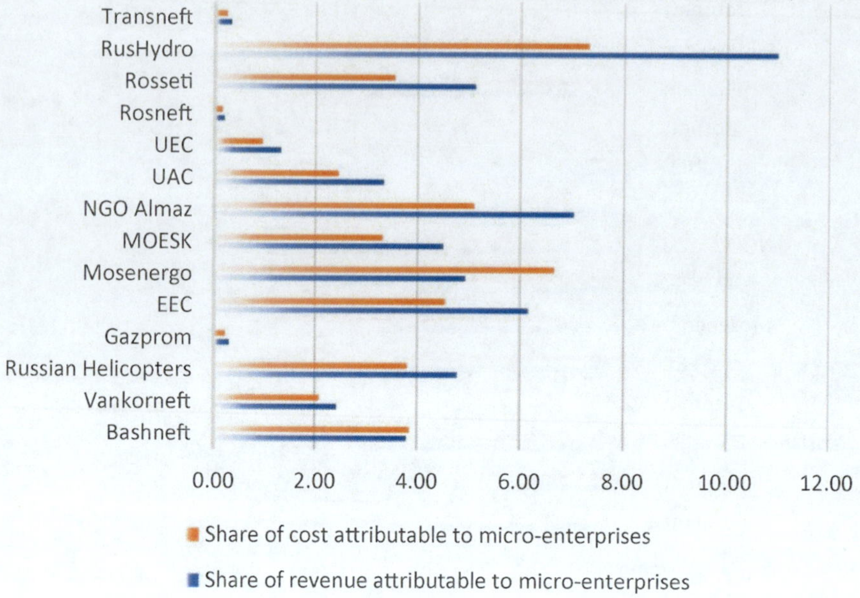

Source: (SPARK-Interfax, 2020; Center for Corporate Information Disclosure Interfax, 2020)

Fig. 3 Shares of revenue and cost of large industrial enterprises attributable to micro-enterprises in 2019, %. *Source* SPARK-Interfax [26], Center for Corporate Information Disclosure Interfax [23]

indicate that the level of internal production localization (autonomy) of large industrial enterprises with state participation in Russia in 2015–2019 decreased; all these enterprises increased the share of orders placed with SMEs. Therefore, there is an expansion of subcontracting as a form of industrial cooperation. The largest share of orders placed with SMEs is observed in large industrial enterprises in the electric power supply industry, and the smallest—in the oil and gas industry. In terms of the volume of orders placed by "anchor" large industrial enterprises, the leaders are medium-sized enterprises; the number of orders placed with such enterprises is 3.8 times higher than the number of orders placed with small businesses, and 31.2 times—with micro-enterprises.

Authors' Contributions and Acknowledgements The present research is part of a study aimed at analyzing the trends in industrial cooperation between SMEs and large businesses in Russia. The results presented in the article were obtained in collaboration with Olga A. Romanona and Evgeny Kuzmin. The study of industrial cooperation in Russia is underway with the expanded team of contributors joined by Marina V. Vinogradova and Olga S. Kulyamina.

References

1. Asaul, A. N., Skumatov, E. G., & Lokteeva, G. E. (2004). *Methodological aspects of formation and development of business networks: Study guide* (p. 55). St. Petersburg: Gumanistika.
2. Tretyak, O. A., & Rumyantseva, M. N. (2003). Network forms of intercompany cooperation: Approaches to explaining the phenomenon. *Russian Journal of Management, 1*(2), 25–50.
3. Gerlach, M. L. (1992). The Japanese corporate network: A block model analysis. *Administrative Science Quarterly, 37*(1), 105–139. https://doi.org/10.2307/2393535.
4. Granovetter, M. (1985). Economic action and social structure: The problem of embeddedness. *American Journal of Sociology, 91,* 481–510. https://doi.org/10.1086/228311.
5. Miles, R. E., Snow, C. C., Mathews, J. A., & Coleman, H. J. (1997). Organizing in the knowledge area: Anticipating the cellular form. *Academy of Management Executive, 11*(4), 7–20. https://doi.org/10.5465/ame.1997.9712024836.
6. Galaso, P., & Kovářík, J. (2018). Collaboration networks and innovation: How to define network boundaries. *Journal of Eurasian Economic Dialogue, 3*(2), 1–17.
7. Lambert, T. E. (2017). Monopoly capital and entrepreneurism: Whither small business? *Journal of Eurasian Economic Dialogue, 2*(3), 1–12.
8. Lambert, T. E. (2018). Monopoly capital and innovation: An exploratory assessment of R&D effectiveness. *Journal of Eurasian Economic Dialogue, 3*(6), 20–35.
9. Petrishcheva, I. V. (2011). Industrial cooperation in the context of interaction between small and large enterprises: Essence and forms. *Almanac of Modern Science and Education, 1*(44), 168–170.
10. Chen, L. (2011). The governance and evolution of local production networks in a cluster: The case of Taiwan's Machine Tool Industry. *GeoJournal, 76,* 605–622. https://doi.org/10.1007/s10708-009-9317-2.
11. Kimura, F. (2002). Subcontracting and the performance of small and medium firms in Japan. *Small Business Economics, 18,* 163–175. https://doi.org/10.1023/A:1015187507379.
12. Kuriyama, N. (2017). The formation of industrial subcontracting in the Japanese Manufacturing Industry. In *Japanese Human Resource Management* (Palgrave Macmillan Asian Business Series). Cham: Palgrave Macmillan. https://doi.org/10.1007/978-3-319-43053-9_4.
13. Park, Y., Shin, J., & Kim, T. (2010). Firm size, age, industrial networking, and growth: A case of the Korean Manufacturing Industry. *Small Business Economics, 35,* 153–168. https://doi.org/10.1007/s11187-009-9177-7.
14. Sprietsma, H. B. (1978). International subcontracting and developing countries. *De Economist, 126,* 220–242. https://doi.org/10.1007/BF01770341.
15. Aydinliyim, T., & Vairaktarakis, G. L. (2011). Sequencing strategies and coordination issues in outsourcing and subcontracting operations. In K. Kempf, P. Keskinocak, & R. Uzsoy (Eds.), *Planning production and inventories in the extended enterprise* (Vol. 151). International Series in Operations Research & Management Science. New York, NY: Springer. https://doi.org/10.1007/978-1-4419-6485-4_12.
16. Sidorenko, E. E., & Chizhova, E. N. (2009). *Production outsourcing as a form of interaction between large and small industrial enterprises: Monograph* (p. 126). Belgorod: BSTU Publishing House.
17. Litau, E. (2018). Entrepreneurship and economic growth: A look from the perspective of cognitive economics. In *ICEME 2018: Proceedings of the 2018 9th International Conference on E-business, Management and Economics* (pp. 143–147). https://doi.org/10.1145/3271972.3271978.
18. Lowry, A. (2020). Industrial policy and technological cooperation in the EAEU: The case of Eurasian technology platforms. In M. Broad & S. Kansikas (Eds.), *European Integration Beyond Brussels. Security, Conflict and Cooperation in the Contemporary World*. Cham: Palgrave Macmillan. https://doi.org/10.1007/978-3-030-45445-6_9.
19. Pochukaeva, O. V. (2006). The interindustry cooperation of production complexes as an economic growth factor. *Studies on Russian Economic Development, 17,* 182–186. https://doi.org/10.1134/S1075700706020067.

20. Toomsalu, L., Tolmacheva, S., Vlasov, A., & Chernova, V. (2019). Determinants of innovations in small and medium enterprises: A European and international experience. *Terra Economicus, 17*(2), 112–123. https://doi.org/10.23683/2073-6606-2019-17-2-112-123.
21. Decree of the Government of the Russian Federation No. 1352. (2014, December 11). *On features of participation of subjects of small and medium business in procurement of goods, works, services by separate types of legal entities.* Retrieved September 24, 2020, from www.pravo.gov.ru.
22. Chernova, V. Y., Golodova, Z. G., Degtereva, E. A., Zobov, A. M., & Starostin, V. S. (2018). Russian industry in global value-added chains. *European Research Studies Journal, 21*(3), 165–178. https://doi.org/10.35808/ersj/1051.
23. SPARK-Interfax. (2020). Retrieved September 24, 2020, from https://www.spark-interfax.ru/.
24. Federal Law No. 209-FZ. (2007, July 24). On the development of small and medium-sized businesses in the Russian federation. Retrieved September 24, 2020, from http://www.pravo.gov.ru.
25. Heywood, J. B. (2002). *Outsourcing: In search of competitive advantages* (p. 174) (Trans. from English). Moscow: Williams.
26. Center for Corporate Information Disclosure Interfax. (2020). Retrieved September 24, 2020, from https://www.e-disclosure.ru/.

Digitization and Sustainability: Smart Working as an ICT Tool to Improve the Sustainable Performance of Companies During the Covid-19 Pandemic

Federica Murmura and Laura Bravi

Abstract The following paper aims to explain to the reader the existing interconnection between the paradigms of sustainability and digitization. In detail, the study will focus on Smart Working, analyzing this tool for its possible improvement of the sustainable performance of companies, and its benefits on the environment, making use of the perceptions that people have about this new way of working. Through the use of a questionnaire, it has been analyzed the perception that people have about this new way of working, which has characterized their lives for about two months during the lockdown period in Italy, caused by the Covid-19 pandemic, considering the time period from 9th March to 1st June 2020. The questionnaire was developed using Google Forms, and it was administered using Computer Assisted Web Interviewing (CAWI) using social networks, primarily Facebook and LinkedIn; 352 workers participated in the survey. The results show that the sample under review is satisfied with this new way of working, both in terms of reducing expenses and increasing the time that can be dedicated to personal activities, and from the point of view of improving the environmental impact. Despite this, a state of skepticism reigns which is characteristic of great changes, since the Covid-19 pandemic we are facing, as a country and globe, forces us to change our habits established over time.

Keywords Digitalization · Covid-19 · Smart working · Sustainability · Industry 4.0

1 Introduction

The goal of mankind is to achieve a sustainable future for all, within a safe and fair operating space of a stable earth system. Ensuring future sustainability for all requires socio-economic development that enhances human well-being, while preserving the resilience of the earth system within planetary boundaries [1].

F. Murmura · L. Bravi (✉)
Department of Economics, Society, and Politics, University of Urbino Carlo Bo, Via Saffi 42, 61029 Urbino, Italy
e-mail: laura.bravi@uniurb.it

V. Kumar et al. (eds.), *Digital Transformation in Industry*, Lecture Notes in Information Systems and Organisation 44, https://doi.org/10.1007/978-3-030-73261-5_10

In 2015, the United Nations adopted the 2030 Sustainable Development Agenda, which provides guidance on aspirations and actions to be achieved by 2030. The Agenda includes 17 Sustainable Development Goals (SDGs) and 169 specific targets to realize the desired future for human development [2].

The document specifies far-reaching objectives, limited in time and often quantified on the basis of a comprehensive consultation between nations and civil society. For the first time, a global development agenda has been adopted that integrates ambitious goals for inclusive social and economic growth for all, with the parallel aim of achieving global environmental goal [3].

The Digital Revolution, which includes virtual reality (VR) and augmented reality (AR), additive manufacturing (AM), artificial intelligence (AI), deep learning, robotics, big data, the Internet of Things (IoT) and automated decision-making systems has entered the public discourse of many countries. It is increasingly clear that digital changes are becoming a fundamental driving force in the transformation of society [4]. The conversion towards sustainability must be harmonized with the threats, opportunities and dynamics of the Digital Revolution and with the objectives of the 2030 Agenda and the Paris Agreement [5]. At the same time, digital transformation will radically change all dimensions of global societies and economies and, consequently, will change the interpretation of the paradigm of sustainability itself. Digitization is not only a "tool" for solving sustainability challenges, but it is also a fundamental engine for disruptive and multiscalary change [6].

The following paper aims to explain to the reader the existing interconnection between the paradigms of sustainability and digitization, what advantages could be gained from them, but at the same time also the negative effects that uncontrolled digitization can have on the environment and society. In fact, although sustainable development and digitization are two phenomena born more or less in the same years, they have been characterized by a different evolution. The goal is therefore to research the possible interactions between sustainability and digital transformation, of how they can affect the current context and the result deriving from their relationship. In detail, the study will focus on Smart Working, analyzing this tool for its possible improvement of the sustainable performance of companies, and its benefits on the environment, making use of the perceptions that people have about this new way of working.

2 Literature Review

2.1 The Concept of Digitalization

The term digitization refers both to widely used technologies related to the advent of the internet and to all those technological innovations that impact the economic system, with the introduction of new services or with the efficiency of industrial production processes.

Several definitions of digitization have been proposed. From an academic perspective, Van Dijk [7] defines digitization through digital communication and the impact of digital media on contemporary social life. In Gartner's IT glossary, digitization is "the use of digital technologies to change a business model and provide new opportunities for revenue and value generation; it is the process of moving to a digital business".

A digital business, therefore, is the result of a multitude of digitization processes such as the transition from traditional supply chains to digital supply chains and represents an essential step towards digital transformation [7].

However, digitalization is often misinterpreted and applied to "digitization". Digitization is the conversion from analog to digital, while digitalization is the use of digital technologies and data to influence the way work is done, transform the way customers and businesses interact and aim to create new income streams. Digitization refers to the internal optimization of processes (e.g., work automation, paper minimization, etc.) and results in cost reduction. On the contrary, digitalization is a strategy or a process that goes beyond the implementation of technology to imply a deeper and more fundamental change of the entire business model and the evolution of work.

The main difference is, therefore, that digitalization is a process that cannot be accomplished without digitization [8].

Digital transformation, on the other hand, requires a much wider adoption of digital technology and a cultural change. Digital transformation is more about people than technology. It requires customer-centered organizational changes, aided by leadership, driven by radical challenges to corporate culture, and the use of technologies that empower and enable employees [7].

The impact of the digital revolution has been slow and silent but over time it has re-modeled work, leisure, consumer behavior, education, etc. [9].

Digital technologies have disrupted production processes in almost every sector of the economy, from agriculture (precision agriculture) transport (self-driving cars) and mining (autonomous vehicles) to manufacturing (robotics; printing 3D), retail (e-commerce), finance (electronic payments, commercial AI strategies), media (social networks), health (AI diagnostics, telemedicine), education (online learning) and public administration (e-governance, electronic voting). Recently, thanks to emerging technologies, the Internet of Things, cloud systems and big data collection, the industrial environment has shown interest in these technological advances, increasingly trying to integrate them to traditional production systems [10].

According to an estimate by the European Commission, the value of the data economy will go from 2.4% in 2018 to 5.8% of EU GDP in 2025 for a total of 829 billion euros. Furthermore, the number of digital professionals in Europe is expected to double in 2025 with 10.9 million experts compared to 5.7 in 2018 [11].

2.2 *Digitalization in Europe and Italy*

Since 2015, the European Commission has been investigating and monitoring the digital competitiveness of member states through the reports on the Digitization Index of the Economy and Society (DESI), a tool aimed at collecting quantitative data from indicators cataloged under five main aspects, with particular focus on the policies adopted by individual countries and the best procedures [12].

DESI is defined as an indicator of European digital performance aimed at providing the results of member states under five dimensions: the provision of a high-speed data connection (connectivity); the progressive increase in the digital skills of citizens (human capital); the frequency regarding the use of online services such as video games, music, online shopping, online banking (use of internet); the digital transformation process in companies and the diffusion of e-commerce systems (integration of digital technology); and the level of digitalization of public services (digital public services) [12]. The first dimension, *connectivity to broadband networks*, is available to 97% of Europeans and 83% of European homes are covered by fast broadband, while ultra-fast connectivity is available to 60% of Europeans. Countries with the highest levels of connectivity include Luxembourg, the Netherlands and Sweden. The average coverage of 4G mobile devices stands at 94% of the European Union population (85% in 2016), while there are 96 mobile broadband subscriptions per 100 people (compared to 67 in 2014). 77% of European households have a fixed broadband subscription and 41% of them with a speed of at least 30 Mbps. The results also show that ultrafast broadband connection is increasingly common. 20% of households subscribe to ultrafast broadband, which is four times higher than in 2014.

The second dimension of *human capital* notes that 43% of Europeans do not yet have basic digital skills. In 2017, there were 8.4 million ICT specialists, an increase compared to three years earlier. In this particular field, Finland, Sweden and Luxembourg have the highest scores [13].

As for the use of *Internet services* in Europe, 83% of the population are active users of the web and regularly carry out various online activities. This figure is flanked by 81% of Internet users who listen to music, watch videos or play online games, 72% read news online, 49% make video or audio calls, 65% use social networks, 69% buy online and 64% use online banking.

Digital transformation within European companies is on the rise, all of which include the use of business software for sharing electronic information (from 26% in 2013 to 34% of companies in 2017), cloud computing (from 11% in 2014 to 18% in 2018) or the use of social media to engage customers and partners (from 15% in 2013 to 21% in 2017). This trend is most advanced in Ireland, the Netherlands and Belgium. The use of e-commerce in Small and Medium size Enterprises (SMEs) has also increased slightly (from 14% in 2013 to 17% of SMEs in 2017). However, less than half of those who trade online sell to other EU Member States [7, 13].

In relation to *digital public services*, 64% of Internet users who sent forms to the public administration used the online channel in 2018 (57% in 2014). While

18% of people used online health services (2017), 50% of general practitioners used e-prescriptions in 2018, nearly double from 27% in 2013. 43% of general practitioners exchange medical data with hospitals or specialists (36% in 2013). The most advanced countries in the field of digital public services are Finland, Estonia and the Netherlands [13, 14].

Despite the developments shown in the last 5 years, Italy with a score of 43.9 (38.9 in 2018) is well below the European average of 52.5. These results place Italy in the 24th place out of 28 member countries of the European Union. In terms of connectivity, Italy records an overall score of 57.6 and ranks 19th among the EU member states, with seven positions higher compared to the previous year. The coverage of fixed broadband networks has slightly increased to exceed 99.5%. Italy has seen a further significant increase in fast broadband coverage, reaching 90% of households and thus exceeding the EU average (83%). Ultra-fast broadband still has a very low percentage value of 24%, ranking Italy in the 27th place. With regard to human capital, Italy is the 26th country in the EU ranking, in fact the level of basic and advanced digital skills of Italians is below the EU average; it was found that only 40% of people aged 16–74 have basic digital skills with an average of 57% in the EU. ICT specialists are 2.6% compared to the EU average 3.7%, although they have a lower incidence on the workforce. Regarding graduates with a degree in ICT, Italy ranks well below the EU average with only 1% of graduates. In relation to the integration of digital technologies by businesses, Italy ranks 23rd.

The national report on the country highlights in particular the need for further systematic efforts to raise the level of digitization of SMEs. Only a few Italian companies have expanded their online business through e-commerce. Quantitatively, only 10% of SMEs have an e-commerce platform (well below the EU average of 17%), of which only 6% sell to international markets and online sales generate a level of revenue equal to 8%. Italy is instead in an advantageous position in sharing information online, in fact 37% of companies use software to communicate within the company compared to the EU average of 34% [13, 15].

2.3 Smart Working as a Tool for Digitalization and Sustainable Development

The Covid-19 pandemic has radically impacted human habits, both social and working. Both are spheres that make up people's daily lives, but which in spite of themselves, are often not reconciled, despite the fact that there is a solution to it, and it is called "smart working". In Italy, also recognized with the term agile work, before the pandemic it was also confused with the teleworking mode, that is a concept very far from the smart philosophy. Agile work is a way of working in which the person worker is placed first at the expense of the machine worker [16]. The worker is granted the freedom of choice, that is, they can independently determine both the hours and the workplaces, with the sole obligation to achieve certain objectives set by the management. This, as it could well be deduced, attributes a concept that is often denied to the employee, namely trust [17]. The pandemic, in addition to having rediscovered the essence of this term, has accelerated the conversion time to this new working philosophy, reaching the figure of approximately 1.3 million smart workers during the lockdown in Italy [18]. The concept behind smart working is the flexibility of the individual professional (employee or freelance), as a crucial point of the entire organization. This approach makes the employee more responsible and autonomous, more serene and able to reconcile private and professional life, thus achieving a balance that is often denied. Everything translates into greater working efficiency and an enhancement of the activities carried out [16]. Smart working is not a completely new concept, in fact in the early 90s several companies tried to work "smart" by reviewing their processes and their business dynamics. Holland was the first nation to start and implement projects related to the current concept of smart working. After about thirty years, is it possible to believe that all Dutch organizations can consider themselves smart? Unfortunately, not. In fact, 75% of the projects started failed. The reasons behind this failure are to be found in the superficial approach that the various companies attributed in its immediate implementation in the corporate culture [19]. Comparing the 1990s with what is happening today, it can be argued that something has certainly changed. Digitization and digital transformation have allowed an increasingly rapid development of this flexible form of working, through the creation of tools that allow the sharing and interaction between workers and also through the change of man who has adapted to new computer technologies and made them part of their daily life.

Analyzing the current scenario, certain elements pivot to digitization are highlighted, such as the transition from web 1.0–2.0, the creation of search engines that have opened knowledge to all, sharing through social media and creation of entire businesses based on digitization that have upset the dynamics of the traditional market [10].

3 Methodology

The following survey aimed to deepen the analysis of the literature carried out from an empirical point of view, trying to detect data coming from both agile and traditional workers on the topic of Smart Working. The main purpose of the research was to analyze the perception that people have about this new way of working, which has characterized their lives mainly for about two months during the lockdown period in Italy, caused by the Covid-19 pandemic, considering the time period from 9th March to 1st June 2020. The questionnaire, divided into three sections, has set itself the objective of collecting data and information relating to different areas, starting from the definition of the socio-demographic profile of the participants, to extend to the perception of the in which employees reach the workplace when they are not in smart mode, which computer they use to perform their duties outside the company premises and the advantages and disadvantages perceived in using this new working mode. These questions were essential for measuring their environmental impact in terms of greenhouse gas emissions, and assessing whether or not employees are able to protect company information, within the devices used, in the event of a situation of "cybernetic vandalism". The questionnaire was developed using Google Forms, and it was administered using Computer Assisted Web Interviewing (CAWI), using social networks, primarily Facebook and LinkedIn; 352 workers participated to the survey.

4 Results

4.1 Respondent Profile

Among the 352 members of the sample, female respondents (53.1%) are in majority compared to males (46.9%). Analyzing the age of the respondents, it can be seen how the interviewed sample is almost equally distributed. In fact, 28.1% of the sample belongs to the age group between 18–30 years, 25.3% between 41–50 years, 23.9% those who are over 51 years and 22.7% of the sample is aged between 31 and 40 years.

As far as the level of education is concerned, the majority of the interviewees obtained a master's degree (40.1%), followed by upper secondary school graduates (26.4%). Almost equally, on the other hand, are those who have obtained a three-year degree and a research doctorate who cover 16.5% and 13.1%, respectively. As regards the geographic area of residence of the sample, the data shows that 148 respondents, that is 42%, are from central Italy, 118 from the south and islands and 75 from the north. Only 10 people have their residence abroad. Finally, investigating the sector and the size of the company to which they belong, for the first category, 40.9% of respondents work in the tertiary sector; only 13.1% of the interviewees work in the advanced tertiary sector. As far as concern to the size of the company they work for, the majority of respondents (41.5%) work in a large company, followed by those who work in a micro company (21.6%), medium-sized company (19.6%) and finally a small one (17.3%).

4.2 Advantages and Disadvantages of Smart Working

Considering the reason why the workers in the sample worked in agile mode, 87.8% of the sample answered the pandemic as the motivation, 4.2% for employment contracts, 2.3% for pregnancy and 1.9% for illness. They were then asked to indicate by which means they reached the workplace when they were not in smart mode.

The interesting, but expected, data sees the majority of smart workers reaching the workplace with their own vehicle, 16% by public transport, 11.8% on foot. Only 6.1%, equal to 16 people, use an eco-friendly vehicle and 1.9% own a company car. These data can be superimposed on ISTAT data and fully reflect the Italian social fabric. Considering the main advantages of smart working, the 39.2%, that is 103 people, are in complete agreement that it allows for a drop in expenses. In reference to more free time, the data express uncertainty on the part of the sample, as although the majority, i.e. 47.6%, agrees, a high percentage (32.3%) do not agree with that, indicating with this working mode a greater number of hours worked daily by at least one in two workers (53.3%). Regarding the environmental benefits, the majority of the sample (58.9%) is in complete agreement with the fact that this modality allows respecting it, while 12.9% of the respondents are uncertain whether this can help protect the environment. Then it has been evaluated the perceived effects of this new working mode on employee performance and greater working autonomy. As far as performance is concerned, the data is interesting, in fact 37.5%—the majority of the interviewees—are indifferent to this benefit; that is, they believe that agile work is comparable to traditional work in terms of work performance. While with regard to autonomy, the interviewees are overall satisfied, given that 177 people out of 263 (67.3% of the total) believe they have more autonomy than traditional work. Hence, the sample was then asked to express, again through the 5-point Likert scale, their level of agreement on the assertion that smart working is characterized by an absence of privacy and/or concentration due to working in non-company offices. The results obtained showed that two thirds of the interviewees (67.4%) do not perceive this problem. As regards, instead, the reduced socialization with work colleagues, deriving from the physical distance, people complain of strong discomfort. As many as 168 people (64.1%), are fully or partially in agreement with the statement. It was subsequently assessed whether or not collaboration within the work team was inefficient due to the distance. Advanced VPN technologies, such as the recent discovery of the Zoom video conferencing system or data sharing such as Microsoft Teams, however, have minimized the inconvenience related to physical distance, as confirmed by respondents (76.1%). Furthermore, only 20.9% of the interviewees complain of the inappropriateness of personal technological equipment and internet connection at home.

4.3 Smart Working and Cybersecurity

In the era of digital transformation, one of the main challenges that companies wanting to adopt new working paradigms, such as smart working, have to face is that of cybersecurity, understood as the security of infrastructures, processes, people and their behavior. Smartphones, tablets and computers help increase productivity, but they expose companies to the risk of cyber-attacks. The higher the risk, the longer the employee remains connected to mobile devices. What is more these tools should be provided by the employer (par. 2, article 18 of the current legislation, law no. 81/2017), and he is the same who have to guarantee constant data security.

The use of company policies and proper training and information for remote workers can be of undoubted advantage; but to protect corporate data it becomes crucial to resort to hardware and software tools built with pre-eminent attention to the protection of information assets [20]. In this context, some "old" security and procedural measures such as IT regulations, or the procedures for creating and maintaining and disposing of VPNs play an even more fundamental role than protecting information, such as highly important corporate assets. Just think of the economic damage that could arise from an act of vandalism caused for example by the cancellation of the entire history of invoices and contracts stipulated over time. Or even more simply, the theft of data relating to corporate projects and therefore encounter the problem of industrial espionage.

But these precautions are not always satisfied, in fact, 44.9% of the participants, that is 118 agile workers, used their personal computer to work in agile mode; furthermore, 43 of them declared that they did not have security systems to prevent a cyber-attack. The situation improves as regards the workers who use the company computer; 143 people, that is 54.4% of the total, declared that they had used a device provided by the employer, although a large part of the interviewees claimed to have security systems installed on their device, 11 people (7.7% of workers with a corporate computer) report a lack of these technologies for protecting corporate information. The number of people who are not aware of the presence of systems for the prevention of any cyber abuse is also relevant, and consist of 53 workers out of the 263 smart workers interviewed. This result confirms a negative side of the Italian working system, namely a little digital preparation of Italian companies; in fact, by analyzing the questionnaire in depth, it can be seen that 26.6% of smart workers say that the company they work for was not ready for smart working before the pandemic, while 34.2% of respondents claim that their company has shown only partial preparation for this change. Furthermore, one out of three companies (30.8%), according to employees, did not provide clear guidelines to their collaborators in order to allow them to perform their duties remotely.

4.4 Smart Working: Environment, Society and Future

Smart working undoubtedly allows a reduction in city traffic and carbon dioxide emissions: according to data from the Smart Working Observatory of the Polytechnic of Milan, in fact, on average, people travel about 40 km to get to work; therefore, if they worked remotely at least one day a week, they could achieve savings in terms of emissions per person equal to 135 kg of carbon dioxide per year. The empirical survey carried out showed that 25.9% (68 people out of 263) of the total are commuters, that is, they go to work in a province or region other than the province of residence; more precisely, 45 people use their own non-eco-friendly vehicle and 16 use public transport, so they have an environmental impact that could be avoided with the help of smart working. This would bring benefits not only from an ecological point of view, but also from a healthy and economic point of view to employees, as it would considerably reduce the level of stress and increase people's free time and mood, as well as reducing related expenses on the commute from home to work; in fact, as many as 59% of commuters declare that they enjoy more free time available when working in smart mode and 72% say they have incurred expenses [21].

The fact that smart working has environmental benefits is also perceived among traditional workers, i.e. those who participated in the survey indicating that they are not engaged in smart working, in fact 86.5% of the them say that agile work has some positive effects on the environment.

Furthermore, among these, despite 38.2% (34 people out of 89 traditional workers), claims not to have worked in smart working as they do manual work, 19.1% (17 out of 89 people) indicated the company unpreparedness as a reason. This last result demonstrates that Italy, unfortunately, is still a decidedly slow country in adopting new flexible working methods, this certainly depends on many factors, but the main reason is to be found in the fact that the Italian entrepreneurial fabric is made up for the great majority of cases of family-run micro-enterprises, in which there is also the problem of attracting qualified personnel capable of managing structural change.

At the conclusion of the survey, the entire sample was asked if they would accept an employment contract exclusively in smart working; despite the fact that 42.6% (150 people out of 352) responded positively, the number of undecided, that is a fifth of the interviewees (21.0%), is noteworthy. Finally, when they were asked whether Smart Working could replace office work tomorrow, 167 people, corresponding to 47.4% of the total, think that in the future agile work could replace traditional work, while 115 (32.7%) argue otherwise, and 70 people (19.9%) are still undecided. This indicates that there are still deep-seated cultural resistances on this issue.

5 Conclusions

The promise of digitization—big data, artificial intelligence, the Internet of Things, cybersecurity, and more—is often described with hyperbole. Both experts and academics have defined big data as the "new oil", demonstrating its usefulness in making statistical predictions or analyzes of a very large sample. Artificial intelligence is receiving a similar hype, compared to the spread of electricity during the Industrial Revolution.

Companies, internally, are using digital tools to map their environmental footprint and assess the impact of environmental changes on their business. New digital technologies are enhancing sustainable innovation, even as they create new vulnerabilities such as cybercrime and loss of privacy. Outside the organization, the digitalization-sustainability convergence is producing a digital transformation in three areas that affect market conditions: investor behavior, urbanization and economic demand.

This study focused on the internal challenge that companies, especially in this historical period, are facing even at the cost of their existence, that is a working paradigm that has allowed them to continue their activities even during the lockdown imposed by governments. Companies have indeed received economic damage, both for the drop in demand and for the adoption of new extraordinary measures, but

Smart Working has established itself as a valid alternative to office work, obviously, type of job permitting, and allowed to companies to cushion the economic recession as much as possible.

Smart Working was born as an ICT tool to reconcile the private life with the working life of employees, and at the same time it is in line with the philosophy of environmental sustainability; since it minimizes all unnecessary journeys and therefore also the CO_2 emissions deriving from them. In this regard, we could safely say that Smart Working is a digital tool consistent with the 3 spheres of Sustainable Development, namely Social, Environmental and Economic.

The sample analyzed is satisfied with this new way of working, both in terms of reducing expenses and increasing the time that can be dedicated to personal activities, and from the point of view of improving the environmental impact. Despite this, a state of skepticism reigns which is characteristic of great changes, since the Covid-19 pandemic we are facing, as a country and globe, forces us to change our habits established over time, and speed up the adoption of new better habits for future generations.

References

1. Rockström, J., Gaffney, O., Rogelj, J., Meinshausen, M., Nakicenovic, N., & Schellnhuber, H. J. (2017). A roadmap for rapid decarbonization. *Science, 355*(6331), 1269–1271. https://doi.org/10.1126/science.aah3443.
2. Bebbington, J., & Unerman, J. (2018). Achieving the United Nations sustainable development goals. *Accounting, Auditing & Accountability Journal, 31*(1), 2–24. https://doi.org/10.1108/AAAJ-05-2017-2929.
3. Rockström, J., Edenhofer, O., Gaertner, J., & DeClerck, F. (2020). Planet-proofing the global food system. *Nature Food, 1*(1), 3–5. https://doi.org/10.1038/s43016-019-0010-4.
4. Domingos, P. (2018). Artificial intelligence will serve humans, not enslave them. *Scientific American, 319*(3).
5. Villani, T. (2018). Ernesto Antonini, Fabrizio Tucci (a cura di). Architettura, Città e Territorio verso la GREEN ECONOMY [Architecture, City and Territory towards the GREEN ECONOMY]. *TECHNE-Journal of Technology for Architecture and Environment, 15*, 377–378. https://doi.org/10.13128/Techne-23591.
6. Vial, G. (2019). Understanding digital transformation: A review and a research agenda. *The Journal of Strategic Information Systems, 28*(2), 118–144. https://doi.org/10.1016/j.jsis.2019.01.003.
7. Van Dijk, J. (2020). *The network society*. Thousand Oaks: Sage Publishing.
8. Gobble, M. M. (2018). Digitalization, digitization, and innovation. *Research-Technology Management, 61*(4), 56–59. https://doi.org/10.1080/08956308.2018.1471280.
9. Reinartz, W., Wiegand, N., & Imschloss, M. (2019). The impact of digital transformation on the retailing value chain. *International Journal of Research in Marketing, 36*(3), 350–366. https://doi.org/10.1016/j.ijresmar.2018.12.002.
10. Rachinger, M., Rauter, R., Müller, C., Vorraber, W., & Schirgi, E. (2019). Digitalization and its influence on business model innovation. *Journal of Manufacturing Technology Management, 30*(8), 1143–1160. https://doi.org/10.1108/JMTM-01-2018-0020.
11. TWI2050—The World in 2050 (2019). *The Digital Revolution and Sustainable Development: Opportunities and Challenges*. International Institute for Applied Systems Analysis (IIASA).

12. Russo, V. (2020). Digital economy and society index (DESI). European guidelines and empirical applications on the territory. In *Qualitative and Quantitative Models in Socio-economic Systems and Social Work* (pp. 427–442). Cham: Springer.
13. DESI. (2019). *The digital economy and society index (DESI)*. Data for 2019. Retrieved October 21, 2020, from: https://ec.europa.eu/digital-single-market/en/desi.
14. Kirov, V. (2017). Digitalization of public services in Europe: Policy challenges for the European trade union movement. *Policy implications of virtual work* (pp. 251–272). Cham: Palgrave Macmillan.
15. Scuderi, A., & Salvetti, F. (Eds.). (2019). *Digitalization and cultural heritage in Italy: Innovative and cutting-edge practices*. Milano: Franco Angeli.
16. Denning, S. (2018). *The age of agile: How smart companies are transforming the way work gets done*. New York: Amacom.
17. Mariano, C., Scacco, A. C., & Crespi, F. (2016). *Smart working. Modelli organizzativi e tecnologie. Spazi e normative*. Milano: IlSole24Ore.
18. IlSole24Ore. (2020). *Work, CGIL: 8 million Italians in smart working with the Covid-19 epidemic*. Retrieved October 21, 2020 from: https://www.ilsole24ore.com/art/lavoro-cgil-8-milioni-italiani-smart-working-epidemia-covid-19-AD7aAMR?refresh_ce=1.
19. Kotter J. P. (2007). Leading change: Why transformation efforts fail. *Harvard Business Review*, January, 2–10.
20. IPSOA. (2017). *Law 22 May 2017 n. 81. Measures for the protection of non-entrepreneurial self-employment and measures aimed at encouraging flexible articulation in the times and places of subordinate work*. Retrieved 21 October 2017 from: https://www.ipsoa.it/normativa/legge/22-05-2017-n-81.
21. Politecnico Milano. (2020). *Smart working at the time of the coronavirus*. Retrieved 21 October 2020 from: https://www.som.polimi.it/lo-smart-working-ai-tempi-del-coronavirus/.

Impact of New Technology on Sustainability of Supply Chains: Empirical Evidence from Manufacturing SMEs in China

Ruibing Shi, Vikas Kumar, and Banu Ekren

Abstract New manufacturing technology can provide useful competitive advantages for enterprises to deal with fierce competition, and help them look for a better solution to production and operation management improving the quality of product services. New technology can also promote enterprises to obtain sustained economic, social and environmental benefits. This study, therefore, focuses on investigating the impact of technology on the sustainability of supply chains in small and medium enterprises (SMEs) in the Pearl River Delta region of China. The findings are based on 100 valid survey responses from SMEs in the region. The study identifies a set of enablers and barriers to new technology implementation in manufacturing SMEs. Our findings show that the economic factors occupy the central position whereas the market pressures from home and abroad; the vision of the enterprise's development; and the apparent advantages of new technologies were identified as other key enablers. On the contrary, the driving force from the government was found to be insufficient, whether it is a relatively free market regulatory environment or tax-free welfare policies for small businesses to promote the use of new technologies. The high production cost appears to be the most critical barrier followed by vicious competition among enterprises in the industry and lack of technical personnel. Our findings also show that enablers and barriers of new technology implementations are significantly correlated with sustainability performance measures (economic, social and environmental performance). Our study hence adds to the limited empirical literature focused on investigating the new technology and sustainability relationship.

Keywords SMEs · Technology · Sustainability · Supply chains · Empirical · Manufacturing

R. Shi
Warwick Manufacturing Group, University of Warwick, Coventry CV4 7AL, UK

V. Kumar (✉)
Ton Duc Thang University, 19 Nguyen Huu Tho Str., Ho Chi Minh City, Vietnam
e-mail: Vikas.Kumar@tdtu.edu.vn

Bristol Business School, University of the West of England, Bristol BS16 1QY, UK

B. Ekren
Faculty of Engineering, Yasar University, Üniversite Caddesi, no. 37-39, İzmir, Turkey

V. Kumar et al. (eds.), *Digital Transformation in Industry*, Lecture Notes in Information Systems and Organisation 44, https://doi.org/10.1007/978-3-030-73261-5_11

1 Introduction

New technology in manufacturing industry refers to the technology used in the production process of enterprises, which can be applied to plan and control processes, manage information and actual production and assembly activities. In the context of rapidly changing market demand, everything needs to be fast and simplified. These advanced manufacturing technologies make the whole production process more systematic. The advantages lie in improving production speed and product service quality, increasing flexibility and reducing costs [1]. However, new technology means high investment costs or import costs, which makes many SMEs in developing countries stand back.

Nowadays, the new technologies used in the manufacturing industry can be divided into two categories: digital technology (the Internet of Things, cloud services, big data and analysis, blockchains) and new manufacturing technology (additive manufacturing, sensors, industrial robots, etc.). These digital technologies can automatically adjust the adaptive system of the production process for a variety of products and changing conditions [2]. Moreover, they can take into account information exchange and supply chain integration to reduce delivery time affected by the bullwhip effect and avoid information distortion [3]. Qrunfleh [4] suggested that by using the technology of information, the firms could manage commodity flow, information flow and capital flow. For example, blockchain facilitates valid and effective measurement of outcomes and performance of key supply chain processes through data transparency and information flow [5]. Robots with artificial intelligence can perform tasks more accurately in production and manufacturing than in the past, improve productivity, ensure early quality control and reduce production costs. Besides, Byrd and Davidson [6] pointed out that the long-term utilisation of information technology leads to better firm performance in terms of return on investment and market share.

Even though people's interest in sustainable issues is generally increasing, the current level of sustainable supply chain management practice is still limited [7]. Enterprises have begun to consider sustainability at the strategic level, but the current production model cannot be considered sustainable. Significant changes need to be made at the technical, managerial and organisational levels [8]. New technology can not only produce high-quality products but also improve the process of enterprise production and operation from a systematic point of view [9]. The high demand for economic and social development for supply chain performance promotes the use of technology in the supply chain. Tracey et al. [10] emphasised the consistency of technology and strategy and thought that new manufacturing technologies in alignment with strategy could differentiate firms from competitors and consequently can enhance their competitiveness. Yawar and Seuring [11] believed that the implementation of technology can not only promote the operation but also directly improve the ability of suppliers, thus improving their ability to deal with social problems.

From China National Bureau of Statistics, by the end of 2016, the number of SMEs in China was 370,000, accounting for 99% of the total number of enterprises, contributing 60% of GDP. Meanwhile, 347,000 SMEs are in the manufacturing industry (93.7%). SMEs in China have played a vital role in China's economic development. Compared with large enterprises, SMEs rely more on the workforce (ordinary workers rather than expertise), resulting in lower productivity, higher costs and lower constant delivery rate [12]. These disadvantages make it more difficult for SMEs to implement new technology development and improve their ability for sustainable development.

Existing studies show that most of the scholars discuss the supply chain strategy solely or the technology implementation separately. Besides, although the benefits of supply chain assessment for enterprise development has been clearly defined, few studies evaluate the supply chain performance in China. SMEs should adopt new technologies consistent with their supply chain development strategy to improve supply chain efficiency and strive to be guaranteed in economic, social and environmental aspects. However, the supply chain development level of SMEs in China and many developing countries and regions are still very elementary, and the utilisation rate of technology is meagre, which is not enough to support the strategic development of their supply chain. Therefore, the objective of this study is to find out the reasons that promote and hinder their use of new technologies to enhance their sustainable development capabilities. Therefore, it is more meaningful to discuss the drivers and barriers of new technology implementation faced by SMEs in China. It is also important to identify how can the use of these new technologies improve lasting economic, social and environmental supply chain performance.

1.1 Enablers of Technology Implementation

The literature identifies several driving factors of technology implementation such as government, market, and social pressures. Luken and Van Rompaey [13] highlighted that when manufacturing industries adopt different technologies, the importance ranking of varying driving factors is different. Local policies set appropriate environmental standards for industries, and the quality of products and their impact on the environment have become the indicators of assessment [13]. Zhu and Sarkis [14] stated that regulations are still the most prevalent pressure for Chinese companies. Government-provided economic incentives for businesses, such as relaxed loan restrictions, grants, and tax exemptions [13], can further increase the adoption rate of new technologies.

The implementation of technology is also influenced by market factors. Kharlamov et al. [15] proposed that social responsibility, investor needs, government regulations and international standards, as well as customer awareness gradually force enterprises to pursue sustainable development. Similarly, these factors also promote the implementation of technology in the supply chain. Companies are facing challenging circumstances: markets are evolving; clients are becoming more and more demanding and unpredictable; product variety is rising; time windows are shrinking, and error tolerance is decreasing. Therefore, technology implementation can solve these problems to some extent. Stakeholders, business partners, investors, primarily supply chain buyers, also impose environmental requirements on enterprises [16]. If the supply chain cannot be sustainable, enterprises will not be able to achieve sustainable development. Although some studies have improved the sustainability of products and services, the pressure from the supply chain is an urgent problem for enterprises to solve. For manufacturing enterprises with export business, entering international markets requires more stringent export product specifications than those produced at home [14], usually manifested in the fact that products are not allowed to contain certain chemicals. The changes in these markets, the needs of partners and customers will promote manufacturing enterprises to choose more technologies to implement production, to ensure the level of environmentally friendly development. Pressure from peers is also one of the social factors. Whether peers adopt relevant technologies has the value of being referenced by enterprises. If competitors can produce more publicly recognised products, it will threaten original company's market share, which means competitor will have higher profits, more significant market share and lower costs [17].

The other factor that also influences the technology adoption in enterprises is social pressure. The public attaches great importance to the environmental impact of manufacturing operations because it will affect their quality of life and environment. Local communities and media exposure will put pressure on manufacturers' factories. Additionally, as natural resources are becoming scarce, manufacturing enterprises that are heavily dependent on natural resources need to improve their technical capabilities and transform and upgrade. Besides, the ownership structure, size and internal capability of the factory are the main enablers to adopt technological means [13]. Enterprise strategy, long-term vision, values and culture, as well as the image and reputation of the company are all internal driving factors for the enterprise to choose technology for development and production [8]. Manufacturing enterprises have high production costs. Using technologies can accelerate the new product development process, reduce long-term production costs, reduce waste of resources and improve economic efficiency. Also, they can improve safety, especially product safety and personal safety of employees, which can meet the needs of employees [18]. The benefits of these technologies themselves drive enterprises to transform and upgrade, and use technology in production and operation.

1.2 Barriers/Challenges of Technology Implementation

Although the role of technology in production and operation has been known, many enterprises do not intend to use new technology. The first kind of enterprises finds themselves unable to face new possibilities in controlling production and planning functions; It is the perceived (lack of) technological capabilities of firms that hinder them from adopting the technology. This idea is manifested in the lack of relevant professionals and operational skills, even if appropriate technical resources have been obtained, some SMEs do not use new technologies in the actual production and operation. Moeuf et al. [12]. The second is the lack of intention to use technology to promote sustainable development. Leleux and Van der Kaaij [19] found that though many firms have the desire, the willingness or even the belief in the impact of sustainability on their businesses, they still failed to identify proper objectives for their efforts, which make them were unable to implement their sustainability strategies successfully.

SMEs also face many difficulties when introducing new technologies and system because of realistic limitation such as the significant initial investment, the burden of maintaining staff to operate it, and continuous payment of maintenance costs. In researching the reasons for the failure of SMEs in Malaysia, Arham et al. [20] also emphasises the influence of the behaviour of leaders and managers on the organisational performance of SMEs and indicates that managers need to show transformational and transactional leadership behaviour to retain talents. The support of senior managers who formulate and define strategies helps build long-term partnerships between supply chains [21]. Wang and Bi [22] stated that a single company could not achieve sustainable manufacturing but a system of enterprises in a global dimension, and proposed services based on cloud computing to tackle this challenge. When new technology products enter the market, most enterprises or individual consumers will take a wait-and-see attitude until more people adopt it. The high R&D costs of the technology itself cause some obstacles in the policy. The existing research shows that scholars have proposed a wide range of impetus and obstacles. However, only by defining the driving factors and challenges of implementing new technology to develop a supply chain for specific types of enterprises is not enough.

1.3 Sustainable Supply Chain Performance

There is no consistent definition of the sustainable supply chain in the existing literature, partly because of the meaning of the supply chain and the demarcation of its boundaries [23]. The concept of a sustainable supply chain focuses on promoting the sustainable development of the supply chain at three levels: economy, environment and society. A majority of studies have advocated that organisational sustainability lies in economic, social and environmental performance. However, Gopal and Thakkar [24] stated that many enterprises focus on measuring lasting performance at the product or functional level, rather than on the sustainability of the entire supply chain and process. This study therefore will measure sustainability performance in these three directions, aiming at solving the economic, social and ecological problems of sustainable supply chain management.

From the economic dimension, sustainable performance improvement should be related to the control of corporate profits, investment and costs. As for the manufacturing industry, it means manufacturers' ability to mitigate procurement-related expenditure, cost produced by energy consumption, abandonment management and fines due to environmental accidents. The innovation ability, total sales, the number of shareholders and the new employment opportunities created by companies are criteria to measure the sustainable economic performance of enterprises [25]. Sustainable profit is the guarantee of sustainable development of enterprises. Therefore, focusing on the durable economic performance of enterprises can help to obtain sustained growth of benefits and resources.

The society has the aspects of 'customers', 'employee', and 'community'. The indicator of social sustainability can focus on work conditions, societal commitment, customer issues, philanthropic contributions, the responsibility to the community; employee turnover rate, health and safety of local communities, equal opportunities and diversity, potential adverse side effect on or from secondary, stakeholders, stakeholders engagement satisfaction [26]. Enterprises have concentrated on the development of a responsible supply chain, and to the help of their products, services and behaviours to the harmonious development of society [27]. Only when enterprises enhance their social influence by improving their behaviour, consumers will generate additional trust in enterprises, and also enable enterprises to attract and retain talents.

Environmental performance relates to the ability of manufacturing plants to reduce air emissions, wastewater, solid waste and the consumption of harmful and toxic substances. Modern enterprises also need to make up for the damage caused by traditional enterprises to the environment, such as in all aspects of the supply chain, focusing on waste and pollution management, recovery and reuse of used products [22]. This kind of behaviour affects not only economic benefits but also environmental benefits. Enterprises that do not pay attention to environmental protection cannot enjoy long-term benefits. At the same time, these three kinds of performance are mutually reinforcing. Improving health, safety and environmental performance of manufacturing enterprises can increase revenue and market share, and promote flexibility, quality and responsiveness in business processes [16].

1.4 Research Gap

When researching how the use of new technology can improve the sustainable performance of the supply chain, most scholars have studied in large multinational enterprises, because there are relatively few obstacles when large enterprises implement new technology. Saad et al. [28] highlighted that SMEs have a different set of challenges. It is evident from the discussions presented in earlier sections that SMEs have the disadvantage of not obtaining economies of scale, and their product portfolio is small. Sources are short and over-reliant on a single market and product. Compared with large enterprises, SMEs rely more on the workforce (ordinary workers rather than expertise), resulting in lower productivity, higher costs and lower constant delivery rate [12]. These disadvantages make it more difficult for SMEs to implement new technology development and improve their ability for sustainable development. So when more substantial companies can quickly produce similar products or provide better services, how to survive in the market and improve profits becomes the key.

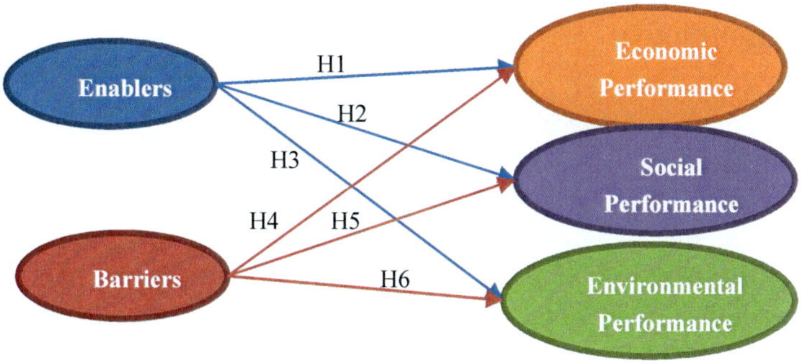

Fig. 1 Conceptual framework

Although the benefits of supply chain assessment for enterprise development has been clearly defined, there is limited literature on the evaluation and optimisation of supply chain performance in China. SMEs should adopt new technologies consistent with their supply chain development strategy to improve supply chain efficiency and strive to be guaranteed in economic, social and environmental aspects. Also, the status quo of implementing new technologies and improving the supply chain in SMEs in China is different from that of large enterprises and SMEs in western developed countries. Therefore, it is more meaningful to discuss the drivers and barriers faced by SMEs in China. The conceptual framework encapsulating the discussion presented earlier is shown below in Fig. 1 together with a set of hypotheses that will be tested in this paper.

H1: The evaluation score of the enablers is positively related to the assessment of the enterprises' economic sustainability performance

H2: The evaluation score of the enablers is positively related to the assessment of the enterprises' social sustainability performance.

H3: The evaluation score of the enablers is positively related to the assessment of the enterprises' environmental sustainability performance.

H4: The evaluation score of the barriers is negatively related to the assessment of the enterprises' economic sustainability performance.

H5: The evaluation score of the barriers is negatively related to the assessment of the enterprises' social sustainability performance.

H6: The evaluation score of the barriers is negatively related to the assessment of the enterprises' environmental sustainability performance.

2 Methodology

This study adopts a survey-based approach. A survey tool was created and distributed to SMEs (employing less than 500 people) in the Pearl River Delta region of China. The Pearl River Delta has always been an essential position for China to carry out different economic activities and has a solid foundation in manufacturing. It includes nine cities in Guangdong Province: Guangzhou, Shenzhen, Zhuhai, Foshan, Huizhou, Dongguan, Zhongshan, Jiangmen and Zhaoqing. In recent years, the survival crisis of manufacturing industry in the Pearl River Delta has become increasingly prominent. Emerging manufacturing industry is continuously rising, so taking SMEs in this region as the research sample can increase the reliability and representativeness of the research. The questionnaires designed using Qualtrics software and are mostly matrix questions measured on five-point Likert scales. The survey data was analysed through SPSS using descriptive statistics, correlations and regression analyses. The study has followed the necessary ethical protocols in data collection and post-study data disposal.

3 Results and Discussions

The survey was distributed to more than 500 SMEs operating in the Pearl River Delta region of China. The survey resulted in 146 survey responses representing a response rate of 29.2%. However, careful evaluation of the data showed that 46 respondents did not fill out the full list of questions and quit the survey halfway, hence these responses were discarded for final analysis. Hence, the effective sample size is 100 respondents with a response rate was 20% which is well aligned with previous studies where an effective survey response between 20–30% is deemed acceptable.

The first part of the questionnaire was focused on collecting demographic information. Around 67% respondents employed less than 250 people whereas 33% respondents employed between 250–500 people. According to the position classification, among the respondents, there were 7 CEOs, 22 general managers, 21 senior managers, 42 general employees, and the remaining 8 included had other roles such as research and design director engineers, professional managers, project managers, etc.

The second part of the questions was focused on evaluating the enablers and barriers to the use of new technologies by SMEs. Table 1 shows the constructs and the measurement items used which were measured on a five-point Likert scale. Findings show that the most critical factor in the enabler is the pressure from competitors in domestic and foreign market competition, which had an average score of 4.02. Which was followed by the enterprise's vision of sustainable development (avg. score 3.90) urging SMEs to use new technologies in production activities. The vision of an enterprise influence the decision-making in its operation and its development vision and culture are strictly related to the willingness of its leaders. The third most important factor was the significant advantages of new technology (avg. score

Table 1 Enablers and barriers of technology implementation in supply chains

Constructs	Category	Code	Influence elements
Enablers of technology implementation in supply chain	Government	GOV1	Policy support (loans/government grants/tax exemption)
		GOV2	Government's attention to production indicators and regulations
	Market	MAR1	Pressure from partners (e.g. stakeholders) in the supply chain
		MAR2	Pressure from competitors (domestic and foreign market)
		MAR3	Quick market changes and large demand for products
	Society	SOC1	Public demand for green manufacturing
		SOC2	Local environmental pollution is serious, shortage of natural resources and energy
	Internal motivations	INT1	Vision promotion of Enterprise's self-development
	Technology	TEC1	The obvious advantages of new technology
Barriers of technology implementation in supply chain	Lack of awareness	LOA1	Lack of awareness of using new technologies
		LOA2	Lack of intention to promote sustainable supply chain
	Lack of resources	LOR1	Insufficient innovation ability of enterprises
		LOR2	Enterprises are underfunded
		LOR3	Lack of technical personnel
		LOR4	Backward management of the enterprises
	Market	MAR1	Vicious competition among enterprises
		MAR2	The high cost of manufacturing
		MAR3	A low level of using new technologies in the whole industry
	Technology	TEC1	Difficult to balance economic benefit, environmental benefit and social benefit

(continued)

Table 1 (continued)

Constructs	Category	Code	Influence elements
	Government	GOV1	Local policies have strict supervision over the use of new technology

3.89), such as productivity, higher delivery rate and lower total cost which was also reported by Birasnav and Bienstock [21]. On the contrary, two government-related items (Policy support and Government's attention to production indicators and regulations) showed the lowest possible contributors (avg. score of 3.22 and 3.47 respectively). This result is inconsistent with Luken and Van Rompaey's [13] analysis of the driving forces behind the adoption of environmentally friendly technologies by several Chinese paper mills.

Concerning barriers, the most likely obstacle was found to be higher production costs (avg. score 3.68). The results of Luken and Van Rompaey's [13] study on obstacles show that the biggest obstacle is the implementation cost of new technologies, which is different from the high production cost proposed in this study. Lu et al. [29] showed that companies prefer low initial investment and high return technologies when studying the use of new construction technologies in Singapore. The second most important factor appeared to be the competition among industry enterprises (avg. score 3.65) which was followed by the lack of skilled personnel (avg. score 3.56). It is worth mentioning that the two most unlikely impediments are lack of awareness of using technology and lack of intention to promote sustainable supply chain, which corresponds to the second most crucial impediment factor (driven by the vision of the enterprise's development). It shows that SMEs in China have a strong sense of sustainable supply chain development and the use of new technologies.

Finally, the enablers and barriers were transformed into single dimension variables, as the Cronbach's Alpha value for enablers was 0.863 and for barriers, it was 0.852, which shows a high internal consistency. A correlation analysis was then carried out together with the economic, social and environmental performance measures. Table 2 shows the outcome of the correlation analysis. It is clearly evident that enablers and barriers are significantly correlated with the performance measures as coefficient were significant at $P < 0.05$ level. Since the overall enablers show a positive correlation with the three performance factors, hence verifying the first three hypotheses (H1, H2 and H3). The barriers also show a positive and significant correlation with the three performance factors, hence H4, H5 and H6 were not supported. Nonetheless, it should be noted that these barriers have a significant impact on these performance measures. The positive correlation between the barriers and performance measures could be due to the way these measures of the barriers were worded. The significant correlation itself indicates that SMEs need to overcome these barriers to take the advantage of new technologies to strengthen their position in the market. To further verify the findings of the correlation, a regression analysis was conducted which shows that altogether enablers and barriers explain around

Table 2 Correlation analysis between the constructs

		Enablers	Barriers
Economic performance	Pearson	**.740****	**.549****
	Sig. (2-tailed)	.000	.000
	N	100	100
Social performance	Pearson	**.696****	**.427****
	Sig. (2-tailed)	.000	.000
	N	100	100
Environmental performance	Pearson	**.645****	**.459****
	Sig. (2-tailed)	.000	.000
	N	100	100

**Significant at 0.05 level

63.3% of the variance (Adj. R^2 0.633). Both coefficients from barriers and enablers were significant at the $P < 0.01$ level.

4 Conclusions

The main aim of the study was to identify a set of enablers and barriers to new technology implementation in manufacturing SMEs in the Pearl River Delta Region of China. Our study identifies government, market, society, internal motivation and advantages of technology as key enablers. The study also identifies a lack of awareness, lack of resources, market factors, government regulations and technological challenges as key barriers. The paper looked at the impact of these enablers and barriers on sustainable performance indicators (economic, social and environmental). The findings show that economic factors still occupy the primary position. Three more likely drivers of the use of new technologies for production activities are (1) market pressures from home and abroad; (2) the vision of the enterprise's development; (3) the apparent advantages of new technologies. On the contrary, the driving force from the government is insufficient, whether it is a relatively free market regulatory environment or tax-free welfare policies for small businesses, to promote the use of new technologies. The three major obstacles to the adoption of new technologies for production activities are: (1) higher production costs; (2) vicious competition among enterprises in the industry; (3) lack of technical personnel. The study showed that enablers and barriers both have a significant impact on the sustainable performance of SMEs. The perceptions of drivers and barriers are similar among the respondents with different enterprise sizes and job backgrounds, but there is no significant difference. This study will enable a deep understanding of the barriers and enablers of new technology implementation in SMEs in China. This study thus adds to the limited empirical research on SMEs in a developing context.

The research scope of this study however is limited to the Pearl River Delta region of China, and hence doesn't represent the same problems faced by SMEs in the whole country when using new technologies. Moreover, findings are based on just 100 survey responses. Future research can thus build on the limitations of the study focus on increasing sample size, adding more industry categories and perhaps collecting and comparing data from different developing regions. Additionally, using a mixed-methods approach will help in triangulation and generalization of findings.

Acknowledgements We would like to express our sincere thanks to Royal Academy of Engineering and Newton Katip Celebi, TUBITAK (Industry-Academia Partnership Programme 2018/2019, No. 4180046) for supporting the collaboration.

References

1. Cheng, Y., Matthiesen, R., Farooq, S., Johansen, J., Hu, H., & Ma, L. (2018). The evolution of investment patterns on advanced manufacturing technology (AMT) in manufacturing operations: A longitudinal analysis. *International Journal of Production Economics, 203,* 239–253.
2. Wang, G., Gunasekaran, A., Ngai, E. W., & Papadopoulos, T. (2016). Big data analytics in logistics and supply chain management: Certain investigations for research and applications. *International Journal of Production Economics, 176,* 98–110.
3. Dalenogare, L. S., Benitez, G. B., Ayala, N. F., & Frank, A. G. (2018). The expected contribution of Industry 4.0 technologies for industrial performance. *International Journal of Production Economics, 204,* 383–394.
4. Qrunfleh, S. M. (2010). *Alignment of information systems with supply chains: Impacts on supply chain performance and organizational performance* (Doctoral dissertation, University of Toledo).
5. Eljazzar, M. M., Amr, M. A., Kassem, S. S., & Ezzat, M. (2018). *Merging supply chain and blockchain technologies.* arXiv preprint arXiv:1804.04149.
6. Byrd, T. A., & Davidson, N. W. (2003). Examining possible antecedents of IT impact on the supply chain and its effect on firm performance. *Information & Management, 41*(2), 243–255.
7. Jakhar, S. K. (2015). Performance evaluation and a flow allocation decision model for a sustainable supply chain of an apparel industry. *Journal of Cleaner Production, 87,* 391–413.
8. Neri, A., Cagno, E., Di Sebastiano, G., & Trianni, A. (2018). Industrial sustainability: Modelling drivers and mechanisms with barriers. *Journal of Cleaner Production, 194,* 452–472.
9. Niaki, M. K., Torabi, S. A., & Nonino, F. (2019). Why manufacturers adopt additive manufacturing technologies: The role of sustainability. *Journal of Cleaner Production, 222,* 381–392.
10. Tracey, M., Vonderembse, M. A., & Lim, J. S. (1999). Manufacturing technology and strategy formulation: Keys to enhancing competitiveness and improving performance. *Journal of operations management, 17*(4), 411–428.
11. Yawar, S. A., & Seuring, S. (2018). The role of supplier development in managing social and societal issues in supply chains. *Journal of Cleaner Production, 182,* 227–237.
12. Moeuf, A., Pellerin, R., Lamouri, S., Tamayo-Giraldo, S., & Barbaray, R. (2018). The industrial management of SMEs in the era of Industry 4.0. *International Journal of Production Research, 56*(3), 1118–1136.
13. Luken, R., & Van Rompaey, F. (2008). Drivers for and barriers to environmentally sound technology adoption by manufacturing plants in nine developing countries. *Journal of Cleaner Production, 16*(1), S67–S77.

14. Zhu, Q., & Sarkis, J. (2004). Relationships between operational practices and performance among early adopters of green supply chain management practices in Chinese manufacturing enterprises. *Journal of Operations Management, 22*(3), 265–289.
15. Kharlamov, A. A., Ferreira, L. M. D., & Godsell, J. (2013). The power of analytical approaches towards the development of differentiated supply chain strategies: Case study. In *Advances in sustainable and competitive manufacturing systems* (pp. 1223–1235). Heidelberg: Springer.
16. Acar, M. F., Aktas, E., Agan, Y., & Bourlakis, M. (2019). Does sustainability pay? Evidence from the food sector. *Journal of Foodservice Business Research, 22*(3), 239–260.
17. Bansal, P., & Roth, K. (2000). Why companies go green: A model of ecological responsiveness. *Academy of Management Journal, 43*(4), 717–736.
18. Govindan, K., Diabat, A., & Shankar, K. M. (2015). Analyzing the drivers of green manufacturing with fuzzy approach. *Journal of Cleaner Production, 96,* 182–193.
19. Leleux, B., & Van der Kaaij, J. (2018). *Winning sustainability strategies: Finding purpose, driving innovation and executing change*. Heidelberg: Springer.
20. Arham, A., Boucher, C., & Muenjohn, N. (2013). Leadership and entrepreneurial success: A study of SMEs in Malaysia. *World Journal of Social Sciences, 3*(5), 117–130.
21. Birasnav, M., & Bienstock, J. (2019). Supply chain integration, advanced manufacturing technology, and strategic leadership: An empirical study. *Computers & Industrial Engineering, 130,* 142–157.
22. Wang, L., & Bi, Z. M. (2013). Challenges for better sustainable manufacturing. In *Advances in sustainable and competitive manufacturing systems* (pp. 1209–1221). Heidelberg: Springer.
23. Sarkis, J. (2012). A boundaries and flows perspective of green supply chain management. *Supply Chain Management, 17*(2), 202–216.
24. Gopal, P. R. C., & Thakkar, J. (2015). Development of composite sustainable supply chain performance index for the automobile industry. *International Journal of Sustainable Engineering, 8*(6), 366–385.
25. Uysal, F. (2012). An integrated model for sustainable performance measurement in supply chain. *Procedia-Social and Behavioral Sciences, 62,* 689–694.
26. Matos, S., & Hall, J. (2007). Integrating sustainable development in the supply chain: The case of life cycle assessment in oil and gas and agricultural biotechnology. *Journal of Operations Management, 25*(6), 1083–1102.
27. Camilleri, M. A. (2017). *Corporate sustainability. Social responsibility and environmental management*. Heidelberg: Springer. https://doi.org/10.1007/978-3-319-46849-5.
28. Saad, M., Kumar, V., & Bradford, J. (2017). An investigation into the development of the absorptive capacity of manufacturing SMEs. *International Journal of Production Research, 55*(23), 6916–6931.
29. Lu, Y., Chang, R., Shabunko, V., & Yee, A. T. L. (2019). The implementation of building-integrated photovoltaics in Singapore: Drivers versus barriers. *Energy, 168,* 400–408.

Digitalization of Supply Chain Management Objects

Alexey P. Tyapukhin

Abstract Digitalization of management objects allows using digital technologies to improve the efficiency of enterprises as links of supply chains. It is particularly difficult to establish communications between various objects of supply chain management—flows, systems, processes, and relationships—as well as to maintain their right combination for solving tasks in the most rational way. The research aims to develop a code of combinations of management objects that can solve the above problem. The research hypothesis assumes the possibility of using a universal code formed by a set of classification features of these objects, each of which is characterized by a binary code. System analysis, grouping, and classification research methods are used. The result is a code that provides digital information processing and increases the efficiency of supply chain management. The scientific contribution is to create a methodological basis for digitalization of management objects. The research results can be used in the development and application of computer software for supply chain management.

Keywords Management object · Supply chain management · Binary code

1 Introduction

Recently, the digital economy or "the combination of several general-purpose technologies and a number of economic and social activities carried out by people through the Internet and related technologies" has developed intensively [1].

According to experts, the digital economy makes it possible to simplify the forms of interaction between economic entities, to decrease the number of intermediate links in supply chains, to reduce the time for concluding commercial transactions, to lower barriers to access various types of markets, to create conditions for enterprises to gain competitive advantages regardless of their size, and to achieve economies of scale and positive returns while reducing costs [2, p. 12].

A. P. Tyapukhin (✉)
Orenburg Branch, Institute of Economics of the Ural Branch of the Russian Academy of Sciences, Pionerskaya St. 11, 460000 Orenburg, Russian Federation
e-mail: aptyapuhin@mail.ru

V. Kumar et al. (eds.), *Digital Transformation in Industry*, Lecture Notes in Information Systems and Organisation 44, https://doi.org/10.1007/978-3-030-73261-5_12

Among other things, the digital economy creates prerequisites for optimizing supply chain management or the "enterprise management concept, which is associated with the impact of the management entity on the linearly ordered links of the logistics system (suppliers and intermediaries) that perform consolidation/disaggregation of resources flow objects in accordance with the values of their end consumers" [3].

Because "digitalization ... refers to the current global trend in the development of the economy and society, which is based on the transformation of information into digital form ..." [4], p. 47), its priority processes are coding and decoding information.

The development of a universal code will allow getting the following advantages for supply chain management: to identify its objects and determine their relationships; to structure these objects; and to make appropriate changes to the parameters and characteristics of supply chain management objects, if necessary.

2 Literature Review

The term "supply chain" refers to the terms, the nature and content of which are still not entirely clear. The supply chain can be perceived as:

- "a group of inter-connected participating companies that add value to a stream of transformed inputs from their source of origin to the end products or services that are demanded by the designated end-consumers" [5, p. 9];
- "the complex network of relationships that organizations maintain with trading partners to source, manufacture, and deliver products. It encompasses all activities associated with flow and transformation of goods and services from the point of origin, through to the end user, as well as the associated information and financial flows" [6, p. 13]; and
- "the flow and management of resources across the enterprise for the purpose of maintaining the business operations profitably" [7, p. 3].

Recall that the flow is a regular and quite large number of something; and the movement of something in one direction (Flow, n.d.). Given the content of the definitions presented above, it is possible to argue that the objects of supply chain management are:

1. the links of the supply chain, as well as their units;
2. the relations (cooperation) of these links;
3. the processes performed by the links of the supply chain; and
4. the resource flows, at the same time: "An integrated supply chain model can generally contain three interrelated flows: material flows (which have three different stages (purchasing, transformation, and distribution), informational flows (electronic data exchange or website linkages) and financial flows (which

include the payment to suppliers and subcontractors for the goods and services and the payment by the customer to the retailer for the final product)" [9].

As follows from the analysis, each of the above management objects, at least does not have an unambiguous definition, cannot be measured with sufficient accuracy; and has an ambiguous effect on other management objects. These findings point to the problem of the potentially low efficiency of the digitalization of supply chain management objects.

Recall that this type of management can be described as "a set of management approaches and information tools that ensure effective integration of suppliers, manufacturers, intermediaries and sellers" [10, p. 4]; and involves the use of the following informatization tools:

- reference models that assume "their own language for describing relationships between participants in the supply chain" such as SCOR (Supply Chain Operations Reference) and DCOR (Design Chain Operations Reference) models [10, pp. 63, 68];
- information systems such as MRP (Material Resource Planning), ERP (Enterprise Resource Planning, including supply chain management modules integrated in ERP systems), PDM (Product Data Management) [10, pp. 99–102];
- instrumental means such as EAI (Enterprise Application Integration), SCEM (Supply Chain Event Management), CPFR (Collaborative Planning, Forecasting and Replenishment) [10, pp. 102–104]; and
- balanced scorecard systems, which assume "the division of key performance indicators (KPIs) into areas of activity..., such as "finance", "customers and marketing", "business processes", "personnel" and "systems" [10, pp. 102–104].

However, the aforementioned tools for informatization of supply chain management do not fully ensure the integration and joint use of its main objects, which hinders the achievement of the goals of their links.

3 Theoretical and Methodological Background of the Research

The theoretical and methodological prerequisites of the research include several elements.

Firstly, the focus of supply chain management objects on the requirements of end consumers of products and/or services, the basis of which is formed by the perceived lack of something, first of all, value. At the same time: "the value construct can explain consumer behavior before and after purchase" [11, p. 180]; and "the value literature emanating from within the marketing discipline consistently refers to value as a complex construct, not well understood" [12, p. 448].

Secondly, using the binary code as the main code, the most reliable for operations with objects described primarily by qualitative characteristics.

Thirdly, the code is generated on the basis of "n" classification features that allow getting 2^n variants of the supply chain management object with the corresponding codes, for example, 16 variants with codes from 0000 to 1111 for n = 4. Each of the selected variants of the management object, in turn, can be structured using the following group of classification features (second-level features), etc.

Fourth, the types of supply chain management objects are formed according to the following scheme: "flow (F)—system (S)—relationship (R)—process (P)", i.e. the required code consists of four parts; and

Fifth, there are various variants of the sought code that can be focused on solving specific problems of supply chain management at its main stages: design, formation, implementation, and optimization.

4 Sequence of Code Formation for Supply Chain Management Objects

The main types of flows in supply chains can be distinguished using the following classification signs: the type of resource flow objects: real or non-real; and the factors of economic activity of supply chain links: economic or managerial. These flows are not three, as shown earlier, but four: material, financial, human, and informational flows (Fig. 1).

If a material flow is selected as the object of structuring, then it is necessary to use such classification signs as the purpose of the flow object: provision or delivery of value; and the relation of the flow object to the value: creation or escort. As a result, the following objects of material flow can be distinguished: products, vehicles, containers (packaging), and loading and unloading devices (Fig. 2).

The information shown in Figs. 1 and 2 allows generating the first part of the sought code. For example, the (material) product located in the container on the vehicle is indicated by a code: 10001110, where 1000—code of the material flow (when other types of flows (Fig. 1) are marked with the symbol "0"); 1110—code of the objects of the material flow (in this case, the loading and unloading device (Fig. 2) is marked with the symbol "0").

Factors of economic activity of supply chain links \ **Type of resource flow objects**	Real (0)	Non-real (1)
Economic (0)	Material flow (00)	Financial flow (01)
Managerial (1)	Human flow (10)	Informational flow (11)

Fig. 1 Classification of resource flows

Relation of the flow object to the value / **Purpose of the flow object**	Provision of value (0)	Delivery of value (1)
Creation (0)	Products (00)	Vehicles (01)
Escort (1)	Containers (packaging) (10)	Loading and unloading devices (11)

Fig. 2 Classification of objects of the material flow

Type of product at the exit of the supply chain link / **Tasks of supply chain links**	Creating value (0)	Escort of value (1)
Product (0)	Technological links (00)	Trade links (10)
Service (1)	Logistics links (01)	Infrastructure links (11)

Fig. 3 Classification of supply chain links

The second part of the code specifies the types of the previous and subsequent links in the supply chain. In this case, the objects of the material flow are under the control of the previous link.

The type of supply chain link is determined based on the following classification signs the tasks of supply chain links: creating or escort of value (product and/or service); and the type of product at the exit of the supply chain link: product or service. It follows from the content of Fig. 3 that such links are: technological, logistics, trade, and infrastructure links.

The data in Fig. 3 allows generating the second part of the sought code. For example, the code 100011100001 indicates that the (material) product in the container on the vehicle (code 1000110) is under the control of the technological link (code 00) currently and then will be transferred to the logistics link in the supply chain (code 01).

In addition to this combination of the code, two main variants are of interest.

The first option takes into account that in practice, as a rule, supply chain links can combine features of several types of links shown in Fig. 3. For example, if a link contains all four types of attributes, then it is a production link (code 1111). If this link does not contain the attributes of a technological link, then it is classified among commercial links (code 0111). If a production link transfers material flow objects to a commercial link, the sought code will appear as follows: 10001110111110111.

The second option for generating the sought code can take into account not only the type of the previous and subsequent links in the supply chain but also the type of links located between them (intermediate links).

In this case, it is possible to specify the type of supply chain (more precisely, the system), which can be distinguished by using the following classification signs:

- the number of previous links: one or more;
- the number of intermediate links: one or more; and
- the number of subsequent links: one or more.

Based on these signs, it possible to distinguish eight types of supply chains (systems) with codes from 000 to 111 (Table 1).

A variant of the sought code, based on the information in Table 1, when using the supply chain in the form of an echelon, can be presented in the following form: 10001110000110 1, where 00 is the technological link, 01 is the logistics link, and 101 is the echelon code (Table 1).

The third part of the sought code can be justified based on the classification of relations between adjacent links in the supply chain using the following classification signs: the share of resources in total purchases (low or high); and the risk level of resource scarcity (low or high).

As a result, it possible to distinguish such types of relationships in the supply chain as selective cooperation, long-term partnership, economically viable relationships, and partial competition (Fig. 4) [3, p. 384].

Table 1 Classification of supply chains (systems)

Number of previous links: one (0) or more (1)	Number of intermediate links: one (0) or more (1)	Number of subsequent links: one (0) or more (1)	Type of resources supply chain
0	0	0	Channel
0	0	1	Front
0	1	0	Chain
0	1	1	Fan
1	0	0	Focus
1	0	1	Echelon
1	1	0	Bundle
1	1	1	Cascade

Share of resources in total purchases

Risk level of resources scarcity	Low (0)	High (1)
High (0)	Selective cooperation (00)	Long-term partnership (01)
Low (0)	Economically viable relationships (10)	Partial competition (11)

Fig. 4 The main types of links relations in the supply chain of consumers and suppliers

Taking into account that there are economically feasible relations between the selected technological and logistics links (code 10), the generated sought code will take the following form: 1000111000011011 0.

The fourth part of the sought code, relating to the process that is performed when managing the resource flow, depends on the type of supply chain link that controls this flow (Fig. 3).

Thus, for example, if the production link is selected as a supply chain link, using such classification features as) the activity planning horizon: current or strategic; and the type of functions and processes of the supply chain link: main or auxiliary. It is possible to distinguish the main types of production activities of this link: production preparation, technological management, resource movement, and concentration/distribution (Fig. 5) [3, p. 65].

If resource movement is taken as an object of structuring, using such classification signs as the state of the flow object: stop or relocation; and the stability of resource flow parameters: stable or unstable. It is possible to distinguish such processes as storage, transportation, assembling/disassembling, and consolidation/unbundling (Fig. 6).

Recalling that the basis of the sought code was selected previously for the product in a container and on a vehicle, which is under the control of the technological link and will later be transferred to the logistics link of the supply chain with economically feasible relations between them (the beginning of the code 10001110000110), then when it moves (code 10) (Fig. 5), more specifically, when consolidating/unbundling (code 11) (Fig. 6), it is possible to get the final structure of the sought code: 100011100001101011.

Type of functions and processes of the supply chain link \ **Activity planning horizon**	Current (0)	Strategic (1)
Main (0)	Technological management (00)	Production preparation (01)
Auxiliary (1)	Resources movement (10)	Concentration / distribution (11)

Fig. 5 Basic production activity types of the supply chain

Stability of resource flow parameters \ **State of the flow object**	Stop (0)	Relocation (1)
Stable (0)	Storage (00)	Transportation (10)
Unstable (1)	Assembling/ disassembling (01)	Consolidation/ unbundling (11)

Fig. 6 Classification of resource movement processes (see Fig. 5)

Similarly, it is possible to get a set of all codes for supply chain management objects that are necessary for its digitalization. In this case depending on the content of the solved task, both simplified and extended versions of the code can be used; and if it is necessary, other coding options for supply chain management objects are available as additions to the main code; based on the results of management by the objects shown in Fig. 1, it is necessary to adjust the principles, methods and forms of supply chain management that ensure their competitiveness.

For example, in [3, pp. 200–203], it is proposed to consider the type of resource flow, the number of resource batches and the number of resources in each batch, the time interval for the flow of resources from the previous link in the supply chain to the next, the costs of resource movement, as well as the date by which the lost profit should be estimated when managing the flow in question; and) to take into account options for consolidating/unbundling resource flows in the course of movement with the corresponding creation (change) of its initial parameters.

5 Conclusion

Thus, the following results have been obtained: the ability to use binary code to digitalize supply chain management objects: flows, systems, processes, and relationships focused on creating and delivering value to end users of products and/or services has been substantiated; the classification of resources supply systems has been proposed; and the code structure for digitalization of supply chain management objects has been developed.

Further research implies specifying the content of the code depending on the specific stage of supply chain management and the specific management situation; and formulating proposals for software developers to implement the results obtained at specific enterprises—links in the supply chain.

References

1. Dahlman, C., Mealy, S., & Wermelinger, M. (2016). *Harnessing the digital economy for developing countries*. Paris: OECD. Retrieved September 28, 2020, from https://www.oecd-ilibrary.org/docserver/4adffb24-en.pdf?expires=1601180676&id=id&accname=guest&checksum=9B45208E3B93F16CE18C80DE0DA098F3.
2. Yakushenko, K. V., & Shimanskaya, A. V. (2017). Digital transformation of information support for economy management of the EAEU member states. *News of Science and Technologies, 2*(41), 11–20.
3. Tyapukhin, A. P. (2018). *Logistics. Supply chain management*. Moscow: KnoRus.
4. Khalin, V. N., & Chernova, G. V. (2018). Digitalization and its impact on the russian economy and society: Benefits, challenges, threats and risks. *Administrative Consulting, 163*, 46–63.
5. Lu, D. (2011). *Fundamentals of supply chain management*. Retrieved September 28, 2020, from https://library.ku.ac.ke/wp-content/downloads/2011/08/Bookboon/Magement%20andOrganisation/fundamentals-of-supply-chain-management.pdf.

6. Chen, H. H., Liu, K.-S., Chen, S.-C., Chang, C.-Y., Hsieh, K. S., & Yang, Y.-W. (2012). An overview of workflow management system structure in the supply chain. *Australian Journal of Business and Management Research, 2*(4), 12–19.
7. Sehgal, V. (2009). *Enterprise supply chain management: Integrating best-in-class processes.* Hoboken: Wiley.
8. Flow. (n.d.). Retrieved September 28, 2020, from https://dictionary.cambridge.org/dictionary/english/flow.
9. Waller, D. L. (2003). *Operations management: A supply chain approach* (2nd ed.). London: Thomson Learning.
10. Krylatkov, P. P., & Prilutskaya, M. A. (2018). *Supply chain management.* Ekaterinburg: Publishing House of Ural State University.
11. Gallarza, M. G., Gil-Saura, I., & Holbrook, M. B. (2011). The value of value: Further excursions on the meaning and role of customer value. *Journal of Consumer Behaviour, 10*(4), 179–191.
12. Loanne, S. S., & Webster, C. M. (2014). Consumer-to-consumer value within social networks. *The Marketing Review, 4*(4), 447–462.

Understanding the Role of Digital Technologies in Supply Chain Risks Management

Jiayan Yang, Vikas Kumar, Banu Ekren, and Evgeny Kuzmin

Abstract Supply chain risks have been regarded as one of the most significant threats to business continuity. Digital technology is considered to reform human production and manufacturing methods. In the recent wake of COVID-19, disruptive digital technologies have emerged as a key tool to manage supply chain risks. Therefore, exploring the impact of digital technology on supply chain risks is considered an important topic in the supply chain management domain. The paper reviews different digital technologies such as 3D printing, IoT, Blockchains, RFID and Big Data Analytics used in supply chains. This exploratory study is based on a survey response from 176 supply chain professionals in China. The findings show the role of digital technologies in managing supply chain risks. The study highlights the current level of implementation of digital technologies in supply chain functions and emphasizes the importance of training. Moreover, the study underlines the significance of supply chain data analysis capabilities for supply chain risk management. The study adds to the limited literature exploring the importance of digital technologies in supply chain risk management.

Keywords Digital technologies · Supply chain · Risk management · Industry 4.0

J. Yang
Warwick Manufacturing Group, University of Warwick, Coventry CV4 7AL, UK

V. Kumar (✉)
Ton Duc Thang University, 19 Nguyen Huu Tho str., Ho Chi Minh City, Vietnam
e-mail: Vikas.Kumar@tdtu.edu.vn

Bristol Business School, University of the West of England, Bristol BS16 1QY, UK

B. Ekren
Faculty of Engineering, Yasar University, Üniversite Caddesi, no. 37-39, İzmir, Turkey

E. Kuzmin
Department of Enterprise Economics, Ural State University of Economics, 62 8 Marta St., 620144 Ekaterinburg, Russian Federation

V. Kumar et al. (eds.), *Digital Transformation in Industry*, Lecture Notes in Information Systems and Organisation 44, https://doi.org/10.1007/978-3-030-73261-5_13

1 Introduction

The world is currently going through a very difficult phase due to the ongoing Coronavirus (COVID-19) pandemic. COVID-19 pandemic has disrupted the global value chains as a result of the lockdown measures adopted by several countries to stop the spread of the disease [1]. Aksoy and Öztürk [2] believes that the process of globalization has brought advantages to businesses and at the same time it has also brought several challenges. Global procurement, the strategies, outsourcing, and production have made the supply chain more geographically dispersed and increased the difficulty level of management. The ongoing COVID-19 pandemic has highlighted the vulnerabilities of the global supply chains. Traditionally, organisations have relied on operating models such as lean, just-in-time production and Toyota Production System (TPS) to reduce costs and improve competitiveness. However, these operating models reduce the company's inventory and increase the risk of supply chain disruption due to shortage of raw materials. According to Berger et al. [3], interruptions caused by supply chain risks have increased costs, reduced revenues and decreased market share for businesses. Therefore, supply chain risks have been regarded as one of the most significant threats to business continuity. A 2011 report by the World Economic Forum (WEF) points out that in the past five years, more than 90% of companies believe that supply chain and transportation risk management has become increasingly important in organizational management [4].

As the whole world is now transitioning towards the fourth industrial revolution, i.e. industry 4.0, many organisations are now relying on disruptive digital technologies to manage the supply chain risks. Park et al. [4] suggest that among the many tools used to prevent and mitigate supply chain risks, digital technology plays a key role. Blockchain, 3D printing, Internet of Things, Cloud Computing, Robotics, Artificial Intelligence, Big Data Analytics and other digital technologies can not only shorten the relationship between enterprises and upstream and downstream partners in the supply chain, improve the efficiency of supply chain operations, but also help enterprises to share information and control responses in a timely and effective manner to deal with risks Wu et al. [5]. The term "Supply Chain 4.0" emphasises the relationships between Industry 4.0 and supply chains [6]. Supply Chain 4.0 has the potential to disruptively transform traditional supply chains [6, 7]. Truong Quang and Hara [8] highlight that digital technology in the supply chain is different from comprehensive management information systems such as MRP II or ERP. Its scope is not limited to the enterprise, but also extends to partners in the supply chain network. The digital technologies in the supply chain have gradually developed and matured with the advancement of supply chain precision, complexity, flexibility and supply chain management theory [8]. Although most enterprises have realized the use of digital technology to strengthen supply chain information sharing and cooperation, to achieve the purpose of preventing and mitigating supply chain risks, the reality shows that enterprises with digital technology resources may not be able to effectively manage and control supply chain risks [8]. Therefore, the main purpose of this study is to explore the impact of digital technology on supply chain risk management.

2 Literature Review

This section provides an overview of the existing literature about supply chain risk management and the application of digital technologies in supply chains. The study mainly explores five emerging technologies namely 3D printing, blockchain, the Internet of Things (IoT), Radio-frequency identification (RFID) and Big Data Analytics (BDA).

2.1 Supply Chain Risk Management

Supply chain risks are "anything that presents a risk (i.e. an impediment or hazard) to information, material and product flow from original suppliers to the delivery of the final product to the ultimate end-user" [9]. There are numerous causes for supply chain risks to occur that varies concerning complexity and completeness [10]. To analyse the effect of modern digital approaches on supply chain mitigations, there is a need to understand these risks in depth. Many authors have grouped these risks in different ways. According to Chopra and Sodhi [11], there are nine specific categories of supply chain risks comprising of forecast, delays, disruptions, systems, inventory, capacity, procurement, receivables, and intellectual property. Christopher and Peck [12] suggested two broad classifications of risks: Internal risk involving process and control and External risks involving demand, supply, and environment. Therefore, supply chain risk includes both its own operational risks and the risks arising from the information transmission process.

Supply chain risk has both the general characteristics of risk and the special nature of the supply chain. The supply chain risk is also dynamic and changes with changes in external factors. The result of supply chain risk comes from the combined effect of internal and external factors. The smooth operation of the supply chain requires each node to cooperate and work together [13]. To achieve the final goal, each enterprise must depend on each other. The complexity of the supply chain also increases the probability of risk. Supply chain risk is directly affected by the company's operating level. The operating level of an enterprise includes budget input, technical level, strategic planning, and information sharing. Therefore, when controlling supply chain risks, we must start from the aspects of enterprise composition and construction principles. Supply chain risks are also transitive [13]. Enterprises in the supply chain depend on each other, which means that the supply chain itself is a whole, and no matter which enterprise node in the chain has a problem, it will affect everyone connected in the chain. Therefore due to the structural characteristics of the supply chain if there is a problem with any node it will affect the entire chain. The supply chain risks also interact with each other. For example, the reduction of one risk may lead to the birth of another risk. Enterprises therefore should pay close attention to the relationship between various risks [14, 15]. One way to solve the complementarity of risks is to keep proper control over the inventory. When inventory is insufficient, the possibility of supply chain interruption is likely to occur, and larger inventory will take up too much liquidity, resulting in problems such as increased costs.

Risk mitigation is a vital part of supply chain management. According to Menoni et al. [16], risk mitigation is a selection of methods and strategies in order to manage risks in a supply chain. Hallikas et al. [17] provide strategies for risk mitigation such as transfer, take, eliminate, reduce, share or assess individual risks, focusing on probability and impact. Similarly, Aqlan and Lam [18] established their mitigation strategies and they are risk avoidance, risk reduction, risk transfer, risk acceptance, ignoring risks, risk exploit. Ho et al. [19] claim that risk mitigation process should be conducted on the same aspects which are relevant to supply chain, i.e., supply chain risk mitigation should include macro and micro risk mitigation, demand, process, supply, finance, manufacturing, information and general risk mitigations. Behzadi et al. [20] highlight that nowadays firms are increasingly global and less vertically integrated, increasing the complexity of supply chains and exposing them to much more risks.

2.2 *Digital Technologies for Supply Chains*

The digital transformation in supply chains has resulted in several benefits such as cost reduction, improved transparency, improved delivery speed, increased efficiency and improved profitability. The modern disruptive technologies are slowly transforming the supply chains and making them more intelligent and efficient. This section will explore the potential some of these Industry 4.0 technologies for supply chains.

As one of the iconic technologies in the context of the new industrial revolution, 3D printing will have a wide-ranging impact on human production and manufacturing methods, life consumption methods and organizational management methods in the future [8]. With the increasing flexibility and capabilities of 3D printing technology, 3D printing has become more and more beneficial to the manufacturing industry and is widely used in materials, automobiles, food and healthcare industries. Scheibe and Blackhurst [21] reviewed the social impact of 3D printing from a technical perspective, including: first, 3D printing can customize healthcare products to improve population health and quality of life; second, 3D printing can reduce the sustainability of manufacturing Environmental impact; third, 3D printing can simplify the supply chain and improve the efficiency and responsiveness of demand fulfilment. Xanthopoulos et al. [22] and Aqlan and Lam [18] studied the advantages of 3D printing over traditional subtractive manufacturing, including printing parts in a short time and improving the manufacturability of highly complex products, shortening production cycles, reducing manufacturing processes to save materials, reduce the need for moulds, increase the density of the final parts and manufacture free-form closed structures. Chen et al. [23] find that 3D printing like industrial manufacturing technology can significantly reduce resource and energy demand and process-related CO_2 emissions per unit of GDP. Basole et al. [24] conducted a sensitivity analysis around supply chain cost changes by establishing a model, indicating that 3D printing technology will reduce sales losses due to product mismatches, as well as increase customer satisfaction due to the full availability of products and increase the market demand. El-Shahat [25] believes that 3D printing technology can reduce costs by maximizing the use of products and equipment. Gladwin and Floyd [26] also analyzed the costs and benefits of a 3D printing technology-based supply chain through case studies to provide technology investment advice. Whereas Bhasin et al. [27] quantitatively estimated the potential impact of 3D printing technology on the global supply chain. Studies have shown that 3D printing technology will significantly change the future supply chain, as manufacturing will move from low-cost regions closer to end customers, which can help companies reduce transportation and inventory costs. It can be seen that the investment in manufacturing technology affects the operation of the entire supply chain by influencing the decisions of the supply chain members.

The main purpose of blockchain technology is to achieve the use of technologies such as cryptography, consensus algorithms and reward mechanisms without the intervention of third-party trust institutions so that each node does not need to trust any other nodes, nor does it require the central certification authority [28]. In a narrow sense, a blockchain is a shared database that connects blocks into a chain in a chronological order to ensure that data is not tampered with [28]. Broadly speaking, blockchain technology is a set of decentralized infrastructure models that combine multiple existing technologies. Li-qun and Zhi-hua [29] discussed the impact of blockchain technology on the factoring business development model and described the possibility of blockchain technology breaking the supply chain financial bottleneck. Hua [30] discussed the role of blockchain in the future supply chain financial innovation application and described the whole process of asset ownership traceability and logistics information. Wang et al. [31] expounded the economic value of blockchain technology on the influence or role of different participants in supply chain finance. Yao et al. [32] combine blockchain technology with supply chain finance, taking reverse factoring products as an example, and integrating supply chain partners into a completely effective and transparent ecosystem for everyone through blockchain. The transparency is used to reduce disputes and transaction costs, maximize the value of financial flows, and help smooth the flow of funds in the supply chain [32]. Blockchains has already shown its potential not only in the financial sector, but also in food safety monitoring and food traceability in the supply chains [33].

The Internet of Things (IoT) refers to a network that connects items to the network through technology, infrared sensors, readers and other devices to exchange information to achieve intelligent identification, location tracking, monitoring and management [34]. The IoT can collect terminal information through sensors and radio frequency identification. The collected information is quickly and stably transmitted to the control system through middleware technology and network so that the operator can analyze the entire system environmental data and items for real-time monitoring of data to discover and solve problems in a timely manner. However, the digital supply chains expose new types of cyber risk in the digital economy from shared infrastructure.

RFID, as one of the important technologies in the New World, has a wide range of applications in many fields, especially industries and fields that have great significance in real life, such as transportation, medical machinery, data statistical management, logistics management, and product anti-counterfeiting [8]. Its working principle is to use radio frequency signals to automatically identify the objects to be identified and visually present it as intuitive data, and the relevant conclusions can be obtained through the analysis [35]. RFID-technologies has been successfully implemented in the supply chains to deliver real-time information about the current status of logistics activities. Geisberger and Broy [36] showed that using REFID the truck-delivery of specific products could be optimized. For example, the delivery information of trans-ported products could be changed in real-time and whenever needed [37]. This way, a product that is already on its way to the initially targeted customer could be routed to another nearby customer if the delivery was aborted. Hence, with the digitalization of all logistics processes through RFID-technologies, even problem management can be carried out centrally and online. Tian [33] highlighted that in the USA and Japan, RFID system had been used for tracking agri-food in the entire supply chain from planting to the distributor and retailer as RFID systems provide management information and safety data of agri-food for the producer, wholesaler, retailer and consumer.

Big Data Analytics (BDA) consists of refined data analysis means that simplifies decision-making procedures by the retrieval of essential and relevant data from an extensive data source within a reasonable time interval [38]. Big Data has been characterized by 5Vs: volume, variety, velocity, veracity, and value [39]. BDA is becoming increasingly popular among manufacturing companies as it helps gain insights and make decisions based on Big Data. It is also becoming an inevitable technology in SCM since it can be used for the smooth functioning of important SC components like barcodes, RFID, and sensors. Its quick and easy data handling capabilities are helping companies to compete well in the fluctuating markets. BDA is enabling better SC agility, enhanced customer delights as well as minimum running expenses [40]. Empirical evidence demonstrates that BDA has multiple advantages in SCM as it helps to reduce operational costs, improve SC agility, and increase customer satisfaction [41].

The evidence presented so far provides a good overview of the application of the industry 4.0 technologies in the supply chains. It also shows that these digital technologies provide numerous benefit to supply chains and hence has seen greater adoption in all facets in recent years. As their ability to provide real-time visualization of the data, improve transparency, better demand forecast, etc. helps supply chains to better deal with the risks and disruptions. As we are currently facing significant disruptions due to the ongoing pandemic, it would be interesting to explore how these digital technologies can assist in supply chain risk management. Next section provides the methodology adopted in this study.

3 Methodology

This is an exploratory study aiming to understand the role that digital technologies play in supply chain risk management. Following the review of the extant literature, a number of digital technologies and their application in the supply chain domain were explored. A survey questionnaire was then designed. The questionnaire was designed to examine participants' understanding of digital technologies, its role in managing supply chain risks and understand challenges associated with the supply chain. The questionnaire designed in this study was divided into four parts:

1) the company's basic information;
2) the company's digital supply chain practices;
3) supply chain risk management;
4) supply chain capabilities.

The questionnaire includes various multiple-choice questions. The study targeted professionals working in the supply chain area and who are familiar with digital technologies. The survey was sent to more than 500+ professionals in China through a personal network and social media platforms such as LinkedIn and WeChat. The data was collected between June–August 2020. The survey resulted in 176 valid responses, with a response rate of 44%. This included responses from 5 CEOs,12 senior/general managers and 159 general employees familiar with the supply chain domain.

4 Findings and Discussions

The first part of the survey was focused on the demographics of the companies. From the perspective of funding sources, 82% of the respondent's organisation belong to Joint Ventures, 11% were private enterprises, 3%—state-owned, and rest (4%)—wholly owned by foreign enterprises. Nearly 81% of those enterprises employed more than 5,000 employees, around 4% were SMEs (employing less than 500 employees) and rest 15% of the enterprises employed between 500–5000 employees (Fig. 1).

The second part of the survey was focused on understanding the supply chain digital practices within the enterprises. When asked about emerging digital technologies that are being used in the supply chain practices of their company (Fig. 2), almost nearly 82% of respondents highlighted the greater reliance on IoT, BDA, AI, robotics, cloud computing, mobile and social technologies, augmented reality/virtual reality, and 3D printing. However, only a small percentage (11%) of respondents mentioned the usage of unmanned/autonomous vehicles.

Figure 3 shows that only 3% of enterprises do not recognize the urgency of the digital supply chain reform, and have not yet started the digital supply chain practice; 5% of them do recognize the urgency of digital supply chain reform, but have not yet begun the practice of digital supply chain; whereas 20% have started either

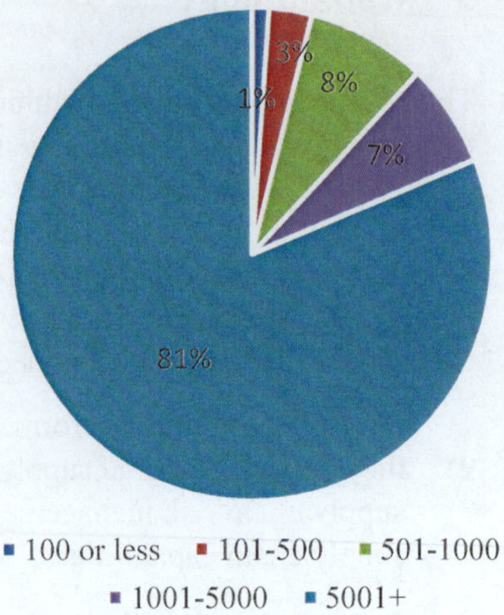

Fig. 1 The total number of employees in the company

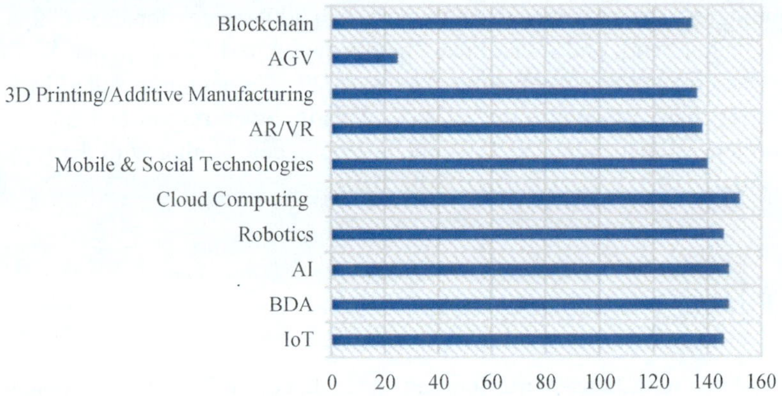

Fig. 2 Which of the following emerging digital technologies are used in your company's supply chain practices?

short-term (less than one year) or long term (more than one year) digital supply chain project. Interestingly, nearly 72% of enterprises have already formulated a mid-to-long-term (more than one year) digital supply chain strategy and are constantly advancing. When asked about the senior leadership support to digital supply chain practices, nearly 74% of respondents agreed that their leaders attach great importance to the company's digital supply chain practices. 78% of participants believe that the return on investment of digital supply chain practices is above 80%. Whereas, 73% believed that the company's digital supply chain practices closely match the company's current development and 76% of enterprises regularly provide technical training to employees. Around 76% of enterprises agreed that their functional departments collaborate in the digital supply chain practice process and 94% of participants

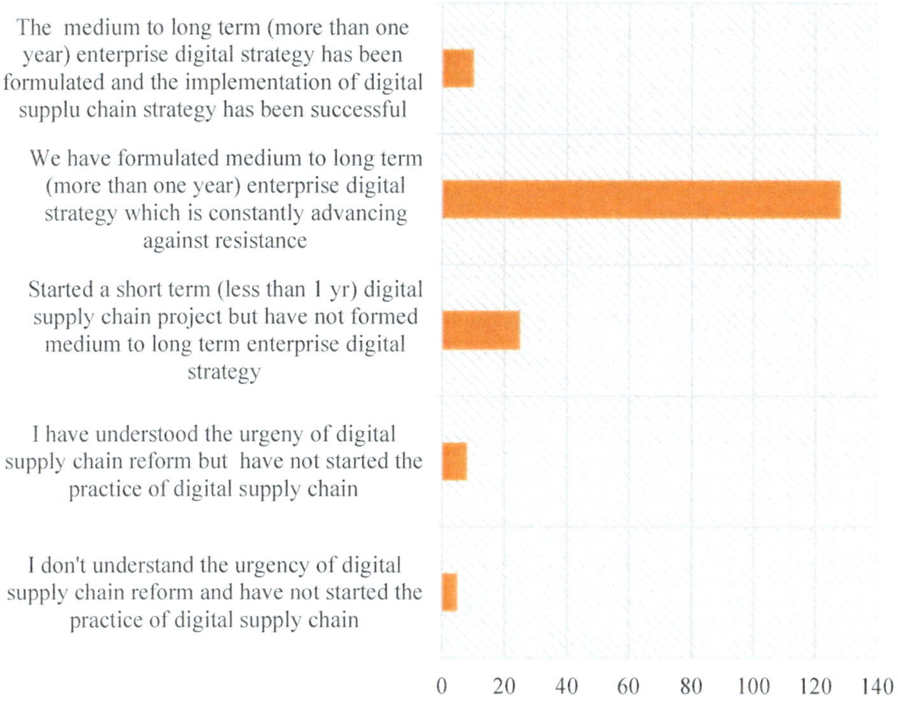

Fig. 3 Digital supply chain practice implementation by companies

supposed that external suppliers were very willing to cooperate in the digital supply chain projects.

The third part of the survey asked questions about supply chain risk management. Around 60% of participants believed that the most likely risk in the supply chain was the risk of information dissemination, and the remaining 11% underlined risks related to the production organization and procurement. In addition, they also stressed the risk related to the selection of distributors (17%), and around 9% highlighted logistics operation risks and around 3% highlighted the corporate culture differences as the risk factor. Regarding the company's measures to deal with supply chain risks (Table 1), respondents were asked to choose a number of potential options that enterprises would normally follow to mitigate supply chain risks. Table 1 shows the respondent's view of these potential measures. Nearly 17% of participants chose to strengthen information exchange and sharing and improving the efficiency of information exchange whereas 20% suggested strengthening enterprise risk management and establishing emergency mechanisms to deal with risks. While nearly 71% noted that all these measures are necessary to manage the supply chain risks.

The final part of the survey focused on exploring the supply chain capabilities. Based on the data stored in the company's digital supply chain system, supply risk warning and automatic generation of flexible response plans, 60% participants believed that the company's supply chain data analysis capabilities can largely

Table 1 Company's measures to deal with supply chain risks

Measures	Volume (%)
Strengthen the risk management of node enterprises	10
Establish an emergency response mechanism	10
Strengthen information exchange and sharing, improve information communication efficiency	17
Strengthen incentives for supply chain stakeholders	10
Optimize partner selection	11
Pay attention to flexible design and maintain the flexibility of supply chains	12
Improve the culture and create common values with supply chain partners	10
Strengthen procurement and optimize logistics and distribution	11
Establish a strategic partnership	10
All of the above	71

support supply chain risk management. Nearly all participant's agreed that when they face product quality-related problems, the digital technologies help trace the supplier, parts batches, and the root cause of the problem in time. Around 52% reported real-time monitoring of their inventory situation whereas only 2% reported that they do not have real-time monitoring of their inventory. In general, more than 80% of participants agreed that the application of digital technology will reduce supply chain risks.

The findings from the survey show that many enterprises have already started adopting emerging digital technologies in their supply chains. The responses show that there is a greater level of awareness among respondents regarding the emerging disruptive technologies. Enterprises also see digital technologies as a great tool to deal with supply chain risks. The study identifies several risk factors such as information collection errors, information security risks, information infrastructure failures, information transmission timeliness, corporate reputation and logistics transportation and storage. The entry point in this regard puts forward suggestions and measures for risk management. Among the six risks, information collection errors, information infrastructure failures and information transmission timeliness are risks that occur at the perception layer, mainly the risks caused by the application of IoT. The implementation of the IoT system in the supply chain needs to be improved for better effectiveness. Information security risks include information asymmetry risks, information risks, information distortion risks, but the proportion of information security risks relative to other risks is relatively large. Corporate reputation risks are often brought about by information security risks. As a result of information security risks, false information cannot be effectively identified, affecting the corporate reputation in supply chain exchanges. Improving the level of the digital technology supply chain can effectively reduce transaction costs, improve the efficiency of information transmission and improve quality issues.

5 Conclusion

This study attempts to establish the role that digital technologies play in managing supply chain risks. The study reviews the application of a number of emerging digital technologies such as 3D printing technology, blockchain, the Internet of Things, RFID technology and Big Data Analytics (BDA) in the supply chains and how these technologies are being used to manage the risks. A survey of the supply chain professionals was conducted that highlights the extent of the usage of emerging technologies in managing supply chain risks. Our findings show that supply chain risk has been regarded as one of the key threats to business continuity. Findings also show that 3D printing technology not only makes the traditional subtractive manufacturing technology obsolete but also provides more choices for designers, manufacturers, sellers and maintenance technicians while bringing more production capacity closer to the end-user. The main purpose of blockchain technology is to realize encryption without the intervention of a third-party trust agency, thereby ensuring the security of supply chain transactions. The key technologies of the Internet of Things include barcode technology, QR code, global positioning system, cloud computing and EPC information network. RFID technology can be applied to multiple industries to ensure that companies can trace their products back to each chain. BDA has shown to improve SC agility, reduce operational costs, and increase customer satisfaction. For large enterprises with multi-level organizational structures and larger scales, the use of digital technology has many benefits in improving procurement efficiency, cost, quality, and standardization, as well as some risks. By analyzing the risks that affect the target of centralized procurement, decomposing the risks, and identifying the influencing factors of the risks, the centralized procurement risks can be analyzed from multiple angles and in all directions, and the supply chain risk problems can be better solved through digital technologies. Our exploratory study thus adds to the limited literature exploring the role of digital technologies in managing supply chain risks.

This study has some limitations. It is based on the 176 valid responses from China and hence future research should increase the sample size and collect data from other regions of the globe. Future studies can also use a combination of qualitative and quantitative methods for broader generalization and triangulation of the findings. Since the research only explores five digital technologies in detail, future studies should also look at the implication of other technologies such as AR/VR, automation and cloud computing to supply chains. Besides, future studies should develop a conceptual framework and empirically explore how these emerging technologies affect supply chain performance. The practical application of these digital technologies in different sectors can also be an interesting area to explore.

Acknowledgements We would like to express our sincere thanks to Newton Katip Celebi, TUBITAK and Royal Academy of Engineering (Industry-Academia Partnership Programme 2018/2019, No. 4180046) for supporting this project.

References

1. Kumar, V. (2020). Adjusting to the new normal: Challenges of the food sector in the wake of COVID-19. *Journal of Supply Chain Management, Logistics and Procurement, 3*(2), 1–18.
2. Aksoy, A., & Öztürk, N. (2011). Supplier selection and performance evaluation in just-in-time production environments. *Expert Systems with Applications, 38*(5), 6351–6359. https://doi.org/10.1016/j.eswa.2010.11.104.
3. Berger, P. D., Gerstenfeld, A., & Zeng, A. Z. (2004). How many suppliers are best? A decision-analysis approach. *Omega, 32*(1), 9–15. https://doi.org/10.1016/j.omega.2003.09.001.
4. Park, Y., Hong, P., & Roh, J. J. (2013). Supply chain lessons from the catastrophic natural disaster in Japan. *Business Horizons, 56*(1), 75–85. https://doi.org/10.1016/j.bushor.2012.09.008.
5. Wu, D. D., Olson, D. L., & Birge, J. R. (2011). Introduction to special issue on "Enterprise risk management in operations". *International Journal of Production Economics, 134*(1), 1–2.
6. Frederico, G. F., Garza-Reyes, J. A., Anosike, A., & Kumar, V. (2019), Supply Chain 4.0: concepts, maturity and research agenda. *Supply Chain Management, 25*(2), 262–282. https://doi.org/10.1108/SCM-09-2018-0339.
7. Tjahjono, B., Esplugues, C., Ares, E., & Pelaez, G. (2017). What does industry 4.0 mean to supply chain? *Procedia Manufacturing, 13,* 1175–1182. https://doi.org/10.1016/j.promfg.2017.09.191.
8. Truong Quang, H., & Hara, Y. (2018). Risks and performance in supply chain: The push effect. *International Journal of Production Research, 56*(4), 1369–1388. https://doi.org/10.1080/00207543.2017.1363429.
9. Peck, H. (2006). Reconciling supply chain vulnerability, risk and supply chain management. *International Journal of Logistics: Research and Applications, 9*(2), 127–142. https://doi.org/10.1080/13675560600673578.
10. Xanthopoulos, P., & Pejicic, J. (2015). *Supply chain vulnerability in the automotive industry.* Master thesis, Jönköping International Business School, Sweden
11. Chopra, S., & Sodhi, M. S. (2004). Supply-chain breakdown. *MIT Sloan Management Review, 46*(1), 53–61.
12. Christopher, M., & Peck, H. (2004). Building the resilient supply chain. *International Journal of Logistics Management, 15*(2), 1–13. https://doi.org/10.1108/09574090410700275.
13. Cruz, J. M. (2013). Mitigating global supply chain risks through corporate social responsibility. *International Journal of Production Research, 51*(13), 3995–4010. https://doi.org/10.1080/00207543.2012.762134.
14. Golicic, S. L., & Smith, C. D. (2013). A meta-analysis of environmentally sustainable supply chain management practices and firm performance. *Journal of Supply Chain Management, 49*(2), 78–95. https://doi.org/10.1111/jscm.12006.
15. Ivanov, D., Dolgui, A., Sokolov, B., & Ivanova, M. (2017). Literature review on disruption recovery in the supply chain. *International Journal of Production Research, 55*(20), 6158–6174. https://doi.org/10.1080/00207543.2017.1330572.
16. Menoni, S., Molinari, D., Parker, D., Ballio, F., & Tapsell, S. (2012). Assessing multifaceted vulnerability and resilience in order to design risk-mitigation strategies. *Natural Hazards, 64*(3), 2057–2082.
17. Hallikas, J., & Virolainen, V. M. (2004). Risk management in supplier relationships and networks. *Supply Chain Risk*, 43–65.
18. Aqlan, F., & Lam, S. S. (2015). A fuzzy-based integrated framework for supply chain risk assessment. *International Journal of Production Economics, 161,* 54–63. https://doi.org/10.1016/j.ijpe.2014.11.013.
19. Ho, W., Zheng, T., Yildiz, H., & Talluri, S. (2015). Supply chain risk management: A literature review. *International Journal of Production Research, 53*(16), 5031–5069. https://doi.org/10.1080/00207543.2015.1030467.

20. Behzadi, G., O'Sullivan, M. J., Olsen, T. L., & Zhang, A. (2018). Agribusiness supply chain risk management: A review of quantitative decision models. *Omega, 79,* 21–42. https://doi.org/10.1016/j.omega.2017.07.005.
21. Scheibe, K. P., & Blackhurst, J. (2018). Supply chain disruption propagation: A systemic risk and normal accident theory perspective. *International Journal of Production Research, 56*(1–2), 43–59. https://doi.org/10.1080/00207543.2017.1355123.
22. Xanthopoulos, A., Vlachos, D., & Iakovou, E. (2012). Optimal newsvendor policies for dual-sourcing supply chains: A disruption risk management framework. *Computers & Operations Research, 39*(2), 350–357. https://doi.org/10.1016/j.cor.2011.04.010.
23. Chen, J., Sohal, A. S., & Prajogo, D. I. (2013). Supply chain operational risk mitigation: A collaborative approach. *International Journal of Production Research, 51*(7), 2186–2199. https://doi.org/10.1080/00207543.2012.727490.
24. Basole, R. C., & Bellamy, M. A. (2014). Supply network structure, visibility, and risk diffusion: A computational approach. *Decision Sciences, 45*(4), 753–789. https://doi.org/10.1111/deci.12099.
25. El-Shahat, A. (2017). 3D printing makes solar power less expensive, gives wider range. *Natural Gas & Electricity, 33*(7), 20–24. https://doi.org/10.1002/gas.21962.
26. Gladwin and Floyd. (2015). Towards sustainable 'Biofriendly' materials for additive manufacturing (Part 2 of 3). Autodesk Inc., November 18, 2015, https://spark.autodesk.com/blog/towards-sustainable-%E2%80%9Cbiofriendly%E2%80%9D-materialsadditivemanufacturing-part-2-3
27. Bhasin, V., & Bodla, M. R. (2014). *Impact of 3D printing on global supply chains by 2020* (Doctoral dissertation, Massachusetts Institute of Technology).
28. Khrais, L. T. (2020, October). Comparison study of blockchain technology and IOTA technology. In *2020 Fourth International Conference on I-SMAC (IoT in Social, Mobile, Analytics and Cloud) (I-SMAC)* (pp. 42–47). IEEE. https://doi.org/10.1109/I-SMAC49090.2020.9243366.
29. Li-qun, Zhou, & Zhi-hua, Li. (2016). Application of block chain in supply chain finance. *Journal of Information Systems Engineering, 07,* 49–51.
30. Hua, S. (2016). *Supply chain finance*, 1st ed. Gale Asia (ISBN-10: 9814698997).
31. Wang, J., He, Q., Xu, Y., Han, Q., & Zhou, Z. (2017, September). An unified payment method of charging piles based on blockchain. In *The 7th International Conference on Computer Engineering and Networks* (Vol. 299, p. 085). SISSA Medialab. https://doi.org/10.22323/1.299.0085.
32. Yao, L., Liu, Y., Zhao, H., & Ding, H. (2019). An improved UKPK-PSO algorithm inspired from block chain technology for flexible job shop scheduling problem. In *2019 Chinese Control Conference (CCC)* (pp. 2260–2265). IEEE. https://doi.org/10.23919/ChiCC.2019.8866111
33. Tian, F. (2016). An agri-food supply chain traceability system for China based on RFID & blockchain technology. In *2016 13th International conference on service systems and service management (ICSSSM)* (pp. 1–6). IEEE. https://doi.org/10.1109/ICSSSM.2016.7538424
34. Zanella, A., Bui, N., Castellani, A., Vangelista, L., & Zorzi, M. (2014). Internet of things for smart cities. *IEEE Internet of Things Journal, 1*(1), 22–32. https://doi.org/10.1109/JIOT.2014.2306328.
35. Sawik, T. (2017). A portfolio approach to supply chain disruption management. *International Journal of Production Research, 55*(7), 1970–1991. https://doi.org/10.1080/00207543.2016.1249432.
36. Geisberger, E., & Broy, M. (Eds.). (2012). *agendaCPS: Integrierte Forschungsagenda cyber-physical systems* (Vol. 1). Berlin: Springer. https://doi.org/10.1007/978-3-642-29099-2.
37. Whang, S. (2010). Timing of RFID adoption in a supply chain. *Management Science, 56*(2), 343–355. https://doi.org/10.1287/mnsc.1090.1121.
38. Tsai, C. W., Lai, C. F., Chao, H. C., & Vasilakos, A. V. (2015). Big data analytics: A survey. *Journal of Big Data, 2*(1), 1–32. https://doi.org/10.1186/s40537-015-0030-3.
39. Wamba, S. F., Akter, S., Edwards, A., Chopin, G., & Gnanzou, D. (2015). How 'big data' can make big impact: Findings from a systematic review and a longitudinal case study. *International Journal of Production Economics, 165,* 234–246. https://doi.org/10.1016/j.ijpe.2014.12.031.

40. Nguyen, T., Li, Z. H. O. U., Spiegler, V., Ieromonachou, P., & Lin, Y. (2018). Big data analytics in supply chain management: A state-of-the-art literature review. *Computers & Operations Research, 98,* 254–264. https://doi.org/10.1016/j.cor.2017.07.004.
41. Ramanathan, R., Olex, A. L., Dozmorov, M., Bear, H. D., Fernandez, L. J., & Takabe, K. (2017). Angiopoietin pathway gene expression associated with poor breast cancer survival. *Breast Cancer Research and Treatment, 162*(1), 191–198. https://doi.org/10.1007/s10549-017-4102-2.
42. Radanliev, P., De Roure, D. C., Nurse, J. R., Burnap, P., Anthi, E., Ani, U., Maddox, L., Santos, O., & Montalvo, R. M. (2019). *Cyber risk from IoT technologies in the supply chain–discussion on supply chains decision support system for the digital economy* (Preprint). https://doi.org/10.13140/RG.2.2.17286.22080.

Artificial Intelligence Disclosure in the Annual Reports of Spanish IBEX-35 Companies (2018–2019)

Enrique Bonsón, Víctor Alejo, and Domenica Lavorato

Abstract This paper explores the information on Artificial Intelligence (AI) that Spanish IBEX 35 listed companies are including in their annual/sustainability reports. The study mainly focuses on the AI systems that companies indicate they are using or developing, the projects they are tackling and the extent to which they follow some principles or ethical guidelines when using AI-based technologies. The study analyses, both from a qualitative and quantitative perspective, the content of the reports of IBEX 35 companies for 2018 and 2019. The findings suggest that although AI reporting is growing because of the interest in these technologies, it is growing in a non-structured way, and that the adoption of ethical approaches to AI is at a very preliminary stage. The paper analyzes some evidence about a part of non-financial disclosure, AI disclosure, which has not been explored yet. It may serve as a starting point for researchers and companies interested in developing clear guidelines on what kind of information is relevant and mandatory for companies to report, what ethical principles or regulations AI applications must follow and how it has to be disclosed.

Keywords Artificial intelligence · Content analysis · Ethical guidelines · IBEX 35 companies · Non-financial reporting · Voluntary disclosure

1 Introduction

In April 2018, the European Commission declared its three main goals regarding artificial intelligence (AI): to increase the technological and industrial capacity of the European Union and the transfer of all those advances in AI to the economy; to prepare for the socio-economic changes brought about by AI; and, to ensure an appropriate ethical and legal framework [6]. This document led us to explore what

E. Bonsón (✉) · V. Alejo
University of Huelva, Calle Doctor Cantero Cuadrado, 6, Huelva, Spain
e-mail: bonson@uhu.es

D. Lavorato
Parthenope University of Naples, Via Amm. F. Acton, 38, 80133 Napoles, Italy

V. Kumar et al. (eds.), *Digital Transformation in Industry*, Lecture Notes in Information Systems and Organisation 44, https://doi.org/10.1007/978-3-030-73261-5_14

Spanish companies were doing in this respect or, more precisely, what they reported to do and what kind of risks and ethical approaches they considered [4].

In this study, which continues the one cited above, we analyze the information on artificial intelligence, machine learning, deep learning and big data, provided by Spanish IBEX-35 companies in their annual reports. We try to answer the following questions: Are companies reporting about artificial intelligence? In what kind of reports? Are they reporting only about general statements? What are the products or applications that these companies are developing and/or using? Have they launched AI projects and initiatives? Have they created or possess units or laboratories dedicated to their development? Do they analyze their potential risks? And finally, do they reflect on the ethical problems arising from their use? [4]. We also conduct a comparative analysis with the data from 2018 and 2019 to check how AI disclosure is evolving. This research constitutes a first approach to AI disclosure to gain insights to develop non-financial information guidelines related to artificial intelligence. These guidelines, should guarantee that the minimum requirements for trustworthy artificial intelligence, such as fairness, explainability, transparency and accountability, are met.

2 Literature Review

Although there is an extensive literature on sustainability reporting [1, 10, 11], the disclosure of information on artificial intelligence as an integral part of these reports has never been analyzed before and, therefore, there is no literature in that field which opens an interesting line of research.

Being a pioneer study in that line of research, we need to explore both current practices and targets to be achieved in terms of key indicators and reporting standards for AI. In that sense, some proposals have been launched on how to regulate artificial intelligence such as the European Commission's White Paper on Artificial Intelligence [7] or the Data Ethics Commission of the Federal Government of Germany [5], in which regulation is proposed to be based on the potential damage of an algorithmic system, addressing it from two fronts, the probability of damage occurring and its severity. On the other hand, we also consider some research that addresses the possibility of carrying out some standardization of all the proposals on ethical principles with "genuine mechanisms of accountability, external to companies and accessible to populations" [9] or some study on how start implementing ethics in AI and stop "AI ethics washing" [8].

3 Material and Methods

The methodology used for this study is that of content analysis. We downloaded all the annual/sustainability reports of these companies and looked into them for mentions in artificial intelligence, machine learning, deep learning and big data. We got a total of 704 mentions that were then classified according to their content within the following categories: general statements, applications/uses, units/laboratories, risk and ethics.

As a "General statement", we consider all those mentions that do not address concrete AI topics, either talking about the future, either listing all these new technologies or talking about the changes that are taking place in business, among others. Here, for example, we expose what would be a typical mention of general matters: "The future of any company will rely on how they can lead in the adoption of Artificial Intelligence. At ArcelorMittal we are committed to being the leader in full enterprise digitalization" [2].

"Applications" include all those mentions explaining some specific developments or projects in which the company is involved and the products or applications they are using. Table 1 shows the main applications reported in 2018 annual reports, grouped into some of the most common functions.

As units/laboratories we imply all those mentions referring to a specific center, within the company, for the study and exclusive development of these new technologies.

In the risk category, we include all those companies that declare a possible negative impact that the development of artificial intelligence could cause. In our study, we found two companies that declare something about this, Bankinter [3], referring to the possible risk of theft of confidential big data, phishing or certain techniques that cybercriminals can develop to steal confidential data; and, Telefonica [13], referring to how they develop their products, applying a rigorous method both at the beginning and at the end of the design of their products and services to avoid possible adverse impacts on human rights.

Finally, our last category, closely related to the previous one, ethics, where we find nine of the 35 companies that make some kind of mention, highlighting the work of Telefónica [12], as one of the first companies to develop, in 2018, its own ethical principles, which include: fair AI, transparent and explainable AI, human-centric AI, privacy and security by design, and working with partners and third parties.

4 Results

The results of this study are presented in the following tables. Table 2 shows how many companies (%) report something related to each category. There is a considerable increase in all categories but the categories of applications and ethics stand out. This suggests that companies are increasingly using artificial intelligence and that they are slightly more concerned about the ethical aspects of the use of these powerful technologies. Appendix provides detailed company-by-company information.

On the other hand, Table 3 summarizes the level of AI disclosure in terms of the number of categories companies are reporting about.

Table 1 AI applications IBEX 35-2018

Category	Description	Company
Detection	Fraud	Amadeus
	Defects to enable predictive maintenance	ArcelorMIttal
	Money laundering and financing terrorism	B. Santander
	Cybersecurity threats	Bankia
	Money laundering and financing terrorism	BBVA
	Product safety issues and harmful substances	Inditex
	Threats to business operations	Telefónica
Diagnosis	Turbine health status	Acciona
	Diagnostic sensors in wind turbines	Siemens Gamesa
Optimization	Platform for massive data analysis	Bankia
	Cognitive platform to automate processes	Bankia
	Customer transaction inquiries	Bankia
	"Now", online banking app	CaixaBank
	Optimizing traffic congestion problems	Ferrovial
	Improving catalyst lifecycle reliability	Repsol
Prediction	Technical data management framework	Amadeus
	Detection of non-technical losses	Endesa
	Automatic report evaluation	Endesa
	Demand	Inditex
	Vehicle damage assessment	Mapfre
Recommendation system	Personalized offers for travelers	Amadeus
	Show offers from advertising partners	Amadeus
	Terminal recommendation	Telefónica
	Customer-based network services	Telefónica
Voice recognition	Chatbot	Amadeus
	Smart contact Center via voice identification	Bankinter
	Chatbot smart assistant	BBVA
	Chatbot	CaixaBank
	Call Center for cognitive assistance, home voice assist	CaixaBank
	Chatbot integrated into the social media platform	IAG
	Virtual Assistant Meliá	Meliá
	Aura digital assistant	Telfónica
Valuation	Personalized offers for travelers	Amadeus
	Show offers from advertising partners	Amadeus
	Terminal recommendation	Telefónica
	Customer-based network services	Telefónica

Table 2 Percentage of companies that report within each category

Category	IBEX 35-2018 (%)	IBEX 35-2019 (%)
General statement	66	77
Applications	63	77
Unit	9	14
Ethics	11	26
Risk	6	6

Table 3 AI disclosure (% of companies)

Type of disclosure	IBEX 35-2018 (%)	IBEX 35-2019 (%)
No disclosure	23	9
Just general statements	11	11
1–2 categories	49	49
3 categories	14	26
$\geq$ 4 categories	3	6

Table 4 AI reporting activity (% of companies)

	No activity (%)	Activity			Risk and ethic concerns (%)
		Low (%)	Medium (%)	High (%)	
IBEX 35 2018	34	49	14	3	17
IBEX 35 2019	20	49	26	6	32

It shows clear evidence that companies stop having so many worthless mentions, and begin to declare more about specific issues and give more information about the uses they give to these new technologies.

Finally, Table 4 shows the level of reporting activity and its progress, it is worth noting that companies that either did not have mentions or only disclosed general matters have dropped by 14%, which means an increase in that amount in AI Reporting Activity. Highlighting the concern of companies for ethical and risk aspects. That is consistent with the results shown in the tables above.

5 Discussion

This study is a first approach to what companies report in their annual and sustainability reports on artificial intelligence, machine learning, deep learning and big data. It is a first analysis where we check how current disclosure is and we begin to think on how it should be, what issues companies should report about to clarify which products/services are using these technologies, in what aspects they are influencing the company and what possible uses are being given. Some standards on what and how companies have to report AI related matters in their non-financial information sections of their annual reports should be developed to guarantee both transparency and accountability for the stakeholders.

6 Conclusions, Limitations and Future Research

According to the results of this preliminary research we conclude the following: (1) AI reporting activity is growing as AI is becoming more used in companies, (2) It is growing in a non-structured way, (3) It will become more important to have a specific sub-section on artificial intelligence in the non-financial information section of the annual reports. (4) There is a need for clear guidelines on what information is relevant and mandatory for companies to report and what ethical principles or regulations these AI applications must comply with so that they can be carried out without negative implications for society.

A series of limitations should be recognized in this research, the most important of which would be that we focus only on the IBEX 35 companies, when we should cover a wide range of companies to obtain a more global sample. In addition, our methodology needs to be automated in order to carry out a more complete and efficient study. Even so, it is a good starting point for researchers and companies interested in digging deeper.

Appendix. AI Disclosure by Company

Company	General statement		Application		Unit/Lab		Risk/Impact		Ethic	
	2018	2019	2018	2019	2018	2019	2018	2019	2018	2019
ACCIONA	1	1	1	1	0	0	0	0	0	0
ACERINOX	1	1	1	1	0	0	0	0	0	0
ACS	1	1	0	1	0	0	0	0	0	0
AENA	–	–	–	–	–	–	–	–	–	–
AMADEUS	1	1	1	0	1	0	0	0	0	0
ARCELORMITTAL	1	1	1	1	0	0	0	0	0	0
B. SABADELL	–	1	–	0	–	0	–	0	–	1
B. SANTANDER	1	1	1	1	0	0	0	0	1	1
BANKIA	1	1	1	1	0	0	0	0	0	1
BANKINTER	1	1	1	1	0	0	1	1	0	0
BBVA	1	1	1	1	0	0	0	0	1	1
CAIXABANK	1	1	1	1	0	0	0	0	0	1
CELLNEX	1	1	0	0	0	0	0	0	0	0
CIE AUTOMOTIVE	1	1	0	0	0	0	0	0	0	0
ENAGAS	0	0	1	1	0	0	0	0	0	0
ENCE	–	0	–	1	–	0	–	0	–	0
ENDESA	1	1	1	1	0	0	0	0	0	1
FERROVIAL	1	1	1	1	0	0	0	0	0	0
GRIFOLS	–	–	–	–	–	–	–	–	–	–
IAG	0	1	1	1	0	1	0	0	0	0
IBERDROLA	1	1	1	1	0	0	0	0	0	0
INDITEX	1	1	1	1	0	0	0	0	0	0

(continued)

(continued)

Company	General statement		Application		Unit/Lab		Risk/Impact		Ethic	
	2018	2019	2018	2019	2018	2019	2018	2019	2018	2019
INDRA	1	1	0	1	0	0	0	0	1	1
INM COLONIAL	–	1	–	1	–	0	–	0	–	0
MAPFRE	0	0	1	1	0	0	0	0	0	0
MASMOVIL	0	1	1	0	0	0	0	0	0	0
MEDIASET	1	1	1	1	0	0	0	0	0	0
MELIA	1	1	1	1	0	0	0	0	0	0
MERLIN	–	0	–	1	–	0	–	0	–	0
NATURGY	1	1	1	1	0	0	0	0	0	0
RED ELECTRICA	1	1	0	1	0	1	0	0	0	1
REPSOL	1	1	1	1	1	1	0	0	0	0
SIEMENS GAMESA	–	0	–	1	–	1	–	0	–	0
TELEFONICA	1	1	1	1	1	1	1	1	1	1
VISCOFAN	–	–	–	–	–	–	–	–	–	–
	23	27	22	27	3	5	2	2	4	9

References

1. Al-Shaer, H. (2020). Sustainability reporting quality and post-audit financial reporting quality: Empirical evidence from the UK. *Business Strategy and the Environment, 29*(6), 2355–2373. https://doi.org/10.1002/bse.2507
2. ArcelorMittal. (2019). Integrated report. Retrieved from https://corporate.arcelormittal.com/sustainability.
3. Bankinter. 2019. Annual report. Retrieved from https://webcorporativa.bankinter.com/www2/corporativa/en/inf_financiera_cnmv/informacion_financiera/memoria/2019.
4. Bonsón, E., & Lavorato, D. (2019). La inteligencia artificial en las empresas del IBEX 35. *Revista AECA, 128*, 127–129
5. Data Ethics Commission of the Federal Government (2019). *Opinion of the data ethics commission*. Retrieved from www.datenethikkommission.de.
6. European Commission (2018). *Artificial intelligence. A European perspective*. Retrieved from https://ec.europa.eu/jrc/en/publication/artificial-intelligence-european-perspective.
7. European Commission (2020). White Paper—On Artificial Intelligence—A European approach to excellence and trust. Brussels.
8. Hao, K. (2019). *In 2020, let's stop ai ethics-washing and actually do something*. Retrieved from https://www.technologyreview.com/2019/12/27/57/ai-ethics-washing-time-to-act/.
9. Hickok, M. (2020). Lessons learned from AI ethics principles for future actions. *AI and Ethics, 1*(1), 41. https://doi.org/10.1007/s43681-020-00008-1.
10. Richarson, A., & Kachler, M. (2017). University sustainability reporting: a review of the literature and development of a model. In J. Arevalo, S. Mitchell (Eds.), *Handbook of sustainability in management education* (pp. 385–405). https://doi.org/10.4337/9781785361241.00027.
11. Romero, S., Ruiz, S., & Fernandez-Feijoo, B. (2018). Sustainability reporting and stakeholder engagement in Spain: Different instruments, different quality. *Business Strategy and the Environment, 28*(1), 221–232. https://doi.org/10.1002/bse.2251
12. Telefónica (2018). Nuestros principios de Inteligencia Artificial. Retrieved from https://www.telefonica.com/es/web/negocio-responsable/nuestros-compromisos/principios-ia.
13. Telefónica (2019). Integrated report. Retrieved from https://www.telefonica.com/en/web/about_telefonica/publications/annual-reports.

Economic Effects of Artificial Intelligence Applications

Maxim Vlasov

Abstract The paper aims to systematize economic effects of using artificial intelligence. The study deals with various approaches to defining the concept of artificial intelligence and identifies their major advantages and disadvantages. Having performed an in-depth analysis, the author gives a broader interpretation of the concept of artificial intelligence. The research results allow framing the concept of artificial intelligence economics, which gives a new avenue for research into the impact of artificial intelligence on the economy. The research focuses on the economic effects of artificial intelligence, discusses the prospects for the use of artificial intelligence and its impact on the global economy, and identifies the negative factors that governments and business leaders should minimize. The theoretical analysis of literature shows that the problem is gaining in popularity. At the same time, there is lack of attention to a number of methodological issues related to the modification of artificial intelligence models that require further research.

Keywords Artificial intelligence · Economic effect · Economics · Models of artificial intelligence

1 Introduction

Starting from the middle of the eighteenth century till the nineteenth century, the world witnessed the industrial revolution which allowed for a transition from manual labor to machinery and building large-scale plants. All that led to the industrialization of society.

In the middle of the twentieth century, Western countries gave rise to new development trends, which made it possible to speak about the transition from industrial to postindustrial society. The main features of postindustrial society include the transition of the economy from manufacturing goods to the creation of services.

M. Vlasov (✉)
Institute of Economics of the Ural Branch of the Russian Academy of Sciences, Moskovskaya St. 29, 620014 Ekaterinburg, Russian Federation

Ural Federal University, Mira St. 19, 620002 Ekaterinburg, Russian Federation

V. Kumar et al. (eds.), *Digital Transformation in Industry*, Lecture Notes in Information Systems and Organisation 44, https://doi.org/10.1007/978-3-030-73261-5_15

Now, one can see ongoing discussions and disputes concerning the fourth industrial revolution. There is an opinion that it is nothing but the continuation of the third industrial revolution or rational continuation of mankind's movement to the top of civilization development: in other words—progress.

Artificial intelligence is the basis for identifying the new phase of the industrial revolution, whereas intelligent services act as the main market of industrial relations. The new concept is based on the use of cyber-physical systems that combine program and computer technologies, with the help of which they can adapt to their environment, analyze incoming information, and react to it.

Artificial intelligence is a catalyst for further development of technologies and improvement of human life and the key to solving mysteries of the twenty-first century. It is important to point out the boundaries and opportunities for applying new technologies in solving intelligent tasks. Therefore, the current research aims to present a systematization of economic models of applying artificial intelligence.

2 Artificial Intelligence Economics

The role of artificial intelligence in business and the international economy can hardly be overestimated, taking into account the developments in this sphere and the growing spread of products and services used in everyday life. All this stimulates the idea that artificial intelligence can lead to radical changes in people's lifestyle, highlights its role in production and the speed of industrial progress.

Technoscience and convergent technologies have a significant influence on the human world, which is formed as an interactive, adaptive, and intelligent information-technological environment for human existence. New technologies and software based on them become interrelated; robotics, computers, and artificial intelligence are combined.

Artificial intelligence is defined in different ways: as the ability of intelligent systems to perform complex tasks; as science and technology of creating intelligent machines and software. These definitions reflect the notion of artificial intelligence which, on the one hand, is a science of creating man-like machines and, on the other hand, a feature of computation technology. Currently, the notion of "artificial intelligence" has exceeded the boundaries of the initial definition; it is a comprehensive concept including several modern technologies and broadening the reach of computer technologies.

Artificial intelligence is a system first developed in the twentieth century. In the twenty-first century, it has become one of the most relevant and debated topics attracting attention of the general public, developers, large corporations, and governments of several countries. This has led to an increase in the artificial intelligence sector in the market but what is the most important—to a large number of innovative and practically applied systems. A number of artificial intelligence systems used in the organization of different business spheres demonstrate high efficacy, quick cost recovery, and evident advantages as compared to previous methods of solving applied tasks.

Despite a considerable number of developments in this sphere, researchers note that currently no universally acknowledged definition of artificial intelligence is approved by all specialists working in this sphere [9].

Several authors broadly define artificial intelligence as a computerized system demonstrating behavior that is widely believed to require the presence of intelligence. Other authors define artificial intelligence as a system able to solve complex tasks and undertake necessary actions to attain its goals irrespective of conditions.

It is believed that artificial intelligence is related to the creation of programmed machines capable of doing things that supposedly require a certain level of intelligence.

The main challenge in designing a precise and universal definition for artificial intelligence is that there is no universal understanding of what intelligence is.

The term "weak artificial intelligence" is used to emphasize that it is limited to one established task, for example, defining the risks of blindness for people with eye diseases or being used as a linguistic and translating device.

When artificial intelligence is developed for a larger scope of implementation or for more efficacy, it is called "strong" [5].

The lack of clarity in definitions means that the term "artificial intelligence" has become a widely used combination for defining a whole range of programs, algorithms, and networks used to achieve a variety of purposes.

Let us look at some of the existing definitions of artificial intelligence.

Ray Kurzweil comes to the interpretation of artificial intelligence as the art of creating machines performing functions requiring intelligence when implemented by humans [8].

Elaine Rich and Kevin Knight define artificial intelligence as "the science of teaching computers to do things at which people excel them at present" [10].

Richard Bellman interprets artificial intelligence via the notion of automation of "activities associated with human thinking, that is, such actions as decision-making, problem-solving, and learning" [4].

Stuart Russel and Peter Norvig mention four main approaches to defining artificial intelligence [11]:

- the approach, which takes human thinking as the basis, meaning that artificial intelligence should be able to implement thinking activities resembling human ones, such as making decisions, solving problems, and learning;
- the approach, which is based on human behavior: artificial intelligence should be able to perform functions which require intelligence from people;
- the approach based on rational thinking;
- the approach based on rational behavior.

The difference of approaches to defining artificial intelligence, as well as the rapid development of technologies in this sphere, makes it difficult to come to one universally acknowledged definition. To formulate the most satisfactory notion, let

Table 1 Artificial intelligence notion

Author	Definition	Remarks
Averkin et al. [2]	Artificial intelligence is usually described as an information and calculation system aimed at solving various intelligent tasks imitating natural (human) ways of thinking, that is, a system that demonstrates functions of human intelligence	lAn almost complete definition, however lacking the part about "strong" artificial intelligence which can achieve or even excel the level of human intelligence
Antipov and Gladilin [1]	This is a scientific area where tasks of hardware or software modeling of those human activities which are traditionally considered intelligent ones are stated and solved	Nothing is mentioned about the ability to learn, self-education, tasks solved with the help of information and computation systems
Benhamou [3]	Artificial intelligence is defined as a combination of technologies for solving cognitive tasks fulfilled by people with the use of information processing devices	The definition is given only for "weak" artificial intelligence which performs only certain tasks and is limited by them

us choose the four most widespread definitions and analyze their advantages and disadvantages, presenting conclusions in Table 1.

Having analyzed the above-mentioned notions and discussed the strong and weak points of each definition, one can offer a more precise interpretation of artificial intelligence.

Artificial intelligence is an informational and computational system capable of learning or self-development. In the framework of this system, intelligent tasks are stated and solved with human methods of thinking.

To define the notion of artificial intelligence economics, it is also necessary to clarify the concept of microeconomics.

Kozyrev [7] sees microeconomics as a part of economic theory studying the behavior of economic actors in the system of the market economy.

According to Kleiner [6], microeconomics is the economics of branch markets from the point of view of companies' interaction.

Having looked at different approaches to defining the term "microeconomics", one can suggest the following definition:

Microeconomics is part of economic science studying relations between economic agents acting and individual local markets.

Having analyzed all the above-mentioned arguments and definitions of artificial intelligence and microeconomics, it is possible to formulate the idea of artificial intelligence economics:

Artificial intelligence economics is a complex economics structure based on the calculation and information system aimed at solving intelligent tasks.

3 Typology of Artificial Intelligence Description Models

The random forest model can be improved by using the knowledge artificial intelligence model as this model has a huge amount of information from Big Data and organizational data (Table 2).

Formula modification:

$$f = \frac{1}{B}\sum_{b=1}^{B} f_b(x') + \sum BigData + \sum KnowledgeManagment \quad (1)$$

Therefore, the random forest model gets more input data for processing multiple supplementary branches and the precision of solving given tasks is improved.

4 Conclusions

The conducted theoretic research aimed at systematizing the economic consequences of applying artificial intelligence provided the following results.

First, the author looked into different approaches to defining the notion of artificial intelligence, identified their advantages and shortcomings to present one's own broader definition of artificial intelligence.

Second, for the first time in economic literature, the author looked into the concept of artificial intelligence economics allowing further research in this area. Based on the results of this work, the author presented the concept of artificial intelligence economics opening a new dimension for studying the influence of artificial intelligence on economics.

Third, the author thoroughly studied the typology of artificial intelligence description models. The article presents the author's artificial intelligence model based on the knowledge models of random forest and manual intelligence. This model allows broadening the scope of solution search for a particular program and decreasing the share of mistakes in decision-making.

Table 2 Typology of artificial intelligence description models

Model's title	Description	Remarks
Artificial neuron network (ANN) model	The ANN model is a powerful technique of machine learning aimed at imitating the brain structure. It is widely used in hydrology for improving the predictability of future hydrologic variables as it considers both linear and nonlinear structures In the general case, the basic structure of the ANN model consists of three layers (input, hidden, and output) The key aim of the ANN is to find the best weight parameters with the help of a learning algorithm. The algorithm of reverse mistake spread is most frequently used for teaching the ANN by means of regulating weight parameters between hidden and output layers in order to minimize output error. The optimal number of hidden units can be defined by trial and error methods as there is no precise method of identifying the number of hidden units. The overall process of the ANN boils down to designing a model that would minimize the mistakes in the learning kit and then apply this model to the test case	Requires a large number of parameters. The result depends on the initialization figures; it is necessary to teach the network repeatedly and choose a quality configuration. Besides, there are several differences in the complexity of the given data evaluation algorithm
Random forest (RF) model	The RF model is a modern technique of machine learning that presents a non-parametric regression model of a white box. For the regression, the RF model uses a learning algorithm based on constructing multiple solution trees on the basis of samples loaded from the teaching data set. The RF model is the most reliable method for processing combinations of nonlinear interactions between input and output variables RF starts from many samples of initial load which are randomly chosen from initial input variables. The solution tree is designed individually from the initially loaded samples. For each solution tree unit, relevant input variables are chosen by means of binary partitioning. The prognostication result can be obtained by uniting results from all trees	The drawback is the large size of obtained models because of the huge number of branches. However, it can effectively process data with a large number of variables

(continued)

Table 2 (continued)

Model's title	Description	Remarks
Artificial intelligence knowledge model	The model of artificial intelligence knowledge was developed based on the academic aspect. It was designed on the basis of theoretic research for providing artificial intelligence systems with all necessary data for making optimal and reassuringly right decisions without interacting with humans. Therefore, the set of available data and information on big data and organization knowledge management will be the core and the foundation of this approach. The knowledge model provides necessary data about organizational areas such as HR management, personnel development, efficacy management, change management, distance learning and data management, development of organization processes, business strategies, or policies and procedures. Big data symbolize processing with obtaining new information in a short period of time with a huge amount of data from different sources and of different quality. This data can be measured with meanings, performance indicators, competitor information, process data and key performance indicators (KPI), as well as e-mail notifications or external environment factors, and so on	Combining organizational data and Big Data, the artificial intelligence system can provide an optimal solution on top of the pyramid of the artificial intelligence knowledge model

Acknowledgements The reported study was funded by RFBR according to the research project No. 19-010-00850.

References

1. Antipov, M. A., & Gladilin, A. V. (2011). Artificial intelligence in the everyday life of modern man. *Conference collections SIC Sociosphere, 40*, 74–77
2. Averkin, A. N., Gaaze-Rapoport, M. G., & Pospelov, D. A. (1992). *Explanatory dictionary of artificial intelligence*. Moscow: Radio and Communications.
3. Benhamou, S. (2018). Quels impacts de l'intelligence artificielle sur l'avenir du travail? *Revue personel, 589*, 46–49
4. Bellman, R. E. (1978). *An introduction to artificial intelligence: can computers think?* San Francisco, CA: Boyd & Fraser Pub. Co.
5. Guihot, M., Matthew, A., & Suzor, N. (2017). Nudging robots: Innovative solutions to regulate artificial intelligence. *Vanderbilt Journal of Entertainment and Technology Law, 20*(2), 385–456
6. Kleiner, G. (2004). Nanoeconomics. *Voprosy Ekonomiki, 12*, 70–93
7. Kozyrev, V. M. (2007). *Fundamentals of the modern economy*. Moscow: Knoruss.
8. Kurzweil, R. (1990). *The age of intelligent machines*. Cambridge, MA: MIT Press.
9. Nilsson, N. J. (2009). *The quest for artificial intelligence: A history of ideas and achievements*. New York: Cambridge University Press.
10. Rich, E., & Knight, K. (1991). *Artificial intelligence*. New York: McGraw-Hill.
11. Russell, S. J., & Norvig, P. (1995). *Artificial intelligence: A modern approach*. Englewood Cliffs, N.J: Prentice Hall.

Industry 4.0-Specific Intellectual Capital and Its Impact on Human Capital and Value Added: Evidence from Russian Regions

Ilia M. Chernenko, Natalya R. Kelchevskaya, and Irina S. Pelymskaya

Abstract The paper aims to study the impact of systemic digitalization, reflected in the Industry 4.0 trend, on the creation of intellectual capital and value added in the regions of Russia. The methodology is based on regression analysis and comparison of statistical data to assess the regional impact of Industry 4.0-specific intellectual capital on the gross regional product and wages in Russian companies. The authors used official data from Rosstat and Higher School of Economics statistical databases on human capital and digitalization. The results of the study show that, on the one hand, digitalization in general and the components of Industry 4.0-specific intellectual capital make a moderate and significant contribution to the value added and revenue of manufacturing and service companies in Russian regions. On the other hand, the authors did not find a significant contribution of Industry 4.0 and digitalization in general to the differentiation of wages of Russian employees in comparison with traditional elements of human capital, such as education and work experience. The originality of the study lies in the fact that the authors developed a theory of Industry 4.0-specific intellectual capital, which can explain the creation of value added and returns from human capital at the level of regional enterprise ecosystems. The authors also propose models that support the assessment of the relationship between the implementation and development of such intellectual capital and the performance of companies.

Keywords Intellectual capital · Industry 4.0 · Russian Regions · Gross regional product · Labor market · Digitalization

1 Introduction

The intellectual capital research program has been in its fourth stage of development over the last few years. During this stage, the potential of network integration of organizations operating in connected ecosystems is revealed [19, 20]. These companies

I. M. Chernenko (✉) · N. R. Kelchevskaya · I. S. Pelymskaya
Ural Federal University, Mira St. 19, 620002 Ekaterinburg, Russian Federation
e-mail: i.m.chernenko@urfu.ru

V. Kumar et al. (eds.), *Digital Transformation in Industry*, Lecture Notes in Information Systems and Organisation 44, https://doi.org/10.1007/978-3-030-73261-5_16

seek to develop intellectual resource management strategies in line with stakeholders' expectations and increase the accountability and transparency of internal business processes. They operate in an interconnected technology environment and networked resource supply chains that support knowledge sharing, intellectual property creation, and business model innovation. This environment ultimately leads to the emergence of intellectual capital of a new quality. Network integration trends are associated with the development of a knowledge-based economy and, in practice, are caused by the promotion of digitalization used to maintain the competitiveness of all businesses. Managers believe digitalization is driving efficiency improvements in key areas: new revenue streams are created by expanding the customer base and product customization, costs are reduced by automating processes and shorter production cycles, and risk management is improved through unprecedentedly accurate predictive analytics and real-time data acquisition [13].

Industry 4.0 is a relevant trend that brings companies around the world closer to the practical implementation of next-generation digitalization based on cyber-physical technologies and big data analytics [8, 16]. Over the past decade, companies have developed a fairly strong practical understanding of Industry 4.0 as the platform for network interaction between suppliers and customers in the value chain, as well as the bundle of IT solutions embodied in products and services [16]. Companies following this trend will experience a profound transformation of internal and external socio-technical systems since digitalization will affect social (primarily related to accumulated human capital) and technical aspects. This leads to the transformation of existing business models aimed at supporting the overall goals of companies that are part of open ecosystems [21].

The digital revolution affects the redistribution of human and technical resources in production [10] and the processes of organizational learning [25], which together leads to the transformation of the existing and creation of new specific intellectual capital. First, cyber-physical elements of production systems lead to a decrease in intellectual routine (for example, when generating reports and performing analytical work) and contribute to the accumulation of technical competencies among employees, which leads to an increase in human capital returns. In modern companies, human and "artificial intellectual" capitals are increasingly competing in solving business problems [7]. Second, network integration and data mining together lead to the formation of structural capital, which is reflected in new instructions and work protocols, technological solutions that are being individualized within each specific company. The organizational structure and the logic of value creation in general are also being transformed. Third, the functioning of companies' ecosystems in Industry 4.0 through broadband Internet and cloud services for sharing knowledge and distributing digital capacities for joint use lead to the building of new strategic alliances between companies from completely different areas, which is reflected in the formation of relational capital.

The vision of companies as participants in digital ecosystems should have certain implications for the accumulation and use of intellectual capital at the national level and in the regional economic environment in general. Research on the implementation of Industry 4.0 at the national level showed varied results. For example, for

Brazilian manufacturers, core technologies of the fourth industrial revolution had a positive impact on organizational learning and operational performance, both at the level of local production teams and companies in general [25]. Chiarini et al. [4], using the example of Italian companies, show that Industry 4.0 has a critical influence on the production strategies of companies, providing a supportive function: five out of six strategies are implemented using network integration technologies, including "green" production strategies, "design-to-cost", integration of supply chains, servitization, and lean-production strategy [4]. The transformative role of Industry 4.0 is also evident in the developing economies. For example, trends of de-industrialization of traditional manufacturing companies in the Croatian Republic and the introduction of Industry 4.0 together will lead to structural changes in the labor market but will require investment in research and development and human capital. This trend emphasizes the need for economic regulators to introduce structural reforms in the field of production policy [24].

Russia is one of the countries with a developing digital economy. Over the past years, national digitalization programs have been approved. They are based on the ideas of the development of national intellectual capital: investments in personnel's technical competencies, formalized research, and development of digital infrastructure to support communication [27]. At the same time, the manufacturing sector in Russia remains fragmented in terms of Industry 4.0 implementation. In particular, network integration is difficult due to localized production chains in the regions, monopolization of resource bases and industries in general. Turovets and Vishnevskiy [26] note that in the Russian context, some companies, due to wide financial support from the government, are becoming pioneers of digitalization, since they have a significant impact on regional development [26]. Small and medium-sized companies are also becoming drivers of Industry 4.0 implementation, competing in the international markets for high-tech products. In such conditions, the study of digitalization and its impact on the processes of added value creation at the regional level and the analysis of consequences of implementing technologies specific for Industry 4.0 for the labor market become relevant.

In this article, using the case of Russian regions, the authors analyze the overall impact of digitalization and specific components of Industry 4.0, which form a qualitatively new intellectual capital, on value added and market value of human capital. The authors suppose that technological advances of Industry 4.0 are generating new components of intellectual capital that have a significant impact on productivity at regional and individual levels. Using regression analysis, the authors investigated the impact on the regional product and human capital of both advanced technologies-related and traditional factors that determine intellectual capital performance, such as the innovative activity of companies, accumulated education of employees, and indicators of digitalization (broadband Internet, the introduction of electronic document management, the use of enterprise resource planning (ERP) systems) and Industry 4.0-specific (use of radio frequency identification (RFID) technologies and cloud services).

2 Industry 4.0-Specific Intellectual Capital: Literature Review and Hypothesis Development

The impact of digitalization on productivity in various sectors of the economy has been the subject of in-depth research for the past several decades [3]. Studies show that the effectiveness of investments in information technology and digitalization is quite difficult to trace in isolation from other factors. It is rational to introduce a system of indicators that would reflect the adoption depth of technological solutions to analyze the contribution of individual factors [13]. Besides, information and digital technologies themselves constitute a platform not only for overcoming organizational routines but also for creating organizational and product innovations [28]. They ensure the education level of employees and their qualifications, the development of intellectual property [14]. This section will consider the impact of Industry 4.0 on the creation and use of specific intellectual capital flows within companies. Since the technological features of cyber-physical elements and data analysis systems mediate the implementation of new formalized intellectual resources, they affect the creation of structural and relational capital, as well as the competencies of employees, and, therefore, their human capital.

Industry 4.0 is considered in the literature as a systematic view of practical digitalization. It is a set of design principles and technological trends such as cyber-physical systems, digital twins, additive manufacturing, and big data mining (for example, based on cloud services) that support service orientation, individualization, modularity, virtualization, decentralization, etc. [8]. Technological solutions in Industry 4.0 primarily affect the transformation of the physical appearance of manufacturing companies by building intensive interconnections between objects of the internal environment (machinery and equipment), company employees, and external stakeholders (primarily customers and suppliers) [29]. Infrastructure changes also affect value chains, which start to operate on a network basis. Companies unite, working according to unified data exchange standards, and create a common field for the exchange of knowledge regarding technological development and marketing strategy [18]. Significant changes also apply to components of intellectual capital, such as structural, human, and relational capital.

Structural capital of Industry 4.0. Elements of cyber-physical systems, based on RFID technologies, various sensors, machine sensors, middleware, and advanced transport equipment, allow the formation of vast streams of data and information that enable predictive analytics with unprecedented accuracy and provide insights in the field of strategic resource planning [8, 12]. Formalized knowledge of the manufacturing environment is collected in real time by ERP systems and other intelligent business systems and forms structural capital specific to Industry 4.0. It represents the results of intelligent data analytics that can be used to make decisions. Unlike traditional automated companies, such structural capital makes it possible to adapt to the production environment in a shorter period, to support elementary machine learning (for example, the so-called "artificial intellectual capital" [7]) to improve quality and make autonomous decisions on capacity allocation, replacement, and repair of equipment [9]. Support for the accumulation and use of the structural capital of Industry 4.0 in operating activities is carried out through the use of relevant technologies, such as smartphones and other smart devices, which can be used to adjust and control the operation of cyber-physical systems [9].

The structural capital of Industry 4.0 accumulates within companies in the long run. For example, big data can be considered as a source of business intelligence, which can be used not only in the operational perspective but also for making strategic, long-term decisions. Companies can analyze text, audio, and video data accumulated over several years, as well as Internet resources to form intellectual insights in the field of production, marketing, research, and development [11]. Big data analytics creates greater transparency in business processes by exposing areas of the organizational continuum where there is room for experimentation, improving the effectiveness of solutions by reducing human error, and offering platforms for innovative business models, products, and services [6]. Thus, Industry 4.0-specific structural capital generates an additional income stream for companies by increasing the business environment transparency and improving the quality of decisions.

Relational capital of Industry 4.0. The network integration of companies using Industry 4.0 also determines the formation of new strategic alliances of companies, which are combined into network structures to create added value. Ecosystems of companies imply the sharing of intellectual resources, digital goal-setting in the distribution of resources and production sites [15]. For example, cloud services allow companies to share computing powers, support information exchange, and regulation of infrastructure and key business processes [8]. Integration with suppliers and buyers also allows the acquisition of universal resources to fulfill highly customized customer orders through e-commerce. Unlike organizations that maintain a mechanistic view of relationships with key stakeholders underpinning value delivery processes, Industry 4.0 companies take an organic approach to organizing knowledge exchange and creating collaborative communities, motivating their partners to build long-term alliances [28].

Practical use of Industry 4.0 network technologies is possible due to technological advances such as broadband Internet, cloud technologies, and external electronic document management systems [12]. Taken together, these technologies reduce the level of the organizational intellectual routine associated with the preparation, sorting, and selection of information [28]. The freed-up time of employees is used effectively to solve the problem of matching the process of creating value to the real needs of customers. Employees of small and medium-sized companies spend more time on dialogue with the client, overcoming the limitations necessary to prepare preliminary technical information, and concentrate on offering innovative solutions [16]. These capabilities of Industry 4.0, which are reflected in the configuration of business models in terms of value delivery mechanisms, improve the company's image and business reputation, creating an additional stream of revenue from new customers and meeting their individualized needs in a strategic perspective. Thus, one can assume that Industry 4.0 forms specific elements of structural and relational capital, which in turn affect regional and local performance and put forward the first hypothesis:

H1. Industry 4.0 stimulates the creation of highly effective structural and relational intellectual capital, which affects the financial performance of companies and added value in the region.

Human capital of Industry 4.0. Digitalization has a significant impact on the social aspects of the working environment, and therefore on the accumulation and use of human capital; it transforms jobs, frees up the labor force, and creates new professions [22]. Intellectualization and digitalization in general allow employees to improve the efficiency of work and decision-making due to the ability to process significant amounts of information. However, they also cause destructive precedents, reducing the competitiveness of workers in low-tech companies [22]. The impact of Industry 4.0 is also reflected in the competencies of workers: in the coming years, the use of cyber-physical systems and data mining technologies will require systemic analytical skills, active learning, and problem-oriented thinking [5].

Human capital specific to Industry 4.0 is obtained due to an increase in employee engagement and job satisfaction by reducing intellectual routine, ensuring a work-life time balance, and high employee autonomy [22]. Workers become more competitive in terms of stakeholder value creation and can qualify for higher wages in the labor market. Industry 4.0-related human capital also requires working experience with cyber-physical systems and data mining technologies, which is more likely to be obtained in regions where companies use the technologies and principles of the fourth industrial revolution. Thus, one can assume that, at the individual level, Industry 4.0 can stimulate additional returns from human intellectual capital in regions with greater systemic digitalization and put forward a second hypothesis:

H2. Industry 4.0 stimulates the creation of highly productive human intellectual capital in the labor market, which demonstrates increased returns in a region where companies are actively using cyber-physical systems.

3 Research Methods and Data

The authors used regression analysis to test the proposed hypotheses. The strength and significance of the relationship between indicators were determined based on the interpretation of coefficients and quality indicators of multiple regression equations. The dependent variables were performance indicators such as employee wages, gross regional product (GRP), and total sales of companies in the region. The independent variables included indicators of specific intellectual capital and control variables, which indicated general digitalization, innovation activity, and GRP.

Measurement of value added and human capital. The economic performance of companies at the regional level was measured based on two indicators, namely the GRP and the total turnover of companies (sales proceeds excluding indirect taxes). The GRP is value added by organizations in the region in all sectors of production and services; it excludes internal turnover, which reflects intermediate consumption [17]. The turnover of companies represents the total revenue of all companies in the region for the year, excluding small organizations, budget organizations, banks, insurance, and other financial and credit organizations (SAL). Wages were measured based on gross individual income net of taxes for a calendar year (W). To measure the effects of Industry 4.0 on human capital, the authors used the indicators of relational and structural capital and general digitalization, which will be presented below. They are expected to have an external impact on productivity in the region. Workers will be trained more intensively in those regions where a larger percentage of enterprises use these technologies, increasing the return on human capital in general. The authors used indicators of human capital from the standard Mincer earnings function [2], such as the number of years of education accumulated (HC_EDU), general (HC_GEN), and special experience (HC_SP), as control variables when testing the human capital hypothesis. For control, respondents' gender (GEND) was added to the equations,it was also specified whether they had subordinates (BOSS) (dummy variables).

Measurement of Industry 4.0 specific intellectual capital and digitalization, innovation activity. The approaches described below were used to measure the components of intellectual capital and performance indicators discussed in the literature review at the regional and individual levels. The authors used the adoption rate of cloud (w_CLOUD) and RFID technologies (w_RFID) and indicators of the spread of electronic sales and electronic data interchange (EDI) systems, external electronic document management (w_EL_SALE). They reflect the percentage of organizations in the region that have implemented these technologies. Cloud and RFID technologies are indicators of structural capital since they allow working with formalized flows of information and data, which will then be converted into knowledge and customer value. E-commerce is a component of relational capital because it supports value creation in relationships with consumers. Besides, general digitalization control variables such as broadband Internet use (w_INT) and integrated ERP systems (w_ERP) were introduced into the equations. They were calculated as the percentage of companies that implemented these technologies. To control when testing the first hypothesis, the authors used the level of enterprises' innovative activity (INNO_ACT). This is the number of organizations in the region that are introducing organizational, marketing, and product innovations.

Data. For the study, the authors integrated several sources of statistical data for 2017, 2018, and 2019. Data from the source [17] for 85 regions were used to determine GRP, company turnover, and innovation activity. Data from the source [1] were used to determine indicators of intellectual capital specific to Industry 4.0 and general indicators of digitalization. The source [23], the Russia Longitudinal Monitoring Survey of the Higher School of Economics, was used to obtain individual data on wages and indicators of human capital. For this source, digitalization indicators from the source [1] were calculated according to the regional characteristics of the respondents.

Models. To test the hypotheses, the authors used direct and lagged effects. That is, the effects of the use of technologies were expected to appear over a year. In the first model, the region acted as an observation unit, in the second one – as a specific person in the region. Models of the following type were initially proposed (a is a constant; the index means the year to which the indicator belongs):

$$
\begin{aligned}
GRP_{\mathrm{t}} = \exp\{a_1 &+ w\_CLOUD_{\mathrm{t},(\mathrm{t}-1)} + w\_RFID_{\mathrm{t},(\mathrm{t}-1)} \\
&+ w\_EL\_SALE_{\mathrm{t},(\mathrm{t}-1)} + w\_INT_{\mathrm{t},(\mathrm{t}-1)}
\end{aligned}
$$

$$+w\_ERP_{t,(t-1)} + INNO\_ACT_{t,(t-1)}\}; \quad (1)$$

$$SAL_t = \exp\{a_2 + w\_CLOUD_{t,(t-1)} + w\_RFID_{t,(t-1)} + w\_EL\_SALE_{t,(t-1)} + w\_INT_{t,(t-1)} + w\_ERP_{t,(t-1)} + INNO\_ACT_{t,(t-1)}\}; \quad (2)$$

$$W_t = \exp\{a_3 + GEND_t + BOSS_t + HC\_EDU_t + HC\_GEN_t + HC\_SP_t + w\_CLOUD_{t,(t-1)} + w\_RFID_{t,(t-1)} + w\_EL\_SALE_{t,(t-1)} + w\_INT_{t,(t-1)} + w\_ERP_{t,(t-1)} + INNO\_ACT_{t,(t-1)}\}. \quad (3)$$

In total, six models were used to test the hypotheses. The authors calculated the effects on *GRP* and *SAL* only for 2018, considering the direct effect of 2018 and the lag effect of 2017. To test the hypothesis about wages, data from 2018 and 2019 on wages in Russian regions were used. Due to the limited statistics on digitalization and Industry 4.0, only lag effects were calculated for human capital models for 2019. Multiple linear regression models after logarithm of both parts and considering direct and lagged effects were as follows:

$$\ln GRP_{2018} = a_1 + w\_CLOUD_{2018} + w\_RFID_{2018} + w\_EL\_SALE_{2018} + w\_INT_{2018} + w\_ERP_{2018} + INNO\_ACT_{2018} \quad (4)$$

$$\ln GRP_{2018} = a_2 + w\_CLOUD_{2017} + w\_RFID_{2017} + w\_EL\_SALE_{2017} + w\_INT_{2017} + w\_ERP_{2017} + INNO\_ACT_{2017} \quad (5)$$

$$\ln SAL_{2018} = a_3 + w\_CLOUD_{2018} + w\_RFID_{2018} + w\_EL\_SALE_{2018} + w\_INT_{2018} + w\_ERP_{2018} + INNO\_ACT_{2018} \quad (6)$$

$$\ln SAL_{2018} = a_4 + w\_CLOUD_{2017} + w\_RFID_{2017} + w\_EL\_SALE_{2017} + w\_INT_{2017} + w\_ERP_{2017} + INNO\_ACT_{2017} \quad (7)$$

$$\ln W_{2018} = a_5 + GEND_{2018} + BOSS_{2018} + HC\_EDU_{2018} + HC\_GEN_{2018} + HC\_SP_{2018} + w\_CLOUD_{2018}$$

$$+ w\_RFID_{2018} + w\_EL\_SALE_{2018} + w\_INT_{2018} + w\_ERP_{2018} + INNO\_ACT_{2018} \quad (8)$$

$$\ln W_{2019} = a_6 + GEND_{2019} + BOSS_{2019} + HC\_EDU_{2019} + HC\_GEN_{2019} + HC\_SP_{2019} + w\_CLOUD_{2018} + w\_RFID_{2018} + w\_EL\_SALE_{2018} + w\_INT_{2018} + w\_ERP_{2018} + INNO\_ACT_{2018} \quad (9)$$

4 Results and Discussion

At the first stage, the authors assessed the distribution of digitalization indicators, both general and specific for Industry 4.0, across Russian regions on average and determined the overall level of digitalization (Table 1). Russian companies in general are characterized by a relatively moderate, close to low level of digitalization. Indicators of business digitalization for the countries of the European Union in 2018 were also provided based on the source [1]. For comparison, four countries were selected, each of which is in a separate cluster in terms of the depth of digitalization implementation in the business environment. For example, Latvia is in the same cluster as Russia, and the data for this country are the most indicative for comparison. Russian companies have succeeded in introducing cloud technologies that support data processing technologies relevant to Industry 4.0, the distribution of computing power, and digital data storage. On the one hand, in terms of other indicators of Industry 4.0 implementation and digitalization in general, Russian companies are inferior to competitors and partners from developed countries. On the other hand, positive digitalization dynamics are observed: a significantly larger number of companies in 2018 compared to 2017 noted an increase in the frequency of electronic sales implementation and usage of electronic document management related to customers and suppliers, as well as government authorities.

Table 2 shows the regression coefficients for the first four proposed models. The analysis of the coefficients allows concluding that the Russian regions received the greatest "digital dividends" in 2018 since the digitalization structure that took place in 2017 explains a significant part of value added exactly in 2018. For the period under review, one can conclude that digitalization in general (and in the particular case of Industry 4.0) yields returns over a period of more than one year. The greatest impact is exerted by the introduction of ERP systems, cloud and RFID technologies. It is obvious that the redistribution of the digitalization structure in the regions, value added and sales in 2018 did not bring a direct significant economic effect. The evaluation of the control variable effects showed a significant result in three of four models—innovative activity makes a positive contribution to the added value generated in the regions and affects the indicators of companies' revenue.

Table 1 Descriptive statistics for variables in models to test the first hypothesis and international comparisons of digitalization indicators

	2018		2017		Illustrative comparisons for 2018 in EU countries			
	Mean	Std. dev	Mean	Std. dev	Belgium	Austria	Latvia	Hungary
Logarithm *GRP*	27.0	1.2	–	–	n.a	n.a	**n.a**	n.a
Share of organizations using broadband Internet, % [w_INT]	85.5	5.7	83.0	7.2	98	98	**99**	91
Share of organizations using cloud services, % [w_CLOUD]	24.6	4.6	21.9	4.9	40	23	**15**	18
Share of organizations using RFID technologies, % [w_RFID]	4.9	1.2	4.5	1.2	21	19	**9**	7
Share of organizations using ERP systems, % [w_ERP]	11.8	3.9	10.5	3.9	54	40	**25**	14
Share of organizations engaged in electronic sales/extranet, EDI systems, in the total number of organizations, % [w_EL_SALE]	15.3	7.3	8.9	3.6	30	18	**13**	15
Level of innovative activity of organizations, as a percentage of the total number of organizations [INNO_ACT]	11.5	5.8	9.8	6.3	68	62	**30**	29

(continued)

Table 1 (continued)

	2018		2017		Illustrative comparisons for 2018 in EU countries			
	Mean	Std. dev	Mean	Std. dev	Belgium	Austria	Latvia	Hungary
Number of regions	85		85		n.a	n.a	**n.a**	n.a

Thus, one can conclude that **the first hypothesis was partially confirmed**. First, there is no stable relationship between digitalization, both general and specific to Industry 4.0, value added, and sales revenue in all the periods considered. Second, there are no direct effects of digitalization on the GRP and revenue of companies in the regions of Russia for a period of less than one year. Third, the specific intellectual capital arising from the application of Industry 4.0 technologies is created only in certain technological areas, such as cloud and RFID technologies. At the same time, the most significant effect is obtained from the introduction of the traditional field of digitalization during the "third industrial revolution"—ERP systems, which, however, are becoming significant components of the Industry 4.0 digital infrastructure. All the results obtained indicate the low significance of the external effects of Industry 4.0 and digitalization in general in the regions where they were implemented. They have a moderate impact on the structure of regional incomes and companies' revenues in a period of more than a year. Therefore, it is *impossible to conclude that stable ecosystems of companies able to jointly use structural and relational capital have formed in Russian regions.*

The authors also examined how Industry 4.0-specific intellectual capital affected the labor market and the use of human capital in Russian regions. For the study, only employed respondents working in organizations were selected. In general, the Russian regions are characterized by a high level of accumulated education. The majority of respondents have a general secondary and at least secondary vocational education (descriptive statistics for the variables are given in Table 3). Moreover, the structure of digitalization, calculated based on the regional characteristics of the RLMS HSE respondents, is comparable to the previously analyzed data for the regions. The same applies to the level of innovative activity of companies in the regions. The gender and professional structure of the samples are also comparable with each other in 2019 and 2018: more than 50% of the respondents are women, about 20% of the respondents are managers with one or more subordinates.

The regression coefficients for the two proposed models used to test the second hypothesis are shown in Table 4. The estimation of the coefficients allows concluding that some digitalization indicators make a moderately negative contribution to wages in Russian regions, and therefore, a decrease in the return on accumulated human capital is observed. For example, if each year of education brings an advantage in the form of income growth by 6.6–7.7%, then an increase in digitalization by 1% in the region of presence may result in a decrease in earnings by 1–2%. In general,

Table 2 Unstandardized regression coefficients for testing the first hypothesis

Models	1.1. (effects of 2018 in 2018 on GRP)		1.2. (effects of 2017 in 2018 on GRP)		1.3. (effects of 2018 in 2018 on SAL)		1.4. (effects of 2017 in 2018 on SAL)	
Variables	Coeff	t	Coeff	t	Coeff	t	Coeff	t
a (constant)	24.241***	11.979	25.569***	23.089	22.374***	8.656	24.300**	18.824
w_CLOUD (structural capital)	– 0.026	– 0.786	0.057***	2.637	– 0.038	– 0.882	0.054**	2.150
w_RFID (structural capital)	0.177	1.265	0.211**	2.069	0.256	1.435	0.332***	2.789
w_EL_SALE (relational capital)	– 0.004	0.462	– 0.037	– 1.285	– 0.004	– 0.189	– 0.064*	– 1.913
w_INT	0.018	0.705	– 0.028*	– 1.811	0.032	0.978	– 0.027	– 1.505
w_ERP	0.023	0.462	0.167***	4.976	0.034	0.548	0.243***	6.213
INNO_ACT	0.067***	3.092	0.007	0.504	0.111***	3.996	0.029*	1.708
R-square	0.183		0.559		0.264		0.669	
R-square, adj	0.121		0.525		0.208		0.644	
F-statistic	2.920**		16.503***		4.673***		26.325***	
Durbin-Watson	1.656		1.698		1.671		1.766	
Number of valid observations	85		85		85		85	

Note *significant at 10%; **significant at 5%; ***significant at 1%

Table 3 Descriptive statistics of variables in the model to test the second hypothesis

	2019		2018	
	Mean	Std. dev	Mean	Std. dev
Logarithm *W* (wage per year, ln RUR)	12.8	0.6	12.7	0.6
Gender male (Male = 1) [GEND]	0.47	0.5	0.49	0.5
Bosses (Boss = 1) [BOSS]	0.19	0.4	0.21	0.4
Special experience, years [HC_SP]	8.8	9.3	8.6	9.4
Years of education accumulated [HC_EDU]	13.5	2.0	13.4	2.0
General experience, years [HC_SP]	23.3	12.5	22.9	12.6
Share of organizations using broadband Internet, % [w_INT]	87.1	5.0	87.2	5.0
Share of organizations using cloud services, % [w_CLOUD]	24.9	4.3	24.9	4.2
Share of organizations using RFID technologies, % [w_RFID]	5.0	1.2	5.0	1.2
Share of organizations using ERP systems, % [w_ERP]	11.8	3.1	11.9	3.2
Share of organizations engaged in electronic sales/extranet, EDI systems, in the total number of organizations, % [w_EL_SALE]	16.3	4.5	16.3	4.5
Level of innovative activity of organizations, as a percentage of the total number of organizations [INNO_ACT]	15.3	8.0	15.0	7.9
Number of respondents	4353		4276	

this factor, in comparison with the traditional components of human capital, can be considered moderate or even economically insignificant.

Thus, one can conclude that **the second hypothesis is rejected**. First, the external effects from the general introduction of digitalization or technologies specific to Industry 4.0 did not form new stocks of human capital in the Russian regions in 2018 and 2019. Second, traditional factors of human capital, such as the level of accumulated education, general and special production experience, used as control variables, make a more significant, tangible contribution to the differentiation of wages in the labor market. The innovative activity of enterprises in the regions also makes a moderate positive contribution.

The research results allow concluding that digitalization, on the one hand, is at the initial stage of development in the Russian economy and has significant potential, on the other hand, its contribution to added value and the turnover of companies is very moderate. Statistically significant effects from digitalization will likely manifest themselves in the long term with a more detailed decomposition of the structure of regional incomes and the sectoral depth of digitalization implementation and, in particular, technologies specific to Industry 4.0.

Table 4 Unstandardized regression coefficients for testing the second hypothesis

Models	2.1. (effects of 2018 in 2018 on wages)		2.2. (effects of 2018 in 2019 on wages)	
Variables	Coeff	t	Coeff	t
a (constant)	9.973***	60.790	10.231***	62.287
GEND	0.238***	14.649	0.243***	15.124
BOSS	0.309***	14.906	0.324***	15.679
HC_EDU	0.075***	17.717	0.064***	15.252
HC_GEN	0.004***	5.643	0.003***	4.320
HC_SP	0.003***	2.762	0.003***	3.204
w_CLOUD	– 0.012***	– 4.428	– 0.014***	– 5.255
w_RFID	– 0.015	– 1.212	0.015	1.119
w_EL_SALE	– 0.008***	– 4.153	– 0.012***	– 6.314
w_INT	0.018***	9.302	0.018***	9.641
w_ERP	0.015***	2.961	0.002	0.346
INNO_ACT	0.013***	10.648	0.015***	11.508
R-square	0.223		0.212	
R-square, adj	0.221		0.210	
F-statistic	111.476***		106.358***	
Durbin-Watson	1.652		1.791	
Number of respondents	4276		4353	

Note *significant at 10%; **significant at 5%; ***significant at 1%

5 Conclusion

Digitalization has a significant impact on companies around the world, increasing competitiveness through increased transparency of business processes, improved control, and the ability to create customized products and services in an unprecedentedly short time. Industry 4.0 can be considered as a special case of the digitalization trend: this is the practice-oriented implementation of advanced information technologies based on cyber-physical and data analytics systems, which are designed to support the individualization of production, increase autonomy and creative decision-making. Technological advances in Industry 4.0 generate additional flows of intellectual capital, creating intangible resources based on unprecedented accuracy and speed of information processing, which determines a qualitatively new level of management decisions. The study has shown that theoretically it is possible to identify Industry 4.0-related flows of structural and relational capital, which affect value added in the regions, company revenues, and regional labor markets. In addition, one can assume that digitalization and the specific intellectual capital of Industry 4.0 have a significant impact on the accumulation and use of human capital in the Russian regions.

The results of the study made it possible to partially confirm the first hypothesis. Digitalization in general and the components of intellectual capital specific to Industry 4.0 make a moderate significant contribution to the added value and turnover of companies in Russian regions. The return on technology implementation has been observed for more than one year; ERP technologies have a significant impact, as well as the components of intellectual capital specific to Industry 4.0, which are formed through the use of cloud and RFID technologies. A more complex situation is observed when trying to assess the impact of digitalization on the Russian regional labor market. The second hypothesis of the study about the impact of Industry 4.0 on the labor market was rejected. Additional flows of intellectual capital arising from the practical implementation of Industry 4.0 do not have a tangible external effect on wages in the regions in comparison with internal factors of human capital, such as education and accumulated work experience. Russian regions are still at the initial stage of creating digital ecosystems. In modern conditions, those ecosystems are based primarily on the achievements of Industry 4.0. Therefore, regional external effects of digitalization and intellectual capital specific to Industry 4.0, estimated for 2018 and 2019 according to the official statistics and databases of the Higher School of Economics, are very moderate and insignificant.

The research results can be applied in the practice of companies and the development of regional policy to assess the impact of digitalization on the socio-economic development of Russian regions and to determine the maturity of the ecosystems of companies that actively follow the trends of Industry 4.0. The limitation of the study is a regional approach to studying the impact of digitalization, in which Industry 4.0 and the specific intellectual capital formed by it are considered as an external factor that determines the quality of the institutional environment in the regions and, accordingly, affects the added value and revenue of companies. In further research, it is necessary to more accurately consider the impact of the competencies formed among workers in the production and service sectors during the implementation of Industry 4.0 on the differentiation of wages. Further research can confirm the presence of Industry 4.0-specific human capital, which will be the source of people's advantages in the labor market. It is also advisable to investigate the impact of Industry 4.0 on the performance of individual companies, assessing the relationship between the implementation depth of cyber-physical systems and the added economic value for each organization.

References

1. Abdrakhmanova, G., Vishnevskiy, K., & Gokhberg, L. (2020). *Digital economy indicators in the Russian Federation: 2020 : Data book*. HSE. Retrieved from https://issek.hse.ru/mirror/pubs/share/387609461.PDF.
2. Björklund, A., & Kjellström, C. (2002). Estimating the return to investments in education: How useful is the standard Mincer equation? *Economics of Education Review, 21*(3), 195–210. https://doi.org/10.1016/S0272-7757(01)00003-6

3. Brynjolfsson, E., & Yang, S. (1996). Information technology and productivity: A review of the literature. *Advances in Computers, 43*(C), 179–214. https://doi.org/10.1016/S0065-2458(08)60644-0.
4. Chiarini, A., Belvedere, V., & Grando, A. (2020). Industry 4.0 strategies and technological developments. An exploratory research from Italian manufacturing companies. *Production Planning and Control, 31*(16), 1–14. https://doi.org/10.1080/09537287.2019.1710304.
5. Cijan, A., Jenič, L., Lamovšek, A., & Stemberger, J. (2019). How digitalization changes the workplace. *Dynamic Relationships Management Journal, 8*(1), 3–12. https://doi.org/10.17708/DRMJ.2019.v08n01a01.
6. Fosso Wamba, S., Akter, S., Edwards, A., Chopin, G., & Gnanzou, D. (2015). How 'big data' can make big impact: Findings from a systematic review and a longitudinal case study. *International Journal of Production Economics, 165*, 234–246. https://doi.org/10.1016/j.ijpe.2014.12.031
7. Gashenko, I. V., Khakhonova, N. N., Orobinskaya, I. V., & Zima, Y. S. (2020). Competition between human and artificial intellectual capital in production and distribution in Industry 4.0. *Journal of Intellectual Capital, 21*(4), 531–547. https://doi.org/10.1108/JIC-11-2019-0275.
8. Ghobakhloo, M. (2018). The future of manufacturing industry: a strategic roadmap toward Industry 4.0. *Journal of Manufacturing Technology Management, 29*(6), 910–936. https://doi.org/10.1108/JMTM-02-2018-0057.
9. Ibarra, D., Ganzarain, J., & Igartua, J. I. (2018). Business model innovation through Industry 4.0: A review. *Procedia Manufacturing, 22*, 4–10. https://doi.org/10.1016/j.promfg.2018.03.002.
10. Inshakova, A. O., Frolova, E. E., Rusakova, E. P., & Kovalev, S. I. (2020). The model of distribution of human and machine labor at intellectual production in industry 4.0. *Journal of Intellectual Capital, 21*(4), 601–622. https://doi.org/10.1108/JIC-11-2019-0257.
11. Jeble, S., Kumari, S., & Patil, Y. (2018). Role of big data in decision making. *Operations and Supply Chain Management: An International Journal, 11*(1), 36–44. https://doi.org/10.31387/oscm0300198.
12. Kosacka-Olejnik, M., & Pitakaso, R. (2019). Industry 4.0: state of the art and research implications. *Logforum, 15*(4), 478–485. https://doi.org/10.17270/J.LOG.2019.363.
13. Kotarba, M. (2017). Measuring digitalization—key metrics. *Foundations of Management, 9*(1), 123–138. https://doi.org/10.1515/fman-2017-0010
14. Lobova, S. V., Alekseev, A. N., Litvinova, T. N., & Sadovnikova, N. A. (2020). Labor division and advantages and limits of participation in creation of intangible assets in industry 4.0: Humans versus machines. *Journal of Intellectual Capital, 21*(4), 623–638. https://doi.org/10.1108/JIC-11-2019-0277.
15. Lokshina, I., Durkin, B., & Lanting, C. (2018). The IoT-and big data-driven data analysis services: KM, implications and business opportunities. *International Journal of Knowledge Management, 14*(4), 88–107. https://doi.org/10.4018/IJKM.2018100106
16. Müller, J. M. (2019). Business model innovation in small- and medium-sized enterprises: Strategies for industry 4.0 providers and users. *Journal of Manufacturing Technology Management, 30*(8), 1127–1142. https://doi.org/10.1108/JMTM-01-2018-0008.
17. Okladnikov, S. M., Boulgakova, N. S., & Gokhberg, L. M. (2019). Regions of Russia: Social and economic indicators 2019. Rosstat. Retrieved from https://rosstat.gov.ru/folder/210/document/47652.
18. Ricciotti, F. (2020). From value chain to value network: a systematic literature review. *Management Review Quarterly, 70*(2), 191–212. https://doi.org/10.1007/s11301-019-00164-7
19. Secundo, G., Dumay, J., Schiuma, G., & Passiante, G. (2016). Managing intellectual capital through a collective intelligence approach. *Journal of Intellectual Capital, 17*(2), 298–319. https://doi.org/10.1108/JIC-05-2015-0046
20. Secundo, G., Massaro, M., Dumay, J., & Bagnoli, C. (2018). Intellectual capital management in the fourth stage of IC research: A critical case study in university settings. *Journal of Intellectual Capital, 19*(1), 157–177. https://doi.org/10.1108/JIC-11-2016-0113
21. Sony, M., & Naik, S. (2020). Industry 4.0 integration with socio-technical systems theory: A systematic review and proposed theoretical model. *Technology in Society, 61*(1), 101248. https://doi.org/10.1016/j.techsoc.2020.101248.

22. The Future of Jobs Report 2018 (2018). Centre for the New Economy and Society. https://www3.weforum.org/docs/WEF_Future_of_Jobs_2018.pdf.
23. The Russia Longitudinal Monitoring Survey—Higher School of Economics (RLMS-HSE) (2020). Retrieved from https://www.hse.ru/rlms/.
24. Tomljanović, M., Grubišić, Z., & Kamenković, S. (2019). Deindustrialization and implementation of industry 4.0-case of the Republic of Croatia. *Journal of Central Banking Theory and Practice, 8*(3), 133–160. https://doi.org/10.2478/jcbtp-2019-0028.
25. Tortorella, G. L., Cawley Vergara, A. Mac, Garza-Reyes, J. A., & Sawhney, R. (2020). Organizational learning paths based upon industry 4.0 adoption: An empirical study with Brazilian manufacturers. *International Journal of Production Economics, 219*, 284–294. https://doi.org/10.1016/j.ijpe.2019.06.023.
26. Turovets, Y., & Vishnevskiy, K. (2019). Patterns of digitalisation in machinery-building industries: *Evidence from Russia. Engineering Management in Production and Services, 11*(4), 7–22. https://doi.org/10.2478/emj-2019-0029
27. Vasin, S., Gamidullaeva, L., Shkarupeta, E., Palatkin, I., & Vasina, T. (2018). Emerging trends and opportunities for Industry 4.0 development in Russia. *European Research Studies Journal, XXI*(3), 63–76. https://doi.org/10.35808/ersj/1044.
28. Wilkesmann, M., & Wilkesmann, U. (2018). Industry 4.0—organizing routines or innovations? *VINE Journal of Information and Knowledge Management Systems, 48*(2), 238–254. https://doi.org/10.1108/VJIKMS-04-2017-0019.
29. Xu, L. Da, Xu, E. L., & Li, L. (2018). Industry 4.0: State of the art and future trends. *International Journal of Production Research, 56*(8), 2941–2962. https://doi.org/10.1080/00207543.2018.1444806.

What Kind of Employees' Team is Necessary for Industrial Digital Transformation? Theoretical and Practical Analysis

Elena Kalabina, Olga Belyak, Vera G. Meister, and Aleksandra Revina

Abstract The article considers cross-functional teams as an alternative to the traditional team-building approach in industrial digital transformation. Based on the contextual analysis of the reasons for creating cross-functional teams, their polyphonic nature and exclusivity signs are revealed. The paper demonstrates particular importance of knowledge sharing in cross-functional teams for efficient work. Knowledge sharing among employees serves as a source for obtaining necessary and useful information and a condition for the successful functioning of cross-functional teams. The purpose of the study was to perform a comparative analysis of the influence of organizational and managerial factors on knowledge sharing in cross-functional teams. The academic environment of two universities in Russia and Germany was used as an example to determine the obstacles and conditions of this process. In the study, two groups of employees from Russian (Ekaterinburg) and German (Brandenburg an der Havel) universities were examined. The paper determines the degree of influence of various organizational and managerial factors on the intensity of knowledge sharing in cross-functional teams under the national context.

Keywords Cross-functional teams · Knowledge sharing · Organizational and managerial factors

1 Introduction

With the digital transformation of industry, there is a demand for who and how will carry out the innovation design processes.

E. Kalabina · O. Belyak (✉)
Ural State University of Economics, 8 Marta/Narodnoy Voli St. 62/45, 620144 Ekaterinburg, Russian Federation

V. G. Meister · A. Revina
Brandenburg University of Applied Sciences, Magdeburgerstr. 50, 14770 Brandenburg an der Havel, Germany

A. Revina
Technical University of Berlin, Straße des 17. Juni 135, 10623 Berlin, Germany

V. Kumar et al. (eds.), *Digital Transformation in Industry*, Lecture Notes in Information Systems and Organisation 44, https://doi.org/10.1007/978-3-030-73261-5_17

One possible way is cross-functional teams as an alternative to the traditional team-building approach in project management. It becomes evident that teams involved in innovation design are built differently from those engaged in typical business processes. Even in the case of modernization changes, the improvements are local but assimilate into all business processes. For such projects, it is enough to build a team with the necessary experts and clear standard roles, find a project manager, calculate a project budget, and wait for the results.

However, this team-building approach is not acceptable for transformation projects. They require a different view on team-building, different coordination processes of team members' actions, and knowledge sharing. Furthermore, transformation projects must be aligned with the organization's business model and the way of creating a new service or product that will affect not only locally but generally the whole organization.

Consequently, there are difficulties in determining: (i) which experts should be part of such a team, (ii) how to implement the processes of interaction between them effectively, (iii) how to set up the exchange and generation of knowledge in the team, (iv) how to manage risks, etc. At present, due to the specificity of their building, cross-functional teams are new agents of the industrial digital transformation [2].

2 Theoretical and Methodological Background

A cross-functional team can serve as a good springboard for overcoming structural and functional silos in an organization that hinder successful business communication [5]. Furthermore, cross-functional teams as a modern work practice allow not only increasing the mobility of functional units [9] but also obtaining a synergistic effect from the joint group activities of employees with different skills working on one task or project [8].

When using the cross-functional teams in the work organization, business leaders need to understand those characteristics inherent in such an approach, which allows the selection of the most effective employee management mechanisms.

The main difference between cross-functional teams and other team interaction types becomes clear from the very name. When working on a project, a cross-functional team "crosses" the adjacent functional areas. On the one hand, this characteristic is a strong advantage (for example, reducing errors in developing solutions due to a comprehensive approach). On the other hand, there is a cornerstone in creating and developing a sense of community in the team, establishing a highly effective knowledge sharing and collaboration. Cross-functional integration for project implementation based on cross-functional teams may require the organization's management to attract additional motivation experience, develop competencies, and improve team interaction [10].

Considering cross-functional teams (hereinafter, CFTs) from various viewpoints, one can see those signs of exclusivity that will allow for a more complete understanding of the possibilities and limitations of their use as well as methods and mechanisms of control.

Firstly, CFTs are project teams, i.e. they follow the standard methods and mechanisms of project management, go through the typical stages of formation, establishment and dissolution, and report to one (project) manager. Hereby, the manager's work in terms of team management aims to create successful interaction between team members and ensure the knowledge sharing process [6].

Secondly, CFT can be viewed as an organizational unit with a clear structure, hierarchy of subordination, and degree of responsibility. In terms of team building, the greatest importance is given to potential team members' soft competencies, for example, the ability to work in a team, flexibility of thinking, and openness to new ideas [1]. From the organizational structure perspective, the CFT is organized according to the principles of an adaptive design structure. At the same time, CFT is built into the organization's existing construct with a matrix type of organizational structure.

Thus, a CFT is a complex, adaptive, dynamic system that, making part of an organization, is organically integrated into its contexts and fulfills the innovative task set in the form of a project with clear resource boundaries (time, financial, organizational, work boundaries).

Thirdly, CFT can act as the basis of a knowledge management system in an organization, since the creation and use of these teams have an innovative focus and, therefore, serve to accept and disseminate new knowledge as well as develop absorptive capacity. Organizations' absorptive capacity is considered a key factor in achieving and maintaining a competitive advantage [4]. The basis of the process of disseminating new knowledge and developing absorptive capacity is the efficient exchange of knowledge between team members. In this context, empirical research on the development of organizations' absorptive capacity shows that CFTs can have a mixed deterrent effect on the organization. Thus, potential absorbency is not easily converted to realized absorbency. The reasons for this phenomenon are not well understood. However, as a possible reason, we can assume the negative influence of the insufficiently developed communicative practice [3].

Finally, the CFT is a cross-cultural phenomenon that brings together people with different professional cultures, vocabulary, and personal goals. The creation of an atmosphere of acceptance for all the team members and the development of internal communication practices to foster knowledge exchange are a priority of the team and business leaders. That is, the three dimensions of cross-functional collaboration (joint focus on task performance, joint communication, and joint interpersonal relationships) directly determine efficient knowledge sharing behavior in CFT [7].

Summarizing the above, we note that the CFT effectiveness is based on knowledge sharing and best communication practices, overcoming cultural, professional barriers, and creating a sense of community in the team. Based on this, the goal of our study was formed: a comparative analysis of the influence of organizational and managerial factors on the knowledge sharing in CFTs in Russia and Germany at present.

To achieve this goal, a number of hypotheses have been put forward regarding the presence and nature of the influence of the following factors on individual activity in knowledge sharing: (1) various coordination mechanisms (managerial factors); (2) organizational environment and organizational conditions (organizational factors); (3) intrinsic and extrinsic motivation to share knowledge. By individual activity in knowledge sharing, we mean the degree of individual participation in knowledge sharing.

In preparation for the study, representative expert groups of employees from the Ural State Economic University (Russia, Yekaterinburg) and the Brandenburg University of Applied Sciences (Germany, Brandenburg an der Havel) were selected. Each expert is a member of the CFT or had such experience in the past.

The research was carried out using a questionnaire constructed based on a 6-point Likert scale and sectional approaches. Some of the questions were taken from foreign scientific sources with translation into Russian and German considering cross-cultural aspects. The questionnaire addresses organizational and managerial factors in the team and the motives for knowledge sharing. The main dependent variable is the individual knowledge sharing activity, i.e. the degree of individual participation.

The questionnaire consists of two blocks—the main content and the socio-demographic part. The main content part includes questions that reflect external and internal factors affecting the exchange of knowledge in CFT. External factors include team coordination mechanisms, the role of the leader (team and functional), organizational environment and organizational conditions factors that facilitate knowledge sharing. Internal factors included the individual characteristics of CFT members, such as motives for knowledge sharing, individual attitudes towards knowledge sharing, which directly influence individual behavior in transferring and accepting knowledge from colleagues. The final socio-demographic part of the questionnaire contains questions about the demographic characteristics of the respondents. See the Appendix for more details.

3 Results

IBM SPSS Statistics data processing program was used for the analysis of the collected data. Average values with standard deviation were calculated for the variables. A paired Student's t-test was used to evaluate the influence of organizational and management factors on the main dependent variable. Spearman's method of rank correlation was used to estimate correlation links between the organizational and managerial factors and the knowledge sharing activity. The differences were considered statistically significant at $p < 0.05$.

The study includes 18 respondents from each university with work experience in cross-functional teams. The main characteristics of the two groups are summarized in Table 1.

The analysis has shown the statistically significant differences in the level of individual knowledge sharing activity between groups from Russian and German universities ($p < 0.05$). Remarkably, the level of knowledge sharing activity in the group from the German university is higher. To compare, the average and ± standard deviation for Germany are 30 and ± 4.0; for Russia—26 and ± 6.78 correspondingly, with $p = 0.0487$ according to the paired Student's t-test.

A correlation analysis was performed to evaluate the relationship between organizational and managerial factors and the knowledge sharing activity. The results are presented in Table 2. See the questionnaire in the Appendix for more details on the factors. The questionnaire consists of 12 sections and a socio-demographic part. Each section is devoted to a different factor listed in Table 2. Section 4 addresses the question if the respondent has the leader role in the CFT. In the case of a positive answer, the following two sections regarding the functional leadership role and team leader role are to be skipped.

Table 1 Characteristics of the groups of the study

Characteristics	Russia	Germany
Gender distribution, number of people		
Men	8	8
Women	10	10
Age distribution, number of people		
25–29 years old	1	5
30–34 years old	4	0
35–39 years old	2	5
40–49 years old	7	5
50–59 years old	3	1
Over 60 years old	1	2
Level of education, number of people		
Academic degree	14	9
Higher (specialist, master)	4	5
Bachelor degree	0	3
Secondary education	0	1
Distribution by the type of task being solved, number of people		
Product	2	4
Process	11	5
Organizational	5	5
Social	0	2
Other	0	2

Table 2 Correlation analysis results

Factors	Correlation with individual knowledge sharing activity			
	Russia		Germany	
	Correlation coefficient	*p*	Correlation coefficient	*p*
Formalization	– 0.200	0.004	0.450	0.000
Direct control	– 0.060	0.002	0.211	0.000
Mutual agreement	0.808	0.025	– 0.101	0.210
Functional leadership role	0.116	0.000	0.197	0.001
Team leader role	0.065	0.000	0.112	0.408
Organizational environment	0.191	0.000	0.065	0.000
Organizational conditions	0.108	0.000	0.266	0.000
Remuneration system	0.051	0.000	0.394	0.000
External motivation	– 0.218	0.225	0.091	0.000
Internal need	0.660	0.000	0.334	0.000

As follows from Table 2, the Russian group can be characterized by the following: (i) statistically significant strong correlation between individual knowledge sharing activity and "*mutual agreement*" factor and (ii) moderate correlation between individual knowledge sharing activity and "*internal need*" factor. In the German group, a statistically significant moderate correlation between individual knowledge sharing activity and (i) "*formalization*" factor, (ii) "*remuneration system*" factor, and (iii) "*internal need*" factor was identified.

Our study's limitations are the small number of participants and a tightly targeted sample limited to university staff. Nevertheless, the results revealed a certain extent to which various managerial and organizational factors and external and internal motivations influenced the individual knowledge sharing activity among CFT members.

4 Conclusion

In the present study, an analysis of the influence of organizational and managerial factors on the sharing of knowledge in cross-functional teams was performed. Cross-functional teams, being a critical success factor of an industrial digital transformation, have become common in academic institutions. Thus, in the article, two universities in Russia and Germany were used as a pilot case study to compare the characteristics of knowledge sharing activities in two different academic settings. Hereby, the individual knowledge sharing activity served as the main dependent variable. In this respect, our results demonstrated the statistically significant differences between Germany and Russia.

The identified higher individual knowledge sharing activity in Germany can be explained by the national specificity of German employees, i.e., structured and responsible way of work. The correlation analysis showed that the "mutual agreement" factor, or "team spirit", of Russian employees mostly drives the process of knowledge sharing. German employees, on the contrary, are mainly guided by the "formalization" factor, i.e., instructions, rules, and regulations.

As a part of future work, it is planned to perform (i) a more comprehensive study with a larger number of participants to clarify the degree of influence of various organizational and managerial factors on individual knowledge sharing activity and (ii) an in-depth analysis of the national context influencing individual behavior in knowledge sharing.

List of Appendices

Appendix. Questionnaire "The impact of organizational and managerial factors on the process of knowledge sharing in cross-functional teams."

Please read the statements carefully. Based on your experiences, rate each statement on a scale of 1–6: 1—"totally disagree", 2—"disagree", 3—"rather disagree", 4—"rather agree", 5—"agree", 6—"fully agree".

1. *Formalization.* How is your work in a cross-functional team regulated?
   (a) The information required for my work is set out in the instructions, recommendations, regulations, and other documents in the organization.
   (b) Our cross-functional team stores information in a large number of reports and documents that we share with colleagues.
   (c) In our team, the interaction between team members is determined by the rules, guidelines, and regulations approved by our managers.
   (d) In our team, discussions of working issues are held at meetings where protocols are written and signed by all participants.
   (e) In our team, all members have clear goals for their daily work as defined by the team leader in the work plan.
2. *Direct control.* How is the control and management in your cross-functional team carried out?
   (a) Our cross-functional team reports to a single project manager.
   (b) I get answers to complex questions and clarification of the tasks that I face during the project implementation directly from the team leader.
   (c) In case of disagreement among our team members during discussions of work issues, our team leader always makes the final decision.

(d) Our team holds meetings to discuss work issues only at the initiative of the team leader.
(e) Meetings to discuss work issues in our team are held formally to report to the team leader on the work done.

3. *Mutual agreement*. How coordinated is the activity in your cross-functional team?

   (a) I feel like part of our cross-functional team.
   (b) I am ready to switch to related functions apart from my usual work duties, if it is necessary to solve the tasks during our project implementation.
   (c) I am ready to make my own decisions concerning my tasks in the project and be responsible for them to the whole team.
   (d) If there is no team leader at work, our team continues to work effectively on the project.
   (e) In our team, it is common to discuss current work issues directly with each other in personal communication.
   (f) Work-related meetings in our team are often held in an informal atmosphere.

4. *Are you the leader of a cross-functional team?* (yes/no question)
   If you answer "yes", please skip sections 5 and 6 and answer further from section 7.
5. *Functional leadership role.* How do you evaluate the business (functional) role of the team leader in your cross-functional team?

   (a) Our team leader tells us and explains our organization's objectives as defined by our management.
   (b) Our team leader is always aware of the current situation in the process of project implementation.
   (c) In a difficult situation during the work process, our team leader carries out a qualified, comprehensive analysis of the situation and develops an understanding of the complex environment.
   (d) I notice that our team leader shows perseverance and will to overcome difficulties that arise during the work on the project.
   (e) Our team leader sets clear working tasks for me and exercises clear control over their execution.

6. *Team leader role.* How do you evaluate the team (emotional) role of the manager in your cross-functional team?

   (a) Our team leader delegates me to make decisions concerning my tasks in the project.
   (b) Our team leader always emphasizes the personal contribution of the team member who has decided to take the initiative in solving current issues.
   (c) I feel the support of our team leader when I discuss my ideas and project proposals with her/him.

(d) Our team leader helps me understand my strengths and weaknesses in working on the project.
(e) In case of an error, I receive constructive comments from our team leader and advice on how to correct them.
(f) If necessary, I can discuss work issues with our team leader in an informal setting.

7. *Organizational environment*. Do your workspace and environment facilitate the search for new information and knowledge sharing in a cross-functional team?

(a) I have access to the information necessary for my professional development and search for new solutions within the project.
(b) Before starting work on the project, our team was assigned a separate room where we work together as a team.
(c) When forming a cross-functional team, I was offered paid training by the organization to improve my professionalism and teamwork skills.
(d) I can take additional training, if necessary, for our project.
(e) Our team regularly discusses new information that may be useful to all participants in the project.
(f) Our team supports the use of non-standard and original approaches, methods, and tools when working on the project.

8. *Organizational conditions*. Are there conditions for obtaining new information useful for your cross-functional team to work on the project?

(a) I have time to search for information that may be useful for our project without affecting the workflow.
(b) Our cross-functional team supports the willingness to participate in development activities in a professional direction if they relate to the current project.

9. *Remuneration system*. Does your cross-functional team have a system to stimulate knowledge sharing activity?

(a) Our team has a system of incentives that considers the activity of searching and discussing new information, which can be useful when working on a project.
(b) In our team, we encourage with material values (e.g. bonuses, material assets, etc.) the use of non-standard, original methods and tools if this has led to increased efficiency and/or optimization of the project and/or workflow.
(c) In our team, we encourage with immaterial values (e.g. public recognition, a designation of professional development prospects, etc.) the use of non-standard, original methods and tools if this has led to increased efficiency and/or optimization of the project and/or workflow.

(d) I know that our organization has a system of recommendations for promotion taking into account the effectiveness of participation in the cross-functional team.

10. *External motivation.* Do you take into account the possible benefits when sharing knowledge in a cross-functional team?

(a) I share my knowledge with my team members because, in our team, you can get rewarded for it.
(b) I share my knowledge with my team members because I think it will help me to climb up the career ladder in the future.
(c) I share my knowledge with my team members because I want to get recognition from my colleagues.
(d) I share my knowledge with my team members because I want to be recognized by our team leader.
(e) Colleagues who actively use their knowledge and experience to improve other team members' work receive rewards and significant awards.
(f) I do not share my knowledge with my team members.

11. *Internal need.* What drives you to share knowledge in a cross-functional team?

(a) I consider it an important part of my work to share knowledge with other members of our team.
(b) I like to share my knowledge with my team members.
(c) When I share knowledge with my team members, it satisfies my internal needs (e.g. desire to feel understood, approved, supported, recognized, etc.).
(d) I feel that my knowledge and experience are useful to our team when working on a project.

12. *Individual knowledge sharing activity.* How do you manifest yourself in the process of knowledge sharing in your cross-functional team?

(a) I often speak out when discussing a complex issue in the course of a project.
(b) I often use the knowledge gained from my team members to improve my skills.
(c) I often use the knowledge gained from my team members to address current work issues.
(d) Usually, I spend much time sharing knowledge with other team members.
(e) I take part in the discussion not only of those issues directly related to my work in the team but also of a wide range of other issues that arise in the implementation of the project.
(f) As a member of a cross-functional team, I actively share my knowledge.

References

1. Denisov, A. F., & Tsybova, V. S. (2018). "Soft" and "hard" qualities of the leader of the company. *Bulletin of St. Petersburg University, Management, 17*(3), 275–296. https://doi.org/10.21638/11701/spbu08.2018.302.
2. Kalabina, E. G., & Belyak, OYu. (2019). Creation of cross-functional teams of parallel design for the development of new products. *Kadrovik, 3*, 62–68
3. Kudryavtseva, E. I., & Volkova, N. V. (2019). The role of network communication activity in the formation of a project team. *Russian Management Journal, 17*(1), 47–70
4. Latukha, M. O., Selivanovskikh, L.V., & Mitskevich E. A. (2019). The practice of managing talented employees and the absorption capacity of Russian companies. *Russian Management Journal, 17* (1), 5–28. https://doi.org/10.21638/spbu18.2019.101.
5. Lustina, T. N. (2019). Modern approaches to building a career in the VUCA world. *Service in Russia and Abroad, 13*(4), 169–177
6. Matushkin, M. A. (2018). Methods and tools of enterprise management in the conditions of VUCA-reality. *Bulletin of the SSEU, 5*(74), 92–95
7. Rozhkova, L. V., Tuguskina, G. N., & Salnikova, O. V. (2019). Management of cross-cultural teams in international and national business. *Models, Systems, Networks in Economics, Technology, Nature and Society, 1*(29), 84–94
8. Santa, R., Ferrer, M., Bretherton, P., & Hyland, P. (2010). Contribution of cross-functional teams to the improvement in operational performance. *Team Performance Management, 16*(3/4), 148–168. https://doi.org/10.1108/13527591011053241
9. Tett, G. (2015). *The silo effect: The peril of expertise and the promise of breaking down barriers*. New York City, NY: Simon & Schuster.
10. Zavyalova, E. K., Alsufiev, A. I., Dominyak, V. I., Zamulin, A. L., Lisovskaya, A. Yu., & Sokolov, D. N. (2018). Organizational and psychological aspects of human resource management in agile companies. *Bulletin of St. Petersburg University, Management, 17*(3), 253–274. https://doi.org/10.21638/11701/spbu08.2018.301.

Digitalization of Talent Management in Russian Companies

Elena V. Maslova, Elena V. Kulchitskaya, and Natalia G. Kizyan

Abstract The paper considers the possibilities for using digital technologies in talent management, presents approaches to defining the concept of talent management, and substantiates the relevance of the subject under study. The authors identify and discuss the main activities in the area of talent management. In the present research, the methods of human resource management associated with the development of digital technologies are specified: robotization, digitalization, systematization of enterprise resource planning, and neuro tools.

Keywords Talent management · Digital economy · HR digitalization

1 Introduction

The digitalization of the economy provides many new opportunities for business in terms of using new technologies in the interests of production, personnel, etc. HR digitalization processes are currently in full swing; in the Russian Federation, they are actively supported by the state. The capabilities of the digital economy in terms of implementing human resource management tools are developing and will continue to develop in the future. In the context of the digitalization of the economy, Russian HR specialists and experts pay special attention to talent management. On the one hand, in a changing environment, the role of talented, highly qualified employees becomes paramount. It is they who create sustainable competitive advantages of modern Russian organizations, generate and implement innovative ideas, allow the organization to keep pace with the times and correspond to the dynamics of the market. On the other hand, the digital economy creates new technological opportunities for HR managers of organizations to manage talent, evaluate employees for their qualifications, consolidate and store information about employees, manage their motivation, the degree of loyalty, etc. Thus, the digital economy opens up many new opportunities and development paths for the talent management system.

E. V. Maslova · E. V. Kulchitskaya (✉) · N. G. Kizyan
Saint Petersburg State University, Universitetskaya Emb. 13B, 199034 Saint Petersburg, Russian Federation
e-mail: e.kulchitskaya@spbu.ru

V. Kumar et al. (eds.), *Digital Transformation in Industry*, Lecture Notes in Information Systems and Organisation 44, https://doi.org/10.1007/978-3-030-73261-5_18

2 Talent Management in Modern Business

The first step is to define how the term "talent management" is interpreted. Armstrong gives the following definition of this concept: "The use of an integrated set of activities aimed at ensuring that the organization attracts, retains, motivates and promotes the talented employees it needs now and in the future" [1, p. 374]. The book War for Talent offers a different approach to the definition of this concept: "Talent management is an area of HR management that deals with attracting skilled workers, integrating new employees, and retaining staff to meet current and future goals of business" [3, p. 26]. It should be noted that Armstrong's view of the talent management concept is broader and more strategically oriented. While a large number of modern theorists and practitioners of HR consulting consider talent management as a separate area of human resource management, the authors of this study, on the contrary, suggest considering it a strategic basis for the entire human resource management system of an organization: recruitment, career management, personnel development, personnel assessment, HR branding, etc.

Modern Russian companies take two approaches to talent management in an organization. The first is to form a talent pool for the preparation of qualified employees for specific vacated positions. The second approach is based on the formation of the so-called pool of talented employees preparing for the implementation of future tasks and projects in the organization. Some Russian companies are using both approaches simultaneously, thus focusing on both current and strategic objectives.

In 2016, the consulting company PwC in Russia conducted a major study on talent management and building a talent management system among CEOs of Russian companies, as a result of which it turned out that 79% of the interviewed managers ranked highly qualified personnel in the first place among the key business needs. The second place in the survey was taken by a successfully functioning tax system, the third place—by developed infrastructure. This indicates the importance of the question posed—business needs talent as a key factor in maintaining and developing competitiveness. In the context of the decline in the working-age population, this issue is especially acute. Therefore, the survey on talent management goals in organizations showed the priority for companies of such benchmarks as retaining key employees, increasing employee performance, and providing the company with personnel of the required qualifications [3].

The talent management system in an organization includes the interconnection of factors and tools that affect human resource management processes, blocks of talent management procedures and system outputs, that is, the results of talent management activities. In the talent management system, external factors of influence include the state of the labor market, socio-cultural and economic aspects, and internal factors include the organizational component, structure and culture of the organization, and the features of the human resource management system as a whole. These factors underlie the implementation of human resource management tools: personnel planning, recruitment, adaptation, training, motivation, career development, personnel assessment, and others. The talent management blocks in the system are represented by four sections: attracting talented employees, organizing the work of talented employees, retaining talented employees, and forming a highly qualified personnel reserve.

The authors pay close attention to these blocks, since they, in their totality, represent the talent management procedures. The result of effective talent management is, on the one hand, the formation of sustainable competitiveness of the organization in the external environment due to the unique advantages that highly qualified employees provide to the organization; on the other hand, the formation of a high business reputation of the organization both as an employer and as an economic entity.

3 Digital Economy and Its Impact on Talent Management

Since this article discusses the talent management system in the digitalization process, that is, in the digital economy, it is necessary to determine what is meant by this concept. The term "digital economy" (in Russian, there are also variants "electronic economy", "web economy", or "Internet economy") was first used in 1995 by the American scientist Nicholas Negroponte to explain to colleagues the advantages of the new economy in comparison with the old one in connection with the intensive development of information and communication technologies. According to this approach, the digital economy is a system of economic, social, and cultural relations based on the use of digital technologies. According to another definition, the digital economy is an activity directly related to the development of digital computer technologies, which includes the provision of online services, electronic payments, Internet commerce, crowdfunding, etc. The Strategy for the Development of the Information Society of the Russian Federation for 2017–2030, approved in Russia, provides the following definition of the digital economy: "The digital economy is an economic activity in which the key production factor is digital data, and their processing in large volumes and the use of analysis results make it possible, compared to traditional forms of management, to significantly increase the efficiency of various types of production, technologies, equipment, storage, sale, delivery of goods and services."

The development of the digital economy is due to the radical changes caused by digital computing and communication technologies in the second half of the twentieth century. Similar to the agricultural and industrial revolutions, the digital revolution marked the beginning of a new informational era, which today is often referred to as Industry 4.0. Industry 4.0 is the production side, equivalent to the consumer-oriented Internet of Things, in which all human-used items will be connected to the Internet. This is a completely new approach to manufacturing—a conglomerate of major industrialists, artificial intelligence experts, economists, and academics. A gradual and consistent transition to a digital economy in society is called digitalization or digital transformation. Digital transformation is changing the form of business in a digital reality based on data. Digital transformation, first of all, means new business processes, organizational structures, regulations, a new responsibility for data, new role models. That is why the digital transformation of management activities in the field of personnel management implies not only individual products that allow digitizing HR processes but also a new digital organization of HR activities in general [4].

The fourth industrial revolution, the transition to fully automated production and the Internet of Things dictate new rules for the functioning of all modern markets. The labor market lends itself to the particular influence of the digitalization process, since automated production implies a radical change in the structure of employment, the risk of total unemployment, and significant changes in the requirements for the qualifications of employees. All these aspects trigger the process of transformation of the labor market, which has already begun. The directions of this transformation must be known and understood by all subjects of the labor market to be able to make decisions and overcome the problems that this process creates.

Changes in the structure of employment in Russia will lead, on the one hand, to unemployment, and on the other hand, to a shortage of qualified personnel to close the vacant positions that arise. Russian employers, as subjects of the labor market, will acutely feel the "staff shortage" arising from the discrepancy between the requirements of the digital economy and the modern system of professional education.

Thus, the personnel problem hindering the process of digitalization of the Russian economy and business today is especially relevant [5]. Today, it is necessary to inform specialists in various fields on the possibilities of digitalization of one or another activity and train them in digital technologies, so that these specialists are in demand in the labor market in the long term.

Today, the share of the digital economy in the country's GDP is 3.9%. According to a study by the McKinsey consulting company, the digitalization of the economy can increase Russia's GDP from 4 to 9 trillion rubles.

Government support for the digitalization process determines the growth dynamics of the markets for new digital technologies. Every year, new tools, programs, and mobile applications appear that allow optimizing the HR activities of a modern company using digital technologies. Since talent management in an organization is today recognized by participants in economic activity as one of the most promising and relevant areas of activity, digital technologies are quite actively used in this area.

4 Digital Talent Management Scheme

Within the framework of human resource management, the most valid digitalization opportunities are robotization, digitalization, systematization of enterprise resource planning (ERP), and neuro tools. Within each block of the organization's talent management system, these capabilities provide digital tools for the successful implementation of management activities. Schematically, the directions and tools of talent management in the digital economy are presented in Fig. 1.

Robotization involves the use of HR bots and robots to implement the simplest procedures for human resource management. The use of robotization in recruiting processes is the most common procedure. The program sets a task that needs to be solved by the robot: what questions to get answers to, how many candidates for vacancies to interview. At this stage of talent management with the help of HR bots and robots, it is possible to determine the level and direction of candidates' education, their ability to answer the formulated questions. It is also possible to program more complex questions and cases related to determining the candidates' IQ levels to expand the capabilities of HR robotization. It should be noted that bots and robots today only conduct primary interviews, thus freeing up specialists' time for other tasks. Those who pass the first stage of the interview, at the other stages of the selection, communicate with employees and managers of the company.

To attract talented employees to Russian companies, in addition to robotization of hiring procedures, it is possible to successfully use ERP systems to centrally store information about candidates for vacancies. This tool is also a very effective basis for building a pool of talented employees and a pool of highly qualified specialists to fill future vacancies.

Today, many Russian companies are very actively using various formats of ERP systems, adapted to the needs of human resource management. For example, SAP is successfully implementing the Human Capital Management platform to solve a wide range of HR tasks, such as information storage, e-learning, professional career management, development of a successful employee profile, and many others. The compliance with the evolving concept of "Employee Happiness" against the background of the general trend of HR consumerization is also very important

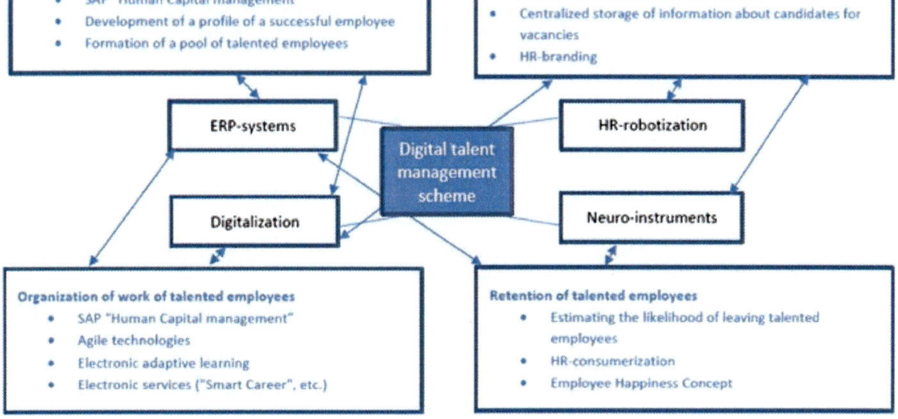

Fig. 1 Digital talent management scheme

for managing talented employees. One of the drivers of digitalization in HR was Sberbank, which tested a device making it possible to assess the emotional state of personnel (collectors, call center employees, and others).

The gadget looks like a badge and records who a person communicates with, the tone of his/her voice, whether his/her heart rate increases, etc. It was also at Sberbank that a product called Team was introduced. The board members installed a special application and regularly gave each other feedback on the principle of traffic lights: red, yellow, and green. These assessments allow controlling information about conflicts and the characteristics of teamwork. Yulia Chupina, Deputy Chairman of the Management Board, Head of Strategy and Development and HR Blocks, commented on these digital innovations as follows: "We have expanded the functionality of the system and extended this practice to at least half of Sberbank's executives. We are planning to build it into SF. Our goal is real-time feedback" [6].

Describing the markets of modern innovative technologies, it is necessary to separate two important terms: automation and digitalization. Automation is the transfer of existing business processes to the basis of computer computing, electronic storage, and data exchange. Digitalization is a change in the business processes of a company in such a way that they are more in line with the new tools and technologies of the digital economy [7]. The field of digital technologies in human resource management today is at the stage of emergence and formation, but today it is obvious that digital technologies in business management and organization are the future. It is necessary to realize that the further expansion of the terminological apparatus of digital HR as an approach based on the principles of the integrity of the management model, measurability, data integration, real-time analysis, and technological flexibility in the field of human resource management will occur in parallel with the development of the digital economy [8]. Human resources experts call this approach HR 3.0 and define the goal of digital HR as combining all areas of human resource management with the capabilities of rapidly evolving digital technologies for transparency, consistency, and measurement of human capital management processes, similar to the management of any other company assets [9].

Neuromarketing in modern business is used to solve a large number of problems related to marketing communications and sales. HR neuromarketing is a new look at the possibilities of using neuro tools in management. The authors understand HR neuromarketing as a set of strategic actions for the application of neuromarketing methods in human resource management, aimed at maximizing the effectiveness of HR management in modern organizations. In other words, HR neuromarketing is an interdisciplinary direction in science at the intersection of neurophysiology, psychology, marketing, and management, which explores the features of work behavior based on sensorimotor, cognitive, and emotional reactions of people [10].

5 Conclusion

Talented employees are not just personnel for a modern Russian company, but the basis of its existence in the context of the global digitalization of business and economy. New business opportunities emerging due to the development of technology are associated, among other things, with an effective personnel policy. It is highly qualified, valuable, educated, creative, and proactive employees who will lead the changes that are taking place in the Russian economy in the era of digitalization.

References

1. Query ID="Q1" Text="Unable to parse this reference. Kindly do manual structure" Armstrong, M. (2010). *Practice of human resource management*. Saint Petersburg: Piter.
2. Michaels, E. J., Handfield-Jones, H., & Axelrod, B. (2001). *The war for talent placed on hold*. Boston: Harvard Business School Press.
3. Levichev, Y., & Vorogushin, E. (2018). *Talent management in Russia and the world: Figures and trends*. Retrieved from https://www.pwc.ru/ru/hr-consulting/assets/talent-management-shtat.pdf.
4. Executive (2019). *What is digitalization?* Retrieved from https://www.e-xecutive.ru/management/itforbusiness/1989667-chto-takoe-tsifrovizatsiya.
5. Shirokova, G. V. (2012). Entrepreneurial orientation: Origins of the concept and the main research approaches. *Russian Management Journal, 10*(3), 55–72
6. Shatz, C. J. (2009). MHC class I: An unexpected role in neuronal plasticity. *Neuron, 64*(1), 40–45
7. Vohs, K. D., & Baumeister, R. F. (2011). *Handbook of self-regulation: Research, theory, and applications*. New York: Guilford Press.
8. Gobe, M. (2010). *Emotional branding: The new paradigm for connecting brands to people*. New York: Allworth Press.
9. Fukolova, Y. (2018). *Personnel under the figure*. Retrieved from https://hbr-russia.ru/management/upravlenie-personalom/776169.
10. Rodionova, E. A., & Kulchitskaya, E. V. (2018). Opportunities for integrating neuromarketing in human resource management. *Economics and Management, 5*(151), 36

Project Management Competences for Next Engineers in the Industry 4.0 Era. A Case Study

Alberto Cerezo-Narváez, Manuel Otero-Mateo, and Andrés Pastor-Fernández

Abstract In the context of training in engineering and technology in the Industry 4.0 era, project competences' acquisition must start from the trainer's perspective as a counselor, facilitator, and sponsor of trainees' learning. This means minimizing master classes to promote their autonomy and collaborative work, not being possible to ensure their development through traditional evaluations. In a recession context (Spain, Andalusia, and Cadiz) with low growth and high youth unemployment rate, it is intended to promote future engineers' entrepreneurship, creativity and innovation. Within this framework, the study reviews the models that highlight the ways of teaching and learning in project management subjects in the engineering degrees of the industrial branch (chemistry, electricity, electronics, industrial design and product development, mechanics, and industrial technology) offered by the University of Cadiz (UCA). This selects project-based learning (PBL), in which learners are the main characters, who evolve through experimentation. This research consists of three stages. In a first phase, education in entrepreneurship is encouraged. Next, culture of innovative entrepreneurship is promoted, propitiating the conditions for the (simulated) creation of innovative companies. Finally, those proposals that potentially contribute to Cadiz improving its business deficit in technological sectors are selected.

Keywords Industry 4.0 training · Project management · Entrepreneurship

1 Introduction

In the Industry 4.0 era, the advance of technology and its social implications has generated in the academic and scientific environment the need to significantly rethink the way knowledge is generated, acquired, shared, capitalized, transferred and applied [6], developing activities that lead to improve their processes to achieve higher levels of quality and sustainability to train future highly trained, innovative and

A. Cerezo-Narváez (✉) · M. Otero-Mateo · A. Pastor-Fernández
Engineering School, University of Cadiz, 11519 Puerto-Real, CA, Spain
e-mail: alberto.cerezo@uca.es

V. Kumar et al. (eds.), *Digital Transformation in Industry*, Lecture Notes in Information Systems and Organisation 44, https://doi.org/10.1007/978-3-030-73261-5_19

entrepreneurial scientific, technological and creative professionals [5]. At the same time, entrepreneurship is having a direct impact on current social and economic progress, which has led the University to rethink its role according to its classic functions, becoming dynamic entities of business activity through the promotion and development of initiatives, as a basis for generating qualified and sustainable employment in the long term [13], particularly in technology.

The educational policies in Europe (Spain included), especially after the implementation of the European Higher Education Area (EHEA) and following the Bologna Declaration, have among their objectives the idea that the University promotes innovative and entrepreneurial attitudes. This requires both a cultural change (social acceptance of the role of companies in society) and an increase in the skills and abilities (competences) of future entrepreneurs [20].

1.1 Project Management and Engineering Competences

According to the European Qualification Framework for Lifelong Learning (EQF), the competence is the demonstrated ability to use knowledge, skills, and personal, social, and methodological abilities, in work or study situations and in professional and personal development. Therefore, the personal level cannot be dissociated from the professional one, once components of professionalism are a combination of personal attributes (capacity, motivation, personality, aptitude, attitude, and values) that are complemented and integrated, in conjunction with other elements related to work contexts (knowledge, skills, abilities, behavior, experience, etc.) [19].

In the university context, competence is the capacity to execute and the degree of preparation, sufficiency and/or responsibility to develop tasks [14, 20, 24]. This framework controls its action thanks to generic and specific competences, in terms of learning, teaching, evaluation and performance. Quality is ensured by the European Credit Transfer System (ECTS), as an accumulation system. In relation to engineering and project management (PM), it is worth highlighting the traceability of a series of competences, mainly of an intrapersonal nature, such as project management, leadership, teamwork, negotiation, ethics, creativity, innovation, and entrepreneurship.

In Spain, competences that graduates must acquire in order to join the labour market after completing their university education are specified in the Memories of University Degrees. They must ensure the basic skills contained in the Spanish Framework of Qualifications for Higher Education (MECES), regulated by the Spanish Royal Decree 1027/2011. In order to achieve it, they are based on the "White Papers" of the National Agency for Quality Assessment and Accreditation (ANECA) under the regulation of the Spanish Royal Decree 861/2010. The acquisition of these competences (such as application of knowledge, transmission of ideas, interpretation of data, and emission of judgments) starts from the perspective of the professor as facilitator, advisor and promoter, leaving behind the traditional master classes, favouring the autonomy of the students, and promoting their resourcefulness.

In the technology sectors, companies demand that future engineers possess a wide range of skills that will allow them to meet the expectations of the labour market and successfully face the challenges presented by a changing context [11]. From this point of view, engineering training should add to the main thematic areas those competences that help them in business contexts [17] and Industry 4.0 environments [7], so that traditional ones are no longer enough. On the contrary, the profile of the engineer must be based on the ability and willingness to learn, on a solid knowledge of the basic natural sciences and any field of technology, together general human and social values [21].

In Europe, the European Network for Accreditation of Engineering Education (ENAEE) creates the European Accredited Engineer (EUR-ACE®) to provide a framework for the accreditation of higher education programs in engineering, as an entry route to the profession. This promotes the quality of engineering graduates in order to facilitate their professional mobility and strengthen their competences. In this way, the EUR-ACE label assures the system prepares graduates who are able to assume relevant roles in the job market [1]. Table 1 shows the competences established by the EHEA and contrasts the dimensions (evaluation criteria) of the EUR-ACE label, as a guarantor of engineering programs in Europe for the promotion of employability (those to be used in the case study are underlined in pink and orange).

In business, in order to survive in a globalized market and especially in technological and industrial sectors, organizations seek a competitive advantage. To achieve this, among the feasible possibilities, it is important to have competent staff [15], so they make a remarkable effort to increase their capabilities, although this effort could be reduced if the gap between what new employees offer and what the market needs were to decrease [5]. In this context, the competences offered by two most widespread professional associations—International Project Management Association (IPMA) and Project Management Institute (PMI)—in their standards (ICB4, PMCDF 3, and PMBOK 6) have to be highlighted. They provide the contextual, specific, and social competences necessary for professional practice, as summarized in Table 2 (those to be used in the case study are underlined in light blue).

The application of knowledge and techniques recognized as good practices is not enough to properly manage projects [2], so that general and specific competences are required, such as quality assurance, leadership, motivation, confidence, resolution or orientation, as IPMA and PMI stress. It is noteworthy that their development through training, mentoring, and coaching allows for better performance in the challenges undertaken, thanks to increased motivation, better self-organization and less need for centralized control [3].

Table 1 EHEA competences and EUR-ACE® dimensions

EHEA Tuning-Project competences	ENAEE EUR-ACE® dimensions
Instrumental:	Organization and development:
• Abstraction, analysis, and synthesis	• Implementation of the plan
• Scheduling and planning	• Organization of the program
• Oral and written communication	• Educational coordination mechanisms
• Information search	• Adequacy of academic regulations
• Application of knowledge in practice	Internal quality assurance:
• Use of applied technology	• Continuous improvement
• Research	• Analysis of objective and verifiable data
• Communication in a second language	• Collection of information
• Problem identification and resolution	Information and transparency:
• Decision-making	• Publication of updated information
• Project formulation and management	Academic staff:
Interpersonal:	• Academic Qualification
• Criticism and self-criticism	• Experience and teaching quality
• Working in international contexts	• Experience and research quality
• Valuing and respecting diversity	Support staff, resources, and services:
• Social Responsibility	• Support staff
• Citizen commitment	• Material Resources
• Ethics	• Support and guidance services
• Motivation	• External internships
• Interpersonal skills	• Compromises and recommendations
• Teamwork	Learning outcomes:
Systemic:	• Training activities
• Work autonomously	• Teaching Methodologies
• Acting in new situations	• Evaluation systems
• Creative capacity	Satisfaction and performance:
• Leadership	• Evolution of indicators
• Initiative and entrepreneurship	• Student Satisfaction
• Permanent learning and updating	• Insertion into the labour market
• Preservation of the environment	Institutional support:
• Quality	• Organizational Structure
• Commitment to the socio-cultural context	• Economic, human, and material support

1.2 Entrepreneurship and Innovation in the University Context

Entrepreneurship in university students links the result of the education obtained at the University and the intention to start a business, according to the training received and the attitude towards self-employment [18]. This also includes entrepreneurial attitudes inside organizations [14] that promote employment, competitiveness, personal development, and even social welfare. Its inclusion in university studies in Cadiz (Andalusia, Spain) can be justified from:

Table 2 Comparative between IPMA and PMI approaches

IPMA ICB 4	PMI PMCDF 3 and PMI PMBOK 6
Perspective:	Strategic and business management:
• Strategy	• Strategy and business
• Governance, structures, and processes	• Organizational process assets
• Compliance, standards, and regulations	• Organizational systems
• Power and interest	• Politics and power
• Culture and values	• Enterprise environmental factors
People:	Personal:
• Self-reflection and self-management	• Managing
• Personal integrity and reliability	• Professionalism
• Personal communication	• Communicating
• Relations and engagement	• Personality
• Leadership	• Leading
• Teamwork	• Being collaborative
• Conflict and crisis	• Dealing with people
• Resourcefulness	• Cognitive ability
• Negotiation	• Getting things done
• Result orientation	• Effectiveness
Practice:	Technical:
• Design	• Tailoring
• Requirements, objectives, and benefits	• Goals and objectives
• Scope	• Scope
• Time	• Time
• Organization and information	• Communication
• Quality	• Quality
• Finance	• Cost
• Resources	• Human resources
• Procurement and partnership	• Procurement
• Plan and control	• Scheduling
• Risk and opportunities	• Risks
• Stakeholders	• Stakeholders
• Change and transformation	• Integration

- The university is an ideal setting for students to acquire and promote entrepreneurial intentions [23].
- The correlation between entrepreneurship and university reveals a connection between the viability and desirability of creating companies (if the creation of a company is perceived as viable, there is a greater desire to do so) [22] and having initiative [12].
- The Plan for the Promotion of Entrepreneurial Culture in the Andalusian Public Education System presented in 2011 involves Andalusian Universities in motivating and promoting innovative and entrepreneurial attitudes.
- The atréBT! competition by the University of Cadiz (UCA) serves as an itinerary for potential entrepreneurs, highlighting the knowledge generated at the UCA and

creating technology-based companies (TBCs), as a tool for transferring research results to its socio-economic environment.

On the other hand, creativity and invention are the pillars of entrepreneurship in science, technology and innovation [10]. Entrepreneurship through innovation is related to economic development, strengthening the productive network environment [9]. In this context, the "Project Based Learning" (PBL) [25], in which students are the protagonists acquiring competences through experimentation, allows undertaking dynamic entrepreneurial and/or innovative incentives. This training daily implies overcoming new challenges, in order to develop future professionals capable of addressing the challenges that arise [16], so there is a latent need to implement new methodologies and teaching models that enable students to face problems and release their full potential.

Given the situation (in Spain, Andalusia and Cadiz) of deep social and economic crisis [4], with low growth rate and high youth unemployment rate, among other differential elements, entrepreneurship, creativity and innovation have been promoted in the educational systems. The link between entrepreneurship and education is perceived in both economic and educational legislation:

- Spanish Royal Decree-Law 4/2013 on Measures to Support the Entrepreneur and Stimulate Growth and Job Creation, which develops a strategy to encourage financing, reduce debt, and promote the competitiveness of the Spanish economy.
- Spanish Law 14/2013 on Support for Entrepreneurs and their Internationalization, which promotes the entrepreneurship in all the stages of the educational system and in teacher training and mentoring.
- Spanish Organic Law 8/2013 for the Improvement of Quality on Education, which proposes to improve the employability and stimulate the entrepreneurial spirit of students, incorporating entrepreneurship into the objectives of the educational stages, reinforcing its transversal character.

2 Objectives

The design of this research is intended to achieve the following purposes:

- To analyze the current situation in order to detect the limitations, deficiencies and needs of the Spanish ecosystem.
- To promote a debate on the specific Andalusian ecosystem of innovation, in which leading companies (e.g., Navantia and Airbus) coexist with high unemployment.
- To identify initiatives and actions to encourage and improve education for innovation and entrepreneurship.
- To undertake the best practices that develop competences to promote entrepreneurship, innovation, and creativity.

3 Methodology

The methodology used in the research is the case study. This does not separate the phenomenon from its context, starting from a preliminary theoretical model to build a theory and reach a more complete explanatory model, creating new theoretical frameworks, checking its practical application, analyzing in depth the complexity and considering the points of view of those involved [8].

The case study is based on an innovation project (π project 17–20), which is being very useful in engineering degrees of the industrial branch offered by the UCA (chemistry, electricity, electronics, industrial design and product development, mechanics, and industrial technology) because of its relationship with innovation and technology. The development of this project consists of three stages:

- Education for entrepreneurship. Promotion of education for entrepreneurship, not only for students, but also for the training provided by university professors.
- Corporate entrepreneurship. Promotion of the culture of innovative entrepreneurship, fostering the conditions for the potential (simulated) "creation" of new innovative companies and encouraging creative initiatives in existing ones.
- Disruptive innovation. Selection of innovative proposals that help to Cadiz and Andalusia improve its business deficit in medium and high technology sectors.

4 Case Study

Since the course 2016–2017 to 2019–2020, the π project is implemented in the subject "Engineering Projects", in the engineering degrees of the industrial branch of the UCA.

It is intended to work and, later, to evaluate, among the competences contemplated in the Memories of University Degrees, which are aligned with the White Books of the ANECA, the following items:

- Basic competences (CB)
  - CB1. Apply knowledge by the defense of arguments and problem solving.
  - CB2. Transmit information, ideas, problems, and solutions to the public.
- General competences (CG)
  - CG1. Direct the activities that are the object of the engineering projects.
  - CG2. Learn new methods and theories in basic and technological matters.
  - CG3. Solve problems with initiative, decision making, creativity and criticality.
  - CG4. Communicate and transmit knowledge, skills, and abilities in engineering.
- Common specific competences (CC)
  - CC1. Organize and plan at a company level.

– CC2. Know the institutional and legal framework of a company.

- Specific competences common to the industrial branch (CI)
  – CI1. Apply knowledge of business organization, logistic systems, and production.
  – CI2. Carry out and interpret schemes in the industrial field.
  – CI3. Organize and manage projects.
  – CI4. Know the organizational structure and functions of a project office.
- Transversal competences (CT)
  – CT1. Communicate orally and/or in writing
  – CT2. Working autonomously
  – CT3. Teamwork
  – CT4. Having initiative and entrepreneurial spirit.

Next, it is necessary to determine the evaluation criteria, as summarized in Table 3, used to measure the level of student performance in the subject.

At the beginning of each course, the subject is presented, and the competences to be acquired, learning results to be achieved, and training activities, are communicated. It is also informed that an individual test will be made, at the end of the course to measure the degree of acquisition of basic knowledge for the management and engineering of projects, and a practical case in which, in group of 4 people, it will be

Table 3 Comparative between IPMA and PMI approaches

Evaluation criteria	Competences				
	CB	CG	CC	CI	CT
EV1. Case study defense (communication and presentation)	CB1	CG4	–	–	CT1
EV2. Entrepreneurship and innovation (value generation)	–	–	–	–	CT4
EV3. Selection of potential technologies (feasibility)	CB2	CG2	–	CI2	–
EV4. Business organization (governance and stakeholders)	–	–	CC2	CI4	–
EV5. Project direction and management (labour organization)	–	CG1	CC1	CI3	CT3
EV6. Technical definition (requirements, deadlines and costs)	–	–	–	CI1	–
EV7. Self-management (planning and execution of tasks)	–	–	–	–	CT2
EV8. Creative problem solving (changes and risks)	–	CG3	-	–	–
EV9. Knowledge (management by processes and competences)	Theoretical knowledge				

necessary to solve an enterprise project from a technological, organizational and/or marketing innovation. The evaluation criteria for its assessment are also presented.

During the academic year, the students receive 20 sessions (2 h each) in which the basic fundamental concepts are transmitted. They are evaluated by means of the EV9 criterion. In addition, they get other 10 practical sessions in which the knowledge acquired is applied in the practical cases. To finish, they defend them in an extraordinary session, in which the teams have 30 min to present their proposals by means of the EV1-8 criteria. In 4 courses, a total of 80 proposals have been approved for development and finally undertaken. The cases cover a wide variety of typologies:

- Energy production and storage devices
- Augmented reality and virtual reality devices
- Software and hardware applications
- Wellbeing services
- Safety devices
- Security and cybersecurity devices
- Household mechatronic devices
- Professional mechatronic devices.

The practical cases, once approved by the professors, who act in the role of the project sponsor, have to address a number of points: value proposition, selection of technology, technical, economic and contextual (both legal and environmental) feasibility, project formulation, governance, work organization, processes definition, change control and risk (threats and opportunities) management. Halfway through the course, in order to actively involve students, a day of entrepreneurship in engineering through innovation is scheduled, for which the Director of Employment and Entrepreneurship and the Entrepreneurship Chair of the UCA are invited to present the atréBT! Programs, as shown in Fig. 1. The conference also aims to ensure students to participate in corresponding atréBT! editions with their practical cases.

Fig. 1 atréBT! competition announcement (from XI edition in 2017 to XIV edition in 2020)

5 Results

In order to assess the achievement of the objectives proposed, a survey is carried out on the 320 students (80 teams of 4 people) enrolled in 2 specific moments of each course: at the beginning of the courses (time 1) and at their end (time 2), whose results are shown in Table 4, being the academic year 2016–2017 the 1st and 2019–2020 the 4th. Statistics at the beginning of courses, through self-assessment, places students at a certain level of "maturity", and at their end, they can measure their own "self-evolution". Questions cover a score from 0 to 10 (0 being the worst and 10 the best) in relation to:

- UTILITY that you give to PM, as part of your training to become an engineer
- IMPORTANCE you give to PM, for your future as an engineering professional
- INTEREST that engineering PM awakens in you as part of your professional future
- KNOWLEDGE you have in engineering PM, to start your career.

In addition, in relation to the degree of performance, by having the learning results, as shown in Table 5 (the 9 evaluation criteria, 8 for competences with a value of 10% each, 1 for knowledge with a value of 20%), which bring together the 16 competences undertaken, the existing gap can be studied. Then, a personal and individualized gap plan can be proposed by the "coordinating" teaching team for the 320 students.

6 Discussion

Thanks to the self-evaluation survey at the beginning and end of courses, the "self-evolution" of the 320 students enrolled in "Engineering Projects" can be measured from their particular initial situation. In relation to PM in the Industry 4.0 era, it is relevant that, although both the usefulness as part of their training and the importance and interest for their professional future barely reach 50% (an average of 51%), at the time of the presentation of practical cases, once courses are finished, the usefulness, importance and interest exceed 80% (an 83%). This means a difference of just over 30% (31%), an increase of more than 60%.

In relation to the knowledge acquired, it is necessary to emphasize the degree of convergence between the self-evaluation and the qualification obtained in the exams. If the knowledge they had at the beginning was self-evaluated with a poor 24%, the "self-evolution" culminates in 71%, very similar to the 67% obtained in the evaluation tests. Likewise, in relation to the 8 indicators that measure the acquisition of the competences trained, the students get a score of 70% (from 64% in the business organization to 81% in the generation of value), aligning themselves both with their theoretical tests and with their "self-evolution".

Table 4 Results of self-evolution

Code	Before the courses					After the courses					Difference				
	1	2	3	4	$\dot{x}$	1	2	3	4	$\dot{x}$	1	2	3	4	Δ
Utility	4.8	5.3	5.6	5.6	**5.3**	8.1	8.4	8.4	8.2	**8.3**	3.3	3.1	2.9	2.6	**3.0**
Importance	4.9	5.2	5.7	5.5	**5.3**	8.4	8.6	8.6	8.3	**8.5**	3.5	3.4	2.9	2.8	**3.2**
Interest	4.1	4.3	5.0	5.5	**4.7**	7.8	8.1	8.1	8.0	**8.0**	3.7	3.9	3.1	2.5	**3.3**
Knowledge	2.2	2.4	2.8	2.5	**2.4**	7.0	7.2	7.1	7.1	**7.1**	4.8	4.8	4.4	4.6	**4.7**

The columns with bolds are the synthesis of the previous four columns (the 4 courses). They measure the weighted mean (weighted average, according to the number of students by course) in the whole fîour courses (before, after and difference)

Table 5 Evaluation

Code	Qualification				
	1	2	3	4	ẋ
EV1. Case study defense (communication and presentation)	7.1	6.0	6.9	7.3	6.8
EV2. Entrepreneurship and innovation (value generation)	7.8	7.7	8.2	8.5	8.1
EV3. Selection of potential technologies (feasibility)	7.2	8.0	8.1	8.3	7.9
EV4. Business organization (governance and stakeholders)	5.2	6.9	6.5	7.0	6.4
EV5. Project direction and management (labor organization)	5.4	7.2	7.2	6.7	6.6
EV6. Technical definition (requirements, deadlines and costs)	6.3	7.0	6.5	6.7	6.6
EV7. Self-management (planning and execution of tasks)	6.8	7.7	7.6	8.0	7.5
EV8. Creative problem solving (changes and risks)	5.9	6.2	7.0	7.4	6.6
EV9. Knowledge (management by processes and competences)	6.7	6.9	7.2	6.0	6.7
Weighted evaluation	6.5	7.0	7.2	7.2	7.0

7 Conclusions

The evaluation by competences allows aligning Memories of University Degrees in engineering of the industrial branch of the UCA with the Tuning project of the EHEA, and its transposition into Spanish regulatory framework, as well as with the most important professional standards in PM (IPMA and PMI). This correlation allows the achievement of a traceability that links what is taught/learned at University with the standards of international excellence in engineering (such as the EUR-ACE® label of the ENAEE). Furthermore, this involves the principles of quality, relevance, transparency, recognition, and mobility contemplated in the EHEA and with the labour market (employability), through the promotion of entrepreneurship, creativity, and innovation in a technological context, thanks to engineering PM.

The chosen topics allow students face the challenges that the paradigm of the Industry 4.0 provides them. The value proposition to make the world a better place for life and work, the selection of the proper technology, the business organization, the management of the project and its technical definition offer students a holistic approach to a better understanding of the relation between technology and society through entrepreneurship, creativity and innovation.

In addition, the coordination of the practical cases is developed according to a collaborative model between equals, facilitating the exchange of information, awareness of the agreed goals and requirements, compliance with deadlines, milestones and dates, as well as the resolution of conflicts that occur during the process. The attendance to the sessions, the active participation and commitment of the students, as well as the degree of progress of the work, allow advancing towards the objectives proposed at the beginning, which are achieved according to the results obtained.

As a continuation of the work started, it is proposed to continue this initiative into the atréBT! competition, evaluating the quality of the proposals presented, noting that both innovation and entrepreneurship can be possible in the current context. On the other hand, it is intended to extend the statistics of self-evaluation at the end with those made at the beginning (self-evolution) but related to the 16 selected competences and 9 learning outcomes. Finally, the lessons learned will be documented according to the professors' evaluation, in order to offer successive improved versions of the program.

Acknowledgements To the INTELPREV TEP-955 Group of the University of Cadiz and the TEP-022 Group of the University of Seville.

References

1. Augusti, G. (2009). EUR-ACE: The European accreditation system of engineering education and its global context. In *Engineering education quality assurance* (pp. 41–49). Springer. https://doi.org/10.1007/978-1-4419-0555-0_3.
2. Besner, C., & Hobbs, B. (2013). Contextualized project management practice: A cluster analysis of practices and best practices. *Project Management Journal, 44*(1), 17–34. https://doi.org/10.1002/pmj.21291
3. Bushuyev, S. D., & Wagner, R. F. (2014). IPMA Delta and IPMA organisational competence baseline (OCB). *International Journal of Managing Projects in Business, 7*(2), 302–310. https://doi.org/10.1108/IJMPB-10-2013-0049
4. Caravaca, I., & González, G. (2017). The crisis of neoliberal globalization and labor markets in Andalusia (Spain). *Cadernos Metrópole, 19*(38), 101–125. https://doi.org/10.1590/2236-9996.2017-3804
5. Cerezo, A., Bastante, M. J., & Yagüe, J. L. (2018). Traceability of intra- and interpersonal skills: From education to labor market. In M. Otero & A. Pastor (Eds.), *Human capital and competences in project management* (pp. 87–110). InTech. https://doi.org/10.5772/intechopen.71275.
6. Cerezo, A., de los Ríos, I., Pastor, A., Yagüe, J. L., & Otero, M. (2019). Project management competences by teaching and research staff for the sustained success of engineering education. *Education Sciences, 9*(1), 44.https://doi.org/10.3390/educsci9010044.
7. Coşkun, S., Kayıkcı, Y., & Gençay, E. (2019). Adapting engineering education to industry 4.0 vision. *Technologies, 7*(1), 10. https://doi.org/10.3390/technologies7010010.
8. Eisenhardt, K. M., & Graebner, M. E. (2007). Theory building from cases: Opportunities and challenges. *Academy of Management Journal, 50*(1), 25–32. https://doi.org/10.5465/amj.2007.24160888
9. Ferreira, J., Coelho, A., & Moutinho, L. (2020). Dynamic capabilities, creativity and innovation capability and their impact on competitive advantage and firm performance: The moderating role of entrepreneurial orientation. *Technovation, 92–93*, 102061. https://doi.org/10.1016/j.technovation.2018.11.004
10. Fukuda, K. (2020). Science, technology and innovation ecosystem transformation toward society 5.0. *International Journal of Production Economics, 220*, 107460. https://doi.org/10.1016/j.ijpe.2019.07.033.

11. Guerrero, D., Palma, M., & La Rosa, G. (2014). Developing competences in engineering students. The case of Project Management course. *Procedia—Social and Behavioral Sciences, 112*(2013), 832–841. https://doi.org/10.1016/j.sbspro.2014.01.1239.
12. He, Q., & Hui, D. (2020). Organizational intrapreneurship policy, entrepreneur subjectivity, and employees' intrapreneurship activity. *International Journal of Information Systems in the Service Sector, 12*(1), 1–15. https://doi.org/10.4018/IJISSS.2020010101
13. Klofsten, M., Fayolle, A., Guerrero, M., Mian, S., Urbano, D., & Wright, M. (2019). The entrepreneurial university as driver for economic growth and social change—Key strategic challenges. *Technological Forecasting and Social Change, 141*, 149–158. https://doi.org/10.1016/j.techfore.2018.12.004
14. Kuratko, D. F. (2017). Corporate entrepreneurship 2.0: Research development and future directions. *Foundations and Trends® in Entrepreneurship, 13*(6), 441–490. https://doi.org/10.1561/0300000082.
15. Lukjanova, J., Sushchenko, O., & Zyma, O. (2019). Educated and competent staff as important factor of innovation development of machine-building and metalworking industry in Latvia. *MATEC Web of Conferences, 297*, 06006. https://doi.org/10.1051/matecconf/201929706006
16. Macías, M. E., Cortés, A. A., & Izaguirre, A. R. (2020). Cyber-physical labs to enhance engineering training and education. *International Journal on Interactive Design and Manufacturing (IJIDeM), 14*(4), 1253–1269. https://doi.org/10.1007/s12008-020-00704-6
17. Mulder, K. F. (2017). Strategic competences for concrete action towards sustainability: An oxymoron? Engineering education for a sustainable future. *Renewable and Sustainable Energy Reviews, 68*, 1106–1111. https://doi.org/10.1016/j.rser.2016.03.038
18. Nabi, G., & Holden, R. (2008). Graduate entrepreneurship: intentions, education and training. *Education + Training, 50*(7), 545–551. https://doi.org/10.1108/00400910810909018.
19. Omidvar, G., Jaryani, F., Samad, Z. B. A., Zafarghandi, S. F., & Nasab, S. S. (2011). A proposed framework for project managers' competencies and role of e-portfolio to meet these competencies. *International Journal of E-Education, e-Business, e-Management and e-Learning, 1*(4), 311–321. https://doi.org/10.7763/IJEEEE.2011.V1.51
20. Sánchez, S. M., & Rodríguez, P. (2015). Promoting entrepreneurship by university teaching innovation in the subject business creation. *International Journal of Educational Research and Innovation, 4*, 41–50
21. Simonette, M. J., Barco, L., & Spina, E. (2016). Considering society and technology in systems: A proposal for systems engineers' education. *IEEE International Symposium on Systems Engineering (ISSE), 2016*, 1–4. https://doi.org/10.1109/SysEng.2016.7753169
22. Torres, J. A., Valencia, A., Bermúdez, J., Díez, L. F., Urrego, M. L., & Maussa, F. O. (2018). Characterization of entrepreneurial intention in university students as from systemic entrepreneurship intention model: A case study. *Cuadernos de Gestión, 18*(2), 95–114. https://doi.org/10.5295/cdg.160670jt
23. Trivedi, R. (2016). Does university play significant role in shaping entrepreneurial intention? A cross-country comparative analysis. *Journal of Small Business and Enterprise Development, 23*(3), 790–811. https://doi.org/10.1108/JSBED-10-2015-0149
24. Wagenaar, R. (2014). Competences and learning outcomes: A panacea for understanding the (new) role of Higher Education? *Tuning Journal for Higher Education, 1*(2), 279–302. https://doi.org/10.18543/tjhe-1(2)-2014pp279-302.
25. Waks, L. J. (1997). The project method in postindustrial education. *Journal of Curriculum Studies, 29*(4), 391–406. https://doi.org/10.1080/002202797183964

Transformation of the Project Space in the Digital Economy: Content and Development

Mira A. Kantemirova, Alla E. Gurina, Marina B. Miroshnichenko, Zaurbek L. Dzakoev, and Lyudmila G. Olisaeva

Abstract The article examines the content and transformation of the project space in the digital economy. It presents a review of the state of the issue in academic sources, clarifies the content of the concept of project space in the digital economy, identifies the prerequisites for its study, and reveals its structure. The project space is considered as a specialized component of the economic space. The research results show that the formation and transformation of the project space in the digital economy require an appropriate institutional environment, system conditions, and infrastructure. The aspects considered in the paper make it possible to expand the scope of possibilities for solving an important problem for the modern economy: the formation of a theoretical and methodological basis for the study of the project space in the digital economy, increasing its role and significance in the processes of socio-economic development of regions and states.

Keywords Digital economy · Project space · Transformation · Lacunarity · Region · Project · Efficiency

1 Introduction

In modern conditions, informatization has become the most important direction of economic development, which ensures progressive changes in all areas of human activity [1, 11, 14, 20]. The process of informatization received its continuation in

M. A. Kantemirova (✉) · A. E. Gurina
North Ossetian State Medical Academy, Pushkinskaya St. 40, 362025 Vladikavkaz, Russian Federation

M. B. Miroshnichenko
Kuban State Technological University, Moskovskaya St. 2, 350072 Krasnodar, Russian Federation

Z. L. Dzakoev
North Ossetian State University, Vatutina St. 44-46, 362025 Vladikavkaz, Russian Federation

L. G. Olisaeva
North Caucasian Institute of Mining and Metallurgy (State Technological University), Nikolaeva St. 44, 362021 Vladikavkaz, Russian Federation

V. Kumar et al. (eds.), *Digital Transformation in Industry*, Lecture Notes in Information Systems and Organisation 44, https://doi.org/10.1007/978-3-030-73261-5_20

the form of the formation of a digital economy, which significantly transforms the project space [3, 4, 6, 9, 17].

In recent years, the project approach to the creation, maintenance, and development of various objects has been widely used. The methodology of the project approach is based on the theories of management, marketing, sociology, economics, and many other sciences. Skillful use of the project approach tools allows considering research objects taking into account the influence of environmental factors, identifying problems and substantiating goals, ways and means of their resolution, identifying risks, objectively assessing the results and cost-effectiveness, achieving the necessary competitive advantage and stable strategic positions.

The basic unit of the project approach is the concept of "project", which, despite the ambiguity of interpretations, is disclosed in sufficient detail in the regulatory and methodological documentation and academic literature [7]. At the same time, the insufficient attention of scientists and specialists to the study of the project space, in which various projects are created, exist, and interact with each other, exerting an integrative influence on the synergy and efficiency of the entire socio-economic system, should be noted.

The purpose of this paper is to study the content and transformation of the project space in the digital economy. To achieve the goal, the following objectives have been set: to generalize about the main approaches to the concept of the project space of the economy; to consider the content of the project space of the digital economy; to identify directions for the formation and development of project spaces of the digital economy.

2 Literature Review

The category "space" refers to general fundamental concepts widely used in various fields of knowledge. The existing approaches to understanding space (substantial and relational) demonstrate the evolution of scientists' views over a long period. In the substantial approach, space and time exist independently of objects and processes. In the relational approach, space is represented by a system of relations between different objects in the process of their coexistence. Both of these approaches within the framework of modern scientific knowledge are developing simultaneously [2].

Many scholars have worked on the scientific development of the concept of space in relation to socio-economic phenomena. Some of them did not use this term in their works, but considered various spatial aspects of economics. For example, Ricardo [13] linked the production specialization of regions and the peculiarities of interregional trade with the influence of the spatial differentiation of resources and labor. The attention of scientists of that period was mainly focused on general economic phenomena, and theoretical issues of the spatial organization of the economy and the methodology of project activities were developed much later.

In the geographical and geopolitical concepts (Ratzel, Challenem, Naumann, Mackinder, etc.), the laws of the spatial organization of states, the structure of political and economic space were presented. Location theories, such as [15], Weber [19], revealed the patterns of agricultural production location. Thünen proposed a number of concepts and tools that allow considering production from the standpoint of the formation of the economic aspects of space. In the classical *standort* theory [19] and the approaches of central places (Kristaller) and of industry specificity (Polander), which develop its provisions, space is also considered as an area of location of enterprises, farms, and factors of production. Lösch's neoclassical *standort* theory [10] supplemented the previous spatial concepts with the boundaries of the region. Further development of the theory of space is associated with macro- and mesoeconomic approaches.

In the middle of the twentieth century, scholars (Greenhatt, Isard, Lefebvre, and others) revealed the spatial features inherent in the regional markets, industrial complexes, production systems of regions, and the location of enterprises. In the spatial models, the size and composition of the region's population, migration, incomes and interdistrict trade balance, etc. were used as factors. Studies of spatial forms of self-organization of companies in one territory in the form of integrated firms, industrial complexes, clusters, economic zones were developed [12], Mailat, Jacobs, etc.), but the methodology of the project approach was virtually not applied.

Project activities are presented in numerous research studies [5, 8], Scott, Kemp, & Jonathan, etc.), reflecting the effective methods of developing and implementing projects: Critical Chain Project Management (CCPM), Theory of Constraint (TOC), Six Sigma, etc., used in the Project Management Body of Knowledge (PMBOK). Modern times are distinguished by the use of many methodological approaches to project management, including PRINCE2, Agile, Scrum, Kanban, etc.

An analysis carried out by the authors has shown that the methodological approaches reflect the content of the project, the ways of its development and implementation, focus on the project management tools, but do not reveal the essential content of the project space.

3 Methods

In the process of developing the problem under study, general academic methods (systemic, formalization, analytical, structural, and others) were used to help identify and substantiate the fundamental properties of the objective reality—the project space—and their interpretation to establish patterns and cause-and-effect relationships of its existence and development.

Among the special scientific methods, the search and analysis of projects presented on the Internet resources of the regions were used, with their main characteristics, indicators and results of implementation, features of the impact on the economy; a study of regional project management systems was carried out to identify the nature of decisions made in the field of project development of the economy. Particular attention was paid to the study of programs for the development of digitalization of the economy, as well as measures for the digital transformation of industries and spheres of the region, their relationship with projects.

4 Results

The theoretical and methodological content of the concept of project space in the digital economy has been disclosed in relation to the trends of modern socio-economic development.

The project space in the digital economy is a set of projects, subjects, and objects carrying out project activities, as well as providing connections and interactions between them based on digital technologies in order to meet the needs and achieve the goals of socio-economic development.

The project space in the digital economy includes:

- projects with their criteria, characteristics, indicators, and results;
- subjects—natural persons and legal entities (individual and collective), directly carrying out the processes of development and implementation of projects or participating in them;
- objects—parts of the objective reality to which cognitive, creative, or transforming project activities of subjects are directed;
- consumers—natural persons and legal entities in need of project products;
- normative and legal support governing the principles, procedures, and rules of interaction of project participants with each other and with elements of the external environment;
- management systems (both within and beyond projects);
- a set of resources (material, financial, labor, etc.) necessary for the implementation of project activities;
- infrastructure (market, information services, energy, transport, etc.).
- digital technologies, products, and services that accelerate project activities and increase business sales.

The study revealed that the need to update the research of the project space in the digital economy is substantiated by the following prerequisites. First, the increasingly widespread use of the project approach and digital technologies to socio-economic development requires the development of the project space as a basis for the implementation of project activities. Project space characterizes not only the number, place, and order of mutual arrangement of projects but also the relationship of actors (subjects, objects, participants in project activities) for their implementation, role in society, struggle for a place in space, etc. The combination of projects and digital technologies leads to the transformation of a business through justifying new goals, changing business strategies, business models, creating and promoting innovative products [16].

Second, in Russia there is still lacunarity and insufficient conjugation of projects and digital technologies with each other, causing a fragmented solution of socio-economic problems and the entire project space. Lacunarity means that lacunae are formed in the project field at the meso-level—voids and gaps, reflecting the absence of modern projects and digital technologies aimed at solving relevant socio-economic problems. Insufficient conjugation of projects and digital technologies with each other is caused by the fact that they do not mutually complement each other, which leads to a decrease in the efficiency of project activities.

Third, the strategic vector of economic modernization is largely determined by the level of development of project activities and digital technologies, which, in turn, presupposes the formation of the project space as a system-specific component integrated within the framework of a single macroeconomic concept of the digital economy. The local unit of the project space in the digital economy is the project itself, and the elements of its infrastructure environment using digital technologies.

The structure of the project space reflects an ordered set of its constituent elements with internal connections between them, possessing the property of reproducibility and invariance in relation to the preservation of specialization within a single economic space [18]. The composition of components of the project space in the digital economy is shown in Table 1.

The project space consists of a number of the following components (subspaces): physical (territorial), administrative (regulatory), scientific and technical (scientific and technological), social, informational, digital, economic, infrastructural, etc.

A block diagram of the digital transformation of the regional economy is shown in Fig. 1.

The effect of transformation of the project space in the digital economy (Etp) can be defined as

$$Etp = \sum_{i=1}^{n} Eti - \sum_{i=1}^{n} Eyi, \tag{1}$$

where Eti is the effect obtained by the i-th project of the region due to transformation (the use of digital technologies); Eyi is the effect obtained by the i-th project of the region in traditional conditions.

With Etp > 0, measures to transform the project space in the digital economy are economically beneficial.

The project space in the digital economy is formed by certain actions of the participants in the project process. This space has a special systemic property, manifested in the ability to "integrate in itself" various types of its many subspaces. The formation of an integral project space that meets the principles of synergy and efficiency requires:

- creation of uniform requirements for projects and digital technologies, ensuring their systemic connectivity, interconnection with each other in terms of the nature of goals and objectives, directions of action, stages of the life cycle, etc.;

Table 1 Composition of components of the project space in the digital economy

Component name	Component content
Physical (territorial)	Zones of the region's existence, hosting the actors, customers, consumers, performers, and project participants; objects to which projects are directed; administration systems, infrastructure facilities, etc
Administrative (legal and regulatory	A set of laws, norms, and rules governing the relationship between actors and stakeholders of project activities to achieve goals and perform relevant functions
Scientific and technical (scientific and technological)	Includes the areas of obtaining and applying new knowledge, contributing to the application of new knowledge, solving technical and technological, engineering, and other tasks on projects as a single system
Social	Zones of connections, relationships, interactions of individuals, project teams, social groups, and society on social issues of projects implementation
Informational	Created in the form of sources and volumes of information necessary for the implementation of projects, ensuring communications between them and presenting them in the external environment
Digital	Is a set of digital technologies that provide flexible behavior of companies, optimization of business processes, increase in the degree of satisfaction of needs, access to new sources of income
Economic	Is a set of individuals and legal entities that realize their needs and interests through the implementation of projects, as well as resources, factors, economic characteristics, indicators, and project results

- implementation of systems (portfolios) of various projects, mutually coordinated by the complexes for resolving socio-economic problems and taking into account the maximization of synergy, performance, and effectiveness;
- formation of a developed infrastructure of the project economy, providing all aspects of the development and implementation of projects.

5 Conclusion

The issues of formation and transformation of the project space in the digital economy have not yet received proper reflection in academic sources. This circumstance, as well as the materials considered above, allow postulating the following provisions, proposed as a basis for the formation and development of the project space. First, the formation and transformation of the project space in the digital economy require

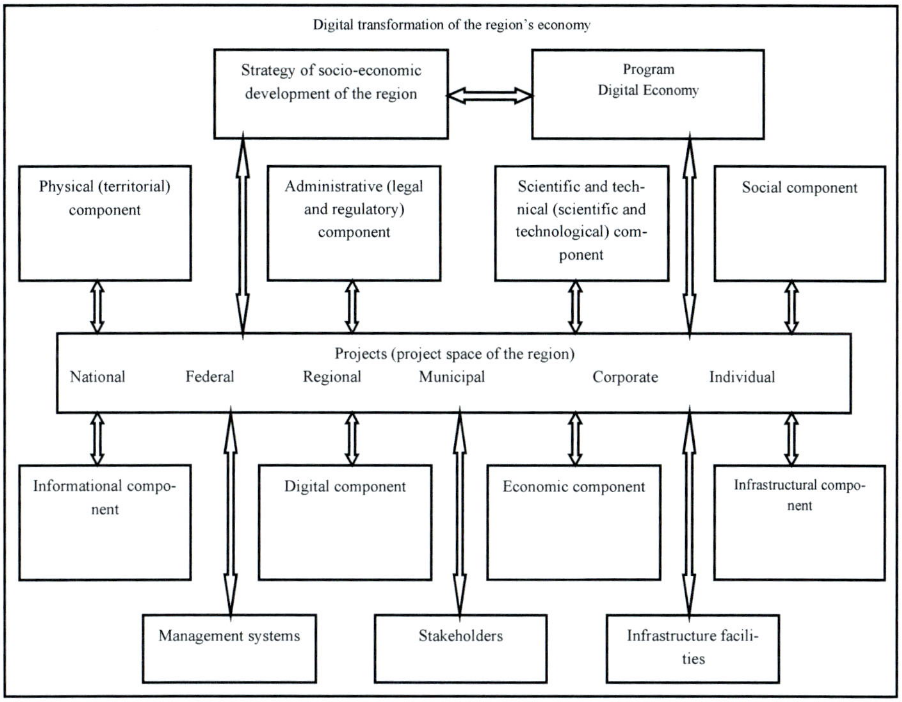

Fig. 1 Block diagram of the digital transformation of the regional economy

an appropriate institutional environment, system conditions, and infrastructure. It is necessary to increase the level of motivation and stimulation of actors for a purposeful and large-scale transfer of the existing economy from predominantly operational principles of activity to project ones. Second, the transformation of the project space in the digital economy goes beyond the service and functional capabilities of project team leaders. This is a strategic task of governing bodies, requiring multi-project regulation of activities in a certain territory and coordinated actions to ensure the conjugation of projects and digital technologies with each other in order to increase the level of synergy and efficiency.

References

1. Arntz, M., Gregory, T., Zierahn, U. (2020). Digitization and the future of work: Macroeconomic Consequences. In K. Zimmermann (Ed.), *Handbook of Labor, Human Resources and Population Economics*. Springer. https://doi.org/https://doi.org/10.1007/978-3-319-57365-6_11-1
2. Biyakov, O. A. (2004). Genesis of the theory of economic space. *Bulletin of KuzSTU, 1*, 75–82
3. Dellis, K., Karkalakos, S., & Kottaridi, C. (2016). Entrepreneurship targeting policies, technological growth, and unemployment. *Journal of Eurasian Economic Dialogue, 1*(6), 19–39

4. Galaso, P., & Kovářík, J. (2018). Collaboration networks and innovation: How to define network boundarieS. *Journal of Eurasian Economic Dialogue, 3*(2), 1–17.
5. Goldratt, E. M., & Cox, J. (2012). *The Goal: A Process of Ongoing Improvement*. (p. 415). Sberbank.
6. Kokuytseva, T.V., Rodionova, I.A., & Damnjanovic, V. (2019). Preconditions for the Transition of Developed and Developing Countries to the Cyber Economy Through the Process of Digital Modernization. In V. Filippov, A. Chursin, J. Ragulina, & E. Popkova (Eds.), *The Cyber Economy. Contributions to Economics*. Springer. https://doi.org/https://doi.org/10.1007/978-3-030-31566-5_6
7. Kompaneytseva, G.A. (2016). Project Approach: Concept, Principles, Factors of Efficiency. *Concept, 17*, 363–368. Retrieved November 16, 2020, from https://e-koncept.ru/2016/46249.htm
8. Leach, L. (2020). *In Time and Within Budget: Critical Chain Project Management* (Trans. from English). Alpina Publishers. (p. 354).
9. Litau, E. (2018). Information flows management as a way to overcome "puberty challenges" of a small enterprise. In *ACM International Conference Proceeding Series* (pp. 34–38). https://doi.org/https://doi.org/10.1145/3278252.3278259
10. Lösch, A. (1959). *Geographic Location of the Property*. (p. 455). Izdatelstvo inostrannoi literatury.
11. Mytareva, L.A., Gorshkova, N.V., Shkarupa, E.A., & Yalmaev, R.A. (2019). The Cyber Economy and Digitization: Impacts on the Quality of Life. In V. Filippov, A. Chursin, J. Ragulina, & E. Popkova (Eds.), *The Cyber Economy. Contributions to Economics*. Springer. https://doi.org/https://doi.org/10.1007/978-3-030-31566-5_3
12. Porter, M. (1993). *International Competition*. (p. 378). Mezhdunarodnye otnosheniya.
13. Ricardo, D. (1955). *Selected Works* (Vol. I). Gospolitizdat. p. 360.
14. Romanova, O. A., Korovin, G. B., & Kuzmin, E. A. (2017). Analysis of the development prospects for the high-tech sector of the economy in the context of new industrialization. *Espacios, 38*(59), 25
15. Thünen, von J. (1926). *Isolated State*. Ekomonicheskaya zhizn. (p. 329).
16. Toomsalu, L., Tolmacheva, S., Vlasov, A., & Chernova, V. (2019). Determinants of Innovations in small and medium enterprises: A European and International Experience. *Terra Economicus, 17*(2), 112–123. https://doi.org/https://doi.org/10.23683/2073-6606-2019-17-2-112-123
17. Trofimov, I. D. (2017). Entrepreneurship and policy dynamics: A theoretical framework. *Journal of Eurasian Economic Dialogue, 2*(3), 13–29
18. Urunov, A. A., Levina, L. F., & Ostapenko, V. A. (2020). Quality of economic space: Measurement problems at the meso-level. *University Bulletin, 4*, 144–151
19. Weber, A. (1926). *Theory of Industry's Location*. (p. 228). Kniga.
20. Xiao, W. (2020). Scientific and technological progress and the transformation of industrial development mode: New-type industrialization. In *Technological Progress and the Transformation of China's Economic Development Mode*. Springer. https://doi.org/https://doi.org/10.1007/978-981-15-7281-4_8

Constructing Cluster-Network Relations in the Oil Sector Based on a Neural Network Model in the Context of Digitalization

Maria Yu. Osipova and Leonid V. Kozhemyakin

Abstract The formation of stable and effective cluster-network connections inevitably increases with the digitalization of all socio-economic relations. The oil sector is one of the key ones in the Russian economy, affecting the determining pace and path of the state socio-economic development, and is subject to the government's greatest regulation as compared to most other industries. Oil companies in Russia are striving to take a dominant role in the global market. The international expansion allows oil companies to diversify state risks and opens up new opportunities. Amid global digitalization, the issue of optimizing big data using new approaches that could be based on classical fundamental knowledge is becoming increasingly critical. One of the methods proposed in the article for working with a broad array of regional indicators in dynamics is neural networks. The paper considers a neural network efficiency model of the cluster-network policy process in the oil sector. The analysis of classical mathematical models allows characterizing the influence of cluster-network connections on the oil and gas industry in the first approximation. The article considers the industry structure and analyzes the Volga Federal District's regions for indicators that characterize the economic state of the regions.

Keywords Cluster-network relations · Oil Industry · Cluster core · Graph theory · Neural network model · Digitalization · Big data analysis

1 Introduction

The key vector of the national economy's successful development in increasing digitalization is to increase competitiveness by creating effective cluster-network links in the socio-economic system. Experience shows that regions with developed cluster-network interactions are becoming the leaders of economic development. The cluster-network approach to the analysis of regional development and industry specifics allows a systematic and comprehensive look at the functioning of economic

M. Yu. Osipova · L. V. Kozhemyakin (✉)
Perm National Research Polytechnic University, Komsomolsky Ave. 29, 614990 Perm, Russian Federation

V. Kumar et al. (eds.), *Digital Transformation in Industry*, Lecture Notes in Information Systems and Organisation 44, https://doi.org/10.1007/978-3-030-73261-5_21

agents included in the economic agglomeration. Besides, the approach allows developing and implementing practical tools to stimulate the socio-economic system of the region and organizations.

A regional socio-economic system is a complex and multidimensional object for management, since, on the one hand, it is a hierarchical state subsystem, functioning within the national space; on the other hand, it is an integrity that functions due to the interaction of many different subjects of various industries and scopes of activities, and, ultimately, the system efficiency as a whole depends on the establishment and formation of their relations. However, currently, there is an imbalance in regional development, accompanied by severe problems and imbalances in socio-economic development, which requires the development of sound strategies and programs, including cluster and network policy.

Although the cluster approach is quite common in scientific works, the issues of formation, development, and evaluation of the effectiveness of cluster-network interactions remain unresolved. Research of the scientific community is based mainly on qualitative methods of cluster analysis (expert, retrospective analysis, analogs comparison method, etc.), but the need for transformation of regional development and the transition to a new economy require the use of economic and mathematical analysis methods, and their range is relatively small, which necessitates the search for new solutions. The process of studying cluster-network connections is associated with the complexity of the phenomena and processes under study and certain information tricks: incompleteness, small time series, and untimely official statistics. These unsolved problems determined the relevance of the research topic.

The theoretical and methodological basis of the work is the fundamental scientific research of leading scientists on the subject under consideration. The analysis shows that the analyzed issue is considered in various directions. The most significant works in theoretical and methodological foundations of the formation and development of clusters and cluster-network connections of socio-economic systems are covered in the works by [2, 3]. The works by Markov and Yagolnitzer [8] and Porter [11–14] are devoted to the formation, development, and improvement of various forms of interaction (intercompany, spatial, cluster, network, etc.). Several works substantiate the use of simulation modeling methods and neural networks for cluster analysis [1, 9, 15].

Despite the variety of existing theoretical, methodological, and applied approaches to the study of cluster-network connections of socio-economic systems, it should be noted that the analyzed studies do not substantiate and specify the impact of the economic space of the region on the development of interaction between oil and gas sector entities. The lack of a systematic view and a single holistic approach to the study of cluster-network interaction of the oil and gas complex entities in the region allows forming the significance of the study.

The significance of the study is to develop methodological foundations for research and forecasting of cluster-network interaction management of economic entities of the oil and gas complex, which ensure the growth of industrial production and the development of the regional system, thereby choosing state regulation tools more reasonably. Moreover, the authors' mechanism for managing cluster-network interaction of the oil and gas sector entities allows its participants to maximize the volume of production of goods and services, increase business profitability indicators, boost tax revenues to the budget, and ensure GRP growth and progressive socio-economic development. This led to setting the work objectives: forming a complex of economic-mathematical models reflecting the processes of formation and development of cluster and network relations of the oil and gas complex at the regional level including advanced mathematical-statistical tools: neural network modeling, mathematical cluster analysis, statistical and adaptive prediction.

Achieving this objective requires setting and solving the following theoretical and practical tasks:

1. Formation of an approach to the development of cluster-network interaction of the oil and gas complex entities of the regional socio-economic system;
2. Development of instrumental and methodological tools for studying the impact of cluster-network interaction on the development of the socio-economic system of the region;
3. Modeling the dependence of the oil and gas sector entities' efficiency on the value of the cluster load index, which characterizes the level of cluster-network interaction at the regional level.

2 Materials and Methods

The mechanism of cluster-network relations is a modern model for forming the network space of the economy, based on the intensity of interactions and the openness of relations that differ not only quantitatively but also qualitatively. The principal difference between cluster-network relations and simple economic relations that arise during the interaction of economic entities is interactive network cooperation, which leads to the formation of centers of mutual interests (Fig. 1).

The shaded area in Fig. 1 conventionally shows a mutual interest (relationships) area that leads to an increase in the speed of solving functional issues for each cluster, so the density of common interest areas indicates the nature of the intensity of cluster-network connections. Consequently, clusters are transformed employing network connections into hybrid systems that work as a single mechanism, which, having received positive qualities from each system (clusters and networks), forms new epicenters of intensive development. The cluster-network nature of connections promotes self-organization and self-development of cluster formations.

If the authors consider the regional structure of Russia, the Volga Federal District occupies the second position in oil production, thus making a significant contribution to one of the prevailing sectors of the Russian economy: oil and gas companies give more than a quarter of the volume of industrial production of Russia, thereby forming substantial tax revenues and other revenues to the state budget [10]. The oil and gas complex refers to industrial production and is a generic name for a group of industries that includes the oil production, transportation, and refining industries.

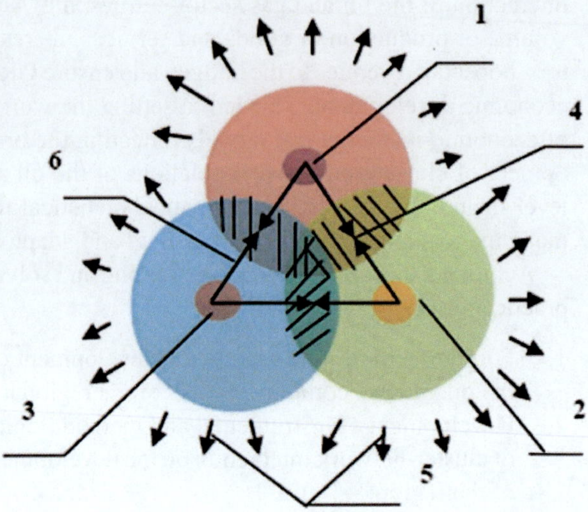

Fig. 1 Flowsheet of cluster-network interactions formation: 1, 2, 3—cluster core; 5—external links; 6—internal links; 4—mutual interest areas (interactive network cooperation)

The branch structure of the object under study—the Volga Federal District is considered (Fig. 2).

Having considered the Volga Federal District's industry structure in detail, it is worth noting the same trend of prevalence of the three industries as in Russia as a whole. About 37% is accounted for by the mining and processing industry. Summing up the interim results, the authors can highlight the leading role of the Volga Federal District and the Perm Territory in particular in the formation of the state oil and gas production complex.

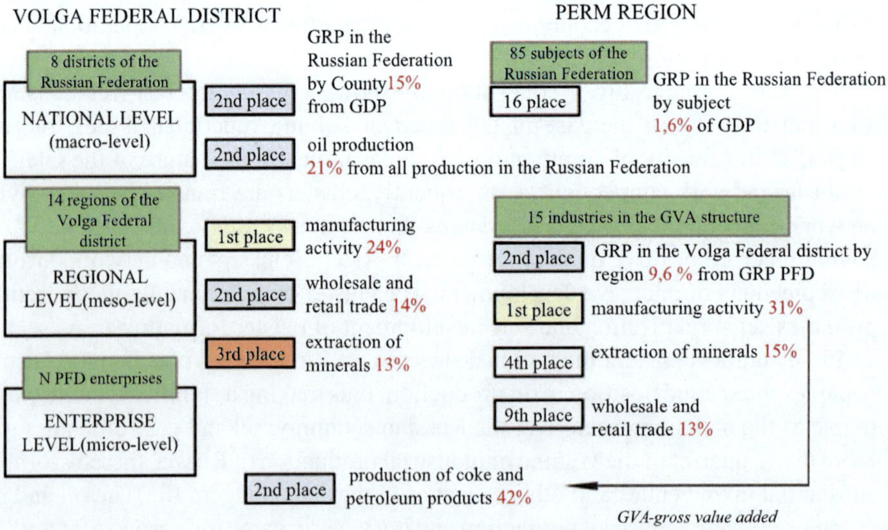

Fig. 2 Leading industries in the Volga Federal District and the Perm Territory

Table 1 Classification of the Volga federal district regions

Group 1 *(Mining)*	Group 2 *(Manufacturing activity)*
Republic of Tatarstan	Republic of Mari El
Udmurt Republic	Republic of Mordovia
Orenburg Region	Chuvash Republic
Perm Territory	Kirov Region
	Nizhny Novgorod Region
	Penza Region
	Saratov Region
	Ulyanovsk Region
	Republic of Bashkortostan
	Samara Region

According to the results of the authors' method for classifying regions with a mixed type of economic activity, the authors have the following distribution of the Volga Federal District regions (Table 1).

For each of the groups, it is necessary to analyze the state of the regional economy (Figs. 3, 4).

Further, the study of the predominance of economic activity and the definition of the main dominant sub-sectors will be conducted for all Russian regions. Based on the results of the analysis of the Volga Federal District, the authors will train a neural network with the following input parameters:

IEM_{ij} production index by type of economic activity "Mining";
IMA_{ij} production index by type of economic activity "Manufacturing";
$rGRP_{ij}$ rate of gross regional product per capita;
k_i cluster load index.

A detailed method for finding the indicator k_i is considered in the previous study; the primary calculations are presented in the published article [6].

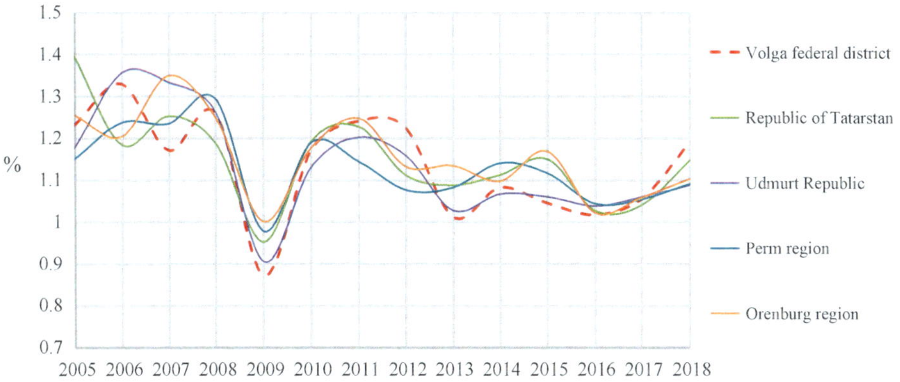

Fig. 3 GRP per capita for group 1 for the period of 2005–2018

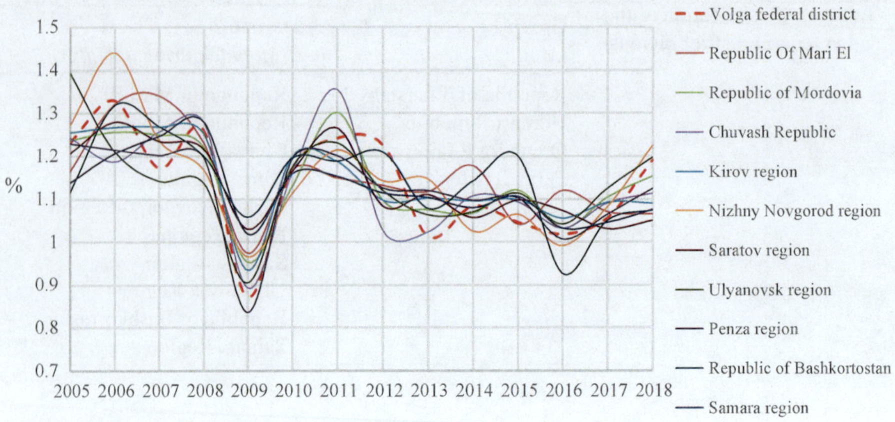

Fig. 4 GRP per capita for group 2 for the period of 2005–2018

Output values will be set by a column vector of the following type: $\mu\{e, m\}$, where e denotes the typical regional industry type "Mining", m– the typical industry type "Manufacturing".

In the work by Yasnitsky [15] "Artificial intelligence", an analysis of the main approaches and methods of neural network modeling is given. The optimal perceptron is proposed. Further, in neural network modeling, the authors focus and rely on the research and conclusions by Yasnitsky.

For a long time, it was impossible to represent a function of many variables as the sum of functions of a smaller number of variables. It turned out that the perceptron, no matter how many neurons it had, could not always construct an approximation of any function of several variables. Doubts about the capabilities of perceptrons were dispelled by the mathematicians [5], who managed to prove that any continuous function n of variables $f(x_1, x_2, \ldots, x_n)$ can always be represented as a sum of continuous functions of a single variable: $f_1(x_1) + f_2(x_2) + \ldots + f_n(x_n)$.

In 1987–1991, Professor Hecht-Nielsen [4] of the University of California (USA) published two articles in which the Arnold–Kolmogorov theorems were reworked in relation to neural networks. It was proved that it was possible to construct a neural network that performs a transformation for any given set of different training examples, and the universal neural network will be a two-layer perceptron, i. e. a perceptron with one hidden layer, and the activation functions of its neurons must be sigmoid.

The required number of neurons in the hidden layers of the perceptron is determined by the formula that is a consequence of the Arnold–Kolmogorov–Hecht-Nielsen theorems:

$$\frac{N_y Q}{1 + \log_2(Q)} \leq N_w \leq N_y \left(\frac{Q}{N_x} + 1 \right) \left(N_x + N_y + 1 \right) + N_y, \tag{1}$$

```
X = tonndata(InputData,false,false);
T = tonndata(OutputData,false,false);

trainFcn = 'trainscg';
inputDelays = 1:5;
feedbackDelays = 1:5;
hiddenLayerSize = 7;
net = narxnet(inputDelays,feedbackDelays,hiddenLayerSize,'open',trainFcn);

[x,xi,ai,t] = preparets(net,X,{},T);

net.divideParam.trainRatio = 70/100;
net.divideParam.valRatio = 10/100;
net.divideParam.testRatio = 20/100;
```

Fig. 5 Representation of information on input parameters of a neural network

```
[net,tr] = train(net,x,t,xi,ai);
y = net(x,xi,ai);
e = gsubtract(t,y);
performance = perform(net,t,y);
view(net)
```

Fig. 6 Option of the best neural network training method

where N_y is the dimension of the output signal; Q is the number of elements in the set of training examples; N_w is the required number of synaptic connections; N_x is the dimension of the input signal.

The authors will use the basic module Neural Net Time Series presented in the Matlab software product to build a neural network. The authors adapt the source code for the required task (Figs. 5, 6).

According to the generally accepted neural network design technology, the entire set of examples was divided into Train, Test, and Validation in the ratio: 70%:20%:10%. The optimal interval $4 \leq N \leq 60$ of the allowed number of neurons in hidden layers is obtained based on the clustering formula.

The neural network was trained using various methods: the error backpropagation method, the elastic backpropagation method, the Levenberg–Marquardt method, etc. Optimization of the neural network structure—selecting the optimal number of hidden neurons and activation functions was performed manually. Thus, there is a dynamic nonlinear autoregressive neural network with an external input for introducing an additional parameter $x(t)$ that affects the value $y(t)$, and the authors consider the option when the data about the additional parameter is unknown, and the external input receives the previous values of the parameter $y(t)$ under study with the following parameters. The main network characteristics:—7 neurons on the hidden layer;—the input delay vector adjusted to the parameter 1:5;—the reverse delay vector adjusted to the parameter 1:5.

The hyperbolic tangent is taken as the activation function on the first layer. On the second layer, a linear transfer function was used. The best result was shown by a

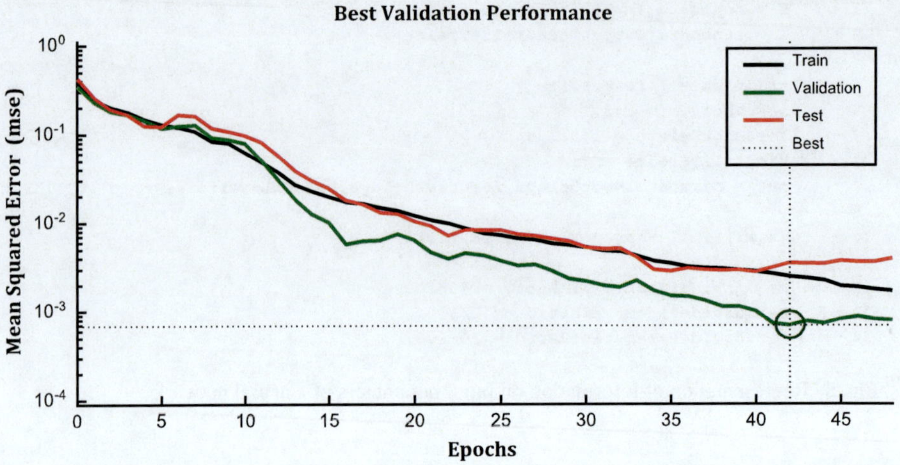

Fig. 7 Representation of the root-mean-square error from the training iteration

network function that updates the weight and offset values according to the feedback of the conjugate gradient method. A closed-loop network was also considered for obtaining a recurrent network, but the error was significantly greater than without closing the loop, so further implementation of this type of network was not considered (Figs. 7, 8).

3 Results

Thus, a table was formed with the leading industries for the predominant types of economic activity "Mining" and "Manufacturing". Sub-sectors that form more than 80% of the corresponding industry are identified (Table 2).

The search for the central vertex of the graph, which is also the possible optimal cluster center, allowed identifying two regions: the Perm Territory for the sub-industry "Crude oil and natural gas production" and the Republic of Bashkortostan for the sub-industry "Production of coke and petroleum products". At the same time, the condition $R_{min} > \widetilde{k}_t$ of critical core mass (studies on finding critical core mass indicators are published in the article [7]) is fulfilled in both cases, which indicates a favorable ground for optimal creation of cluster-network connections in a mixed type of economic activity in regions with dominant industries: "Mining" in the context of the sub-industry "Production of crude oil and natural gas" and "Manufacturing" in the context of the sub-industry "Production of coke and petroleum products".

Thus, the inhomogeneity of the percentage of leading industries within the region and the cluster-network load, in general, suggests the need to redistribute the subsequent processing of production to nearby regions or those located on the logistics route, which will make the clusters more complete.

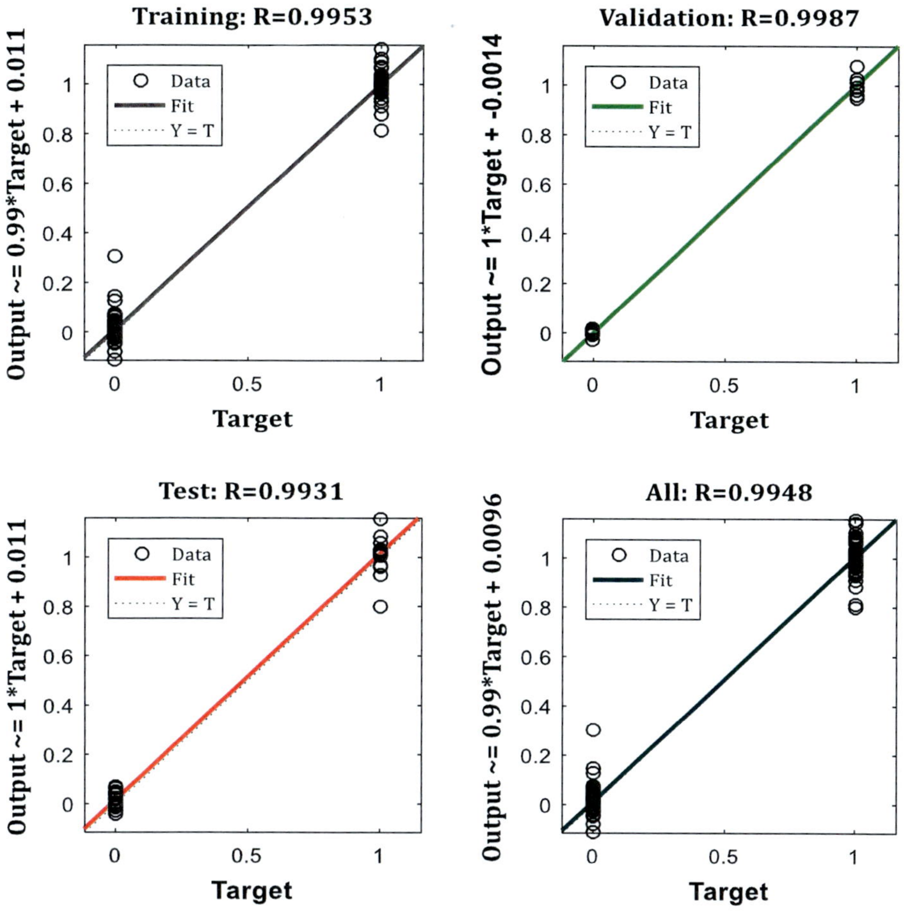

Fig. 8 Generalizing ability of a neural network

Next, an attempt is made to construct a predictive econometric model of the gross regional product level based on the variability of the cluster load index of regions with dominant industries: "Mining" of the Volga Federal District. The main econometric models are presented in Table 3a, b.

Such models cannot adequately describe the studied dependencies due to the curvelinear input parameters, and checking the forecast values on retrospective data has a high deviation from the actual indicators. In this regard, a neural network model was used, the results of the forecast of which on average did not deviate from the real data by more than 1.15%.

The next stage of the study was the enterprises that are possible centers cluster cores of regions: Perm Territory and the Republic of Bashkortostan. Considering the regions, the Perm Territory is of greater interest since it occupies high positions in the rating with its mixed type of economic activity, and the leading activity is the oil industry, led by companies of the LUKOIL group (Fig. 9).

Table 2 Leading industries and corresponding sub-industries of Russian regions

Industry	% of industry	Sub-industry	Region
"Mining"	70.7	crude oil and natural gas production	Khanty-Mansi Autonomous Area, Tyumen Region without autonomous areas, Arkhangelsk Region, Komi Republic, Yamal-Nenets Autonomous Area, Sakhalin Region, Yamal-Nenets Autonomous Area, Tomsk Region, Perm Territory, Republic of Tatarstan, Udmurt Republic, Orenburg Region
	8.6	coal mining	Kemerovo Region, Republic of Khakassia
	6.6	mining of metal ores	Chukotka Autonomous Area, Belgorod Region, Magadan Region, Republic of Tyva
	3.4	extraction of other minerals	Republic of Sakha (Yakutia)
"Manufacturing activity"	25.8	production of coke and petroleum products	Omsk Region, Volgograd Region, Ryazan Region, Republic of Bashkortostan
	19.2	metallurgical production and production of finished metal products	Krasnoyarsk Territory, Vologda Region, Lipetsk Region, Sverdlovsk Region, Chelyabinsk Region, Vologda Region, Irkutsk Region
	15.2	production of food products, including beverages and tobacco	Republic of Adygea, Stavropol Territory, Tambov Region
	13.4	production of machinery and equipment	Tver Region, Ulyanovsk Region, Samara Region
	8.7	chemical production	Tula Region, Astrakhan Region, Kirov Region, Novgorod Region

Table 3 Multivariance of the main models

a

Function type	Russian regions	
	Republic of Tatarstan	Udmurt Republic
Linear	$y = -46.374x + 403.61$	$y = -59.423x + 356.52$
	$R^2 = 0.0053$	$R^2 = 0.0733$
3rd order polynomial	$y = 724.42x^3 - 756.54x^2 - 892.89x + 1207.2$	$y = -70.664x^3 - 706.59x^2 - 1841.1x + 1591$
	$R^2 = 0.4985$	$R^2 = 0.6501$
Power	$y = 323.18x^{0.234}$	$y = 293.89x^{0.477}$
	$R^2 = 0.0155$	$R^2 = 0.0855$
Exponential	$y = 326.87e^{0.004x}$	$y = 311.89e^{0.187x}$
	$R^2 = 9E - 05$	$R^2 = 0.034$
Logarithmic	$y = -120.3\ln(x) + 358.51$	$y = -136.5\ln(x) + 327.49$
	$R^2 = 0.0399$	$R^2 = 0.1489$

(continued)

Table 3 (continued)

a

Function type	Russian regions	
	Republic of Tatarstan	Udmurt Republic

b

Function type	Russian regions	
	Perm Territory	Orenburg Region
Linear	$y = -176.33x + 125.31$	$y = -7.5947x + 299.17R^2 = 0.0007$
	$R^2 = 0.1589$	
3rd order polynomial	$y = -2107.9x^3 - 7826x^2 - 9217x + 3732.2$	$y = -461.76x^3 + 2295.9x^2 - 3393.2x + 1753.9$
	$R^2 = 0.2454$	$R^2 = 0.7553$
Power	$y = 283.47x^{0.7613}$	$y = 270.15x^{0.174}$
	$R^2 = 0.1824$	$R^2 = 0.0208$
Exponential	$y = 134.56e^{0.722x}$	$y = 268.15e^{-0.008x}$
	$R^2 = 0.1934$	$R^2 = 5E - 05$
Logarithmic	$y = 183.11\ln(x) + 307.21$	$y = -53.57\ln(x) + 295.32$
	$R^2 = 0.1454$	$R^2 = 0.0298$

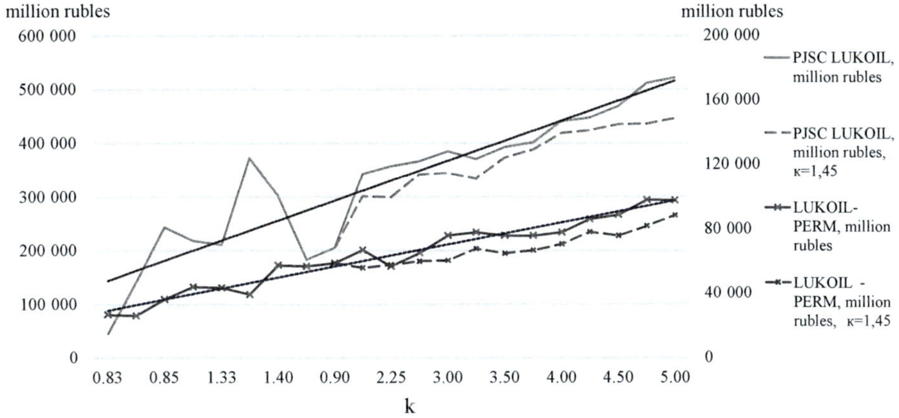

Fig. 9 Relationship between k and the profit of enterprises

The Perm Territory is one of the few in Russia and the only one in the Volga Federal District that combines the entire oil and gas vertical: from exploration to petroleum products sales. Consequently, the LUKOIL structure as a vertically integrated company has all formal characteristics of a cluster. The authors interpret the response of the forecast values of the industrial enterprise's profit when the cluster load index changes as the management of cluster-network connections at industrial enterprises (in this case, an enterprise in the oil and gas sector—LUKOIL group of enterprises), focused on the dominant industry of the enterprise region [10].

The forecast results confirm the hypothesis on the favorability of strengthening—the creation (concentration) of a cluster with the leading sub-industry of oil production. In particular, the profit of large enterprises focused on the dominant industry will increase much more intensively with an increase in the cluster load index, which is typical for a cluster economy [6].

4 Conclusion

Thus, the development of a fuel and energy cluster based on the existing structure of the vertically integrated oil company (VIOC) LUKOIL, where the cluster core can be the VIOC LUKOIL, will be possible optimal management of the region with a characteristic mixed type of industrial production. This can contribute to the growth of strategic initiatives and profit growth of the oil and gas company, as well as increase the likelihood of strengthening and improving socio-economic indicators through the influx of new labor and investment in various projects, thereby increasing the efficiency of both the region and the enterprise itself.

The article considers the industry structure and analyzes the Volga Federal District's regions for indicators that characterize the economic state of the regions. A holistic system view and a unified theoretical and methodological approach to studying various forms of cluster-network interaction of oil and gas industry entities are formed. Predictive models are constructed using neural network modeling in the classification of regions by dominant industries, making a short-term forecast of the profit of oil and gas enterprises while managing the level of cluster-network connections of the enterprise understudy as the cluster core.

References

1. Andreychikov, A. V., & Andreychikova, O. N. (2004). *Smart Information Systems: Textbook for Higher Education Institutions*. Finance and Statistics.
2. Query ID="Q1" Text="Unable to parse this reference. Kindly do manual structure" Borisevich, V.I., Geisler, P.S., & Fateev, V.S. (2002). *Regional Economy. Study Guide*. BSEU. (p. 432).
3. Goldratt, E.M., & Cox, D. (2014). *Objective: The Process of Continuous Improvement* (E. Fedurko, Trans.). Popurri. (p. 400).
4. Hecht-Nielsen, R. (1987). Kolmogorov's mapping neural network existence theorem. *IEEE First Annual Int Conf. on Neural Networks, 3*, 11–13
5. Kolmogorov, A. N. (1957). On the representation of continuous functions of several variables as superpositions of continuous functions of one variable and addition. *Reports of the USSR Academy of Sciences, 114*, 953–956
6. Kozhemyakin, L.V. (2020). Determination of the Critical Mass of the Oil-Producing Cluster Core Using Graph Theory. *Simulation, Optimization, and Information Technology, 8*(3). Retrieved November 21, 2020, from https://moit.vivt.ru/wp-content/uploads/2020/08/Kozhemyakin_3_20_1.pdf.
7. Kozhemyakin, L.V. (2020). On Managing Cluster-Network Interaction of Oil and Gas Complex Facilities Using Neural Network Modeling. In *Questions of Technical Sciences: New Approaches to Solving Actual Problems. Collection of Scientific Papers on the Results of the International Scientific and Practical Conference, No. 7, Kazan*. ICRON. (p. 39).
8. Markov, L. S., & Yagolnitzer, M. A. (2006). *Clusters: Formalization of Relationships in Informal Production Structures*. (p. 194). IEOPP SB RAS.
9. Mikhalev, D.A. (2015). *Modeling the Processes of Formation and Development of Regional Industrial Clusters* (Ph.D. Thesis). (p. 223).
10. Pervadchuk, V. P., Osipova, MYu., & Kozhemyakin, L. V. (2019). Econometric modeling of cluster-network interactions. *Economics and Entrepreneurship, 10*(111), 978–983
11. Porter, M. E. (2003). *Competitive Environment*. (p. 495). Williams.
12. Porter, M.E. (2007). *Competitive Strategy: Methods for Analyzing Industries and Competitors* (Trans. from English, 3rd ed.). Alpina Business Books. (p. 453).
13. Porter, M.E. (2014). *International Competitive Environment* (Trans. from English). International Relations. (p. 896).
14. Porter, M.E. (2015). *Competitive Advantage: How to Achieve a High Result and Ensure Its Sustainability?* (Trans. from English). Alpina Business Books. (p. 715).
15. Yasnitsky, L. N. (2011). *Artificial Intelligence. Elective Course: Study Guide*. BINOM. Laboratorya znanyi.

Modeling a Development Strategy for Petrochemical Enterprise Organizational Structures

Alexey I. Shinkevich, Vladimir I. Petrov, and Naira V. Barsegyan

Abstract The study aims to identify the determinants that affect the efficiency of production processes and personnel development as a key component of modernization transformations and the dominant factor of production in Industry 4.0. To solve this problem, a strategy for developing a lean organizational structure to manage a petrochemical enterprise is modeled using the production function proposed by Cobb and Douglas. The results of the analysis show that taking into account the achievement of total indicators for the petrochemical industry as a cumulative result, the efficiency of innovation activity expressed in the calculation of the shipment of innovative products per highly productive workplace will increase from 0.7 million rubles on average per petrochemical enterprise to 1.6 million rubles by 2024. The proposed methodology can be used not only at the industry level when designing lean management structures in the petrochemical industry but also at the micro-level for individual enterprises in the industry.

Keywords Development strategy · Lean strategy · Organizational structure · Petrochemical enterprises

1 Introduction

In the modern conditions of transition to Industry 4.0, the organization of production in the petrochemical industry is based on the use of optimization models, which requires new directions for increasing the industrial complex efficiency to be taken into account.

The optimization of management systems becomes feasible when the existing tools and approaches are comprehensively taken into consideration. This approach is the only way to define mechanisms, indicators, resources, and a system of measures to achieve the set goals. The key value of integration is that it facilitates the transition to

A. I. Shinkevich · V. I. Petrov · N. V. Barsegyan (✉)
Kazan National Research Technological University, K. Marx St. 68, 420015 Kazan, Russian Federation

V. Kumar et al. (eds.), *Digital Transformation in Industry*, Lecture Notes in Information Systems and Organisation 44, https://doi.org/10.1007/978-3-030-73261-5_22

a set of production processes and improves them by applying innovative technologies and appropriate methods.

Identifying the determinants that affect the efficiency of production processes and personnel development as a key component of modernization transformations and the dominant factor of production in Industry 4.0 is of great importance for developing a strategy for implementing a lean management structure for petrochemical enterprises. In this regard, the purpose of the study is to identify the factors that affect the organizational structure of management by modeling and constructing a production function.

2 Literature Review

The organizational structure of management is one of the tools for improving the management system, the units of which are subject to constant changes and adjustments—creation, reduction, division, and unification of links as enterprises develop and grow. For the same enterprise, one can design different organizational management structures depending on the selected development strategy and create different organizational structures for the same selected strategy. Consequently, it is necessary to identify the most effective and optimal organizational structure. This task requires the development of appropriate methods or a set of them.

Special attention is paid to the management system in the works by Gölzer and Fritzsche [1, 2]. The studies by Shinkevich et al. [3], Zinovyeva et al. [4], Kudryavtseva et al. [5] solve the problems of identifying factors that influence the management system of industrial enterprises. Tolstykh et al. [6] present methods and models for analyzing the performance of industrial enterprises. Works by both Russian and foreign scientists are devoted to automated systems for supporting decision-making on resource conservation management in the industry in the context of digitalization of the economy. The works by Petrik et al. [7], Shinkevich et al. [8] are dedicated to a study of the Internet of Things platform. Remane et al. [9] assess the digital maturity of organizations in two aspects—the impact of digitalization on the organization and organizations' readiness for transformation. Lubnina et al. [10] study the influence of the management system on the rational use of resources.

However, in the presence of an extensive theoretical and methodological array of data and practical solutions, the possibilities of mathematical and system engineering methods, Big Data, and Industry 4.0 achievements are not fully used when designing organizational management structures and developing approaches to their assessment, which would take into account the features of petrochemical enterprises' development strategies in the period of digitalization. Insufficient elaboration of these issues predetermined the choice of the study topic, its purpose and objectives.

3 Material and Methods

According to the OPEC data published in the World Oil Outlook, the demand for petrochemical products will only increase in the medium term. Consequently, the issues of resource and energy saving at petrochemical enterprises require a thorough solution.

The efficient use of hydrocarbon resources and the development of integrated oil refining require a diversified strategy of petrochemical production. The organizational structure of enterprise management is built according to the strategy for its development.

For modeling organizational management structures at petrochemical enterprises, it is appropriate to use a production function taking into account the indicators of the use of human and material capital in organizing production. Considering the directions of digitalization, the increasing level of innovation in production, and the development of industry 4.0, the authors suggest using shipment of innovative products per one petrochemical enterprise as a result variable, i.e. an indicator of production effectiveness. Explanatory variables are the utilization of labor resources, expressed through the share of jobs in total employment at petrochemical enterprises, and the utilization of tangible capital as the coefficient of renewal of fixed assets in the petrochemical industry. The calculations are based on the average values for the petrochemical industry, which includes such subtypes of activity as "chemical production" and "production of rubber and plastic products". The choice of these indicators for modeling was determined by the results of component and factor analysis, which showed that human resources, innovation, technical and technological potential of production exerted the greatest influence on the design of organizational management structures in the petrochemical industry. These factors will be considered when constructing the production function.

Let us use the classical model of the production function proposed by Cobb and Douglas:

$$Y = A \times K^{\alpha} \times L^{\beta}, \quad (1)$$

where, in this case Y is the volume of shipped innovative products per one petrochemical company, million; K is coefficient of renewal of fixed assets (financial component); L is the share of jobs in total employment at petrochemical enterprises, percentage (human component); α, β are the elasticity of the model; A is the independent variable of the model.

The initial data for modeling, as well as logarithms for indicators, are summarized in Table 1.

Table 1 Source data to build the model of the production function

Year	Innovative products shipped per 1 enterprise, mln rubles	Share of high-performance jobs in the total headcount, %	The coefficient of renewal of fixed assets	Ln		
	Y	L	K	Y	L	K
2010	4.3	42.4	5.9	1.5	3.7	1.8
2011	5.4	45.7	6.4	1.7	3.8	1.9
2012	6.0	54.7	6.5	1.8	4.0	1.9
2013	5.7	57.7	6.9	1.7	4.1	1.9
2014	5.6	60.0	6.9	1.7	4.1	1.9
2015	7.3	55.1	6.3	2.0	4.0	1.8
2016	8.6	57.4	5.2	2.1	4.1	1.6
2017	7.7	65.3	5.9	2.0	4.2	1.8
2018	9.1	71.6	5.7	2.2	4.3	1.7
2019	10.0	78.4	5.7	2.3	4.4	1.7

4 Results

As a result of modeling, the following model of the production function was obtained:

$$Y = 0.75 \times K^{-1.22} \times L^{1.08} \quad (2)$$

The model is statistically reliable, as indicated by the statistical significance of the coefficients of the equation (p-value less than 0.05). The coefficient of determination is 89%. The Fisher criterion also corresponds to the standard—the p-value is less than 0.05. The average model residuals tend to zero. There is no autocorrelation in the model residuals, as confirmed by the Darbin-Watson criterion, which is 2.1 (with a standard value equal to 2) (Table 2).

Table 2 Results of modeling the production function of petrochemical enterprises (calculated by the authors)

Regression Summary for the Dependent Variable: Y (Spreadsheet1) R = 0.94277537; R^2 = 0.88882540; Adjusted R^2 = 0.8570612; F(2.7) = 27.982 $p < 0.00046$ Std. Error of estimate: 0.10212

	b*	Std.Err	b	Std.Err	t(2)	p-value
Intercept			−0.29	1.17	−0.25	0.81
L	0.75	0.13	1.08	0.19	5.73	0.00
K	−0.41	0.13	−1.22	0.39	−3.15	0.02

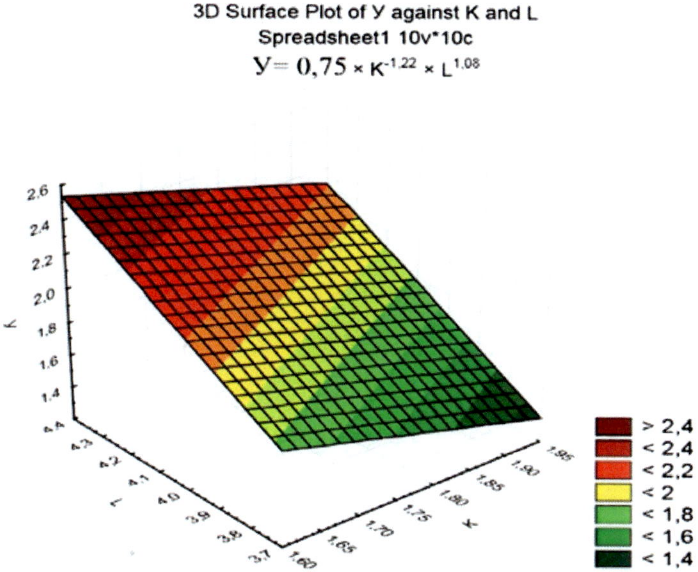

Fig. 1 Diagram of the surface of the production function of petrochemical enterprises for the use of labor and material capital (constructed by the authors)

The three-dimensional visualization of the model of the production function of petrochemical enterprises by the components of human, material, and innovation potential is shown in Fig. 1.

Unstable dynamics of the renewal of fixed assets affected the negative sign for the variable that characterizes material capital. At the same time, the increase in the share of high-performance jobs reflected an increase in innovative products shipped per petrochemical enterprise. Consequently, the component of human resource management was crucial in the development of innovative activities in the petrochemical industry. Therefore, when designing organizational management structures at petrochemical enterprises, these development programs should be focused primarily on the goals of innovative development with labor costs and their productivity as the dominant factor.

The results of modeling the production function made it possible to prepare a medium-term forecast for shipment of innovative products at petrochemical enterprises. Taking into account the current trends, in which the average growth rate of the share of high-tech jobs in 2010–2019 was 2%, and the average rate of decline in the coefficient of renewal of fixed assets -1%, substituting the values of independent variables in the model, the authors calculated the forecast values of shipment of innovative products per petrochemical enterprise for the period up to 2024. According to the forecast, this indicator will rise from 10 million rubles per petrochemical enterprise in 2020 up to 18.4 million rubles per petrochemical enterprise in 2024 (Fig. 2).

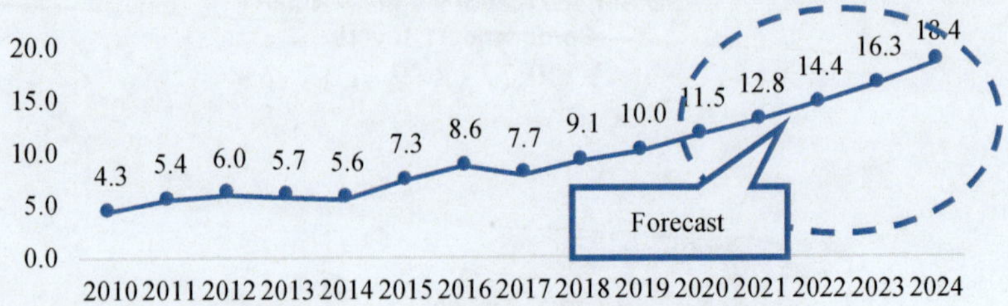

Fig. 2 Forecast values of shipment of innovative products per petrochemical enterprise (million rubles) (calculated by the authors)

Thus, the design of organizational structures of management at petrochemical enterprises, taking into account the level of manufacturability of production and personnel involved in high-performance workplaces, will provide an increase in the shipped innovative products. The competitive advantage of petrochemical companies also owes to a more flexible factor of production—labor and its components, such as using skills, knowledge, and abilities of staff in high-tech manufacturing.

5 Discussion

A new organizational structure of a petrochemical enterprise focusing on managing value streams is a prerequisite for the successful implementation of lean production methods, tools, and principles.

Under modern conditions of transition to the digital economy, advanced manufacturing technologies, the Internet of Things, and additive manufacturing play an important role in creating an innovative product and bringing it to the market. Based on digital platforms that are flexible and scalable, it becomes possible to analyze the market, predict its needs, and plan the production of new products, which will allow manufacturers to create the goods consumers need. Manufacturers are now using technological opportunities to complement or optimize their lean manufacturing initiatives. Digital platforms combine the most important functions for business, allowing productivity and efficiency to be increased through the automation of tasks and improvement of the visibility of processes in the enterprise.

More and more manufacturers will use digital platforms to organize a demand-driven supply chain. The advantage will be data continuity, which allows the flow of available information to be tracked. Currently, projects are being developed to determine and standardize methods for implementing intelligent production systems. Advanced production technologies allow employees to focus on more useful activities, freeing them from performing numerous tasks. Repetitive tasks that do not require high skills will be performed automatically, and employees will have access to the Internet of Things data and implement improvements. Digital platforms will create a more collaborative environment and provide more opportunities for innovative change.

6 Conclusion

The study has simulated a strategy for developing a lean organizational structure for managing a petrochemical enterprise. The results of modeling show that, taking into account the achievement of cumulative indicators for the petrochemical industry, the efficiency of innovation activity expressed in the calculation of shipment of innovative products per high-performance workplace will increase from 0.7 million rubles on average per petrochemical enterprise to 1.6 million rubles by 2024. The proposed method can be used not only at the industry level when designing lean management structures in the petrochemical industry but also at the micro-level for individual enterprises in the industry.

Russian scientists and specialists have accumulated positive experience in developing effective principles, tools, and methods for organizing production systems and their application. The modern system of lean production in high-tech industries should take into account the specifics of Russian approaches to organizing and managing petrochemical production systems.

Acknowledgements The research was carried out within the framework of the grant of the President of the Russian Federation for state support of leading scientific schools of the Russian Federation, project number NSH-2600.2020.6.

References

1. Gölzer, P., & Fritzsche, A. (2017). Data-driven operations management: Organizational implications of the digital transformation in industrial practice. *Production Planning and Control, 28*(16), 1332–1343
2. Mintzberg, H. (1979). *The structuring of organization: A synthesis of the research*. Englewood cliffs, 4.
3. Shinkevich, A. I., Kudryavtseva, S. S., & Ershova, I. G. (2020). Modelling of energy efficiency factors of petrochemical industry. *International Journal of Energy Economics and Policy, 10*(3), 465–470
4. Zinovyeva, I. S., Savin, A. G., Brizhak, O. V., & Shchinova, R. A. (2020). Natural management of a modern region: Assessment of effectiveness and perspectives of improvement. *Lecture Notes in Networks and Systems, 73*, 717–723
5. Kudryavtseva, S. S., Shinkevich, M. V., Malysheva, T. V., & Ishmuradova, I. I. (2020). The specifics of training for the industrial sector in the context of digitalization. *Journal of Physics: Conference Series, 1515*, 022014
6. Tolstykh, T., Savon, D., Safronov, A., Shkarupeta, E., & Ivanochkina, T. (2020). Methods and models for analysis the effectiveness of industrial enterprises. In *Proceedings of the 32nd International Business Information Management Association Conference*, pp. 7710–7722.

7. Petrik, D., Straub, D., & Herzwurm, G. (2020). Potentials of Platforms for the Realization of Digital Services for Component Manufacturers. *The 53rd CIRP Conference on Manufacturing Systems, 93*, 652–657.
8. Shinkevich, M. V., Vertakova, Yu. V., & Galimulina, F. F. (2020). Synergy of digitalization within the framework of increasing energy efficiency in manufacturing industry international. *Journal of Energy Economics and Policy, 10*(3), 456–464
9. Remane, G., Hanelt, A., & Wiesboeck, F. (2017). Digital maturity in traditional industries—an exploratory analysis. Twenty-Fifth European Conference on Information Systems (ECIS), from https://www.en.wim.bwl.uni-muenchen.de/pubdb_en/art_proc_i/2017-04.html.
10. Lubnina, A. A., Bashkirtceva, S. A., Rajskaya, M. V., & Zaripov, R. N. (2020). The rationalization model of the use of enterprise resources. *IOP Conference Series: Materials Science and Engineering, 862*, 042009

Regional Specifics of Digitalization the Oil Midstream Soil Monitoring

Alla Yu. Vladova

Abstract A review of literature related to frozen ground engineering showed that the number of publications and datasets has been increasing in the last five years. Based on the North Siberian crude oil pipeline that crosses continuous, discontinuous, sporadic, and non-permafrost areas, an exploratory data analysis of soil condition is conducted to investigate the influence of pipelines on the freezing and thawing of frozen soil around the pipeline and thermal stability of permafrost. The contribution of the study is the hypothesis concerning the possibility of clustering water-saturated and frozen layers along with the right-of-way areas.

Keywords EDA · Exploratory data analysis · Frozen Soil · Right-of-way areas

1 Introduction

Transit infrastructure is crucial to the successful midstream phase of energy development. The 500-km North Siberian pipeline intakes crude from new oilfields in Yamal-Nenets Autonomous Area and the north of Krasnoyarsk region. Northern Siberia is among Russia's most promising new oil provinces and is expected to sustain the country's crude output in the face of natural declines in West Siberia [1]. The pipeline overcomes water barriers, goes through difficult soils and draining wetlands. Swamps and wetlands took up most of the route [2] and required the construction of several brides and one hundred and half river and stream crossings (Fig. 1).

As the greenhouse effect develops, Northern Siberia is feeling it the most: temperatures are rising at about twice the global average. That's having a huge impact on

A. Yu. Vladova (✉)
V. A. Trapeznikov Institute of Control Sciences of the Russian Academy of Sciences, Profsoyuznaya St. 65, 117997 Moscow, Russian Federation
e-mail: avladova@mail.ru

Financial University Under the Government of the Russian Federation, Leningradsky Ave. 49, 125993 Moscow, Russian Federation

V. Kumar et al. (eds.), *Digital Transformation in Industry*, Lecture Notes in Information Systems and Organisation 44, https://doi.org/10.1007/978-3-030-73261-5_23

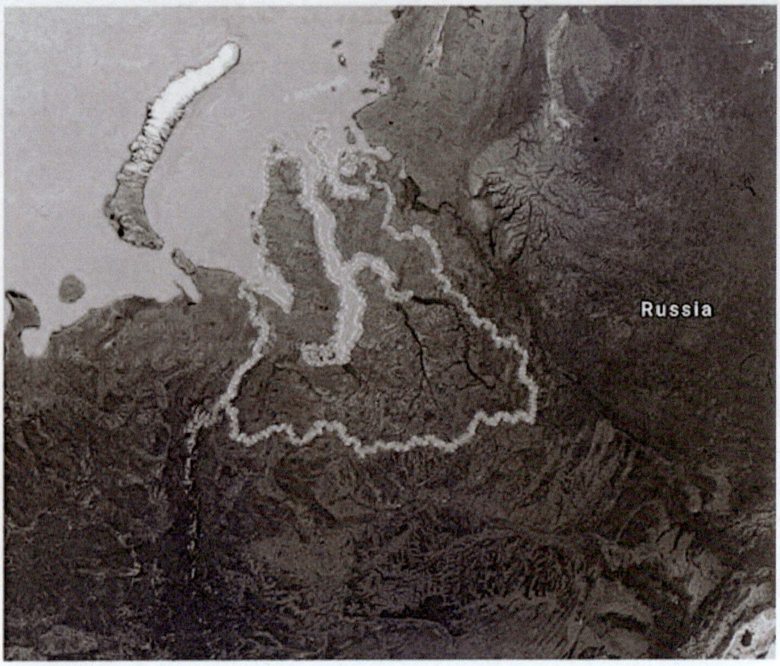

Fig. 1 Map of the region

the region's permafrost, ground that typically stays frozen all year round [3]. Table 1 reflects the soil description at a certain distance of the route.

A characteristic of the route of this crude oil pipeline is the discontinuous development of permafrost. The depth to the top of permafrost ranges from 5 to 20 m. The

Table 1 Soil description

Rider, m	Depth of the soil layer, m	Power of the soil layer, m	Soil description
19.8	0.1	0.1	Moss
19.8	3.5	3.4	Loam
19.8	6	2.5	High plasticity loam
19.8	8.3	2.3	Sand
19.8	17	8.7	Frozen sand
26.6	0.1	0.1	Moss
26.6	3	2.9	Fine sand
26.6	5.4	2.4	Sand saturated with water
26.6	9.5	4.1	Clayey sand
26.6	17	7.5	Sand

study aims to estimate the effect of midstream heating on permafrost to prevent the development of hazardous processes at the operation stage.

2 Literature Review

As [4] puts it, 'The pace and nature of Russia's development, both in the economic and geopolitical spheres, largely depends on the pace and nature of the development of Siberia and vice versa'. According to the platform dimensions.ai, which provides access to grants, publications, patents, and other sources, there is a significant number of publications in the field of frozen ground engineering (Fig. 2). Shi et al. [5] showed that adverse effects of pipeline construction on soil properties mainly occurred in the right-of-way areas and the impaired zones were in the order trench and working areas. The soil restoration cycle may be complete within six years of construction. Based on one planned arctic natural gas pipeline which will cross continuous, discontinuous, sporadic, and non-permafrost areas from north to south, with different pipeline temperatures set, a thermal model of the interaction between pipeline and permafrost is established to investigate the influence of pipelines on the freezing and thawing of frozen soil around the pipeline and thermal stability of permafrost. The results show that different pipeline temperatures influence the permafrost table greatly [6].

Ding et al. [7] studied the ground temperature fluctuates over time, and the fluctuation characteristics are determined by soil properties, climate, depth, and other factors. The seasonally thawed layer is in the shallow of undisturbed frozen ground and backfilled soil. The maximum thawing depth of backfilled soil was about 2.3 m more than the permafrost table of the undisturbed frozen ground. Soil near the foundation slab was keeping a frozen state. The results showed that the construction of

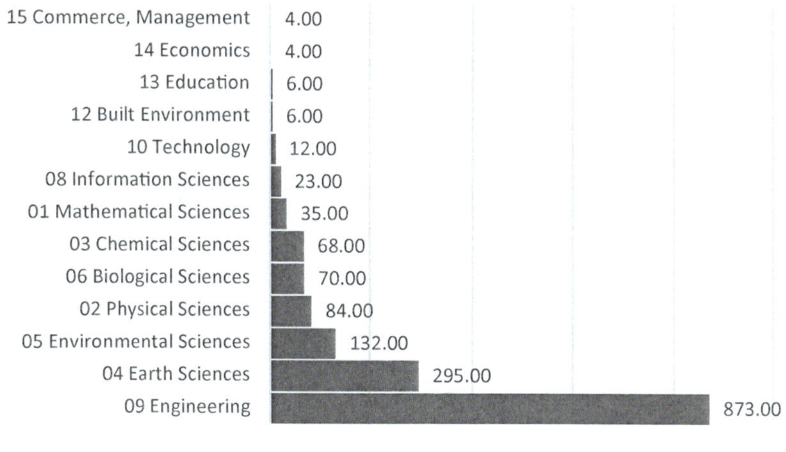

Fig. 2 The number of publications in each research category

frozen ground in the cold season is helpful to refreeze and keep the frozen state of the ground.

Today Python and R languages present the most powerful libraries to support extended data analysis (i.e. *pandas, sklearn*) and visualization (*seaborn, matplotlib*). They offer scripts or wrappers for commonly needed functionality, especially for visualization that data scientists created for themselves to perform repetitive tasks. McKinney [8] describes tools to load, clean, transform, merge, slice, dice, summarize, and reshape dataset, to analyze and manipulate regular and irregular time series, and to create informative visualizations.

3 Material and Methods

The original data sample retrieved from a geological database contains almost 6,000 entries across 7 different features (Table 2). At the first step, entitled Statistics, we applied the Python's open-source library, named *pandas_profiling* to our dataset in the hope to perform automated exploratory data analysis [9]. It displayed a descriptive overview by showing the number of variables, observations, total missing cells, duplicate rows, memory used, and the variable types.

Then, it generates a detailed analysis for each variable, class distributions, interactions, correlations, missing values, samples, and duplicated rows. It seems (Fig. 3) that values of two float features, named depth and power of the soil layer, are distributed according to the exponential law (with outliers at the tail in case of the first listed feature).

Exponential distribution means that the most frequent values are the values that are closer to zero. It means that we have a deal with a pie of thin geological layers.

Table 2 Soil description

Feature	Type	Range	Outliers
Km	int64	151–358	
Picket	float64	1517–3589	
Rider, m	float64	0–102	
Depth of the soil layer, m	float64	0–30	30 m—3; 29, 27, 25, 24 m—4
Power of the soil layer, m	float64	0–24.2	24.2, 17, 16.8 m—1; 16.9—4; 16.5 m—2
EGE element	float64	0–939	
Soil description	object	Sandy loam—Sand	

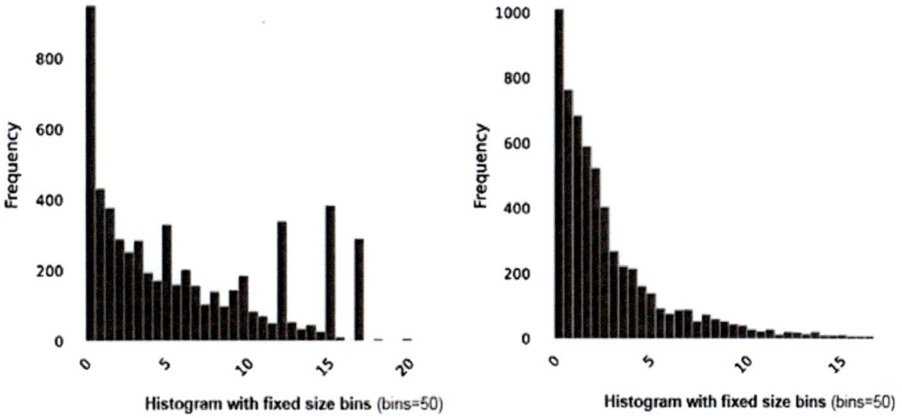

Fig. 3 The distributions of the features, named depth and power of the soil layer

The distribution of the feature, named *EGE element*, that encodes soil types according to the Unified Soil Classification System [10], seems to be binomial (Fig. 4). It contains all codes, excluded gravel, granite, and other hard ground.

According to Fig. 5, there is a strong linear correlation between features named Km and Picket as well as Power of the soil layer and Depth of the soil layer. It associates with the physical meaning of these features.

We reviewed the stages of data analysis proposed by Kandel et al. [11], and the generalized result is shown in Fig. 6.

Trying to understand the semantics of the categorical feature and what it represents, we studied contained values. Figure 7 reflects a semantic map of the feature, named Soil description that we got with help of the Python's WordCloud library.

As it shows, the most frequent words are *soil* and *water* that give us soil saturated with water. The frozen ground still has a significant place in the semantic map as well. The final category of our exploration process is storytelling.

Fig. 4 Distribution of soil types

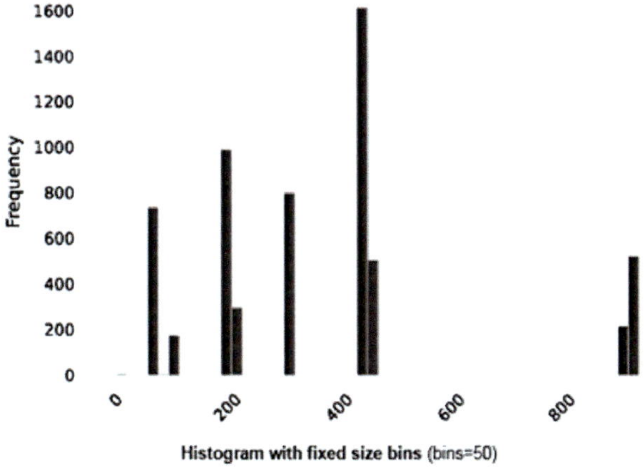

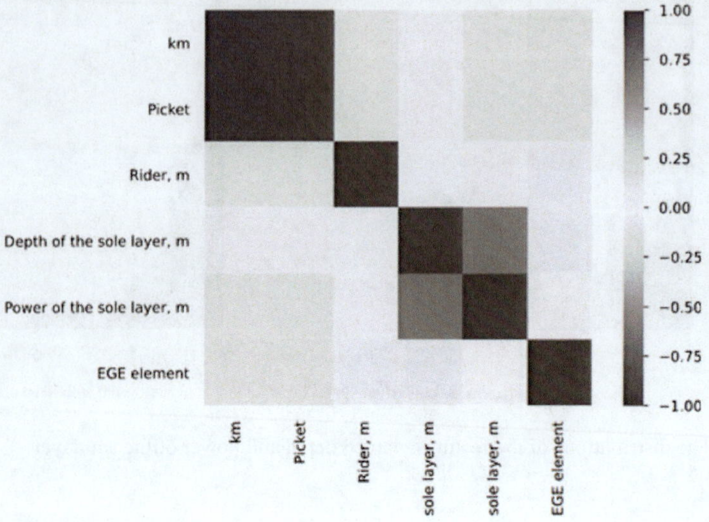

Fig. 5 Linear correlation of the dataset features

Fig. 6 Exploration process

Fig. 7 Semantic map of the categorical feature

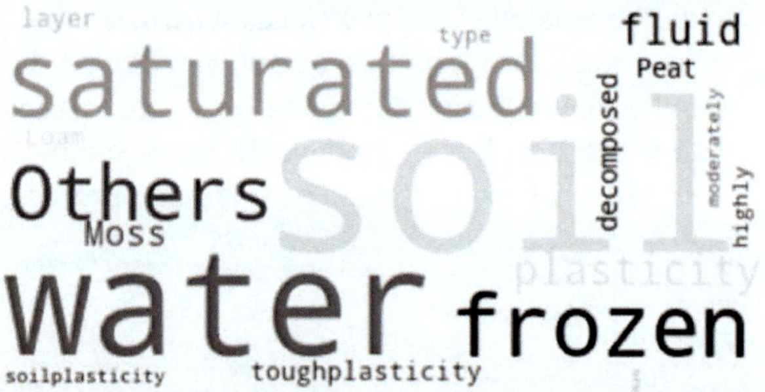

It involves exploring different approaches to identify the best way to present the data for downstream consumers and relate the data to what they care about or to operationalize the analysis.

Fig. 8 The ratio of soil types

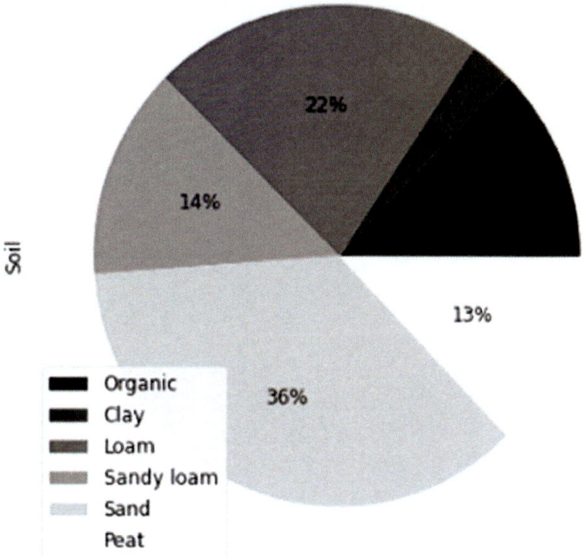

4 Results

For the categorical feature *Soil description*, we created a pie chart to understand the share ratio between different types of soil (Fig. 8).

It demonstrates that the most frequent type is sand, and it can be frozen, plasticity, water-saturated, dusty (as well as all other types of soil). It is known that dry soil has lower thermal conductivity. With regard to water, the thermal conductivity of dry sand is 3 times, dry loam—4 times, and peat—6 times less. However, it increases 4–10 times if the soil becomes water-saturated. This is because the air that fills the pores has 28 times less thermal conductivity than water. Scientists have found that the larger particles (pebble, gravel, and sand) in the soil define the greater thermal conductivity [12]. That is the reason why sand conducts heat faster than loam.

5 Discussion

The important soil property is lower ability to conduct heat from top to bottom (vertically) compared to the horizontal direction (along the route). And the depth of winter freezing greatly depends on this property [13]. In one climatic area, the size of the freezing zone can change significantly (in the case of different thermal conductivity of the soils). Soil types distribution along the oil pipeline route is presented in Fig. 9.

It is found that 280–340 km of the route contains the most significant frequency of peat. It means that in further research we will possibly localize that 20 km for a

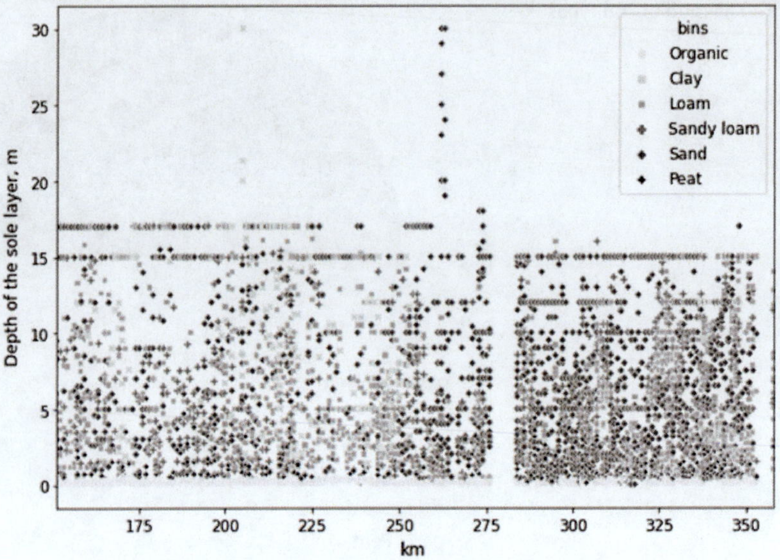

Fig. 9 Soil types distribution along the oil pipeline route

separate study. Figure 9 also shows that there is a gap in data at 275–278 km and it should be approximated with existing data.

6 Conclusion

Our explorative analysis pops up several qualifying questions for further drilling: why there is a gap in data at 275–278 km; if it is possible to segregate water-saturated and frozen soil layers to study them as one cluster, should we cluster layers taking into account the whole pie of layers or we may study them independently; and so on. As an additional stage of analysis, it will be useful to enrich our data with a known thermal conductivity coefficient.

Summing up, our 3-stage analysis helped us to formulate several hypotheses to check.

References

1. Rodova, N. (2019). Transneft sees fast growth in Arctic, E Siberian crude pipeline flows. Retrieved October 10, 2020, from https://www.spglobal.com/platts/en/market-insights/latest-news/oil/040519-transneft-sees-fast-growth-in-arctic-e-siberian-crude-pipeline-flows.
2. Vladova, A. Yu. (2016). The retrospective analysis of temperature condition of soil in the information measuring system. *Bezopasnost truda v promyshlennosti, 12*, 46–53.

3. Jones, N. (2018). Redrawing the Map: How the World's Climate Zones Are Shifting. Retrieved October 16, 2020, from https://e360.yale.edu/features/redrawing-the-map-how-the-worlds-climate-zones-are-shifting.
4. Kryukov, V. A., Lavrovskii, B. L., Seliverstov, V. E., & Suslov, N. I. (2020). Siberian development vector: Based on cooperation and interaction. *Studies on Russian Economic Development, 31*, 495–504. https://doi.org/10.1134/S1075700720050111.
5. Shi, P., Xiao, J., Wang, Y.-F., & Chen, L.-D. (2014). The effects of pipeline construction disturbance on soil properties and restoration cycle. *Environmental Monitoring and Assessment, 186*(3), 1825–1835. https://doi.org/10.1007/s10661-013-3496-5.
6. Xinze, Li, Jin, H., Wei, Y., Wen, Z., Li, Y., & Li, X. (2020). Numerical analysis of temperature fields around the buried arctic gas pipeline in permafrost regions. *Thermal Science*, 248–248. https://doi.org/10.2298/tsci200521248l.
7. Ding, S. J., Cheng, Y. F., Lu, X. L., & Yang, Y. P. (2012). Monitoring and analysis of fine-grained frozen soil temperature and permafrost table for transmission line foundation. *Applied Mechanics and Materials, 204–208*, 694–698.
8. McKinney, W. (2012). *Python for data analysis: Data wrangling with Pandas, NumPy, and IPython*. O'Reilly Media, Inc.
9. Ismail, A. (2020). How to use Pandas-Profiling on Google Colab. Retrieved October 31, 2020, from https://medium.com/python-in-plain-english/how-to-use-pandas-profiling-on-google-colab-e34f34ff1c9f.
10. Unified Soil Classification System (1985). Retrieved October 31, 2020, from https://en.wikipedia.org/wiki/Unified_Soil_Classification_System.
11. Kandel, S., Paepcke, A., Hellerstein, J. M., & Heer, J. (2012). Enterprise data analysis and visualization: An interview study. *IEEE Transactions on Visualization and Computer Graphics, 18*(12), 2917–2926.
12. Heat and soils. Retrieved November 1, 2020, from https://catalogmineralov.ru/cont/255.html.
13. Golofast, S. L., Vladova, A. Yu., & Lobodenko, I. Yu. (2016). Design, development and maintenance of geotechnical monitoring information system for trunk pipeline. *Science and Technologies: Oil and Oil Products Pipeline Transportation, 2*(22), 80–87.

Assessment of Online Courses Control Materials Using Information Theory Methods

Alexander Tolmachev and Galina Astratova

Abstract The digital transformation of industry poses new challenges for related industrial fields, in particular for education. Universities must transform accordingly and provide the digital economy with qualified personal. Online technologies, including online learning, play an important role in digital transformation, opening up new opportunities and posing challenges that the education system has never faced before. The problem of making justified decisions on the selection and assessment of the quality of online courses and their control materials is one of these challenges. Data mining and machine learning analytics tools that work with learners' digital footprint data can be used to solve this problem. To do so, this work uses the methods of information theory. The indicator of the informativeness of control materials provides differentiation of standalone checkpoints and online courses in general and minimizes the subjective factor present when using existing assessment methods. Another indicator that assesses the mutual informativeness of checkpoints allows determining how much information about the final test results can be obtained by monitoring current academic performance. This indicator is applicable both to individual checkpoints and their series (assembled by type—test assignments, homework assignments, etc.; or by the chronology of the course—¼, ½, etc. of the course length). With its help, it is possible to evaluate the course checkpoints and make a decision on how to improve the course materials. In addition, this indicator can be useful for assessing the marginal accuracy of the prediction of the test results according to the current academic performance of a student. The proposed methods have been tested on online courses of the Ural Federal University with positive approbation results.

Keywords Digital transformation · Online education · Information theory · Learning analytics

---

A. Tolmachev (✉) · G. Astratova
Ural Federal University, Mira St. 19, 620002 Ekaterinburg, Russian Federation
e-mail: avtolmachev@urfu.ru

V. Kumar et al. (eds.), *Digital Transformation in Industry*, Lecture Notes in Information Systems and Organisation 44, https://doi.org/10.1007/978-3-030-73261-5_24

1 Introduction

The digital transformation of industry poses new challenges for related industrial fields, in particular for education. Universities supply the digital economy with new specialists and participate in the processes of improving the qualifications of existing specialists working at industrial enterprises. Ural Federal University is an active participant in such processes: it organizes special master's and additional education programs for industrial enterprises while performing its own digital transformation program.

Online technologies and, especially, online learning, play an important role in digital transformation. As shown in papers of [1–6], they open up numerous opportunities for all participants in the educational process, such as extending reach and access, improving educational outcomes, innovations in teaching and learning, research on teaching and learning. At the same time, new opportunities arise due to the formation of a digital footprint by students during online learning and the use of learning analytics tools based on data mining and machine learning methods [8], which are used to solve the problems related to the assessment of online courses, decision-making on how to choose online courses and evaluation of the effectiveness of online learning [7]. These tools expand and supplement the capabilities of widely used psychometric methods, which are also being developed now [9].

The paper examines the methods of information theory applied to the tasks of assessing the quality of online courses, which is understood as the correspondence of the study results to the set goals [7]. Evaluation of the quality of online courses is carried out through the analysis and assessment of their control materials, which can be viewed as a digital image of online courses. When taking online courses, learners go through different types of checkpoints—test assignments, homework assignments, project work, etc., for which they receive grades. These grades can be considered not only as a means of measuring the level of knowledge of students, but also as a means of measuring the quality of the control materials of the course and as a verification of their compliance with the content of the course. The purpose of this analysis is the differentiation of students, checkpoints (control materials) and online courses. A separate problem that can be encountered is subjectivity in the choice of parameters of assessment models. The authors' studies are also aimed at minimizing the influence of this factor.

The proposed methods can be useful for direct participants in the educational process (students, teachers, online course authors, academic managers) in their current activities, and for the development of automated recommendatory decision support systems.

2 Literature Review

Research in the field of assessing the quality of test materials and measuring the level of students' knowledge has been conducted for a long time. Psychometric methods have become widespread, including Classical test theory (CTT), Item response theory (IRT) and Generalizability theory (G theory) [10]. To assess the tasks constituting the tests, the indicators of difficulty and discriminative ability of tasks are commonly used [10]. However, these indicators are not always effective in assessing both individual tasks and checkpoints in general. As an example, Table 1 presents the difficulty index and discrimination index for some tests of the MOOC "Engineering Mechanics" (UrFU, Spring 2019).

Based on the values of the indices it is possible to conclude that control materials of the test # 12 (blue) and test # 15 (red) are identical. However, an analysis of the graph of the distributions of student ratings presented in Fig. 1 shows that there are differences in the students' tests results, which are not shown by the difficulty index and discrimination index. The subjective factor is present in determining the acceptable limits of the values of both indicators, their interpretation and the sample sizes of strong and weak students used to calculate the discrimination index.

Table 1 Indicators for the MOOC "Engineering Mechanics" (UrFU, Spring 2019)

Checkpoint name	Sample size (learners)	Difficulty index	Discrimination index
Test #12	611	0.87	0.51
Test #15	541	0.87	0.50

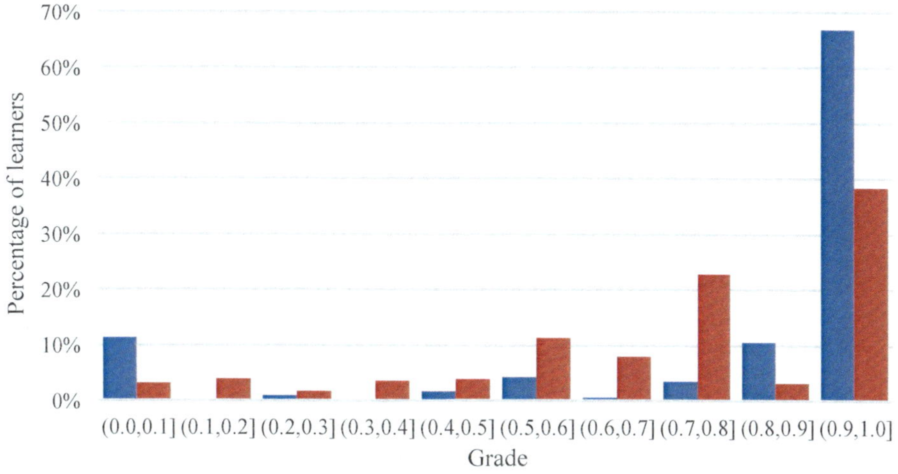

Fig. 1 Percentage of learners with different grades for the MOOC "Engineering Mechanics" (UrFU, Spring 2019)

To overcome the aforementioned problems encountered during the evaluation of control materials of online courses, the authors have previously proposed fundamental tools based on information theory [7]. The current paper presents further research on information theory methods and their application to the assessment of online course control materials. To describe them, the main definitions and conclusions from [7] are given below.

While studying the materials of the online course, the student passes a series of N checkpoints $\{x_i\}_{i=1...N}$, which are accompanied by assessment. To describe the results, a vector of dimension N with grades awarded for completion of the tasks of these checkpoints is used. At the same time, we will distinguish between checkpoints that characterize the current state of the educational process (for example, current control tests, homework assignments, etc.) and its result (final testing in the form of an exam or test). In the higher education system, this division is justified because of the high importance of learning outcomes that confirm the achievement of the set goals, and their relationship to current academic performance. A vector with components consisting of assessments that characterize current academic performance and learning outcome will be called the individual digital profile (IDP) of the student:

$$Y = \{\, x_1, x_2, \, \ldots, x_N | y\} \tag{1}$$

Generally, the components of the vector Y are real numbers ranging from 0 to 1. The work uses discrete values that characterize academic performance depending on the score obtained (such a gradation is common in the higher education system) in accordance with Table 2.

The information contained in the message about how the listeners handled the tasks of the checkpoint x_i can be determined using the information entropy $H(x_i)$ [11]:

$$Inf(x_i) = H(x_i) - 0 = -\sum_{j=2,3,4,5} P_{x_i(j)} \log_2 P_{x_i(j)} \tag{2}$$

The probability of obtaining a discrete grade j, according to (2), based on the results of the checkpoint x_i is calculated as the frequency ratio (statistical probability):

$$P_{x_i(j)} = \frac{N_{x_i(j)}}{\sum_{j=2,3,4,5} N_{x_i(j)}} \tag{3}$$

Table 2 Values of discrete variables of student's academic performance

Discrete grade	Grade	Grade scale
«Unsatisfactory»	2	[0.0, 0.4]
«Satisfactory»	3	(0.4, 0.6]
«Good»	4	(0.6, 0.8]
«Excellent»	5	(0.8, 1.0]

Table 3 Informativeness index for the MOOC "Engineering Mechanics" (UrFU, Spring 2019)

Checkpoint name	Sample size (learners)	Informativeness index
Test #12	611	0.55
Test #15	541	0.92

Information (2) is measured in bits (binary units). It reaches maximum when all states are equally probable:

$$P_{x_i(j)} = \frac{1}{4}, Inf(\max) = 2\,bit \tag{4}$$

Based on (2) and (4), it is possible to determine the informativeness index of the checkpoint—a dimensionless quantity normalized to unity:

$$I(x_i) = \frac{Inf(x_i)}{Inf(\max)} \tag{5}$$

The results of applying the informativeness index to the assessment of control materials from Table 1 are presented in Table 3. The informativeness index allows us to identify distinctions in the control materials of the course that are inaccessible to the difficulty index and discrimination index.

Below we will consider the informativeness for a series of checkpoints, as well as their mutual informativeness, which, as a special case, allows us to determine how much information about the results of the final test gives the observation of the current academic performance. Such indicators will be useful to participants in the educational process in the field of higher education:

- authors of online courses will be able to make data-driven decisions how to improve course materials;
- students will be able to make an informed choice of online courses during the formation of their individual educational trajectory;
- academic managers will be able to make informed decisions when including online courses in the educational program.

Moreover, an automatic system of recommendation services can be created based on these indicators to support decision-making of participants in the educational process.

3 Material and Methods

3.1 Informativeness of a Series of Checkpoints

Formulas (2) and (5) can be generalized to the case of a series of checkpoints described by individual digital profiles of students (1). In this case, the information contained in the message about the results of passing a series of N checkpoints $X = \{x_1, x_2, \ldots, x_N\}$, will be defined as:

$$Inf(X) = H(X) - 0 = -\sum_{\{x_1,x_2,\ldots,x_N\}} P_{\{x_1,x_2,\ldots,x_N\}} \log_2 P_{\{x_1,x_2,\ldots,x_N\}} \tag{6}$$

The practical use of formula (6) is difficult due to the large number of possible system states (individual digital profiles). For example, for a discipline that includes 20 checkpoints, the number of possible states will be $4^{20} \approx 10^{12}$. By the standards of online courses, this number of checkpoints is not large—there can even be 40 or 100 of them, but even in this case the direct calculation of the statistical probability becomes impossible, because the number of listeners to any online course will be much less than the number of possible states. According to this, for direct calculation of probabilities in (6) it is possible to reduce the number of possible states by aggregating checkpoints using average group grades. Aggregation is possible both by the types of checkpoints, such as "test tasks", "homework", etc., and by the time of their completion, for example, checkpoints for 1/4, 2/4, 3/4, 4/4 parts of the course. In addition to this, for direct calculation of probabilities in (6) one can make assumptions about the probabilities of unobservable states. As the total number of observed states increases, the probability of the appearance of some previously unobserved state decreases exponentially, i.e. the deviations of the distribution of the observed individual digital profiles from the real distribution become random with an increasing level of confidence. In this case, by choosing unique individual digital profiles and counting their number, the calculation of probabilities in (6) can be performed according to Table 4.

The informativeness index for a series of checkpoints, by analogy with (5), is defined as the ratio of information (6) for this series to the maximum value of information:

$$I(\{x_1, x_2, \ldots, x_N\}) = \frac{Inf(\{x_1, x_2, \ldots, x_N\})}{Inf(\{x_1, x_2, \ldots, x_N\})_{\max}} \tag{7}$$

The obtained informativeness index (7) can be used for assessing the course and its control materials. Such assessments are interesting when working on improving the course materials.

Table 4 The probabilities of unique individual digital profiles (IDP)

ID IDP	IDP vector	IDP frequency	IDP probability
ID_1^{IDP}	$\{x_1, x_2, \ldots, x_N\}_1^{\mathrm{IDP}}$	N_1^{IDP}	$N_1^{\mathrm{IDP}}/N^{\mathrm{IDP}}$
…	…	…	…
ID_P^{IDP}	$\{x_1, x_2, \ldots, x_N\}_P^{\mathrm{IDP}}$	N_P^{IDP}	$N_p^{\mathrm{IDP}}/N^{\mathrm{IDP}}$
		$N^{\mathrm{IDP}} = \sum_{i=1..P} N_i^{\mathrm{IDP}}$	$\sum_{i=1..P} N_i^{\mathrm{IDP}}/N^{\mathrm{IDP}}$

3.2 Mutual Informativeness of Checkpoints

If we consider the vector *Y (1)* as a set of two connected systems, where.

$X = \{x_1, x_2, \ldots, x_N\}$ is an N-dimensional vector characterizing the current performance when passing the course checkpoints, $Y = \{y\}$ is a one-component vector characterizing the success of the final testing, then the entropy of these systems will be bound by the ratio:

$$H(Y, X) = H(Y) + H(X|Y) = H(X) + H(Y|X) \tag{8}$$

The one-dimensionality of the vector Y is used for simplicity of reasoning and due to its widespread use in practice (one test or an exam at the end of the course); however, generalization to the case with a higher dimension can be performed as well.

The total conditional entropy of the system Y included in (8), provided that the state of the system X is completely determined, can be calculated in the general case using the partial conditional entropies:

$$H(Y|X) = \sum_{\{x_1,\ldots,x_N\}} P_{\{x_1,\ldots,x_N\}} H(Y|X_{\{x_1,\ldots,x_N\}}) \tag{9}$$

Further, *H(Y|X)* can be expressed in terms of $P_{\{y|x_1,\ldots,x_N\}}$—the conditional probability of finding system Y in state $\{y\}$ provided that system X is in state $\{x_1, \ldots, x_N\}$:

$$H(Y|X) = -\sum_{\{x_1,\ldots,x_N,y\}} P_{\{x_1,\ldots,x_N\}} P_{\{y|x_1,\ldots,x_N\}} log_2 P_{\{y|x_1,\ldots,x_N\}} \tag{10}$$

The total conditional entropy of the system X, provided that the state of the system Y is completely determined, $H(X|Y)$, can be calculated in a similar to (10) way. The entropies $H(Y)$ and $H(X)$ are calculated according to (6).

Based on (8), it is possible to evaluate the control materials of the course by determining how much information about the system Y (final test) can be acquired by the observation of the system X (current performance). Index

$$I(X \to Y) = H(Y) - H(Y|X) \tag{11}$$

can be considered as a decrease in the entropy (measure of uncertainty) of the system Y after obtaining information about the system X. Similarly to the entropy in this section, $I(X \to Y)$ is complete information about the system Y contained in the system X.

On the one hand, if systems Y and X are completely independent (the results of the final testing are not related to information about the current academic performance), then $H(Y|X) = H(Y)$ and $I(X \to Y) = 0$.

On the other hand, if the state of system X completely determines the state of system Y, i.e. the result of the final test can be clearly determined according to the current performance, then $H(Y|X) = 0$ and $I(X \to Y) = H(Y)$.

It is possible to determine partial information $I(X_p \to Y)$ about system Y, contained in the message that system X is in state $X_p = \{x_1, \ldots, x_N\}_p$:

$$I(X_p \to Y) = \sum_{\{y\}} P_{\{y|X_p\}} \log_2 \frac{P_{\{y|X_p\}}}{P_{\{y\}}} \tag{12}$$

For one checkpoint x_s, considering discrete grades from Table 2, partial information (12) will take the following form:

$$I(x_s \to Y) = \sum_{y=2,3,4,5} P_{\{y|x_s\}} \log_2 \frac{P_{\{y|x_s\}}}{P_{\{y\}}} \tag{13}$$

The computation of the conditional probabilities included in (13) can be performed by analogy with the method shown in Table 2 by calculating the frequencies of individual digital profiles corresponding to various grades for the final test.

To evaluate control materials, we establish an indicator that characterizes the reduction in the uncertainty of the final test in fractions of one when receiving information about passing a separate checkpoint:

$$r_s = \frac{I(x_s \to Y)}{H(Y)} \tag{14}$$

The r_s indicator can be used to evaluate the quality of the x_s control materials, as well as to make recommendations on how to improve them.

Following similar logic, it is possible to define the index characterizing the decrease in the uncertainty of the final test when receiving information about passing a series of checkpoints:

$$r_{\{x_1,\ldots,x_N\}} = \frac{I(X_{\{x_1,\ldots,x_N\}} \to Y)}{H(Y)} \tag{15}$$

If the contributions from the course checkpoints differ significantly, then with the help of (15) it is possible to develop algorithms for reducing the dimensionality of the space of vectors X, the main goal of which is to use checkpoints which lead to a maximum reduction in the uncertainty of the final testing and to recommend the author of online course to revise the control materials that do not lead to a noticeable decrease in the uncertainty of the final testing. In fact, we are talking about the analysis of the distribution of the uncertainty reduction level of the final test between the control materials of the current academic performance.

As an example of such algorithm, we can consider the step-by-step selection of checkpoints:

- at the first step, the indicator (14) is calculated for all checkpoints $\{x_1, \ldots, x_N\}$ and the checkpoint with the maximum value of the indicator is selected (let it be x_s);
- at the second step, the pairs $\{x_s, x_i\}, i \in [1 \ldots N], i \neq s$, are made up, (15) is calculated for them and the pair with the maximum value of the indicator is selected;
- at the third step, using the pair from the second step, triples of checkpoints are created, (15) is calculated for them and the triple with the maximum value is selected;
- these steps are repeated until the reduction in uncertainty reaches a certain predetermined threshold, for example, 80–90%.

Once the algorithm is completed, the number of checkpoints used for this reduction is examined. Based on the analysis results, it is possible to suggest the authors of online course to make a decision regarding the remaining checkpoints and their control materials.

Index (15), which shows a decrease in the uncertainty of the final test after receiving information on the results of the course checkpoints before the final test, can be used to assess the limits of the predictive accuracy of the final test based on the data of current academic performance.

4 Results

As an example, to test the methods for assessing control materials proposed in the work, several UrFU online courses posted on the National Open Education Platform (https://openedu.ru/) were analyzed. The list of courses is presented in Table 5.

All courses include three types of checkpoints: 1) theory tests or self-control tests (A), 2) home or study assignments (B), 3) project assignments or control tasks (C). At the end of the course, students take the final test (R).

Table 5 List of UrFU online courses considered in the article

MOOC ID	Course name	Semester	Sample size (learners)	Number of checkpoints
ENGM 40	Engineering Mechanics	Fall 2019	429	40
ENGM 41	Engineering Mechanics	Spring 2019	729	40
ENGM 42	Engineering Mechanics	Spring 2020	310	30
RUBSCULT 77	The culture of Russian business speech	Fall 2019	878	54
RUBSCULT 78	The culture of Russian business speech	Spring 2019	210	54
RUBSCULT 79	The culture of Russian business speech	Spring 2020	195	54

Checkpoints are grouped in series by type as suggested in Sect. 3.1 «A-B-C». For each group, an average grade was calculated and converted into discrete grades according to Table 2. As a result, each state is characterized by three grades such as "5–5–5", "5–5–4" … "2–2–2". The maximum number of states in this case is $4^3 = 64$, and the maximum information contained in the message about the results of passing such a series of checkpoints, according to (6), is 6 bits. With the help of (7), the informativeness (7) for the series of checkpoints is calculated. The results are presented in Table 6. The number of unique IDPs is shown to demonstrate how many states out of 64 possible are occupied by at least one profile.

Figures 2 and 3 show the indicator (14) for all checkpoints of the ENGM 41 and RUBSCULT 78 courses, characterizing the decrease in the final test uncertainty in unit fractions when receiving information about the completion of a separate checkpoint.

Using the indicator (15) for a series of checkpoints, it is possible to evaluate how the information about the completion of several checkpoints affects the uncertainty of the final one. In Sect. 3.2, an algorithm was described, the purpose of which was to find out by what minimum amount and which checkpoints the uncertainty of the final test can be reduced by 80–90%. The result of its application to the control materials of the ENGM 41 course is shown in Fig. 4 ($r\{x_1 \ldots x_N\}$—line #1). Figure 4 also

Table 6 Informativeness index for a series of checkpoints

MOOC ID	Semester	Number of unique IDPs	Informativeness index	Probability of the IDP "5–5-5"
ENGM 40	Fall 2019	33	0.53	0.51
ENGM 41	Spring 2019	49	0.75	0.22
ENGM 42	Spring 2020	31	0.58	0.43
RUBSCULT 77	Fall 2019	30	0.28	0.78
RUBSCULT 78	Spring 2019	19	0.30	0.73
RUBSCULT 79	Spring 2020	17	0.28	0.78

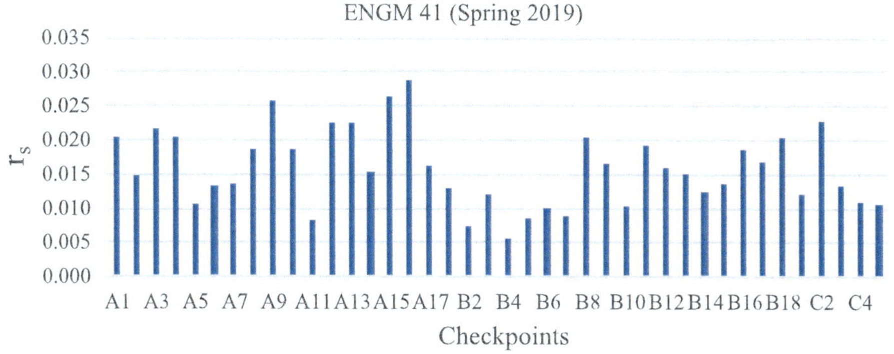

Fig. 2 Indicator r_s (14) for the ENGM 41 course

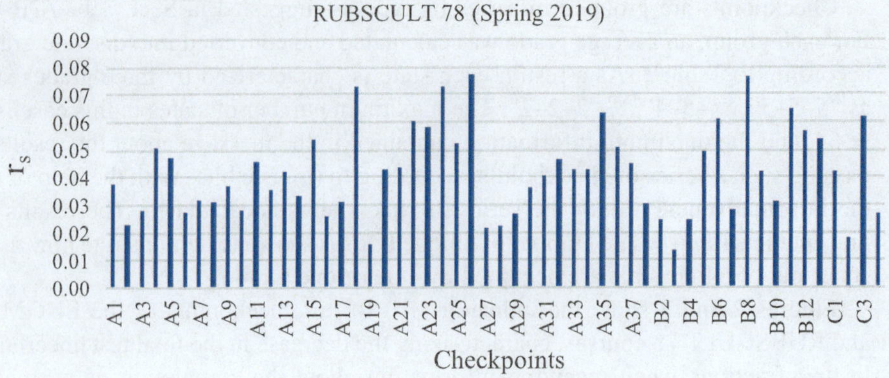

Fig. 3 Indicator r_s (14) for the RUBSCULT 78 course

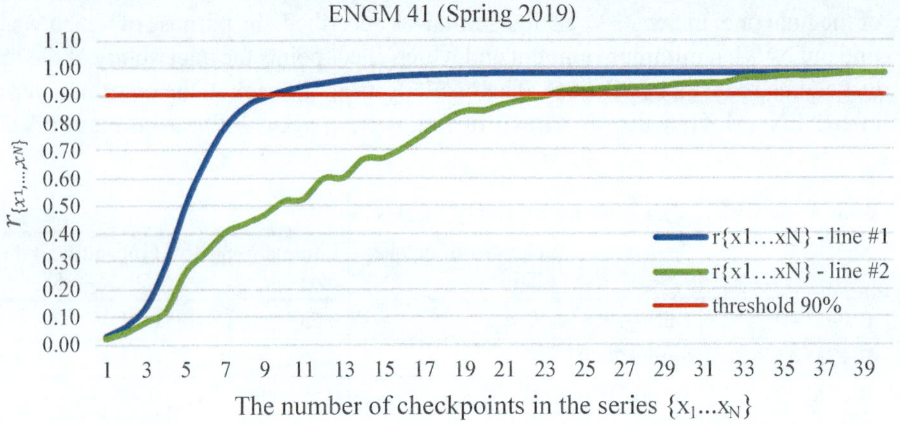

Fig. 4 Index $r\{x_1 \ldots x_N\}$ (15) for the ENGM 41 course series

shows a graph for a series of checkpoints formed in the order of their chronological completion ($r\{x_1 \ldots x_N\}$ - line #2).

The threshold value of 90% reduction in the final testing uncertainty for line # 1 is obtained after the formation of a series of 10 checkpoints (value of the indicator $r_{X_{ENGM}(\text{line \#1})} = 0.91$):

$$X_{\text{ENGM41}}(\text{line\#1}) = \{\text{A16} - \text{A2} - \text{A15} - \text{B11} - \text{A9} - \text{A1} - \text{B18} - \text{A7} - \text{B9} - \text{C3}\} \tag{16}$$

The threshold value of 90% for line # 2 is obtained after the formation of a series of 24 checkpoints (value of the indicator $r_{X_{ENGM}(\text{line \#2})} = 0.91$):

$$X_{\text{ENGM41}}(\text{line \#2}) = \{\text{A1} - \text{B1} - \text{A2} - \text{B2} - \text{A3} - \text{B3} - \text{A4} - \text{B4} - \text{C1} - \text{A5} - \text{B5} - \text{A6} - \text{B6} - \text{A7} - \text{B7} - \text{A8} - \text{B8}$$

$$- A9 - B9 - C2 - A10 - B10 - A11 - B11 \quad (17)$$

The value of the $r_{X_{ENGM}}$ indicator for a series of all 40 checkpoints of the course is 0.98.

5 Discussion

Analysis of the informativeness index of the series of checkpoints in Table 6 shows that among all the three launches of the RUBSCULT online course the share of individual digital profiles "5–5-5" is high (over 70%). This suggests that fairly simple control materials were selected in all types of checkpoints, so most students pass them perfectly. Such an approach can be justified, for example, if this course is not the students' specialization and does not affect the formation of key competencies. The indicator of the informativeness of the series of checkpoints, proposed in the work, detects this situation well with a low output value of less than 30%.

The launch of the ENGM course in the spring semester of 2019 had a high indicator of informativeness (75%) and a low share of IDP with all grades of "5" (0.22). However, in the subsequent launches of Fall 2019 and Spring 2020, the share of IDP "5–5-5" increased to 0.51 and 0.43, respectively, which, apparently, was due to the simplification of the course assignments by the authors.

The analysis of the informativeness of a series of checkpoints can be useful when making decisions about the choice of courses by students and academic managers, as well as when working on improving the control materials of the course, as it helps to do this in a balanced way based on quantitative indicators.

The graphs in Figs. 2 and 3 show that each checkpoint taken separately makes a relatively small contribution to the reduction of the uncertainty of the final test. For ENGM 41—no more than 3%, for RUBSCULT 78—no more than 8%. However, even a small contribution varies between different checkpoints and can be used for decision making on changing control materials or generating automatic recommendations for course authors. For example, authors of the ENGM course should pay attention to control materials B4, B2, A11, B5, B7. If we consider the final test as a reflection of the learning goals, it is important to comprehend whether these milestones correspond to these goals. For RUBSCULT these points are B3, A19, C2.

Analysis of the graphs of the indicator (15) in Fig. 4 shows that when using the algorithm described in Sect. 3.2, the threshold value of 90% reduction in the uncertainty of the final testing is achieved with a minimum set of a series of 10 checkpoints, or 24 checkpoints if passing them in chronological order. At the same time, the remaining checkpoints make a minimal contribution in terms of information; however, they may be necessary and useful in methodological terms. This can also be a used as a reason for revising the control materials of the final test.

The values of the indicator (15) can be used to evaluate the limits of the predictive accuracy of the final test based on the data of the current academic performance. Hence, based on (17), we can say that the forecasting accuracy limit of 90% is achieved after students have completed about half of the course, and as a result of passing all 40 checkpoints, the forecasting accuracy can be close to 100%.

6 Conclusion

The indicators for the quality evaluation of control materials of online courses based on information theory considered in the work—the informativeness of checkpoints and their series, the mutual informativeness of checkpoints and their series, their influence on the reduction of the uncertainty of the final test are quantitative metrics and allow participants in the educational process (students, academic managers, course authors) to make informed data-driven decisions. According to the authors, the proposed indicators can be used both independently and in combination with psychometric methods that are widespread in evaluating online course assignments complementing them.

Acknowledgements This work was carried out within the framework of an internal UrFU grant on the topic "Modeling the process of forming the values of University students in the context of implementing mass open online courses (MOOCs)".

References

1. Hollands, F. M., & Tirthali, D. (2014). MOOCs: Expectations and Reality. Full report. Online Submission. Retrieved October 24, 2020, from https://files.eric.ed.gov/fulltext/ED547237.pdf
2. Abrami, P. C., Bernard, R. M., Bures, E. M., et al. (2011). Interaction in distance education and online learning: using evidence and theory to improve practice. *Journal of Computing in Higher Education, 23*, 82–103. https://doi.org/10.1007/s12528-011-9043-x
3. Aguaded Gómez, J. I. (2013). The MOOC revolution: A new form of education from the technological paradigm? *Comunicar, 41*, 7–8
4. Fidalgo-Blanco, Á., Sein-Echaluce, M.L. & García-Peñalvo, F.J. (2016). From massive access to cooperation: Lessons learned and proven results of a hybrid xMOOC/cMOOC pedagogical approach to MOOCs. *International Journal of Educational Technology in Higher Education 13*(24). DOI: https://doi.org/10.1186/s41239-016-0024-z
5. Filatova, L., Abankina, I., Abankina, T., & Nikolayenko, E. (2012). Education development trends in Russia. *Journal of US-China Public Administration, 9*(10), 1198–1214
6. Jacoby, J. (2014). The disruptive potential of the massive open online course: A literature review. *Journal of Open, Flexible and Distance Learning, 18*, 73–85
7. Bystrova, T., Larionova, V., Sinitsyn, E., & Tolmachev, A. (2018). Learning analytics in massive open online courses as a tool for predicting learner performance. *Educational Studies Moscow, 4*, 139–166. https://doi.org/10.17323/1814-9545-2018-4-139-166
8. O'Farrell, L. (2017). Using learning analytics to support the enhancement of teaching and learning in higher education. National Forum for the Enhancement of Teaching and Learning in Higher Education. Retrieved from https://www.teachingandlearning.ie/publication/using-learning-analytics-to-support-the-enhancement-of-teaching-and-learning-in-higher-education/

9. Abbakumov, D., Desmet, P., & Van den Noortgate, W. (2020). Psychometrics of MOOCs: Measuring learners' proficiency. *Psychologica Belgica, 60*(1), 115–131. https://doi.org/10.5334/pb.515
10. Crocker, L. M., & Algina, J. (1986). *Introduction to Classical and Modern Test Theory*. Holt, Rinehart, and Winston.
11. Wentzel, E. S. (1969). *Probability theory, Main edition of physical and mathematical literature*. Nauka.

Role of the Banking Sector in Shaping the Financial Potential of the Economic Development of Territories

Ilya V. Naumov

Abstract In the context of the lack of financial resources in the real sector of the economy and enterprises of various economic activities, low budgetary security of territorial systems to solve acute problems of socio-economic development and implementation of spatial strategies, bank capital becomes an important strategic resource. The wide range of investment instruments available to banks and credit institutions improves financial security economic actors, to form the financial potential of the progressive development of territorial systems. The main purpose of the work is to justify the role of the banking sector of the economy and its investment resources in shaping the financial potential of progressive socio-economic development of territorial systems. To achieve this goal, the study proposes the use of methods of statistical and multiple regression analysis on the method of the smallest squares based on panel data on subjects of the Russian Federation for the period 2008–2016, as well as methods of spatial analysis. The study found that the progressive socio-economic development of territorial systems depends not only on the volume of investment resources of enterprises of the real sector of the economy, incoming foreign direct investment, but also on investments of the banking sector of the economy in government and corporate debt securities and shares, the volume of lending to financial and non-financial institutions, households. The study showed that the banking sector has a strong investment potential, its volume of investments during the period 2008–2016 it significantly exceeded the volume of investments in the fixed capital of enterprises and the volume of foreign investment, and since 2014 it has exceeded the size of the GDP of the Russian Federation. Comparison of GRP of Russian entities and the amount of investment resources concentrated in them allowed to identify the regions where bank investments are most in demand.

Keywords Banking sector · Financial capacity · Spatial analysis · Economic development · Regional economy

---

I. V. Naumov (✉)
Institute of Economics of Ural Branch of the Russian Academy of Sciences, Moskovskaya St. 29, 620014 Ekaterinburg, Russian Federation
e-mail: Ilia_Naumov@list.ru

Ural State Mining University, Kuybysheva St. 30, 620014 Ekaterinburg, Russian Federation

V. Kumar et al. (eds.), *Digital Transformation in Industry*, Lecture Notes in Information Systems and Organisation 44, https://doi.org/10.1007/978-3-030-73261-5_25

1 Theoretical Review of the Role of the Banking Sector Socio-Economic Development of Territorial Systems

Banking capital plays a key role in the development of the economy of territorial systems of various levels. Banks and credit institutions perform one of the most important functions in its development, namely, providing the real sector of the economy with the necessary financial resources for the implementation of important investment projects aimed at modernizing and expanding production, construction of transport, engineering and energy infrastructure. In today's environment of rebuilding production, Enterprises' processes for an innovative type of development, as the researchers note, "it is important to provide them with long-term resources. In such circumstances, the weak development of financial markets makes the banking sector the main source of such resources for enterprises." [9]. According to most researchers, and in particular, [7], it is banks and other credit institutions that contribute to the creation of a resource base for the implementation of infrastructure and socio-economic projects, maintain financial stability in crisis situations, and they fall the burden of providing the regional economy with cash.

A theoretical review of scientific papers in this direction has shown that the investment opportunities of the banking sector are underestimated by many authors, and lending is considered among all possible instruments of capital investment by this sector. Researchers such as [1, 2, 5, 6, 8, 10, 13], as well as a number of foreign researchers: [3, 4]. In particular, Abel Aganbegyan in one of his last works stated that Russia «needs 15 years with 10% growth of investments and their effective use thanks to the predominance of retribution investment loan in order to technologically update all major sectors of the national economy, transferring them to the use of modern technologies», but today «the volume of investment loans in the assets of our banks is only 1.1 trillion 1.5%». We agree with the position Banking is a key part of attracting investment to the real economy, but in addition to lending, there are other tools for attracting investment, such as investing in securities (stocks, various types of debt securities) of manufacturing plants. The use of such investment instruments by banks and other credit institutions contributes to the inflow of long-term financial resources into the real economy. Investments of the banking sector in government debt securities, federal bonds regional and municipal budgets form the financial foundations for the implementation of infrastructure projects, strategic programs and projects of the respective territorial systems. In the context of the need to attract long-term investment in the implementation of the socio-economic development strategies of the territories, this investment tool of the banking sector of the economy becomes the most effective mechanism for attracting financial resources [11, 12]. Investments of the banking sector in the debt securities of government agencies, federal loan bonds, regional and municipal budgets form the financial basis for the implementation of infrastructure projects, strategic programs and projects of relevant territorial systems. In the context of the need to attract long-term investment in the implementation of the socio-economic development strategies of the territories, this investment tool of the banking sector of the economy becomes the most effective mechanism for attracting financial resources.

2 A Methodical Approach to Justifying the Role of the Banking Sector in Shaping the Financial Potential of the Territories' Economic Development

To justify the key role of the banking sector of the economy and its investment resources in shaping the financial potential of the progressive socio-economic development of the territories, it is envisaged the use of statistical analysis and economic and mathematical modelling tools. The initial information is to use official data from the Federal State Statistics Service on GRP volumes and fixed investments, foreign direct investment, as well as regional statistics from the Central Bank of Russia on the volume of investments of credit institutions in securities, volume and structure of lending for the period from 2008 to 2016 to 85 subjects of the Russian Federation. At the initial stage of the study, it is expected to calculate and analyze the dynamics of the ratio of investment resources of the banking sector in the regions of Russia with a key indicator of their socio-economic development, gross regional product (IR_{BS}).

$$IR_{BS} = \frac{(I_{DS} + V_{BL})}{\text{GRP}} \tag{1}$$

where IR_{BS} is Index of the ratio of banking investment resources to the gross regional product of Russian regions; I_{DS} is Investments of banks and other credit institutions in securities (government and corporate debt securities, shares and discounted promissory notes), million rubles; V_{BL} is The volume of bank lending to financial, non-financial organizations, individuals, million rubles; GRP is Gross Regional Product, million rubles.

This study will allow us to establish not only the size of investment resources of banks in the regions, but also to assess their contribution to the economic development of these territories. Comparison of investment resources of banks and other credit institutions with the achieved level of GRP in each territorial system will allow us to assess the investment attractiveness of the regions. Differentiation of territorial systems based on the index of the ratio of investment resources of the banking sector and their gross regional product is assumed using the following threshold values:

1. Territorial systems with a high value of the ratio index, exceeding the upper limit of the standard deviation of the index from the average value for the Russian Federation:

$$IR_i > \left(\overline{IR_i} + \sqrt{\frac{\sum\left(IR_i - \overline{IR_i}\right)^2}{n}}\right) \tag{2}$$

2. Territorial systems with an average index of the ratio of banking investment resources to the GRP of Russian regions ($\overline{IR_i}$).
3. Territorial systems with a low value of the index of the ratio of banking investment resources to the GRP of Russian regions:

$$IR_i < \overline{IR_i} \quad (3)$$

As a result of the study, we intend to identify the concentration centers of investment resources of the banking sector of the economy, as well as regional systems that are difficult to attract the investments of banks necessary for the implementation of strategic initiatives.

At a later stage, space–time construction is to be built to justify the key role of the banking sector in shaping the financial potential of the territories' economic development. regression model of the dependence of GRP entities of the Russian Federation on the investment resources of the sector of non-financial corporations (investments of enterprises in fixed capital), financial corporations (investments of credit institutions) and foreign investors (foreign direct investment). As a result of the modelling, it is planned not only to establish the impact of the investment potential of the banking sector of the economy on the key indicator of the socio-economic development of the territory, but also to identify the main tools for attracting investment in this sector of the economy.

3 Research Results

As of the beginning 2019, the volume of assets of the banking sector of the economy in Russia amounted to 94,083.7 million rubles. The share of investment resources of the banking sector, to which we include investments in shares, state, municipal and corporate debt securities, accounted bills, lending to financial, non-financial institutions and individuals, from their existing assets is 82.9% (78,054.9 million rubles). In the structure of investment resources Of course, the Russian banking sector is dominated by lending, with a share of 89.3% (Fig. 1). The largest amount of credit resources by banks is used to finance investments in the real sector of the economy (42.7%). and the social needs of households (individuals) – 19.1%. This ratio of credit allocation directly demonstrates the key role of the banking sector of the economy in the socio-economic development of territorial systems. Credit institutions actively attract financial resources to state and municipal budgets. Thus, the amount of funds raised in the budgets as of 2019 amounted to 3,238.8 million rubles or 4.1% of the investment resources of the banking sector.

The investment resources of the banking sector of the economy far exceed the investment of the real sector of the economy in fixed capital and foreign direct investment. In 2016, the investment resources of the banking sector exceeded the amount of investment in the fixed capital of enterprises 4.6 times and foreign investment 7.3 times. Despite the difficult financial and economic situation in the country in

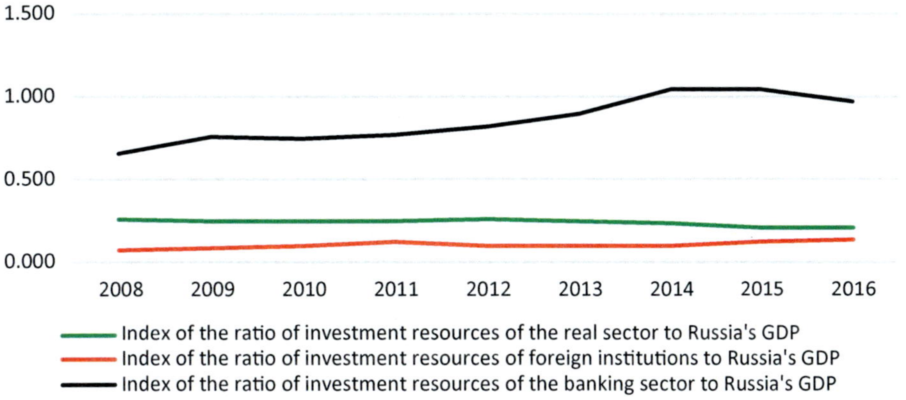

Fig. 1 Dynamics of the indices of the ratio of investment resources of the real, banking sector, foreign institutions to GDP

2008, 2012–2016, the size of bank investments, in contrast to foreign and investments of enterprises of the real sector of the economy, only increased every year. A similar trend was observed when comparing the dynamics of the change in investment resources and gross domestic product in Russia (Fig. 1).

Figure 2 shows that during the entire period under review, the volume of investment resources of the banking sector of the economy in Russia was close to the values of GDP, and since 2014 even slightly exceeded it, while investments of the real sector of the economy and foreign institutions did not exceed 30% of GDP. This

Fig. 2 The result of spatial comparison of GRP and the volume of investments in the banking sector of the economy for 2016, million rubles

speaks not only of the high importance of the banking sector in the socio-economic development of our country, but also of its significant investment potential, which, if used correctly, can create the necessary financial conditions for the implementation of the planned strategic programs of progressive technological development of the regions.

It should be noted that not all regions have such a significant amount of investment resources in the banking sector. Calculation of the average index of the ratio of bank investment resources to GRP for 85 Russian regions for the period from 2008 to 2016 showed that only three regions have a really high value. These include Moscow, where the volume of investments of credit institutions exceeds the GRP by 3.53 times, the Kostroma Region (1.49 times), and the Amur Region (the index value equaled the GRP). In seven regions, this index exceeded the average value of the index, calculated for 85 constituent entities of the Russian Federation for the entire study period. These regions include St. Petersburg (0.49), Novosibirsk region (0.45), Samara region (0.32), Sverdlovsk region (0.24), Vologda region (0.15), the Republics of Tatarstan (0.36) and Altai (0.22).

The spatial comparison of gross regional product with the volume of investments of banking institutions for 2016 allowed us to establish 3 types of regional systems (Fig. 2). The first group of regions (with the volume of bank investment resources and the volume of GRP above the average level) includes Moscow, St. Petersburg, Krasnodar Territory, the Republic of Tatarstan, Rostov, Samara, Sverdlovsk, Chelyabinsk and Novosibirsk regions. Attracted investment resources of the banking sector of the economy play a key role in the socio-economic development of these territorial systems. None of the regions except Moscow and St. Petersburg attracts a large amount of foreign investment, investments of enterprises of the real sector of the economy.

The regions in this group are potential innovative centers of Russia, they have a powerful scientific and technical potential, developed innovation infrastructure, intellectual human resources potential for progressive innovative socio-economic development. The lack of financial resources for the active deployment of innovative processes in these territorial systems is the only deterrent. Investment resources of the banking sector of the economy can solve the problem of limited financial resources and create favorable conditions for innovation in all areas of human life in these regions.

The second group of regions with above-average banking investment potential and low GRP volume included such regions as Kostroma, Amur regions, the Republic of Crimea, Primorsky territory. These territorial systems have recently attracted significant bank investment resources for the development of transport, logistics and engineering infrastructure.

In the third group of regions with below-average banking investment resources the level and high volume of GRP included such regions as the Republic of Bashkortostan, Sakha (Yakutia), Krasnoyarsk, Perm region, Khanty-Mansi, Yamalo-Nenets Autonomous District, city of Moscow, Leningrad, Nizhny Novgorod, Tyumen, Irkutsk and Kemerovo regions (Fig. 2). These regions have high rates of economic development as they are the mineral and raw materials centers of the Russian Federation for the production of natural gas, crude oil, metal ore and coal. They actively attract investment from the real sector of the economy and are less in need of additional banking investment resources.

To substantiate the key role of banking investment resources in the socio-economic development of regions, we carried out a regression analysis using the least squares method using panel data for 85 Russian regions for the period from 2008 to 2016. As a result of the analysis of 738 observations, we built a spatio-temporal model of the dependence of the GRP of Russian regions on the investments of enterprises in the real sector, foreign direct investment and bank investment resources:

$$\mathrm{GRP} = 66029.25 + 2.886 * \mathrm{IFA} + 1.336 * \mathrm{FI} + 0.047 * \mathrm{BL} + 0.237 * \mathrm{BIS} \quad (4)$$

where GRP is Gross regional product of Russian regions, million rubles; IFA is Investments in fixed assets, million rubles; FI—Foreign investment, million rubles; BIS is Banks investments in government and corporate debt securities, shares, discounted bills, million rubles; BL is the volume of bank lending to financial, non-financial corporations, individuals, million rubles.

The results of the regression analysis are presented in Table 1. Evaluation of these results allowed us to draw a conclusion about the reliability of the constructed model and the statistical significance of its parameters.

The correlation coefficient in the model is equal to one, the null hypothesis of insignificance of the determination coefficient is rejected (Prob (F-statistic) <0.05), the statistical significance of the regression coefficients is confirmed (Prob. <0.05). The model lacks multicollinearity, autocorrelation between residuals, residuals are normally distributed.

Table 1 Results of regression analysis

Variable	Coefficient	Std. Error	t-Statistic	Prob
C	66,029.25	10,506.76	6.284452	0.0000
IFA	2.886844	0.051297	56.27668	0.0000
FI	1.335713	0.107790	12.39177	0.0000
BIS	0.237193	0.122966	1.928929	0.0491
BL	0.046504	0.021654	2.147594	0.0321
R-squared	0.968799	Mean dependent var		605,986.6
Adjusted R-squared	0.968628	S.D. dependent var		1,335,759
S.E. of regression	236,590.5	Akaike info criterion		27.59280
Sum squared resid	4.10E + 13	Schwarz criterion		27.62399
Log likelihood	− 10,176.74	Hannan-Quinn criter		27.60483
F-statistic	5689.869	Durbin-Watson stat		0.730875
Prob (F-statistic)	0.000000			

As a result of modeling, we came to the conclusion that there is a close direct relationship between the gross regional product of the constituent entities of the Russian Federation and three types of investment resources. Attraction of additional investment resources of banks and other credit institutions, enterprises of the real sector of the economy and foreign institutions will lead to an increase in the GRP of the considered territorial systems. At the same time, these resources are used extremely irrationally, and the generated space–time model is a good example of this. Despite a significant preponderance in the size of investment resources in the banking sector, their additional growth in the regions will contribute to an increase in the volume of GRP to a lesser extent than the growth in investments of enterprises in the real sector of the economy. For example, attraction of bank investments in securities in the amount of 1 million rubles. will lead to an increase in the GRP of Russian regions by 0.23 million rubles. Allocated additional loans in the same amount will lead to an increase in GRP by 0.05 million rubles. At the same time, attracted foreign investments in the amount of 1 million rubles. will contribute to the growth of the GRP by 1.34 million rubles, and the investments of enterprises of the real sector of the economy in fixed assets in the same amount will contribute to the growth of the GRP by 2.9 million rubles.

There are many reasons for the irrational use of investment resources by credit institutions. The central problem, in our opinion, is the high key rate set by the Central Bank of the Russian Federation. Its size does not allow attracting credit resources necessary for the real sector to modernize production processes, introduce technical and technological, organizational, economic and other innovations. It does not solve many social problems of households. High volatility in financial and commodity markets, uncertainty in the development of the domestic economy contribute to an active outflow of investment resources of the banking sector abroad. To attract these resources to the Russian economy, to develop the real sector, we consider it necessary to change the monetary policy pursued by the state in terms of regulating the key rate. It is necessary to use mechanisms of state support for credit institutions, such as: subordinated lending, subsidizing part of the interest rate on bank loans attracted for the implementation of investment projects, projects to modernize production processes, introduce innovations, etc. The monetary policy implemented by the state should be subordinate to development goals economy, should stimulate financial institutions to participate in its development, create conditions for progressive innovative socio-economic development of territorial systems.

4 Conclusion

The banking sector plays a key role in the development of territorial systems of various levels, it performs one of the most important functions in their development: provides the real sector of the economy with financial resources necessary for the modernization and technological renewal of production processes, budgets of various levels means to implement the most important investment projects aimed at the construction of transport, engineering, energy infrastructure, implementation of strategic plans for socio-economic development of the territories.

Research has shown that Russia's sector has a strong investment potential that exceeds GDP over the past five years. The volume of investment resources of the banking sector exceeds the volume of investments of enterprises of the real sector of the economy in fixed capital by 4.6 times and the volume of foreign investments—7.3 times. In contrast to the investments of the real sector of the economy and foreign direct investment, the size of bank investment resources is actively increasing every year despite the difficult socio-economic situation in Russia. Spatial comparison of the volume of GRP of Russian entities with the volume of investments banking institutions have allowed us to identify regions where bank capital is most in demand and necessary to build the financial potential of progressive economic development. These regions include the city of Moscow, St. Petersburg, Krasnodar Territory, the Republic of Tatarstan, Rostov, Samara, Sverdlovsk, Chelyabinsk and Novosibirsk regions.

The performed regression analysis by the method of least squares using panel data made it possible to form a spatio-temporal model of the dependence of the GRP of Russian regions on investments in fixed assets of enterprises in the real sector, foreign direct investment and bank investment resources. This model showed that investment resources by the banking sector are used extremely inefficiently because of the speculative financial policy implemented and supported by the Central Bank of the Russian Federation. We believe that a progressive socio-economic territorial system requires a different approach to using the investment resources of the banking sector of the economy attracted to the economy.

Acknowledgements The article was prepared with the support of the Grant of the Russian Foundation for Basic Research No. 19-010-00660 "Scenario design of a model for reproducing the investment potential of institutional sectors in the regional system".

References

1. Aganbegyan, A. (2016). New model of economic growth of Russia. *Administrative Consulting, 1*(85), 31–46
2. Aganbegyan, A. (2017). How to resume social and economic growth in Russia? *Economic Revival of Russia, 3*(53), 11–20
3. Belke, A., Haskamp, U., & Setzer, R. (2015). Regional bank efficiency and its effect on regional growth in "normal" and "bad" times. *ROME Discussion Paper Series, 15*(7), 1–39. https://doi.org/10.4419/86788680
4. Bernini, C., & Brighi, P. (2018). Bank branches expansion, efficiency and local economic growth. *Regional Studies, 52*(10), 1332–1345. https://doi.org/10.1080/00343404.2017.1380304
5. Glazyev, S. (2019). Priorities of the outstripping development of the Russian economy in the context of changing technological structures. *Economic Revival of Russia, 2*(60), 12–16
6. Igonina, L. (2015). The role of banks in the financial support for investment in fixed capital. *Finance and Credit, 2*(21), 2–13

7. Koroshchenko, N., Mishina, N., & Simonova, I. (2016). The role of regional commercial banks in the development of regions. *Young Scientist, 1*, 381–385
8. Kostina, N., Danilenko, N., & Ivlev, A. (2016). Lending to small businesses by state and commercial banks: analysis and development prospects. *Financial Analytics: Problems and Solutions, 38*(320), 20–33
9. Meshkova, E., & Butnikov, N. (2018). The role of banks in stimulating the development of the real sector of the economy (pp. 34–41). In: *Modern aspects of banking development*. Rusines.
10. Motovilov, O. (1994). *Banking and commercial lending and innovation financing*. Publishing House of St. Petersburg State University.
11. Naumov, I. (2018). Dynamic balance model of the movement of financial flows between institutional sectors in the regional system. *News of the Ural State Mining University, 3*(51), 155–164
12. Naumov, I. (2018b). Scenario modeling of the processes of movement of financial flows between institutional sectors in the regional territorial system. *Finance: Theory and Practice, 1*(22), 32–49. https://doi.org/https://doi.org/10.26794/2587-5671-2018-22-1-32-49
13. Sukharev, O. (2015). Changes in the doctrine of monetary and budgetary policy in a recession. *Federalism, 1*, 93–110

Assessment of the Industrial Development Rates of Russian Regions in the Context of the Digitalization of the Economy

Olga Smirnova and Alena Ponomaryova

Abstract The paper is devoted to the urgent problem of the growth of the regional industrial sector and the development of a methodological toolkit for assessing the level of digitalization of Russia's regions as compared with the industrial production output. The study examines the aspects of sustainable economic development of industry, considering the development of digital technologies. The industry is a backbone sector of the economy. A drop in the level of industrial production in industrially developed regions of Russia was recorded in 2020. Given the good rates of economic growth of the country in recent years, the current crisis, which is based on non-economic reasons, poses a threat to the development of manufacturing industries. In conditions of instability, support for a digital transformation of the backbone industry of the Russian economy becomes a matter of ensuring its national security. For the progressive and uniform development of digitalization in the real sector, it is necessary to enhance innovation activity in the regional industrial sector. At the same time, the government should share the risks of introducing fundamentally new technology and high technologies with industrial enterprises. In this regard, questions arise about the value that technological innovation brings both to the industrial sector and society as a whole.

Keywords Digital economy · Regional industrial sector

1 Introduction

The processes of informatization and automation are now firmly entrenched in the processes of industrial production, digitalization being the next stage in the transformation of the economy of the real sector. The main goal of this process is to reduce

O. Smirnova (✉) · A. Ponomaryova
Institute of Economics of the Ural Branch of the Russian Academy of Sciences, Moskovskaya St. 29, 620014 Ekaterinburg, Russian Federation
e-mail: smirnova.op@uiec.ru

O. Smirnova
Ural Federal University, Mira St. 19, 620002 Ekaterinburg, Russian Federation

V. Kumar et al. (eds.), *Digital Transformation in Industry*, Lecture Notes in Information Systems and Organisation 44, https://doi.org/10.1007/978-3-030-73261-5_26

costs by optimizing the processes of production, management, sales, and promotion of products in the market. It is becoming more and more obvious that the digitalization of the Russian economy will become an important source of long-term economic growth. In this regard, it is natural that the resources spent on the development of the digital economy in recent years have been increasing: in 2016, they amounted to 1.7% of GDP, and in 2019, this share was already 2.1% [1]. The share of Russia's GDP, which currently accounts for the sector of information and communication technologies, is 2.8%, while in countries such as the USA, China, and the UK it was more than 10% back in 2017. According to experts from McKinsey, the potential effect of digitalization of the economy by 2025 will amount to 4.1–8.9 trillion rubles, the forecasted rate of GDP growth being 19–34% (Bhattacharjee et al., 2017).

In the context of globalization of the world economy, the effect of the economy of scale is achieved in production, while an increase in services forces an economic entity to diversify sources of supply and work in various geographical markets. Increasing competition is forcing industrial enterprises to implement new development strategies in the context of the digitalization of the economy, including the reorganization of production chains using firms operating in the network. This leads to partnership strategies and new power relationships that affect the productive and technological capabilities available to countries and societies.

2 Literature Review

The basic technologies that underlie the previous stages of economic transformation are replaced by new solutions in the form of digital platforms. This is how digital solutions currently connect their users and business partners and form entire ecosystems. A digital economy, like any complex system today, has many different interpretations. The following definition by a number of specialists seems to be the most justified. A digital economy is a kind of economic structure, it is the economy of data, within the framework of which they are created, transmitted, and stored. However, the main thing is that based on the analysis of these data, management decisions are taken making it possible to increase the efficiency of the economy and management efficiency, which means also an improvement in the quality of life [13, 14, 20]. That is, data in the digital economy become a leading resource of production and have a number of unique advantages [20]:

- data are a practically inexhaustible resource, easily replicated and disseminated;
- data allow saving other resources, that is, they can provide a transition to more environmentally friendly types of production;
- data per se are an environmentally friendly resource that does not harm the environment;
- when working with data, universal software and equipment are used making it possible to work with their various types.

More and more countries are creating digital development strategies, including Russia, where the digital economy is developing under the government program of the same name, as well as a national project. Currently, in Russia, the service sectors, the banking and public sectors of the economy are more susceptible to digitalization processes, while, according to a number of experts, the basic sectors for the formation of the digital economy are fundamental science and the industrial sector.

The digital transformation of industry, as a backbone branch of the economy, will entail the development of related industries and infrastructure. At the same time, the digitalization of the social sphere cannot have the same effect on production. In these conditions, the economic security and competitive development of the Russian economy become directly dependent on the level of digitalization of the real sector. Of course, many innovative and technological changes lead to improved business results. The peculiarity of the impact of digital transformation lies in its ability to accelerate the business cycle and bring new technologies and products to the market.

The issues of the concept of networkization and digitalization of the economy are scrutinized by Russian and foreign researchers: [2, 16, 7, 6, 19, 3, 11, 15, 8, 13, 14, 9, 13, 10, 12].

Studies of the digital economy are increasingly converging to the general conclusion that the widespread development and implementation of digital platforms both in the social and industrial life of society will radically change the models of relationships between economic entities. In the context of the scale of Russia and the extremely differentiated development of regions, a study of industrial growth in the context of digitalization at the regional level is especially relevant.

3 Materials and Methods

This study adopts the point of view of the Institute for Statistical Studies and Economics of Knowledge of the Higher School of Economics and other leading Russian economists that the degree of digitalization of the economy can characterize the level of use by enterprises and households of broadband Internet, radio frequency identification technologies, cloud services, enterprise resource planning systems, as well as the degree of involvement of organizations of all types of economic activity in e-commerce.

Industry, as a backbone industry, deserves special attention to assessing the impact of the digital economy on its development. It should be noted that there is currently no universal methodology for assessing the impact of digital technologies on the dynamics of industrial production.

In this work, to assess the level of digitalization of Russia's regions in the context of its comparison with the volume of industrial production, it is proposed to use a model based on an overlapping set of initial indicators collected by Rosstat and OOO *Rating Agency RIA Rating* (Tables 1, 2) to characterize the development of the information society. The simplicity and transparency of the model are noted, aimed at facilitating the procedures for collecting and processing data, as well as reducing the possibility of manipulating the results. The adopted methodology is tested on Russia's regions.

In the study, the average value of the level of digitalization in the industry was calculated, a significant deviation of 37.9% or more was taken, that is, this value will be the threshold value for a particular indicator taken [18].

The integral rating score was calculated in three stages. An integrated methodological approach includes:

- indicator of industrial production of Russia's regions;
- indicator of digitalization of Russia's regions;
- an integral rating score of Russia's regions.

The initial indicator for identifying the level of digitalization of Russia's regions is the share of organizations using the Internet in the total number of organizations (Id).

$$I\text{i} = \sqrt{I\text{ip} \cdot I\text{d}} \tag{1}$$

where Ii is integral rating score of a region, %; Iip is index of industrial production of a region, %; Id is share of organizations using the Internet in the total number of organizations, %.

The rating was built by ranking the regions of Russia in descending order according to the value of the integral rating score. In the process of diagnosing the number of groups, the scale of variation of the indicator (R) should be taken into account, which makes it possible to evaluate the variation of the indicator between the extreme values of the indicator—the limiting (Xmax) and the minimum (Xmin) and is formed according to formula 2, the width of the interval is found according to formula 3:

$$R = \text{Xmax} - \text{Xmin} \tag{2}$$

$$R = 108.4 - 70.5 = 37.9$$

$$h = \frac{R}{N} \tag{3}$$

where h is width of the interval; N is number of qualitative assessment groups.

$$h = \frac{37.9}{3} = 12.7$$

The level of digitalization of the regions of Russia has significant territorial differentiation. It depends on the availability of an appropriate innovation and information and communication infrastructure, as well as on the level of socio-economic development of the region. In this regard, the boundaries of the qualitative assessment groups were adjusted: 72.4–83.14% being low level; 83.15–95.85%—middle; 95.86–107.6%—high.

4 Results and Discussion

Dynamic (index) indicators characterize trends in the development of industries. In the methodology, they include the industrial production index. The share of organizations using the Internet characterizes the share of enterprises using the Internet in the total number of enterprises. In 2019, this indicator in 75 regions of Russia exceeded 80%, and in two regions (the Republic of Dagestan and the City of Sevastopol) it was less than 70%. They use Internet technologies in their activities. A clear change in the indicators of digitalization of the industrial sector of the regions in 2020 in comparison with 2019 is shown in Figs. 1, 2.

In 2020, the leaders of the rating in terms of industrial production are the Tyumen and Tula Regions, as well as the Kabardino-Balkarian Republic—the production growth exceeded 120%. This growth was provided by the mining and processing sectors. The decline in the industrial production index in the country as a whole amounted to 2.4%, due to a decrease in the industrial production index in 38 regions of the country. The strongest drop was noted in the Republic of Tyva (39.5%), the Kostroma Region (over 20%), and the Nizhny Novgorod Region (9%). A decrease in the rate of industrial production is observed in such industrially developed regions

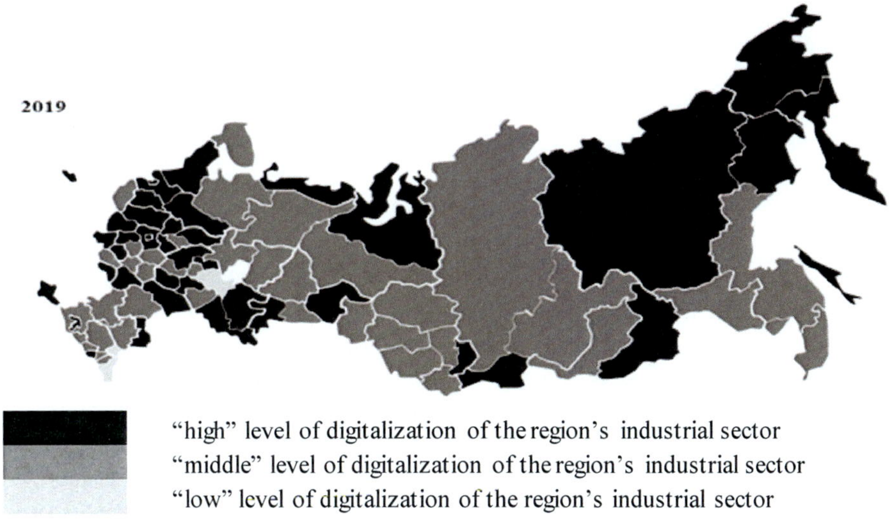

Fig. 1 Localization of regions with different values of the industrial production index in the space of the Russian Federation, 2019

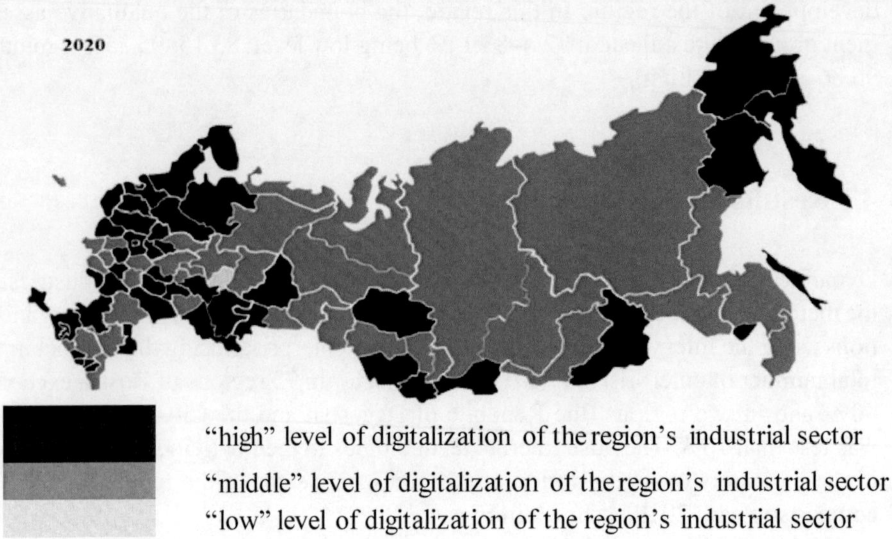

Fig. 2 Localization of regions with different values of the industrial production index in the space of the Russian Federation, 2020

as the Chelyabinsk Region, the Republic of Bashkortostan, the Samara Region, the Perm Territory, and others.

According to the results of the industry in 2019, industrial production growth was 2.2%. Currently, the unstable situation, both in the domestic and foreign markets, has a negative impact on the development of the industrial sector of Russia. Given the good rates of economic growth of the country, the current crisis, which is based on non-economic reasons, poses a threat to manufacturing industries in their development. At first glance, it seems that it will not affect all industries, but those that are accepted by the government as the most affected are air travel, trade, leisure, entertainment, hotels, catering, etc.

The manufacturing industry, according to experts, belongs to the second risk group and the economic downturn in this industry will manifest itself over time. This will be affected by the rupture of production chains associated with the closure of borders, delays in the supply of components, equipment, and a decrease in investment in the industry. Pilot projects and new product launches may be at the highest risk. The economic recession is inevitable and the main measures of state support, including that for the industrial sector, in addition to the existing ones, may be not only a tax deferral but also the introduction of tax holidays, as well as investment support for pilot projects, which include the digitalization of production.

In these conditions, the entrepreneurial function of the government as an investor in the most priority and strategic sectors of the economy becomes especially urgent and necessary. One such priority tasks is obviously the digital transformation of the industrial sector. Technological changes associated with digital technologies and the development of a new production paradigm are transforming the Russian industrial sector, ensuring the security of the national economy, reducing the country's dependence on the development of its commodity sector.

5 Conclusion

The analysis of the industrial sector in the context of the digitalization of the economy of Russia's regions confirms the conclusions of leading researchers in industrial development on the need for the digital transformation of the industry. The study revealed that in the context of the currently observed decline in the level of industrial production, the issue of ensuring a stable level of digitalization of the industrial sector remains acute. Since the competitive development of such a system-forming branch as the industry is directly related to the country's successful recovery to the pre-crisis level and ensuring its economic security level.

The ongoing large-scale scientific and technological transformations already have a significant impact on the sphere of finance and pose threats to the stable functioning and development of the industry [17]. Under these conditions, the government can share the risks associated with the use of modern electronic technologies. In addition, the risks of digitalization can be reduced in the context of the introduction of digital platforms in the industrial sector. Networkization and systematic use of digital platforms are among the essential conditions for the effective development of both individual companies and the industrial sector as a whole.

Acknowledgements The paper was prepared with the support of the Russian Foundation for Basic Research project No. 18-010-01156 "Modeling the technological transformation of the industrial sector of Russia in the context of the digitalization of the economy".

References

1. Abdrakhmanova, G. I., Vishnevsky, K. O., Gokhber, L. M., et al. (2020). *Indicators of the Digital Economy: 2020: Statistical Bulletin*. Moscow: National Research University Higher School of Economics.
2. Akberdina, V. V., Grebenkin, A. V., & Smirnova, O. P. (2017). Comprehensive Toolkit for Assessing the Sustainability of Economic Sectors: Regional Aspect. *Economy of Region, 13*(4), 1264–1279. https://doi.org/10.17059/2017-4-23
3. Avdeenko, T.V., & Aletdinova, A.A. (2017). Digitalization of the Economy Based on the Improvement of Expert Knowledge Management Systems. Scientific and Technical Bulletin of the St. Petersburg State Poly-Technical University. *Economic Sciences, 10*(1), 7–18.
4. Bhattacharjee, T., & Pal, R. (2013). Network Externalities and Strategic Managerial Delegation in Cournot Duopoly: Is There a Prisoners' Dilemma? *Review of Network Economics, 12*, 343–353. https://doi.org/10.1515/rne-2013-0114

5. Digital McKinsey. (2017). Digital Russia: New Reality. Retrieved May 2, 2020, from https://www.mckinsey.com/~/media/McKinsey/Locations/Europe%20and%20Middle%20East/Russia/Our%20Insights/Digital%20Russia/Digital-Russia-report.ashx
6. Ericson, R. E. (2009). Eurasian Natural Gas Pipelines: The Political Economy of Network Interdependence. *Eurasian Geography and Economics, 50*(1), 28–57. https://doi.org/10.2747/1539-7216.50.1.28
7. Gabdrakhmanov, O. F. (2017). Network Economy: Features and Types of Informal Economic Networks in the Service Sector. *University Bulletin, 3*, 42–47
8. Gulin, K. A., & Uskov, V. S. (2017). On the Role of the Internet of Things in the Transition to the Fourth Industrial Revolution. *Problems of Territory Development, 4*(90), 112–131
9. Hou, H., Hong, S., & Zhao, C. (2017). On the Role of Network Externalities in Strategic Delegation Contracts with an Industry-Wide Union. *Applied Economics Letters, 24*(21), 1621–1628. https://doi.org/10.1080/13504851.2017.1368980
10. Makarov, V.L., & Popov, E.V. (2020). *Network Economic Interactions*. 2nd ed. Moscow.
11. Pogodina, T. V., Aleksakhina, V. G., Burenin, V. A., Polianova, T. N., & Yunusov, L. A. (2019). Towards the Innovation-Focused Industry Development in a Climate of Digitalization: The Case of Russia. *Entrepreneurship and Sustainability Issues, 6*(4), 1897–1906. https://doi.org/10.9770/jesi.2019.6.4(25)
12. Popov, E. V., & Semyachkov, K. A. (2020). *Smart Cities*. Moscow: Yurayt.
13. Romanova, O.A., & Ponomaryova, A.O. (2017). Priorities of Regional Industrial Policy during the Formation of the Digital Economy. In Yu.G. Lavrikova (Ed.), *Materials of the IV All-Russian Symposium on Regional Economics* (pp. 122–127).
14. Romanova, O. A., & Ponomaryova, A. O. (2020). Multi-Vector Industrial Policy of Russia in the Conditions of the Formation of a New Industrial Landscape. *Journal of Economic Theory, 17*(2), 276–291
15. Schmidt, A. V., Antonyuk, V. S., & Francini, A. (2016). Urban Agglomerations in Regional Development: Theoretical, Methodological and Applied Aspects. *Economy of the Region, 12*(3), 776–789
16. Sheresheva, MYu., & Dunaeva, S. O. (2019). Network Interaction as the Basis for the Creation of the Value Proposition of Transport Companies in the Segment of Railway Transit Traffic. *The Manager, 10*(3), 47–57
17. Smirnova, O.P. (2019) Economic security of the industrial complex in the context of digital transformation. *Regional Economy: Theory and Practice*. (pp. 2096–2113).
18. Vasina, N. V., Danilov, A. N., & Nedelko, G. V. (2017). Identification of Threshold Values of Indicators for Assessing the Financial Condition of an Organization. *Bulletin of the Novosibirsk State University of Economics and Management, 2*, 162–173
19. Voronkova, OYu., Yakimova, L. A., Frolova, I. I., Shafranskaya, Ch., & Ya., Kamolov, S.G., & Prodanova, N.A. . (2019). Sustainable Development of Territories Based on the Integrated Use of Industry, Resource and Environmental Potential. *International Journal of Economics and Business Administration, 7*(2), 151–163. https://doi.org/10.35808/ijeba/223
20. Yusupov, R. M. (2009). Informatization as a Factor of Innovative Economic Growth. *Economics and Management, 10*, 5–10